AMERICAN CYCLONE

THEODORE ROOSEVELT
AND HIS 1900 WHISTLE-STOP CAMPAIGN

JOHN M. HILPERT

UNIVERSITY PRESS OF MISSISSIPPI / JACKSON

www.upress.state.ms.us

The University Press of Mississippi is a member of the
Association of American University Presses.

First printing 2015

∞

Library of Congress Cataloging-in-Publication Data

Hilpert, John M.
American cyclone : Theodore Roosevelt and his 1900
whistle-stop campaign / John M. Hilpert.
    pages cm
Includes bibliographical references and index.
ISBN 978-1-4968-0339-9 (cloth : alk. paper) — ISBN 978-
1-4968-0340-5 (ebook) 1. Presidents—United States—
Election—1900. 2. Roosevelt, Theodore, 1858–1919. 3.
Presidents—United States—Biography. 4. United States—
Politics and government—1897–1901. I. Title.
E738.H55 2015
324.973'0911—dc   2015009821

British Library Cataloging-in-Publication Data available

To Pat

who has made all of life's whistle stops with me

CONTENTS

PROLOGUE

When Theodore Roosevelt entered the nation's political conversation as the Republicans' nominee for the vice presidency in 1900, he was only forty-one years old. However, he had caught the public's attention with the popular version of his life story. Child of East Coast privilege. Sickly, bespectacled youth. Naturalist and author. Harvard graduate. New York assemblyman. Young widower. Badlands cowboy. Civil service reformer. Urban police commissioner. Assistant secretary of the navy. Rough Rider and war hero. Enemy of political bosses as governor of the nation's most important state. Attentive husband to his second wife, Edith, and the father of six children.[1]

Few candidates for the presidency or vice presidency have enjoyed the elevated level of recognition and admiration accorded Theodore Roosevelt in the waning days of the nineteenth century. To millions he seemed of a set with the likes of George Washington and Ulysses S. Grant, each of whom captured the nation's attention with his wartime leadership. Even as Roosevelt exited the troop ship carrying him home from the war with Spain in September 1898, there was talk of election to New York's governorship and of the presidential opportunity likely to occur in 1904.

Revolutionary War hero Washington was ushered into the presidency by a unanimous decision of the electors.[2] His military service had spanned several difficult campaigns over a period of years, and his victories meant independence for the new nation. When voters elected Grant to become commander in chief, it was in the shadow of his grueling years of battlefield failures and successes in a war that threatened the very sovereignty of the United States.

When Theodore Roosevelt joined the ranks of the nation's military heroes, he had led an assault on a hill in Cuba, assumed combat leadership for a period of weeks, and defiantly stood up to the federal bureaucracy on behalf of the soldiers in his command. Although the colonel claimed victory in the skirmishes involving him and the Rough Riders, his celebrity was arguably outsized in contrast to Washington, Grant, and other military heroes who sought the presidency or vice presidency before him. Not only is this clear to us in hindsight, but it was also apparent to some of

Roosevelt's contemporaries, particularly his opponents, who were not shy about making the point that the attention paid to him had been purchased with comparatively modest battlefield experiences.[3]

Roosevelt's life story, his frequently bold behavior, his quirky visual appeal, and the image of his dashing company of Rough Riders—combined with his energy and winning personality—gained for him a following among the newspapermen covering the battles with Spanish troops in Cuba. In turn, these representatives of dailies from New York and Chicago, as well as writers from the national newswire services, reported regularly to their readers on the colonel's accomplishments and antics. His wartime achievements may have merited reasonable attention, but, to his good fortune, he became the chosen one, the adopted focus for the journalistic narrative of the war with Spain.

Roosevelt was the name citizens began to connect with national success. From his three years as a state assemblyman, his stint with the Civil Service Commission, and his time as New York's police commissioner, Roosevelt understood the value and potential of positive relationships with newspapermen. When the stirrings of journalistic attention came his way in Cuba, he was ready to seize the opportunity. Roosevelt proved himself strategic and wily in courting the right relationships with those reporting the news, and these skills stood him in good stead throughout the rest of his life.

After his triumphal return from Cuba, his election as governor, and his widely reported tiffs with machine politicians and big businessmen, Theodore Roosevelt was positioned for national office. Despite the misgivings of some Republican leaders, Roosevelt was a proven politician who could manipulate circumstances and voters to benefit himself and his party. When the vice presidential nomination came his way, he cultivated the image of the reluctant candidate wooed by demanding convention delegates to accept a role he would have preferred to avoid. Humbly, he accepted the nomination for the sake of strengthening the ticket.

Part 1 of this book's narrative summarizes in chapter 1 Roosevelt's rise to the status of national hero, his gubernatorial campaign, and his service as New York's chief executive. Chapter 2 briefly recaps those particulars of Roosevelt's nomination for the vice presidency that bear on the interpretation of his subsequent campaign for the office. Information on the period covered in part 1—roughly the spring of 1898 to the early summer of 1900—is available to the reader in much greater detail in the extensive biographical canon on Theodore Roosevelt. Only those developments in his life directly related to later events in the summer and fall of 1900 are presented herein.

Parts 2 and 3 comprise the primary focus of this book, presenting in detail materials from primary sources that tell the story and analyze the significance of his vice presidential campaign in the election of 1900. Nowhere else does the Roosevelt literature present as broadly the time from the Republican National Convention in June 1900 to the national election in November 1900.

This period proved highly significant in the life of the man who would quickly and unexpectedly become the twenty-sixth president of the United States. For four months Roosevelt campaigned tirelessly through many regions of the nation on behalf of William McKinley's reelection, and in the process he burnished his own shining image, gained political influence by expanding Republican support, demonstrated his steel by standing up to naysayers, and sharpened his sense of the public's response to him and his message.

Part 2 discusses image, strategy, platforms, and public policy, as well as trips taken early in the summer of 1900 that showed the candidate what was awaiting him in the campaign to come. Part 3 covers the period from the beginning of September to Election Day on November 6, 1900, detailing Roosevelt's message, his experiences, and critical elements that created variations in the political environment state by state, and even community by community.

Campaigning for William McKinley's reelection as president, his own election as vice president, and the election of regional candidates on the foundation of the Republican platform moved Theodore Roosevelt beyond the image of hero turned politician, and he evolved into his party's most forceful champion. Roosevelt scholars generally treat the election of 1900 in a cursory fashion, reciting gross statistics on the number of communities visited and speeches made, then moving abruptly to his restlessness as vice president and his unanticipated ascension to the presidency. This book explains why the events of 1900 between the months of June and November should not be overlooked by those interested in understanding Theodore Roosevelt.

Never was the public's adulation of Teddy—a moniker he reportedly despised[4]—more enthusiastically displayed than during his time on the national ticket with William McKinley. Nearly everywhere Roosevelt visited, the nation's citizens eagerly demonstrated their fondness for him. Nowhere was this more evident than in the West, the Midwest, and the states bordering the Old South. These were the regions where Roosevelt spent seven weeks in 1900 traveling by train on an extensive whistle-stop campaign tour.

Journalists who traveled on the Roosevelt special—known colloquially as Camp No. 2 of the Rough Writers—reported extensively on the candidate, including details on demonstrations by both his many enthusiastic supporters and a few vocal opponents who were occasionally quite threatening. Newspaper readers during September and October 1900 were treated regularly to stories on the great adventure of the vice presidential campaign trip, and these narratives fed the national interest in Theodore Roosevelt. Much of what follows is based on reports that ran in the pages of daily and weekly publications serving up news and opinions to American communities large and small.

William F. "Buffalo Bill" Cody met the Roosevelt train at Junction City, Kansas, on September 28, 1900—reportedly surprising the candidate—and this icon of the West proclaimed, "Ladies and gentlemen, Governor Roosevelt is the American Cyclone, and I don't wonder that some have taken to their cellars. The Wild West is not here to make political speeches. The ticket Governor Roosevelt represents is already elected, and all they have got to do is to show down and take the pot."[5] Those words of one American hero on behalf of another provided the fitting title of this book, *American Cyclone*.

Cody's voice joined the chorus of several hundred thousand citizens who shouted their greetings to Theodore Roosevelt at the whistle stops on his campaign tour. Neither Buffalo Bill nor the ambitious politician whose praises he proclaimed could have guessed what was one year down the tracks of history. This book tells the story of a few short months in the life of the "American Cyclone" that positioned him to become the president of the United States.

Part One

RISING TO PROMINENCE: SPRING 1898 TO JUNE 1900

CHAPTER 1

FROM HERO TO GOVERNOR

Among the Americans for whom there are multiple biographies, Theodore Roosevelt occupies a lengthy space on our bookshelves. His was a life of achievement, and he exhibited a character of such strength, determination, and engaging quirkiness that we are endlessly fascinated by his story. This is an examination of one small part of that story that has thus far escaped detailed treatment—namely, his campaign for the vice presidency. That it has been glossed over by most scholars is not surprising because it seems a brief moment in a thoroughly studied life of public accomplishments.

Roosevelt walked onto the national political stage in the summer of 1900, and this review of his campaign shows that both his image and the voting public's response to him evolved day by day. When an assassin's bullet felled President William McKinley, his recently elected vice president had held office for barely six months. Theodore Roosevelt became the twenty-sixth president of the United States on September 14, 1901, and overnight the campaign of 1900 retroactively took on greater significance.

This chapter briefly recounts events in Roosevelt's life from the spring of 1898 to the fall of 1900 that carried him from a position within the federal bureaucracy through military service to the governorship of the state of New York. It was a remarkable period of acceleration and elevation, even for one already on a pathway to success because of his well-known and assertive leadership in public service.

April to August 1898

If not for the cruel intervention of fate and political maneuvering, Melvin Grigsby might have become president of the United States. Indeed, if charging up the San Juan Heights in Cuba at the head of the Rough Riders won

Theodore Roosevelt favorable national attention, that same recognition could have come to the leader of Grigsby's Cowboys, another of the three volunteer regiments authorized by Congress and gathered for the war with Spain in 1898.[1]

In the end, however, Colonel Grigsby, South Dakota's attorney general and a hero of the nation's Civil War, could only dream of what might have been. Bureaucratic tangles mired him and his Third US Volunteer Cavalry at Camp Thomas in Chickamauga, Georgia, for the 115-day duration of the conflict.

The Second US Volunteer Cavalry, known popularly as Torrey's Rocky Mountain Riders, also saw no action. Only the Rough Riders, the First US Volunteer Cavalry, made it to Cuba for the fight.

Grigsby had announced in May 1898 to an enthusiastic crowd in Sioux Falls, "Patriotism is up and politics is down!" He was mistaken, according to Robert Lee Mattson in his review of the treatment accorded Grigsby's Cowboys versus Roosevelt's Rough Riders. "Political pull and pressure had been all important in obtaining congressional authorization for these regiments," Mattson wrote, "and would play a major role in the decisions that would cause one of the regiments to win immortality while the other two became lost in obscurity."[2]

Political action was Grigsby's intent when he planned a trip to Washington, DC, after the sinking of the battleship *Maine* in Havana Harbor in February 1898. His visit in mid-April was to persuade key members of the Senate that national readiness for war required volunteer regiments.[3]

Meanwhile, Theodore Roosevelt was working with his friend Dr. Leonard Wood to convince President McKinley, cabinet officials, and congressional leaders of the same need. Both were well known to the top echelon of the administration, as Roosevelt was the outspoken and aggressive assistant secretary of the navy and Wood was the personal physician to both the president and the secretary of war, Russell Alger. Roosevelt wrote in his 1899 account, "I had preached, with all the fervor and zeal I possessed, our duty to intervene in Cuba . . . [and] if a war came, somehow or other, I was going to the front."[4]

In his 1913 autobiography, Roosevelt openly discussed the politics that handed him the government position he held as an assistant cabinet secretary, a placement that subsequently gave him the opportunity for glory with the Rough Riders. He wrote, "In the spring of 1897 President McKinley appointed me Assistant Secretary of the Navy. I owed the appointment chiefly to the efforts of Senator H. C. Lodge of Massachusetts, who doubtless was actuated by his long and close friendship for me."[5]

That politics and self-dealing became rife in the nation's capital when a war with Spain appeared unavoidable is illustrated by this anecdote from Roosevelt's autobiography: "One Congressman besought me [as assistant secretary of the navy] for a ship to protect Jekyll Island, off the coast of Georgia, an island which derived its sole consequence because it contained the winter homes of certain millionaires."[6]

In another instance, Roosevelt recorded that after much badgering by influential members of the House and Senate seeking protection for a city in their home state, "finally the President gave in and notified me to see that a ship was sent to the city in question." Owing to his disgust with the demand, Roosevelt satisfied the order by sending a nearly useless ship; namely, "a Civil War Monitor, with one smooth-bore gun . . . under convoy of a tug . . . [that was not] a formidable foe to any antagonists." However, he gleefully reported that "joy and peace descended upon the Senator and the Congressman, and upon the President whom they had jointly harassed."[7]

Throughout the winter and early spring of 1898, Roosevelt and Wood pressed the need for volunteer regiments and pushed for their own participation at the front. "The President and my own chief, Secretary [of the navy] Long, were very firm against my going," Roosevelt wrote, "but they said that if I was bent upon going they would help me. . . . So we started with the odds in our favor."[8]

As Roosevelt told the story, once Congress had "authorized the raising of three cavalry regiments from among the wild riders and riflemen of the Rockies and the Great Plains,"[9] he was offered command of the First US Volunteer Cavalry, but he demurred. Instead, Roosevelt asked that Dr. Wood be named colonel, owing to his military experience, and that his own rank be lieutenant colonel assigned to assist Wood with the command. (Wood had served for years on the western frontier and had received a medal of honor.)

This command structure of the regiment also proved to be a winning strategy designed by Roosevelt in response to the political realities. Because he knew little about the needs of a regiment destined for battle, Roosevelt recognized that Wood's experience would bring efficiency to the recruiting, training, and equipping of their regiment. Here is Roosevelt's firsthand summary of their political gamesmanship and the results: "By ceaseless worrying of excellent bureaucrats, who had no idea how to do things quickly or how to meet an emergency, we succeeded in getting our rifles, cartridges, revolvers, clothing, shelter-tents, and horse gear just in time to enable us to go on the Santiago expedition."[10] This ability to assess fairly his own capabilities and to craft political strategy accordingly stood Theodore Roosevelt in good stead in this instance and in many situations in years to come.

By contrast, the commander of the third volunteer regiment, Melvin Grigsby, "had great troubles equipping his regiment" because he did not remain in Washington "harrying the bureaucrats as Roosevelt had done." Mattson concluded, "The problems of the Third Regiment were due to its Colonel's lack of influence."[11] This disparity in political influence played out in other areas as well—for example, in the recruitment of volunteers and the availability of transportation to the front.

Because citizens of the late nineteenth century counted on daily and weekly newspapers for reports on the major stories affecting the nation, it became obvious to the American people that Theodore Roosevelt had captured the minds and hearts of correspondents reporting the war and of editors determining which stories would find ink. From the East Coast to the West Coast and from large cities to small towns, Roosevelt became the face of the war with Spain, and the Rough Riders were the darlings of the news media.

In his biography of Roosevelt, Edmund Morris wrote that the Rough Riders' colonel came home "to find himself the most famous man in America."[12] On September 15, 1898, the volunteer military unit was honorably discharged. Less than two months later, on November 8, Roosevelt was elected governor of New York, arguably the most important state in the Union at the end of the nineteenth century. Even more remarkably, key Republicans in Chicago had already announced the formation of a "Roosevelt 1904 Club," proclaiming him their choice to succeed William McKinley.[13]

It was a nearly incomprehensible elevation of political fortune, even for one as ambitious as Theodore Roosevelt. He had, after all, held only the elective office of New York state assemblyman, and although he briefly made a mark in that post, he lost a bid to be the assembly's speaker in 1884. In 1886 he came in third in a three-way contest for mayor of New York City, and he ran in no other elections prior to the war. Roosevelt's leap to prominence in 1898 resulted not only from his accomplishments, but also from the whims of history, self-promotion, media hunger for a hero, and his winning personal characteristics.

Newspapermen were in the thick of the action with the unit, as Roosevelt acknowledged in his retrospective on the war. He wrote, "There were also with us, at the head of the column, two men who did not run away, who, though non-combatants—newspaper correspondents—showed as much gallantry as any soldier in the field. They were Edward Marshall [*New York Journal*] and Richard Harding Davis [*New York Herald*]."[14]

In a brief biography of Davis, historian Ray Cresswell wrote that the war with Spain brought the journalist a golden opportunity: "Roosevelt, the Rough Riders, and Davis had converged at the right place and time. Roosevelt and his regiment provided the rich material Davis wanted, and Davis became their best publicist. It was an ideal relationship."[15] According to Cresswell, Roosevelt eventually gave Davis an honorary membership in the Rough Riders. (A photograph from the war shows Roosevelt and Davis in earnest conversation.)

Demonstrating the national pervasiveness of the news generated by these journalists, an editorial ran in the *Anaconda Standard* from southwestern Montana near the end of July, when the Rough Riders were in their second month of fighting. The following opinion had already crystalized in the small western mining community: "If this war winds up in a reasonably short time, we shall, in all probability, be hearing about Theodore Roosevelt in state politics in New York." The piece mentioned that many favored him for the governorship. It continued, "Before the war he would hardly have been slated. . . . But Roosevelt is a good deal bigger man than he was before he was a Rough Rider."[16]

Reports from the battlefields in Cuba prompted the public's favorable assessment of Roosevelt, the soldier. Some examples follow.

> He was heroic in the *San Francisco Call* on June 26: "Lieutenant Colonel Roosevelt led his men with a rifle he picked up from one of the wounded and charged the iron building that the Spaniards had fortified themselves in."[17]
>
> He was a leader in the *St. Landry Clarion* of Opelousas, Louisiana: "Col. Wood at the right and Lieut. Col. Roosevelt at the left led a charge which turned the tide of battle and sent the enemy flying over the hills to Santiago."[18]
>
> He was humble in South Carolina's *Anderson Intelligencer*: "I want to say a word for our own men. Every officer and man did his duty up to the handle. Not a one flinched."[19]

One story after another built Roosevelt's image, sometimes enhancing the narrative for effect. For example, on June 25, the *San Francisco Call* ran a full-page, front-page feature complete with a portrait of Theodore Roosevelt in uniform at the top of the sheet and an artist's rendition of a battle scene across the bottom depicting a savage charge with Roosevelt brandishing his sword and leading the way for a troop of mounted cavalrymen.[20] This idealized scene existed only in the artist's mind because the Rough Riders' horses did not arrive in Cuba and they fought on foot. Also, Roosevelt wrote later that he left his sword behind because the scabbard tangled in his legs in battle.[21]

Recalling that the US forces fighting in Cuba included the regular army, the navy, and units of the National Guard with many times the number of fighting men than were there with Roosevelt and the Rough Riders, the attention paid to this single volunteer unit was all the more striking. Throughout the conflict, each development affecting the Rough Riders and Roosevelt found its way into print.

When Colonel Wood was assigned broader authority with the troops in Cuba, Roosevelt's star continued to climb. On July 9, the *Times* of Washington, DC, reported on Roosevelt's promotion to colonel, as the Senate agreed to the action shortly after it was introduced. The report concluded, "There has been no promotion since the war began that has been met with more hearty approval, not only in the War Department, but with the public generally."[22]

On the same day (July 9, 1898), Virginia's *Williamsburg Gazette* ran a subhead calling the Rough Riders "Teddy's Terrors." Below the subhead were the words of a ballad that included this stanza:

> *With Devil's Lake Imps at his left and his right*
> *Our Teddy will be in the thick of the fight*
> *Then out with your guns, boys, and let the air ring*
> *Hip, hurrah for Ted Roosevelt, the cow-punchers' king!*

Accompanying the piece was an illustration of a battlefield conference with Wood standing on the ground looking up at Roosevelt elevated on horseback.[23]

As the war on the Cuban front ground to a conclusion, a leading newspaper in Los Angeles, the *Herald*, broke the story that Secretary of War Alger had delayed the return of the troops to US soil and that "fearful conditions"—disease and poor sanitation—were threatening lives. Roosevelt wrote a letter demanding action and earning the ire of Washington-based officials.[24] Confronting authority on behalf of US soldiers earned Roosevelt more positive attention. An editorialist with the *Dalles Daily Chronicle* of Oregon wrote: "Secretary Alger shows a persistent determination to convict himself of littleness and incapacity . . . [in contrast to] the courageous and manly course taken by Theodore Roosevelt to save the army at Santiago from annihilation by disease."[25]

For nearly everyone, save a few naysayers who had an ax to grind, Theodore Roosevelt presented an almost perfect vision of an American hero: courageous, determined, patriotic. Yet when lauded, the *Wichita Daily Eagle* reported, "He refused absolutely to talk about his achievements, but gladly spoke of the work of his men."[26]

As W. Joseph Campbell, professor at the American University, wrote, "The Rough Riders' charge was crucial to promoting an ambitious political agenda that catapulted Roosevelt to the White House in a little more than three years."[27] Beyond the world of reality, there developed a metaphysical dimension, a place where this man was elevated to near-divine status by historical circumstances, a media frenzy, and a national hunger for heroes.

August to November 1898

Joseph Wheeler was a colorful character who had fought in the Civil War for the Confederate States of America and subsequently served in the US House of Representatives as a congressman from Alabama. Although he was in his sixties and still held his congressional seat at the outbreak of the war with Spain, he volunteered to serve, and President McKinley commissioned him as a major general. He was given command of cavalry units and became the superior officer to the commanders of the volunteer regiments, including the Rough Riders.

When the troops returned home from Cuba, the Rough Riders disembarked on August 14, 1898, at Montauk Point in New York. General Wheeler strode off the ship to loud cheers from the crowd of onlookers. However, newspapermen reported that the most enthusiastic welcome was reserved for Colonel Theodore Roosevelt.[28] William Roscoe Thayer, Roosevelt's biographer and his classmate at Harvard, wrote that from this moment on Long Island, there was "direct proof that every war breeds a president."[29]

Whether Roosevelt accepted the truth of that aphorism in the late summer of 1898 is uncertain, but he surely understood that the public accepted him as a hero and that political opportunities were open to him. He had barely stepped foot on his home state's soil when local journalists crowded around shouting the day's pregnant question: "Will you be our next governor?"[30] Wisely, Roosevelt avoided answering by touting the bravery of the Rough Riders. Of course, he also knew that an affirmative response to the political question was not his alone to give.

When Theodore Roosevelt campaigned for election as governor of New York in 1898, he effectively manipulated the political environment to his benefit and developed strategies that would serve him well in his 1900 campaign for the vice presidency. There were several similarities between the two elections. First, powerful political personalities influenced and, to a degree, controlled both the gubernatorial and vice presidential nominations Roosevelt sought and the course of both campaigns.

Second, during each of the two campaigns, negative revelations or public relations missteps threatened to derail a successful outcome. Understanding how these challenges were met is instructive regarding Roosevelt's acumen in accepting and applying political solutions.

Third, campaign strategies evolved in each case to use Roosevelt's talents and the widespread eagerness to see him in the flesh and to hear him speak assertively about American ideals and public policy. These strategies illustrate why the bigger-than-life image he carried into the twentieth century has outlived him, enduring to become part of the national mythology.

These similarities illustrate how the 1898 one-state effort prefigured aspects of Roosevelt's 1900 national campaign. Recounting some details of his run to become New York's governor helps to interpret events that occurred twenty-four months later and explains, in part, strategies eventually adopted by the vice presidential candidate and his handlers.

In his autobiography first published fifteen years after the triumphal weeks in Cuba, Roosevelt wrote a straightforward statement describing the political situation he encountered upon returning home: "The Republicans realized that the chances were very much against them. Accordingly the leaders were in a chastened mood and ready to nominate any candidate [for governor] with whom they thought there was a chance of winning. I was the only possibility."[31] Biographer Edmund Lester Pearson put it even more succinctly when he wrote in 1920: "The Republican Party in New York was in a bad way."[32]

Scandal had tainted the Republican incumbent, Frank Swett Black, who had the misfortune of holding the governor's office while public ire rose over the misuse of funds for the deepening of the Erie Canal. Statewide media fanned the flames of controversy, and the power brokers of New York's Republican Party began to cast about for an alternative candidate.[33]

Black was not eager to relinquish his office, but Senator Thomas Collier Platt, universally acknowledged as a classic nineteenth-century party boss and the maker of political careers in New York, knew he faced a conundrum. "If he supported Black's bid for reelection he would lay himself open to charges of cynicism and irresponsibility," wrote Edmund Morris. However, despite the fact that the governor "had not been personally involved in the scandal," if Platt turned to someone else, "it would be tantamount to admitting there had been high-level corruption."[34]

Louis Auchincloss and Arthur M. Schlesinger Jr. assessed the situation in much the same stark terms as Roosevelt himself. They wrote, "TR's wartime popularity almost required the New York Republicans to run him as candidate for the governorship, as they had no other candidate so likely to win." Still, they acknowledged uneasiness among the party leaders: "Thomas Platt . . . would rather have lost the election than gain a chief executive who would loosen his iron grip on the party."[35]

"Tom Platt did not want him at all," surmised Harold Howland, an early Roosevelt biographer. "But he did want to win the election. . . . So he swallowed whatever antipathy he may have had and offered the nomination to Roosevelt."[36]

Two years later Platt would play a significant role in Roosevelt's nomination for the vice presidency. With the Frank Black problem out of the way and a growing eagerness to move Roosevelt away from New York politics, Platt would see an opportunity to foist the governor on another of the nineteenth-century political bosses, Marcus Alonzo Hanna, US senator from Ohio, campaign manager for William McKinley, and chief king maker for the Republican Party. Hanna's resistance and the eventual outcome of the political back and forth would be eerily similar to the Platt-versus-Roosevelt tilt of 1898 (see chapter 2).

Even though Senator Platt and his colleagues among the party regulars eventually decided that Roosevelt in the governor's chair was better than allowing a Democrat to occupy the seat, the seemingly smooth ride to the nomination abruptly encountered a deep pothole. Just a few days before the nominating convention, a question arose that potentially affected Roosevelt's eligibility to become the party's candidate. Morris wrote, "No sooner had Roosevelt decided he was strong enough to run for Governor . . . than a sensational private revelation threatened to destroy his candidacy overnight."[37]

On September 24, 1898, there was a shocking headline in New York City's *Sun* that read "Plot to Beat Roosevelt" and a subhead that said "Gov. Black's Friends and Tammany Democrats Make a Most Interesting Discovery."[38]

The front page of the *New-York Tribune* offered more insight as to the subject of the revelation. The headline was "Roosevelt's Personal Tax," and the subhead read "Scheme to Spring a Surprise at Saratoga Discovered."[39] The opening of the Republican state convention in the picturesque community of Saratoga was imminent and the primary business was to nominate the party's candidate for governor on September 27.

At the head of the September 24 story in the *Sun* was a question that would stir the leadership of Republican insiders to immediate and furious action: "Did Roosevelt lose citizenship in New York when he went to Washington as Assistant Secretary of the Navy?"[40] At the heart of the accusation was a document that Roosevelt had signed claiming legal residency in Washington, DC, as of October 1897, when his lease on a New York property terminated and he was living in the district serving his federal post as an assistant cabinet secretary. This change-of-residency status was intended to save him fifty thousand dollars in taxes he would otherwise have owed to the city of New York.[41]

Article 4, section 2, of the constitution of the state of New York read: "No person shall be eligible to the office of Governor or Lieutenant Governor except a citizen of the United States, of the age of not less than 30 years, and *who shall have been five years next preceding his election a resident of this State*" (italics added).[42]

Implied by the charge was not just the legal challenge to Roosevelt's eligibility, but also the ethical question whether "the man who faced Spanish bullets unflinchingly at Santiago had attempted to dodge the payment of personal taxes in New York." Typically, Roosevelt lashed out, claiming to be "amazed that any set of politicians could rely for support upon the affidavit he had filed with the Tax Commissioners."[43]

Senator Platt and party chairman Benjamin Odell called the Republican leadership to a conference at the Fifth Avenue Hotel the very evening the anti-Roosevelt strategy became known. Elihu Root presided at the conference.[44] Root was a powerful attorney in New York City, a respected member of the elite class who spent his career moving between key federal positions in Republican administrations and his private law practice. The meeting was publicly announced as an investigation of the charge, and Roosevelt hurried into the city with all pertinent documents.[45]

On the table was the offending affidavit which read, in part: "[As of April 19, 1897] I had no residence in New York City and did not vote and could not vote there at the last election . . . and [I] do not now own or lease any dwelling-house there whatsoever. Last June I rented the house in which I am now residing with my family at No. 1810 N St., Washington. . . . I have been and am now a resident of Washington." The statement was signed by Roosevelt on March 21, 1898.[46]

Despite this damaging and seemingly incontrovertible evidence, Chairman Odell made a bold statement following the conference. Speaking for himself and others in the group, he said, "We can say that Colonel Roosevelt will be nominated for Governor to a certainty. He has decided to accept the nomination and stand for election, and he will be elected."[47]

Roosevelt was sent to cool his heels away from the press and public at his family home in Oyster Bay. It fell to the unassailable Elihu Root to explain and to establish Roosevelt's credentials in front of the convention. According to Morris, "Root must research, and if necessary invent, enough scholarly argument to reassure the Saratoga Convention that they were in fact voting for a citizen of New York State." Convention officials arranged for Root to take a delegate's seat and to have the floor at the appropriate moment.[48] After yet another lengthy meeting at the convention site, the media reported that Root's "opinion in favor of Roosevelt was even stronger."[49]

As the convention moved toward the nominating session, Roosevelt attempted to address the situation with a message redefining the term *resident* and an assertion that he was trying to preserve personal resources to meet the expenses required to raise the regiment of Rough Riders in service to the nation. He said he had reviewed all relevant correspondence between himself and his attorney and "that the letter [of March 25, 1898,] will be all that is necessary to refute the assertions of the opposition."[50]

In the end, the determination of the delegates to nominate Roosevelt and the politically effective oratory of Elihu Root held sway. Roosevelt became the nominee by a unanimous vote, after an initial delegate tally of 753 to 218. The supporters of Frank Black came up more than five hundred votes short and immediately announced their wholehearted endorsement of Theodore Roosevelt's candidacy for election as governor.[51]

Hindsight suggests the question of nonresidency could have damaged or destroyed his gubernatorial candidacy. Perhaps that is why neither the serious threat posed by this challenge nor the successful outcome to the incident receives mention in his autobiography.

One additional aspect of the 1898 gubernatorial election informs the understanding of his vice presidential run two years later—namely, the whistle-stop methodology Roosevelt embraced as a statewide strategy. It would become his most visible campaign tactic in 1900, even though his goal had shifted to a national office.

In her study of the transformational presidency of Theodore Roosevelt, *The Bully Pulpit*, Doris Kearns Goodwin examined closely the relationship of the man to the influential journalists of his day. Roosevelt understood intuitively that those ties potentially expanded his audience and polished his image as a heroic figure willing and ready to offer courageous leadership. He cultivated these friendships, and the press repaid his courtship with favorable coverage.[52] From his earliest political service as an assemblyman to his appointed positions to his triumphs during and after the Rough Rider experience, Roosevelt and the print media evidenced a special bond that worked to his benefit.

As the gubernatorial campaign launched, Republican leaders trumpeted an assured victory, but a positive outcome was by no means certain. The stain of scandal in Frank Black's administration, the hesitancy of party bosses to nominate their war hero, questions about residency status, and a relatively strong opponent combined to create a challenge that could not be ignored. In typical Roosevelt fashion, his instinct was to charge to the fore, and he forced the hands of party leaders to create a strategy centered on his assertive and personal involvement. "Unwilling to accept failure without putting forth his utmost effort, Roosevelt demanded a statewide push. Machine leaders, who customarily controlled the entire campaign, initially resisted his requests; candidates rarely took the stump on their own behalf."[53]

Thayer characterized Roosevelt's first larger-scale campaign in this way: "Roosevelt stumped the state at a pace unknown till then. . . . [H]e went from place to place in a special train speaking at every stop from his car platform or, in the larger towns, staying long enough to address great audiences out of doors or in the local theatre."[54]

"After being nominated," Roosevelt wrote, "I made a hard and aggressive campaign through the state . . . and against all probabilities, I won."[55]

Of course, everywhere Roosevelt traveled, media representatives were both his companions and unofficial promotional team, and his own notion of a winning image for the public was visually evident. "To be sure he was seen and heard at every whistle-stop, he would take along a party of six Rough Riders in full uniform," wrote Morris. "By the time Roosevelt's twin-unit Special left Weehawken, New Jersey, at 10:02 on Monday morning, 17 October, his party had been enlarged to include several other aspirants to high state offices, and a half dozen newspaper correspondents."[56]

On the first day of the statewide tour, there were seventeen stops over a course of two hundred miles, and more than twenty thousand people heard Roosevelt speak. At each stop, a Rough Rider bugler called the faithful to hear the candidate's speeches.[57] Two weeks later, the *New-York Tribune* summarized the results of the train travel, terming it a "remarkable campaign tour." According to this newspaper's tally, Roosevelt traveled more than twelve hundred miles and made more than one hundred speeches. "The number of speeches does not matter," the report went on, "but the quality of them does, and it may be candidly said that Colonel Roosevelt won votes for the Republican Party all over the state."[58]

Roosevelt's success in 1898 using public appearances to make bold statements and as a means to positively affect the course of events would inform his strategic decisions for the rest of his political career. His hard-won New York victory—by a slim margin of eighteen thousand votes—was surely proof to him that he had chosen and tailored an effective campaign methodology.

To be sure, several politicians of the era campaigned by train. Just two years before the 1898 New York gubernatorial race, William Jennings Bryan took railroad tours through more than twenty states, seeking votes for his presidential election at stops along the way. In 1898, Theodore Roosevelt mastered the technique and by 1900 he was ready to spend his considerable energy on a national whistle-stop tour, addressing crowds at venues large and small. It was a methodology perfectly suited to his style and his eccentricities, and those millions of voters fortunate enough to live along his route were treated to a memorable spectacle in the history of American politics.

CHAPTER 2

FROM GOVERNOR TO VICE PRESIDENTIAL CANDIDATE

Like many successful yet relatively young professionals, Governor Theodore Roosevelt reached a moment rife with internal conflict over a career decision. Quite simply, he wanted to play out his ambitions on the world stage, and by most assessments, to Roosevelt that meant becoming secretary of war, governor general of the Philippines, or president of the United States.[1] However, the lines of history had come together to lay at his feet the near certainty of becoming the Republican nominee for vice president of the United States. The vice presidency appeared to be Roosevelt's next job, if he would agree to join the incumbent president, William McKinley, on the ticket.

As other accomplished individuals before and after Roosevelt have experienced, deciding whether to accept candidacy for the vice presidency is a difficult choice. That it is an honor to be considered is undeniable. It is, after all, a prestigious title, and it dangles the prospect that one might be elevated to the presidency whether at a moment of national tragedy upon the death of the president or as the party's nominee in a subsequent election. Yet the vice presidency in and of itself is of little consequence except in those rare cases where the president chooses to share defined responsibilities that give the position more substance.

Theodore Roosevelt was understandably reluctant to accept the Republican nomination for the vice presidency. He was governor of New York, a position that could eventually propel him toward a presidential nomination, and he judged that his first two-year term was going well. In April 1900, he wrote to one of his supporters, "I have been absolutely successful . . . for my two years I have been able to make a Republican majority in the Legislature do good and decent work and have prevented any split within the party. . . . There has been an enormous improvement in the administration of the government, and there has also been a great advance in legislation."[2]

Almost from the moment of his triumphal return from the war with Spain there was talk of the likelihood of Roosevelt's service as president of the United States. He had captured the nation's attention, helped in that regard by friends in the media.

Many voters loved the Rough Rider image, his reformer's zeal, and his seemingly unconventional approach to life generally. The public's fascination had carried him into the executive mansion in Albany, despite the misgivings of Boss Thomas Platt and other powerful men who historically controlled both the state's Republican platform and access to elected and appointed positions. Popular support for Roosevelt in 1898 forced those party leaders to put him at the head of their statewide ticket and to deal with his unwelcome, maverick ways in the governor's chair. Not long into his term, they were searching for a means to displace him.

Several developments were pushing Roosevelt in the direction of the vice presidency as he pondered his political future in the state and national elections of 1900.[3] These combined with his own ambitions were powerful motivators. The list included the following:

First, there was no certainty he would win reelection as New York's governor. He had won the office by fewer than eighteen thousand votes in 1898—his percentage of the overall vote was slightly less than fifty-one—and the corporate sponsors of the Republican Party were threatening to withhold financial support because his policy decisions and his appointments were often not in their interests.

Second, Platt was scheming to off-load Roosevelt into the vice presidency, thereby moving him out of New York politics. There was even the possibility they might seek to deny his renomination as governor.

Third, close friends and supporters were urging Roosevelt to accept vice presidential candidacy as an affirmative step toward the presidency in 1904. Of course, the history of the position suggested that elevation by this means was anything but certain.

Fourth, the nomination was open and available because the incumbent vice president, Garret Hobart, had died in November 1899. He was only fifty-five years of age when heart disease claimed him.

Fifth, the groundswell of public support for Roosevelt's nomination became abundantly clear during a trip to the heartland in the summer of 1899. That this support extended to those who would be delegates to the Republican convention in June 1900 was obvious, and it appeared to be growing exponentially.

Sixth, the appeal to Roosevelt was that his presence on the ticket would strengthen the Republican chance for victory. This was perhaps the most difficult rationale for a man of his political convictions and ego needs to resist.

There was, however, an equally weighty list of countervailing reasons that caused Roosevelt to hesitate in giving a positive response to the call to the vice presidential nomination.[4] This list included the following:

First, he was fully aware of the effort by Boss Platt to exile him to Washington, DC, as a means of reasserting the power of the Republican machine to set New York's political agenda. As an aggressive and naturally pugnacious individual, Roosevelt could hardly tolerate any decision that would suggest he backed away from a fight.

Second, he recognized the impotence and lackluster character of the vice presidency. By contrast, his self-assessment was that he preferred active engagement with issues and decision makers.

Third, his wife did not favor a vice presidential run, and his financial circumstances would be diminished by service as the vice president. At the time, the vice president annually earned 20 percent less than the New York governor. Also, the vice president secured and paid for his own housing in Washington, DC, and he was expected to spend personal funds for lavish social events. Roosevelt was concerned that the situation would stress family finances and diminish educational opportunities for his children.

Fourth, the key Republican political strategist and certain highly placed members of the McKinley administration did not favor a Roosevelt candidacy for many of the same reasons Platt wanted to move him out of New York. Washington insiders had seen his outspoken activism as assistant secretary of the navy, and there was concern that he was both self-absorbed and uncontrollable.

These dynamics—whether compelling a favorable decision or supporting a negative choice regarding candidacy for the vice presidency—exercised powerful and varying influence on Governor Roosevelt over the months leading to the Republican Convention in Philadelphia from June 19 to 21, 1900. When his friend Henry Cabot Lodge urged him in the summer of 1899 to consider the vice presidency, Roosevelt wrote that his wife opposed it and the position was vacuous.[5] Six months later he maintained a similar stance, when Platt said publicly that Roosevelt ought to accept the vice presidential nomination. The governor replied by letter that it was not an office he favored.[6]

Whether Roosevelt's actions and responses to entreaties regarding his candidacy for the vice presidency represented dissembling, waffling, or self-designed campaign strategy is unclear. During the twelve months prior to the Republican convention, he made statements ranging from definitive declarations of his determination to retain his position as governor of New York to unmistakable hints that he would accept a nomination to become vice president.

No recorded instances of Roosevelt's on-again, off-again posture are more striking or illustrative than his letters to his friend and confidante Henry Cabot Lodge, who was urging him to accept the opportunity to join McKinley on the Republican ticket. On July 1, 1899, the governor wrote that his wife, Edith, opposed a vice presidential candidacy while he was "inclined to be for it."[7] On February 2, 1900, Roosevelt wrote to Lodge, "I am going to declare decisively that I want to be Governor and do not want to be Vice President."[8] Then, during the last week of April 1900, he wrote to Lodge, "By the way, I did not say . . . that I would not under any circumstances accept the vice presidency."[9]

One of the pivotal events in the life of Theodore Roosevelt in the year leading to his decision in favor of the vice presidential candidacy was the first Rough Rider reunion in Las Vegas, New Mexico, from June 24 to 26, 1899. He traveled from New York to New Mexico round-trip by train, and at stops along the way he was hailed as a hero and even urged to seek the presidency. Not only had he come home from the war a darling of the media, but he had courted good and open relationships with journalists during his year as governor as well. In turn, newspapers across the nation rewarded him with laudatory coverage. Following is a sampling of quotations that illustrate the reports read by voters in newspapers coast to coast.

In the *Kansas City Journal* on June 24, 1899, there was this praise: "Roosevelt subjugated Kansas yesterday. As he stormed the heights of San Juan at the head of the Rough Riders he laid siege to the thousands who greeted him and completely captured their hearts. Roosevelt is nothing if not magnetic. People are irresistibly attracted toward him."[10]

The *El Paso Daily Herald* ran a full-page feature on the Rough Rider on June 24, 1899, in which Roosevelt was described as "the man who had bearded the New York corruptionist in his den and tamed him."[11]

The *Evening Herald* of Shenandoah, Pennsylvania, reported on June 24, 1899: "At Topeka the governor spied Lieutenant Parker of Gatling Gun fame at San Juan hill. . . . 'Hello, Parker,' he shouted. . . . 'Three cheers for the next president of the United States,' was Parker's rejoinder. The cheers were given."[12]

The *Saint Paul Globe* on June 25, 1899, told the story of the hero's advent at the reunion: "Gov. Roosevelt arrived here at 1:30 o'clock this evening [June 24], and was greeted as he stepped off the platform of the rear car with tremendous cheering from 5,000 people massed around the depot."[13]

The *Record-Union* of Sacramento, California, reported in its June 25, 1899, edition this detail of the arrival in New Mexico: "The noted New Yorker . . . was almost lifted bodily from his feet by the press of persons anxious to grasp his hand."[14]

The *Wichita Daily Eagle* shared with its readers on June 25, 1899, that several Wichita groups sent Roosevelt the following telegram: "The G.A.R. Posts, the Commercial Club, and the citizens of Wichita earnestly invite you to stop here on your way home. You will be greeted by 20,000 people."[15]

The *Salt Lake Herald* reported an honor for Roosevelt in its June 26, 1899, edition: "The troopers [Rough Riders] were standing at attention in front of the grand stand. . . . [B]efore Colonel Roosevelt could realize why he was being spoken to, Hon. Frank Springer, acting on behalf of the people of New Mexico, began a speech, presenting Colonel Roosevelt with a handsome gold medal."[16]

The *Evening Times* of Washington, DC, asserted on June 27, 1899, that the trip back to New York was also eventful: "Governor Roosevelt arrived here [Kansas City] this morning [June 27] en route to Milwaukee to attend the carnival. All along the route from Las Vegas he was given a succession of ovations."[17]

The *Kansas City Journal* described on June 28, 1899, the widespread nature of the receptions: "Governor Roosevelt's daylight journey across Missouri, Iowa, and Illinois was a delightful one from every point of view. A crowd met him at Marceline [Missouri] and another at Bucklin [Kansas]. Galesburg [Illinois] sent a delegation to the train. . . . Fully 3,000 people were at the station." In this same piece it was reported that Roosevelt gave brief speeches at stops along the way.[18]

In these snippets culled from the hundreds of wire service and local reports that appeared in newspapers nationwide in the week between June 21 and 28, 1899, are the essential elements of the Roosevelt image and the underpinnings of his political strengths. He had a personality that drew people to him, and he enjoyed a broad base of support that stretched seemingly from coast to coast. He was a military hero. He was not only a leader, but he was also willing to exercise his office in the face of corruption to bring reforms. Voters wanted to see him and be close to him, and the media treated him favorably, promoting him by mixing editorial commentary into their reporting of events.

If Roosevelt needed confirmation that he had national appeal, surely the trip to New Mexico provided that assurance in an undeniable fashion. So fulsome was the praise he received at his stops and in the media that he announced upon his return to New York that there were no plans to launch a Roosevelt candidacy for the presidency in 1900, thereby hoping to calm any uneasiness William McKinley might have felt about a rival.[19]

Despite the accolades and the apparent support from many across the United States, Roosevelt knew the political situation in New York was less certain, even perilous. In barely a year in office, the governor had pushed civil service reforms and insisted on stronger enforcement of protections for factory workers. He supported increased taxes for corporations with public franchises, such as the street railways and quasi-public utilities.[20] "Legislatures existed simply to do the bidding of big business," wrote William Roscoe Thayer, twenty years after Roosevelt's gubernatorial service. "Merely to suggest that the special privileges of the corporations might be open to discussion was sacrilege. No wonder, therefore, that the holders of public franchises marshaled all their forces against the Governor."[21]

When Roosevelt declared his determination to appoint his own candidate as superintendent of insurance, rather than reappoint the favored candidate of Boss Platt and the Republican machine, the rift widened. "Although the proceedings (of the Republican National Convention) did not open until 19 June 1900," wrote Edmund Morris, "Theodore Roosevelt's trajectory toward the vice-presidential nomination began to accelerate from the moment the New York Senate confirmed Hendricks as Superintendent of Insurance on 31 January."[22] Francis J. Hendricks was Roosevelt's nominee; Platt supported Louis F. Payn, the incumbent in the position.

As the months between January and June 1900 rolled past, the political maneuvering by Platt and others of the machine politicians in New York intensified. They were determined that Roosevelt would be a one-term governor, despite his popular appeal, and they adopted the strategy of moving him to a relatively harmless plateau—namely, that of the vice presidency. To that end they formed alliances with Republican power brokers in other states and sought to escalate the public's demand for Roosevelt's nomination.

Platt made no secret of his wish that the governor accept a place on the national ticket, and in early February 1900 Roosevelt wrote to him, "I should like to be Governor for another term. . . . Now, as Governor, I can achieve something, but as Vice-President I should achieve nothing."[23] More achievements of the sort Roosevelt sought were nowhere on the agenda of Platt and the business interests of New York.

On April 16, 1900, Governor Roosevelt wrote in a letter to Norton Goddard, a supporter and leader of a Republican district organization in New York, "Nobody can tell, and least of all the machine itself, whether the machine intends to re-nominate me next fall or not. . . . [T]he big corporations undoubtedly want to beat me."[24] Roosevelt felt the uncertainty of his situation.

Of course, the governor could not have missed the irony that voters across the nation held him in high esteem, while powerful forces in his own backyard hoped to drive him out of the elected position he declared to prefer. Just as strongly, he could not have misunderstood that his continuing progress in high-profile politics would more likely be abetted by a decision to accept the vice presidential nomination that friends and foes alike were urging upon him.

One day after writing the letter to Goddard—on April 16, 1900—Roosevelt accepted election to serve as a delegate at large to the Republican National Convention meeting in June in Philadelphia. Henry Cabot Lodge had earlier warned him that attending the convention would likely result in his nomination, and Judge Alton Brooks Parker told Roosevelt's wife Edith just three weeks prior to the convention, "You will see your husband unanimously nominated for the office of Vice-President." Edith was not pleased, and she called Parker a "disagreeable thing" for sharing his prediction about her husband's fate.[25]

While the stars were aligning for a Roosevelt nomination both in New York and among delegates to the convention from several states, one powerful individual stood against the New York governor moving into the vice presidency. Senator Marcus Alonzo Hanna of Ohio was a close friend and advisor to President William McKinley. He was also the acknowledged political leader of the Republican Party. Thus, he had become to the national organization what Senator Thomas Platt was to the party in New York. Hanna did not favor a Roosevelt nomination. Indeed, when the governor's vice presidential candidacy eventually became unavoidable, Hanna famously said, "Don't any of you realize that there's only one life between this madman and the presidency?"[26]

Power, uncertainty, and compelling characters are the elements of a good drama, and media then, as now, could not resist reporting dramatic stories in great detail. For weeks, the vicissitudes of the Roosevelt vice presidential quandary played through the daily and weekly newspapers of the nation. The public had regular updates on the hero and the villains, and Roosevelt's shining image was surely burnished in the minds of voters everywhere.

While the nitty-gritty of the events surrounding the convention makes fascinating reading, the following front-page headlines from more than a dozen communities tell the story crisply and rather comprehensively:

The *Bismarck Daily Tribune* (June 18): WANTS ROOSEVELT: GREAT TIDE OF SENTIMENT AT PHILADELPHIA FOR THE ROUGH RIDER[27]

The *Evening Bulletin* of Maysville, Kentucky (June 19): WILL TEDDY YIELD?[28]

The *San Francisco Call* (June 19): ADMINISTRATION TO PUT FORTH ITS OWN CANDIDATE TO DEFEAT ROOSEVELT[29]

The *Indianapolis Journal* (June 19): ROOSEVELT BOOM DEAD[30]

The *Wichita Daily Eagle* (June 19): HE LOVES ME; LOVES ME NOT: ROOSEVELT IS SO COY[31]

The *San Francisco Call* (June 20): HANNA DECLARES ROOSEVELT WILL NOT GET THE NOMINATION[32]

The *Times* of Washington, DC (June 20): THE DELEGATES IN DOUBT[33]

The *Guthrie Daily Leader* of Guthrie, Oklahoma (June 20): KANSAS TO DO IT: ROOSEVELT'S NAME TO BE PRESENTED BY THE SUN-FLOWER STATE[34]

The *Omaha Daily Bee* (June 21): EVERYBODY FOR ROOSEVELT[35]

The *Scranton Tribune* of Scranton, Pennsylvania (June 21): LOOKS LIKE ROOSEVELT[36]

The *Richmond Dispatch* (June 21): ROOSEVELT THE MAN: HANNA THROWS UP THE SPONGE[37]

The *St. Paul Globe* (June 21): MR. ROOSEVELT RESIGNED: WILL GO TO HIS GRAVE SMILING[38]

The *Rock Island Argus* of Rock Island, Illinois (June 21): McKINLEY AND ROOSEVELT COMPOSE THE TICKET[39]

The *El Paso Daily Herald* (June 21): McKINLEY AND ROOSEVELT WILL LEAD THE GRAND REPUBLICAN PARTY ON TO GLORIOUS VICTORY[40]

Those engineering Roosevelt's candidacy for the vice presidency were tireless in their efforts. While Boss Platt did his work before the convention and with the New York delegation, his enlisted coconspirator, Boss Matthew Quay of Pennsylvania, mapped and managed a political strategy at the convention that brought Senator Hanna to heel. Various state delegations traipsed to Roosevelt's hotel room to demonstrate support and to implore the governor to accept the nomination. Much to Hanna's chagrin, President McKinley refused to become involved in the decision, publicly stating his preference from the White House that the convention delegates should choose the candidate.[41]

For his part, Roosevelt was indeed coy, as one of the headlines mentioned previously reported. He slid daily, or even hourly, from private refusals to a muddled public position that seemed to say, "I would rather not, but I will accede to the overwhelming will of the party." He behaved as a bride-in-waiting, expecting to be wooed. He listened to advice from friends and supporters who urged an affirmative decision. He hosted more than four hundred pleading party members in his room for a series of meetings with state delegations. He agreed to second the nomination of William McKinley, thus giving himself presence at the podium prior to the choice of the vice presidential candidate. He even made a regal entry into the hall after other delegates had arrived, moving slowly to his seat while acknowledging the cheers and cries for his candidacy. Through it all, he played to the crowd masterfully and used the strength of his popularity to great effect.[42]

Each turn of the drama surrounding Roosevelt's nomination was observed and reported by journalists through newspapers nationwide. Surely no other vice presidential selection in the history of the United States has so engaged the public over such a prolonged period. Whether a voter was inclined toward one party ticket or the other made no difference. Front-page stories everywhere were about the determined efforts to draft Roosevelt despite his proclaimed reluctance.

In the end, the delegates attending the Republican Party Convention of 1900 would not be denied the hero of San Juan on their ticket. They nominated only Theodore Roosevelt for the vice presidency, and they unanimously elected him to be their candidate.[43] As subsequent chapters shall demonstrate, he did not disappoint the party with his enthusiasm or his effort during the campaign.

Part Two

PREPARING TO CAMPAIGN: JULY AND AUGUST 1900

CHAPTER 3

CRAFTING IMAGE AND NEGOTIATING STRATEGY

On the cover of the May 16, 1900, issue of *Puck* magazine was a full-page political cartoon featuring an unmistakable caricature of Theodore Roosevelt in Rough Rider attire along with four fetching young women in summer dresses and bonnets labeled respectively, "North, South, East, and West." *Puck* was a humor magazine published in New York City, but it served a nationwide audience. Biting political cartoons were its stock-in-trade, and this Roosevelt cover was among its best.

One of the young women ("East") has her foot in a pool labeled "Vice-Presidential Waters," and she is coaxing "Teddy," the label on his hat, to join her. Another maiden wearing the bonnet labeled "South" has a hank of the governor's hair, urging him forward. "North" and "West" are applying steady pressure with their hands on his back while casting provocative looks his way. Beneath is the caption, "The Struggle for Life."[1]

Understanding the political context led readers to one apparent interpretation of the cartoon. There was a message from voices across the United States, and these sirens represented the nearly irresistible pressure for Roosevelt to accept his party's nomination for the vice presidency. While the not-so-gentle pulling and the flattery were alluring, accepting the invitation could be politically fatal. Assuming the governor saw the May 16 issue of *Puck,* he would surely have nodded his agreement with this explanation.

However, a quick glance at the image or a less perceptive understanding of contemporary party politics might have meant the reader would reach another conclusion. One could see Roosevelt frolicking with the four young women, dancing them in the direction of the "Vice-Presidential Waters," and thus "Teddy" took the role of coaxer rather than coaxed. It would surely have been a faulty interpretation of *Puck's* intention, yet it was a rather obvious alternative.

Roosevelt would have disapproved the latter interpretation. As his letters written in the shadow of the Republican National Convention show, he went to great lengths to formulate and promote an authorized interpretation for his friends and for the public. He would have no one thinking he was exiled from the governor's office or driven to the vice presidency by personal ambition.

We are fortunate that Roosevelt was a literary man who obviously enjoyed writing and that so much of his correspondence has survived and is accessible. Likewise, we can be grateful that he was always concerned with shaping his own image among friends, family, and other associates, as well as for the public generally. To the very end of his life, he was determined that his autobiography would tell his story in the way he wanted it told. These sources, his letters and his autobiography, offer remarkable insights into Roosevelt's mind in the days and weeks following the nominating convention in June 1900 and then retrospectively near the end of his life.

Of primary importance to Roosevelt both during the summer of 1900 and still two decades later was to carefully craft the narrative of the nomination to ensure that the themes he preferred were emphasized with bold underlines. Two letters written within days of the end of the convention in Philadelphia already showed the basics of what we shall refer to as the authorized interpretation.

Just two days after the convention's final gavel fell, Roosevelt wrote this account to his friend, Seth Low, who was serving as president of Columbia College (later Columbia University): "It was simply impossible to resist so spontaneous a feeling. When I stood the state machine on its head and forced them to decide against me, the only effect was to make the rest of the country absolutely unanimous and neither Hanna nor anyone else could stop it."[2]

Shortly thereafter he wrote to his older sister, Anna Roosevelt Cowles, whom he affectionately called Bamie: "It was the feeling of the great bulk of the Republicans that I would strengthen the national ticket and they wanted me on it at all hazards."[3]

Time and again in his correspondence, Roosevelt used the phraseology *standing the state machine on its head*; that is, he was defining a pivotal political moment as one he managed and manipulated to his preferred ends, thereby seeking to exclude any suggestion in the authorized interpretation that he fled a threatening situation in New York or that others controlled his fate. Just as the *Puck* cartoon could suggest two nearly opposite meanings, so it was that an account of the Republican convention could obviously lead to differing views. Indeed, one could say that it was not the state political machine that Roosevelt set on its head; rather it was the interpretation of history he intended to shape by turning it topsy-turvy.

During the convention, Senator Hanna met with Roosevelt. Out of a determination to dissuade his vice presidential candidacy, Hanna told the governor that New York's Boss Platt was setting the course that would end with a Roosevelt nomination and that only a definitive withdrawal from availability would prevent it. Roosevelt, in turn, issued a statement that left the matter muddled and appeared to open the door to action by those delegates who favored his nomination.[4]

What Roosevelt described as standing "the state machine on its head" is clearly defined in his 1913 autobiography: "Most of the [New York] delegates were under the control of Senator Platt. The Senator notified me that if I refused to accept the nomination for Vice President, I would be beaten for the nomination for Governor. I answered that I would accept the challenge, that we would have a straight-out fight on the proposition, and that I would begin it at once by telling the assembled delegates of the threat, and giving fair warning that I intended to fight for the Governorship nomination, and, moreover, that I intended to get it. This brought Senator Platt to terms. The effort to instruct the New York delegation for me was abandoned."[5]

In Roosevelt's authorized interpretation, this moment of victory for him was when he assumed the prospect of the vice presidential nomination was behind him. It was also the moment of greatest surprise in his narrative because it was then that the undeniable force of popular will overtook him, and he was unable to avoid the pressure in favor of his nomination. It is a tidy package and a good story. In fact, many of the events occurred as they are represented in the authorized interpretation.

What Roosevelt intended to convey with the details of his narrative was that he wrested control of the situation from Platt, staving off an attempt by the New York machine to force the governor to accept the vice presidential nomination. This so impressed the remainder of the delegates that Roosevelt could not resist their determination to draft him. As he wrote six days after the convention to Dr. Lyman Abbott, a theologian who supported governmental reforms, "The delegates . . . said: "So Roosevelt has stood Platt on his head has he? Well, that settles it. We might not have wished him placed on the ticket by Platt, but now we have got to have him anyway."[6]

However, what the newly minted candidate completely overlooked in the authorized interpretation were the behind-the-scenes machinations of Platt working with Quay of Pennsylvania and other powerful party leaders to engineer the Roosevelt nomination over Hanna's objections. Most tell-ingly, the governor's narrative ignores the most obvious and honest per-spective on the outcome—namely, that Platt achieved his goal in the end. While events may have dictated detours at this or that point in the journey, Platt and his coconspirators reached their desired destination. When every-one left Philadelphia, Roosevelt was on the national ticket and would soon be exiting New York politics.

These glimpses of Roosevelt creating his authorized interpretation are significant in what they reveal about the man and his motivations. He needed to portray himself standing strong in the face of that which he viewed as evil—whether Platt, machine politicians, corrupt businessmen, civil service cheats, or foreign oppressors—both for his psyche and for those whose good opinion he sought. He wanted the admiration of family, friends, voters, and the public generally, and he spent great effort crafting his desired image. Indeed, one would not be disappointed in an attempt to understand the life of Theodore Roosevelt by viewing his decisions and actions through the lens of this personality dynamic.

Understanding the months between the nominating convention and his election to the vice presidency abets the interpretation of Roosevelt's contributions to American history. For him it was a time of transition and uncertainty. Had he made the right political choice to accept the nomi-nation? Would the McKinley-Roosevelt ticket be elected? Would the vice presidency be a springboard to greater success or a plank walking him into obscurity?

These broad questions mixed in his mind with the more practical con-cerns of the moment. How could his actions in the campaign further bur-nish his image? What efforts were expected by party leaders and what could he tolerate? He knew the importance of humility, as he wrote to Presi-dent McKinley, "It is entirely unimportant what I say compared with the immense importance of what you say."[7] He also knew the fickle nature of fame. To his oldest daughter, Alice Lee, he wrote, "This popularity of mine is in its very nature evanescent."[8]

At least twice in his correspondence from the period, Roosevelt reveals that dignity has importance to his image of himself. In the letter to Seth Low there is this reflection on recent events: "I was not entirely satisfied with Depew's speech in reference to me [at the convention]. He spoke of me as a cowboy and the like as undignified."[9] And in correspondence with Sena-tor Hanna regarding campaign tactics, Roosevelt wrote, "I must avoid at all hazards giving the belief that I am going to do anything undignified."[10] Yet, he gave clear evidence that he would control his dignified mien, when writing to Cecil Arthur Spring Rice, a British diplomat who had been the best man at Roosevelt's marriage to Edith. Of his appeal to voters in the western states, he wrote to his close friend, "They regard me as a fellow barbarian and like me much."[11]

Was he truly revealing in this letter to Rice an aristocratic air in his view of the nation's citizenry? It is unquestionably true that Roosevelt's perspectives were informed by the stereotypical ideas of the privileged, eastern community of nineteenth-century Americans, and this feature of his character makes his subsequent actions on the vice presidential campaign trail all the more interesting.

Roosevelt was, for example, quite cynical about the electorate. To John Hay he wrote, "I should suppose we would re-elect the President but at times I feel rather melancholy when I realize the infinite capacity of the American mind to look at facts from a queer angle."[12] Even more sharply, he complained about the voters to his beloved sister Bamie: "The combination of all the lunatics, all the idiots, all the knaves, all the cowards and all the honest people who are hopelessly slow-witted is a formidable one to overcome when backed by the solid South. . . . Moreover the best interests are curiously apathetic. . . . So there is plenty of room for alarm."[13]

That Roosevelt chose to rationalize his acceptance of the vice presidential nomination in altruistic terms is demonstrated everywhere in his correspondence. "The great bulk of the party insisted upon having me," he wrote to New York's civil service commissioner, Silas Wright Burt, "feeling that I was absolutely necessary in this crucial contest for what I regard as the salvation of the Nation."[14] To Paul Dana, editor in chief of the *New York Sun,* he complained that while he would have preferred to stay in his current position, "it is evident that I help the ticket."[15] And to his close political friend and eventual successor in the presidency, William Howard Taft, Roosevelt was quite blunt: "I could not refuse without giving the ticket a black eye."[16]

Roosevelt extended this thought in a letter to George Hinkley Lyman, a fellow Harvard graduate and member of the Republican National Committee: "Every real friend of mine will consistently speak of me as exactly what I am, the man chosen because it is believed he will add strength to a cause."[17] That cause could not have been clearer in Roosevelt's mind—namely, "the definite overthrow of Bryanism, a movement which is fraught with such terrible menace to the country."[18]

Despite his claim that he was enlisting in a righteous crusade, Roosevelt was careful to remind friends of one overriding theme, as he did his comrade in arms, General Leonard Wood: "The office [of vice president] meant nothing to me, indeed meant only sacrifice."[19] Yet the governor was also careful not to express total disdain for his situation, surely to avoid the image of the besieged dilettante, as in his letter to John Hay: "Well, now I join the innumerable throng of New York's vice presidential progeny *in esse* or *posse*. I should have liked to stay where there was real work; but I would be a fool not to appreciate and be deeply touched by the way I was nominated."[20] Roosevelt added a positive spin, when writing to New York Harvard Club chum Winthrop Chanler, whom he addressed as Winty: "In one way I shall be glad to get a little in touch with national affairs again because I am really down at the bottom more interested in them than in state and municipal affairs."[21]

Several of Roosevelt's letters from the latter half of August relate to an issue that had vexed him since his wartime service in Cuba. While his heroic character was widely celebrated by citizens across the nation, official recognition had been less generous, perhaps because the colonel had written a publicly released letter after the hostilities in which he demanded the troops be conveyed at once to the United States. Conditions were abysmal for the encamped and idle soldiers, and Roosevelt led the advocacy effort to hasten their return.

The public nature of this volunteer colonel's actions were an affront to secretary of war Russell Alger, and the specter of official unhappiness with his military service arose to trouble Roosevelt in subsequent political campaigns. Indeed, it may have cost him the Congressional Medal of Honor during his lifetime. He had been nominated and certainly coveted the award, but it would not come his way until 2001, more than eighty years after his death.[22]

Roosevelt must have heard rumblings that his political opponents intended to claim his military heroism was mostly fantasy, and his correspondence shows he was preparing to defend himself. The following are four telling quotations demonstrating this to be an important issue to the candidate:

To Elihu Root, who had succeeded Russell Alger as secretary of war: "That pleasant creature Senator Pettigrew [of South Dakota], and divers other Democrats, have started to attack my military record. . . . I should like to have copies of the letters sent to the War Department recommending me for a Medal of Honor."[23]

To Charles Henry Burke, Republican congressman from South Dakota: "Tomorrow I shall consult Senator Hanna as to whether it would not be well to have published the recommendations of my officers that I be given a Medal of Honor for gallantry at San Juan."[24]

To Henry L. Turner, a fellow veteran of the war against Spain in Cuba: "I am rather amused at Pettigrew's stating that I was two miles in the rear of my men at San Juan, while Altgeld gave me the credit of shooting the Spaniard in the back on the firing line. The two positions are hardly consistent."[25]

To Charles Richard Williams, editor of the *Indianapolis News:* "Please do not quote me personally, as I do not care to be involved in personal denials. The facts are simply that without any suggestion of mine, Generals Shafter, Wheeler, and Wood wrote to the War Department recommending me for the Medal of Honor."[26]

As he readied himself for the national campaign, Roosevelt naturally worried over the details, communicating regularly with Senator Hanna and other party leaders. To Hanna, for instance, he offered his full effort: "I am strong as a Bull Moose and you can use me up to the limit," with a single caution, "taking heed of but one thing and that is my throat. Two years ago in the New York campaign I only managed to hold out just barely to the end and could not have spoken for three days longer. . . . I do not want my throat to give out."[27] This request came within a week of the end of the convention.

There were also other things on Roosevelt's mind as he negotiated his campaign activities with Hanna, the same Republican boss who had opposed his nomination. Still thinking of his dignity, he wrote: "I most emphatically do not wish to appear like a second-class Bryan." Democrat William Jennings Bryan had traveled thousands of miles in his 1896 presidential campaign and made hundreds of whistle-stop speeches in towns and cities across the nation. This concern, related to Roosevelt's desire to maintain his dignity, was also expressed within days of the convention's conclusion. However, in the same letter, he acknowledged that he knew "it was desired that I should go over the country and make a certain number of speeches in the doubtful western states as well as in my own."[28]

Then there was this more definitive statement to Hanna during the second week of July: "Do remember not to make me do a rear platform canvass, save where it is absolutely unavoidable. I can do far more satisfactory work by a set speech."[29] In hindsight following the campaign, it is obvious that party leaders paid this directive absolutely no heed.

By mid-August the outline of the vigorous whistle-stop campaign schedule was known by Roosevelt and party leadership, yet the candidate continued to plead, as in this letter to Henry Clay Payne, a key Republican committeeman from Wisconsin who would eventually become postmaster general during Roosevelt's presidency: "I must make the most emphatic protest against the plan for me to speak all day long in the open air from the tail end of the car. I do not think such a course is wise or dignified, and I know that it means that in the middle of the campaign you will have to pull me out and stop my speaking entirely because my voice will give out. . . . The real point is for me to appear in [each] state and make one speech which can be read throughout it, and then go on."[30]

As the events of September and October would show, the candidate's plea fell on deaf ears. Rough Rider Roosevelt had agreed to run, and run he would at full speed all day, every day, throughout the fall campaign.

CHAPTER 4

PARTY PLATFORMS AND PUBLIC POLICY

When Theodore Roosevelt wrote the narrative of his life in 1913, he described the public policy concerns during his vice presidential campaign thusly: "In 1896, 1898, and 1900 the campaigns were waged on two great moral issues: (1) the imperative need of a sound and honest currency; (2) the need, after 1898, of meeting in manful and strait forward [sic] fashion the extraterritorial problems arising from the Spanish War. On these great moral issues the Republican party was right."[1]

While Roosevelt's summary offers a tidy package of two issues as he recalled them more than a decade after the 1900 campaign, the actual statements provided by the Republican and Democratic platforms do not fall quite so conveniently into these neat categories. Furthermore, the speech-making on the campaign trail strayed occasionally beyond these boundaries.

When the Republicans met in Philadelphia from June 19 to 21 and the Democrats gathered in Kansas City from July 4 to 6, the platforms discussed by the delegates included not only Roosevelt's two issues, but also a range of other public policy matters. Some of these occupied the candidates and their supporters during the campaign; others were not aired except in the formally adopted documents. From the party platforms of 1900 come the following statements that provide an outline of the parties' positions.[2]

On McKinley's Performance

REPUBLICANS: "President McKinley has been in every situation the true American patriot and the upright statesman, clear in vision, strong in judgment, firm in action, always inspiring and deserving the confidence of his countrymen."

DEMOCRATS: "Believing that our most cherished institutions are in great peril, [and] that the very existence of our constitutional republic is at stake

... we earnestly ask for ... the hearty support of the liberty-loving American people."

On the Spanish War

REPUBLICANS: "The American people ... have conducted and in victory concluded a war for liberty and human rights. . . . It was a war unsought and patiently resisted, but when it came the American Government was ready."

DEMOCRATS: "The burning issue of imperialism growing out of the Spanish war involves the very existence of the Republic and the destruction of our free institutions. We regard it as the paramount issue of the campaign."

On Sound Currency

REPUBLICANS: "We renew our allegiance to the principle of the gold standard . . . and we favor such monetary legislation as will enable the varying needs of the season and of all sections to be promptly met in order that trade may be evenly sustained, labor steadily employed, and commerce enlarged."

DEMOCRATS: "We reiterate the demand of [the 1896 Democratic] platform for an American financial system made by the American people for themselves, and which shall restore and maintain a bi-metallic price-level, and as part of such system the immediate restoration of the free and unlimited coinage of silver and gold at the present legal ratio of 16 to 1."

On Trusts

REPUBLICANS: "We recognize the necessity and propriety of the honest co-operation of capital to meet new business conditions and especially to extend our rapidly increasing foreign trade, but we condemn all conspiracies and combinations intended to restrict business, to create monopolies, to limit production, or to control prices."

DEMOCRATS: "The dishonest paltering with the trust evil by the Republican Party in state and national platforms is conclusive proof of the truth of the charge that trusts are the legitimate product of Republican policies, that they are fostered by Republican laws, and that they are protected by the Republican administration, in return for campaign subscriptions and political support."

On Tariffs

REPUBLICANS: "The Republican Party . . . promised to restore prosperity by means of two legislative measures—a protective tariff and a law making gold the standard of value. . . . No single fact can more strikingly tell the story of what Republican Government means to the country than this—that while during the whole period of one hundred and seven years from 1790 to 1897 there was an excess of exports over imports of only $383,028,497, there has been in the short three years of the present Republican administration an excess of exports over imports in the enormous sum of $1,483,537,094."

DEMOCRATS: "Tariff laws should be amended by putting the products of trusts upon the free list, to prevent monopoly under the plea of protection. . . . We condemn the Dingley tariff law as a trust breeding measure, skillfully devised to give the few favors where they do not deserve and to place upon the many burdens which they should not bear."

On Labor

REPUBLICANS: "In the further interest of American workmen we favor a more effective restriction of the immigration of cheap labor from foreign lands, the extension of opportunities of education for working children, the raising of the age limit for child labor, the protection of free labor as against contract convict labor, and an effective system of labor insurance."

DEMOCRATS: "In the interest of American labor and the uplifting of the workingman, as the cornerstone of the prosperity of our country, we recommend that Congress create a Department of Labor, in charge of a secretary, with a seat in the Cabinet."

On Annexing the Philippines

REPUBLICANS: "Our authority could not be less than our responsibility; and wherever sovereign rights were extended it became the high duty of the government to maintain its authority, to put down armed insurrection, and to confer the blessings of liberty and civilization upon all the rescued people."

DEMOCRATS: "We condemn and denounce the Philippine policy of the present administration. . . . [It has] placed the United States . . . in the false and un-American position of crushing with military force the efforts of our former allies to achieve liberty and self-government."

◆ ◆ ◆

It should be noted that the Republican platform contained statements on several other issues. The party favored the liberal administration of veterans' benefits, an efficient civil service system, attention by the states to better roads, an extension of rural free delivery, and the annexation of Hawaii. This election being held two decades before the implementation of the Nineteenth Amendment, Republicans also congratulated "the women of America upon their splendid record of public service . . . [and for] their faithful co-operation in all works of education and industry." Thus, the Republican delegates intended to broaden their appeal with positions and statements on several issues.[3]

It was the Democrats who focused most of their platform's attention on the two issues Roosevelt recalled from 1900 when he later wrote his autobiography. Indeed, the Democrats clearly saw vulnerability in the opposition party over a growing national concern regarding imperialism and militarism. Also, faithful to their recent past, Democrats chose to emphasize their traditional sixteen-to-one stance on monetary policy.[4]

As the campaign proceeded, the two issues Roosevelt later highlighted in his autobiography did, indeed, define much of the territory upon which the political battle was fought. As we shall discover, the vice presidential candidate made one statement after another in regard to these matters in towns and cities across the United States, even as William Jennings Bryan was offering voters the opposing view. However, local and regional interests often forced additional issues into the candidate's speeches, and some of these situations created the most colorful and interesting moments of the campaign.

Before we begin the long campaign journey with Theodore Roosevelt, there are useful insights regarding his views on the public policy questions in his formal letter accepting the party's nomination for the vice presidency. These perspectives would play out again and again in his whistle-stop speeches. The acceptance letter was published with the date of September 15, 1900, a day Roosevelt spent campaigning in North Dakota, but the candidate had written much of the document during the two summer months immediately following his nomination.[5]

As the vice presidential candidate on the Republican ticket, it might have gone without saying that Roosevelt assessed the first four years of the McKinley presidency favorably, but he underscored his view of "the work which has so well begun during the present administration."[6] He wrote: "Under administration of President McKinley this country has been blessed with a degree of prosperity absolutely unparalleled, even in its previous prosperous history."[7] However, if the economic success was to continue, "the currency of this country must be based upon the gold dollar worth one hundred cents."[8] The Democrats' proposed sixteen-to-one ratio of silver to gold to expand the money supply would prove ruinous in Roosevelt's view.

Among the few ambivalent situations in which Roosevelt found himself was that of the Republican position on—and, more generally, cozy relationships with—big businesses and the trusts. He had built a reputation as governor of New York by standing up to businessmen and their abuses; indeed, a principal reason he was leaving the governor's chair was the threat that big business would not support a Roosevelt reelection campaign to return to Albany. The Democratic platform took a strong antitrust position, but the Republicans found a middle course more satisfying for their friends and supporters. Thus in his official acceptance letter, Roosevelt termed the issue of trusts "a serious problem," but he quickly followed with the acknowledgment that "the problem is an exceedingly difficult one." In a circuitous argument he condemned "indiscriminate denunciation of corporations generally, and of all forms of industrial combinations in particular." Yet he attempted to maintain his own tough reputation by recognizing unspecified "real abuses," and stating for the record that "there is ample reason for striving to remedy these abuses."[9] He came down squarely astride the two positions on these issues.

Matters on which Roosevelt took a more focused stance were the charges of imperialism and militarism leveled by Democrats against McKinley and his Republican administration. As there was controversy swirling around the annexation of the Philippines following the end of the Spanish War with the Treaty of Paris, Roosevelt sought to justify the action of the United States by comparing it to Jefferson's acquisition of the Louisiana Territory in 1803. He wrote:

"The doctrine of 'the consent of the governed' . . . was not held by [Jefferson] or by any other sane man to apply to the Indian tribes in the Louisiana territory which he thus acquired, and there was no vote taken even of the white inhabitants, not to speak of the negroes and Indians, as to whether they were willing that their territory should be annexed. The great major-ity of the inhabitants, white and colored alike, were bitterly opposed to the transfer. An armed force of the United States soldiers had to be hastily sent into the territory to prevent insurrection . . . exactly the same purpose [for which] President McKinley has sent troops to the Philippines . . . [because they are] not fit or ready for self-government."[10]

By this logic that he would repeat frequently during the campaign, Theo-dore Roosevelt explained his view that US actions in the Philippines were appropriate, even righteous. Here was a candidate for the nation's second-highest office writing not only the words cited previously, but also sharpen-ing his thought as follows: "The reasoning which justifies our having made war against Sitting Bull also justifies our having checked the outbreaks of Aguinaldo and his followers."[11]

Roosevelt was about to campaign by train across South Dakota and neighboring states, home to Sitting Bull and the tribes of the great Sioux Nation, yet he felt completely comfortable publishing these comments in late nineteenth-century America. He and his campaign advisors were revealing not only their perspectives, but also their understanding of the views held by people he was about to visit. Soon after writing his official acceptance letter, Roosevelt made similar remarks at stops throughout the western states. In several communities, he was greeted by members of American Indian tribes seemingly supportive of his candidacy.

Such comments and contradictions have drawn scholarly attention. For example, Sarah Watts recalled that Sitting Bull's horse was featured in Buf-falo Bill's Wild West show after the chief's death doing tricks and perform-ing in dramas that portrayed battles between the US cavalry and American Indian tribes. She wrote that such demonstrations "alternatively teased and boggled the public's imagination . . . [and] helped dissociate war against the Indians from its brutality and misery and reestablished it as vaudeville entertainment that appealed to the nation's romantic sense of itself."[12]

Leroy G. Dorsey wrote: "Roosevelt used his public rhetoric to shape a diverse collection of people—white and non-white alike—into one mythi-cal, cohesive identity. . . . [His] rhetorical treatment of Indians perhaps hurt them as much as any other racist dialogue of the day. His portrayal of their supposed savagery echoed other popular works of the time, perhaps affirm-ing rather than submerging that notion in the public's consciousness. . . . As myths can do, Roosevelt's Americanism simultaneously offered desired change for one group [American Indian] and reestablished the status quo for another [White Americans]."[13]

CHAPTER 5

JULY AND AUGUST TRAVEL

If a voter in 1900 was the proud owner of a Columbia graphophone and purchased the wax cylinder featuring the most popular song of the day, he would have been singing the words, "I love you as I never loved before."[1] Though the intended object of affection in the ditty was a wife or girlfriend, the line might as easily have applied to the newly nominated Republican vice presidential candidate. Why was he so beloved? As the aptly titled "McKinley and Roosevelt" campaign song promoted: "Then let us praise McKinley's name from Mexico to Maine / And Teddy Roosevelt just the same for whipping treacherous Spain."[2] As the campaign began, the Rough Rider halo still floated above Theodore Roosevelt.

Less than two weeks following the close of the Republican convention, it was time for Roosevelt to travel to the second Rough Riders' reunion scheduled for July 1 to 4 in Oklahoma City, Oklahoma Territory. During the previous summer's journey to the first reunion in New Mexico, Roosevelt's heroism had been celebrated at stop after stop, and the widespread affirmation undoubtedly encouraged thoughts of national office. This trip to the second gathering, overlaid as it was by his recent vice presidential nomination, surely added to the candidate's confidence.

Fully seven thousand people greeted Roosevelt at his stop in Kansas City. At small communities between that grand reception and another celebration in Topeka, Kansas, "the applause was without limit," the *St. Louis Republic* reported. However, the same story included this observation: "[The acclaim] was not so much for Roosevelt as a candidate for vice president as for 'Teddy,' the Rough Rider and man." This reporter's conclusion was that Roosevelt had transcended politics, a stature few politicians achieve.[3]

Some journalists interpreted events more modestly, as with this report in a small-town Oklahoma newspaper: "The nomination of Governor Roosevelt as the Republican vice presidential candidate has augmented the great interest in the southwest in his visit here."[4] Still, when Roosevelt arrived at the reunion on July 2, the reception was anything but subdued: "A typical frontier demonstration and a rousing welcome from Rough Riders, cow punchers, and citizens of all classes, white, black, and red, were accorded today to Governor Theodore Roosevelt. . . . He rode a black charger in the procession. . . . He was cheered along the line, the cry, 'Hurrah for Teddy' being the prevailing sentiment."[5]

From stories that filled newspapers nationwide, voters could hardly have seen the second Rough Riders' reunion as anything short of a campaign launch. In Wichita, Kansas, readers learned that "when Roosevelt was introduced, he was met with cries of 'Vice President, Vice President!'"[6] And in Prescott, Arizona, the media account of the reunion portrayed events focused squarely on one particular hero: "At night a pyrotechnical display, 'The Battle of San Juan,' will be given, and there will be a military ball in honor of Governor Roosevelt."[7]

What had been almost universally positive media reports on the Roosevelt trip to the 1899 reunion eroded somewhat during the 1900 journey precisely because of the vice presidential nomination. Newspapers with a Democratic bent could not allow the Republican candidate's perceived failings to go unremarked. This editorial observation from a journalist in Hutchinson, Kansas, is an example of the new political dynamic: "Bryan seldom repeats himself in a speech, seldom uses the same phrases and illustrations. But in his 'non-political' speeches along the road to the Rough Riders Reunion, Teddy made the same speech he made a year ago on his way to New Mexico. . . . Teddy had better take a day off and learn a new one."[8]

During his Oklahoma trip that lasted from July 2 to 6, Roosevelt stopped in several smaller communities. These include such places as: Newkirk, Oklahoma; Holliday, Lawrence, Osage City, Emporia, Florence, Winfield, Arkansas City, Peabody, and Newton, Kansas; and Galesburg, Illinois. Additionally, he took care of campaign business with Mark Hanna in Cleveland and with William McKinley in Canton, Ohio, where the president was summering at his home.[9]

At Emporia, the always-charming Roosevelt said to his listeners, "I am glad that I should be making my first speeches since I was nominated here in Kansas, because it was your delegation that forced me to become a vice presidential candidate." He also told the good folks of Kansas that it was not his intention to talk about politics on this particular trip. However, he said about this resolve, "I don't know that I can very well help it, because this year the issues that are at stake in politics are those in which I believe with my whole heart and soul; because to me the honor and welfare of the country are at stake." At one point in the speech, the *Indianapolis Journal* reported that a woman waved her arms and shouted, "Thank God, we don't want 16 to 1 anymore, and we won't have it."[10]

During a brief stop in Osage City, Roosevelt shook hands and received a large bunch of Kansas sunflowers. He left the train at Newton to the cheers of two thousand people and addressed the crowd at an auditorium. While visiting Florence, the candidate spoke favorably of the African American soldiers with whom he had fought in Cuba, some of whom had graduated from the nearby Haskell Institute at Lawrence. He extended this line of thought with the awkward comment, "If we ever have another war, which I earnestly hope we will not, maybe I will have some Filipinos in my regiment."[11]

Coverage of Governor Roosevelt's long train trip to Oklahoma City was summarized thusly by a newspaper back home in New York City: "Something very like a triumphal tour was the Governor's dash across Kansas. . . . At every station along the line, after leaving Kansas City about 10 o'clock in the morning, crowds of enthusiastic Kansans gathered to cheer him on his way, whether the Governor's train was scheduled to stop there or not. The Governor made 18 speeches in all today."[12]

Three days later and following his reunion with comrades in arms, Roosevelt made a brief stop in Cleveland, Ohio, to confer with Senator Hanna and another to visit William McKinley at his home in Canton, Ohio. This was the site of the famous front porch where the president had made a show of hosting 750,000 visiting voters during the 1896 campaign, thereby garnering significant media attention sitting in a rocking chair, while William Jennings Bryan raced around the country to one whistle stop after another. One could not miss the image of McKinley, again in the 1900 campaign, enjoying conversations on his stoop, while Bryan and Roosevelt traveled the nation battling each other for votes.[13]

Hanna had visited McKinley earlier in the week to talk campaign strategy and to arrange the formal notification of nomination in Canton for the following week. In the local newspaper was a curious report: "[Hanna and McKinley were] talking over the little surprise party that is to be held when the president is notified. . . . It was a very delicate subject as McKinley had to be told all about it without having him understand what it was all about, but Mr. Hanna looked as if he had been quite equal to the task and was in a jolly humor."[14]

Roosevelt's visit to Canton drew national attention. For example, San Francisco voters read: "The home city of the President today accorded to his colleague on the Republican National ticket an ovation almost unprecedented even in Canton. It would be hard to say whether the citizens of Canton voiced a more demonstrative welcome to President McKinley or Governor Roosevelt."[15]

This being the first public appearance of the two together, it is not surprising that a wire service reporter wrote that "[Roosevelt's] only companions from Cleveland to Canton were the newspapermen who have accompanied him on his long trip to Oklahoma." Indeed, local folks wanted to give the visiting reporters a show: "As the Governor alighted from the train whistles blew and cannon boomed and an immense crowd gathered about the station and gave him a mighty cheer of welcome."[16]

The story of the reception in Canton ran coast to coast, so that voters in cities such as Wheeling, West Virginia, also had the opportunity to read Roosevelt's speech. He said of McKinley, "I shall follow and support [him] with every ounce of strength that there is in me." Of his opponents, the Democrats, he said, "In Kansas City [at the Democratic convention] they have had a little difficulty in finding out what they believe." Then, he couldn't resist this brief and memorable statement on the issue of sound money in light of a disagreement within the Democrats' platform committee: "I see by the papers that they had some difficulty extending finally to a vote of 27 to 25 in putting in free silver. . . . Now we believe with all our faith in a dollar worth 100 cents. Apparently they had 52 per cent of faith in a 48 cent dollar."[17]

It was Roosevelt at his most personable, and the more subdued McKinley must have dealt with mixed emotions as he stood beside his vice presidential running mate on the most famous front porch in America. In fact, when the crowd sought a statement from McKinley, he offered simply a rather weak announcement that he would again campaign from his rocking chair. The president said, "I only appear that I may say that I am going to be with you most of this summer." Unsurprisingly, a journalist noted that given this brief remark, "the crowd soon afterward broke up."[18]

Following this show of traveling to Ohio to honor and confer with McKinley and Hanna on their turf, Roosevelt returned to his family home on Long Island. Other than a four-day train trip later in July to St. Paul, Minnesota, and a quick overnight to Washington, DC, in August, he spent two months in Oyster Bay with infrequent trips into the city for meetings at the Union League Club.[19] He did not occupy the governor's mansion in Albany, nor did he make regular campaign appearances on behalf of the Republican ticket. Between the end of his party's convention on June 21 and the departure for his major campaign trip to the west on September 2, he spent fifty-eight of the seventy-one days in summer retreat.

Of singular interest during these weeks of little or no public campaigning is Roosevelt's trip to St. Paul, Minnesota. He left New York City on Sunday evening, July 15, 1900, spoke at the National Republican League convention on Tuesday, July 17, made quick stops on Wednesday in Milwaukee and Chicago, and arrived back in New York City on Thursday, July 19. This entire trip covered nearly twenty-five hundred miles and offered Roosevelt yet another foretaste of the cross-country campaign travel that was to come.

Several aspects of this trip early in the campaign season are interesting in retrospect. One dustup was reported by the *Minneapolis Tribune* three days prior to Roosevelt's departure from New York. Although Minneapolis, the larger of the two twin cities, had expected a speaking stop after the vice presidential candidate addressed the gathering in St. Paul, the announcement came that rail schedules and the need to visit Chicago would not allow for another appearance in Minnesota.[20] Coverage of this announcement made the community's disappointment and the risk of political damage obvious.

Demonstrating the same competitive spirit between these two adjacent metropolitan areas, leaders of the St. Paul event sought and received assurances that Roosevelt would not stop along the way to speak to any other community or group. This allowed the National Republican League, an organization of local Republican organizations from around the country, to bill the candidate's speech as the "Keynote of the Republican National Campaign of 1900."[21]

Roosevelt's day in St. Paul was to include a breakfast with the Commercial Club, a small and informal luncheon with key local and statewide leaders, and a formal dinner with still another group of influential individuals at the Minnesota Club. Also there was to be a parade in the evening.[22] This was the schedule as announced by Minneapolis media.

St. Paul journalists, on the other hand, were considerably more effusive in their coverage after the visit: "St. Paul yesterday gave Gov. Roosevelt of New York a welcome worthy of the man. . . . [He was] cheered liberally en route to the hotel. . . . During the afternoon he grasped the hands of thousands at the Ryan Hotel, and at the Auditorium he delivered what must be regarded as the opening speech of the campaign." Even the smallest detail was noted by the St. Paul newspapermen because this was an event for the ages in their eyes, made more important as it was theirs exclusively:

"There's nothing perfunctory about Col Roosevelt's handshake. He just takes your hand—not like a pump handle either—[and] gives it a hearty grip that makes you feel good all over."[23]

Minnesota's Republican leadership must have found a way to salve any injured egos because the Minneapolis media were also enthusiastic on the day following the event. The report in the *Minneapolis Tribune* after the candidate had departed carried this headline: "Greatest Political Demonstration in the History of the Northwest."[24] As we shall see, this was but the first of many instances that a community claimed its welcome of Theodore Roosevelt was the most extraordinary political celebration any person ever experienced.

Celluloid jugate buttons promoting the major party candidates for president and vice president of the United States in the election of 1900. The Republican candidates were William McKinley and Theodore Roosevelt. The Democratic candidates were William Jennings Bryan and Adlai Stevenson. Note in the lower-right image that the donkey has Bryan's face. (Upper and middle: *Private Collection. Photographer—Pat Hilpert.* Lower left: *Anderson Americana Auction, July 2014.* Lower right: *Old Politicals Auction, October 2014.*)

Upper: *Puck* centerfold from April 18, 1900, showing President William McKinley pondering the choice of running mates for the upcoming campaign. Middle: *Puck* cover from September 12, 1900, illustrating Theodore Roosevelt as a maverick cowboy who was "branded" the Republican Party's vice presidential candidate but "not broken." Lower: *Puck* cover from May 16, 1900, depicting Governor Roosevelt of New York in Rough Rider attire being enticed toward a vice presidential candidacy by sirens representing all regions of the nation. (All: *Library of Congress* and *Theodore Roosevelt Digital Library, Dickinson State University.*)

Upper left: Ribbon badge likely worn at the Republican National Convention in Philadelphia from June 19-21, 1900. Upper right: William McKinley and Theodore Roosevelt on the front porch of the president's home in Canton, Ohio. Lower left: Roosevelt with his second wife, Edith Carow, and his six children. Lower right: Roosevelt vice presidential celluloid portrait button. (Upper left and lower right: *Private Collection. Photographer—Pat Hilpert.* Upper right: *Almanac of Theodore Roosevelt.* Lower left: *Wikimedia Public Domain Document.*)

Photographs of Theodore Roosevelt campaigning from a train and from a speakers' platform. (Upper: *Private Collection. Photographer—Pat Hilpert.* Lower left: *Almanac of Theodore Roosevelt.* Lower right: *Wikimedia Public Domain Document.*)

Theodore Roosevelt's heroic image as leader of the Rough Rider volunteers during the 1898 War with Spain was a ubiquitous element of his 1900 campaign for the vice presidency. (Lower right: *USAmericana Auction, November 2013*. All others: *Private Collection. Photographer—Pat Hilpert*.)

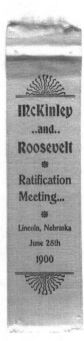

Upper left: Celluloid jugate button worn by supporters of the McKinley and Roosevelt ticket in Montana. Others: Five campaign ribbons from Republican events during the 1900 campaign; those from Deadwood, the St. Louis Coliseum, and Cedar Rapids were produced for Theodore Roosevelt's whistle stops. (Upper right: *Adams Museum in Deadwood, SD. Photographer—Tia Lanphear.* All others: *Private Collection. Photographer—Pat Hilpert.*)

Upper and middle: Celluloid buttons worn by supporters of the Republican ticket in the election of 1900. Theodore Roosevelt visited in or near these communities during his whistle-stop tour. Lower: Two coattail buttons depicting McKinley and Roosevelt with candidates for statewide offices. Aaron T. Bliss was the Republican nominee for governor of Michigan. Samuel R. Van Sant was the Republican nominee for governor of Minnesota. Both Bliss and Van Sant won their races. (All: *Private Collection. Photographer—Pat Hilpert.*)

THEODORE ROOSEVELT'S RECENT VISIT TO WEST COLUSA MINE, BUTTE, MONTANA.

THE ROUGH RIDER'S START ON THE ROUND-UP.

Newspapers across the nation covered every aspect of Theodore Roosevelt's 1900 campaign on behalf of the Republican ticket. Upper: Hand-drawn illustration of the candidate's visit to a copper mine near Butte, Montana. Lower: Cartoon of Rough Rider Roosevelt holding two placards related to the campaign issue of gold versus silver standards. (Upper: San Francisco Call, *September 23, 1900, p. 15.* Lower: Salt Lake Herald, *September 17, 1900, p. 1.*)

The Roosevelt Wild West Show Hits Utah.

GOLDEN INGOTS OUTWEIGH SILVER BRICKS.

Upper: Newspaper cartoon showing Theodore Roosevelt as the leader of a Wild West show troupe riding into Utah. Lower left: Image from a campaign poster promoting the McKinley and Roosevelt ticket. Lower right: Hand-drawn illustration from a newspaper supporting the Republican position that the gold standard was to be preferred over silver. (Upper: Salt Lake Herald, *September 21, 1900, p. 1.* Lower left: *Almanac of Theodore Roosevelt.* Lower right: San Francisco Call, *October 21, 1900, p. 13.*)

GOVERNOR ROOSEVELT STOOD WITH UNCOVERED HEAD ACKNOWLEDGING
THE CHEERS OF THE PARADERS.

Cornelius N. Bliss stood at his side.

Upper: Photograph of Governor Theodore Roosevelt reviewing the McKinley and Roosevelt Business Men's Sound Money Parade in New York City on November 3, 1900. Lower: Republican campaign poster for the election of 1900 highlighting achievements during President McKinley's first term. (Upper: New-York Tribune, *November 4, 1900.* Lower: *Hake's Americana and Collectibles Auction, January 2010.*)

Part Three

RUNNING TO WIN: SEPTEMBER TO NOVEMBER 1900

CHAPTER 6

MICHIGAN, INDIANA, ILLINOIS, AND WISCONSIN

Each summer, the citizens of Aberdeen, South Dakota, together with hundreds of visitors celebrate the memory of L. Frank Baum and his popular books enjoyed by children and adults alike. Baum once ran a dry goods store and published a newspaper in the community. He became known for his satirical editorials that never shied away from biting comments on political issues. Though the author left Aberdeen prior to the publication of *The Wonderful Wizard of Oz* (1900) and subsequent books in the series, locals find the inspiration for his characters and images in his Aberdeen experiences.

On the other hand, reviewers and historians have argued since almost the time the tales were published that Baum had other and better-known references in mind. Did the Yellow Brick Road symbolize the gold standard? Was the Emerald City a stand-in for Washington, DC, or perhaps the color had something to do with greenbacks? Was Dorothy a fictionalized image of a naive American public? And most interesting for our study of the 1900 election, could the Cowardly Lion have been William Jennings Bryan in allegorical form?[1]

Bryan, whose name notably rhymes with *lion,* seemed to his supporters anything but cowardly. His roaring oratory grabbed the attention of the Democratic Party convention in 1896 and vaulted him to the first of his three presidential nominations as the youngest candidate ever to head a major party ticket. His two terms in the US House of Representatives showed his electability. He gathered volunteers from his adopted home state of Nebraska to fight against Spain in Cuba and was appointed a colonel. However, illness kept him in Florida and away from the fighting. Yet it is not his recuperation that historians cite as the reason Baum may have painted Bryan with the cowardly lion image. Some offer the candidate's critique of the nation's policy on the annexation of the Philippines; others suggest the weakness of his arguments for revised monetary policies. L.

Frank Baum provides no definitive answers; thus, the academic controversies may continue undeterred.

There is no question that Bryan adopted positions and fought for them, often beyond reason. When the Democrats were writing their 1900 platform and Bryan's preference for sixteen-to-one silver-to-gold coinage was drawing heavy fire, the candidate wrote to party leaders: "If by any chance the committee on resolutions decides to report a platform in which there is not a silver plank . . . I will come to Kansas City on the fastest train available, make a fight for silver on the floor of the convention, and then decline to take the nomination if the convention omits the ratio."[2] Clearly, Bryan was an idealist ready to fight for his principles, as the infamous Scopes trial would demonstrate much later in his life.

Those who met, knew, or just observed Bryan during his campaigns often found much to admire. Journalist Sewell Ford was a well-known political commentator at the end of the nineteenth century. When Bryan secured his second presidential nomination, Ford wrote these words published in various newspapers across the nation: "A big man with a big mind and a big heart. This is the impression William Jennings Bryan makes on persons. . . . A man of ideas and ideals." Ford also commented on Bryan's vigorous pursuit of the presidency: "In his remarkable campaign of four years ago [Bryan] traveled over 18,000 miles. Since then he has been on the go for the better part of three years. His total mileage since his first nomination would equal three times around the distance of the earth."[3]

Thus the champions for the 1900 election were ready for the contest. In early September, presidential candidate Bryan and vice presidential candidate Roosevelt began chasing around the country on trains, soliciting votes, shaking countless hands, and delivering hundreds of speeches. They spoke from the rear of their railcars, from station platforms, from outdoor speakers' stands constructed for the occasions, and from auditorium stages. They marched in parades, attended receptions, and ate countless meals with business and political leaders. They patted children's heads, tasted grandmothers' cakes, listened to proud parents' stories of children's accomplishments, and complimented event planners. They recognized local heroes and addressed regional sensitivities, even as they promoted their party platforms and parried attacks by their opponents.

While President McKinley made occasional campaign appearances, he spent much of his time on his front porch in Canton, Ohio, or in the White House in Washington, DC, receiving visitors and acting presidential. Roosevelt's vice presidential counterpart on the Democratic ticket, Adlai

Stevenson, did some traveling, but he generated little publicity or attention compared to the two principal contenders who campaigned in the limelight. McKinley and Stevenson were older political warhorses, one having a term as president on his résumé and the other a stint as vice president during Grover Cleveland's second administration. McKinley was fifty-seven years old during the campaign, and Stevenson celebrated his sixty-fifth birthday a few weeks before the election. By contrast, Bryan was forty years of age, and Roosevelt turned forty-two on October 27, 1900.

As August passed, the starter's pistol was about to fire for the sprint to Election Day on November 6. Roosevelt's principal assignment was to win voters in the West, Midwest, and states bordering the Old South where he would spend most of his time during September and October. Chicago was his first major stop. Local labor organizations had invited both Roosevelt and Bryan to appear at a large Labor Day celebration on Monday, September 3. They arrived in Chicago within hours of one another on Sunday evening and stayed in the same hotel complex—rooms in the Auditorium and the Auditorium Annex. Both initially refused to discuss campaign issues with newspapermen because the event organizers had billed the celebration as nonpartisan. However, the presence of each political party's most assertive champion certainly created a stir.

Here is how the *Rock Island* (Illinois) *Argus* described the first public encounter between the two candidates: "The number in the parade of labor organizations is figured at 30,000 and it was reviewed from the loggia of the Auditorium Hotel. . . . At 10:30 when the column passed, Mayor Harrison stood alone on the balcony. Five minutes later Bryan made his appearance . . . greeted by a volley of cheers. Then came the Colonel of the Rough Riders, who was cheered by the great crowd that lined the east side of Michigan Avenue. Governor Roosevelt reached across the heads of a number of committeemen and gripped the hand of Colonel Bryan and the crowd renewed its cheering."[4]

Perhaps the handshake was intended to demonstrate sportsmanship or collegiality, but it proved to be the only nonpolitical gesture of the day. Supporters of both candidates openly expressed their opinions: "The procession as it passed the reviewing stand was a series of continuous cheering. The men in line shouted the names of their favorites and swung their hats and canes in the air. First it was Bryan and then Roosevelt who were cheered. 'Hooray for Bryan. You're all right, Billy!' was answered by 'Hello, Teddy. Hooray for Roosevelt!'"[5]

Immediately after the parade concluded, the candidates were taken to a meal in the hotel billed as a flag-of-truce luncheon with union leaders, and from there the two went to nearby Electric Park for open-air speeches. While newspaper accounts varied on their assessment of which candidate was more eloquent or persuasive, there was general agreement that Roosevelt, who spoke first and left for his return trip, observed the nonpartisan expectation, while Bryan stepped across the line blatantly, particularly as he brought up the subjects of militarism and imperialism.

This is a quotation characteristic of Roosevelt's two o'clock speech: "To do our duty—that is the summing up of the whole matter. We must do our duty by ourselves and we must do our duty by our neighbor. . . . There can be no substitute for the world-old, humdrum, commonplace qualities of truth, justice and courage, thrift, industry, common sense, and genuine sympathy with and fellow-feeling for others. The nation is the aggregate of the individuals composing it."[6]

Demonstrating the difference in Bryan's four o'clock remarks are these words: "A law already enacted makes subjects of the Porto [sic] Ricans, withdraws from them the guarantees of the Constitution, and asserts the power of the President and a Congress to govern them without their consent and tax them without representation. . . . On Election Day [laboring men] with their silent ballots can shape the destiny of this nation and either bring the government back to its ancient landmark or turn it into the pathway followed by the empires of the Old World."[7]

"Bryan Not Fair," proclaimed the next day's headline in the *Indianapolis Journal,* and the subhead offered a sharp contrast: "Injected Politics into His Chicago Labor Day Speech, While Roosevelt Declined to Violate the Truce and Delivered a Nonpartisan Address."[8] Some newspapers around the country more supportive of the Democratic cause were not as pointedly accusatory in their coverage of Bryan's trespass, yet it appeared that round one had gone to the Republicans.

This trip to Chicago had a whirlwind character. Roosevelt departed New York on Sunday, joined the festivities on Monday, and left Illinois that same day to return to New York. Upon arrival in his home state on Tuesday, he went immediately to Saratoga to address the New York State Republican Convention, the gathering that would nominate a candidate to succeed him as governor.

Delegates to the convention in Saratoga warmly welcomed Governor Roosevelt. He used his time on the dais to support strongly the newly nominated Republican candidates for statewide offices and to offer a list of his administration's accomplishments. Of course, he could not resist a media opportunity to campaign for a McKinley and Roosevelt victory in

November, veering strangely toward the extreme of apocalyptic rhetoric. He said: "The interests at stake for the state are great, but those at stake in the nation as a whole are greater. . . . We appeal to all men who are in heart and purpose, and not merely in name, Americans, to stand with us for the re-election of President McKinley, because against him are arrayed the forces of chaos and evil, the forces of repudiation and dishonor."[9]

Furthermore, he had this warning for those who dared to support the Democratic candidate: "The men who directly or indirectly aid Mr. Bryan in this contest must understand . . . [that] upon all such men will rest forever afterward the heavy responsibility of having plunged the business world into disaster, the laboring world into misery, and of tainting with dishonor the national name."[10] No delegate left the hall with any doubt about Roosevelt's passion, but some may have wondered whether his tiring journey and the stress of his pending transition had exaggerated his frequent tendency toward hyperbole.

Also, there was surely no delegate leaving the hall facing a more demanding schedule. The *Evening Times* from Washington, DC, reported his quick turnaround as the candidate left to fulfill the principal campaign assignment: "Governor Roosevelt's western campaign car 'Minnesota' was attached to the rear end of train 23 [leaving Albany]. . . . The Governor came down from Saratoga in time to fix up a few of his personal affairs in Albany before leaving his official home for six weeks."[11]

So far-reaching was the interest in everything Roosevelt that newspaper readers in El Paso learned: "Governor Roosevelt will start from here [Saratoga] this evening on a stumping tour of the west. . . . He will make a rapid tour of all the principal cities of the west and northwest, returning to New York about Oct. 15."[12]

Journalists of the period acknowledged the unusual nature of the election of 1900, one in which a vice presidential candidate received so much attention. An editorial from Scranton, Pennsylvania, pointed to this historical quirk: "Not often does a candidate for the vice presidency receive as much attention from the opposite party as has been accorded to Theodore Roosevelt by the Democrats this year. That the Democrats are engaged in a desperate attempt to smother him in mud is obvious. . . . In brief, Theodore Roosevelt is too well-known and too well-liked a man to be successfully lied about."[13]

Of course, those offering criticisms were not deterred by Roosevelt's reputation, as they sought weaknesses to highlight. From the wonderfully named *Kansas Agitator* came this jab: "New Yorkers have the same sort of a kick coming as have Kansans. Their Governor Teddy Roosevelt spends very little time at the capital."[14] Ohioans read: "Before Theodore Roosevelt closes his campaign he will have all kinds of explanations to make. To the general public Mr. Roosevelt must explain how he happens as a candidate to advocate a policy of imperialism and colonization which as an author he so vigorously condemned. To Democrats Mr. Roosevelt must explain the libel he uttered upon a class of patriotic men when he said: 'The Democrats stand for lawlessness and disorder.' . . . [And] Mr. Roosevelt must explain his insult to the American volunteer . . . when he wrote, 'The Rough Riders are as good as any regulars and three times as good as any state troops.'"[15]

As the words flew back and forth, Roosevelt boarded his special train and headed west accompanied by a small staff and an ever-changing entourage of politicians and luminaries who sought to enhance their own reputations by association. Officials of the national party worked with state committees to plan the trip, city by city and event by event.

Before Roosevelt returned to New York, he would make campaign stops through the following states (in order of first stop): Michigan, Indiana, Illinois, Wisconsin, South Dakota, Iowa, Minnesota, North Dakota, Montana, Idaho, Utah, Wyoming, Colorado, Kansas, Nebraska, Missouri, Kentucky, Ohio, West Virginia, and Maryland. Occasionally, the route took him to one or another state a second time; for instance, he made stops in eastern South Dakota between September 11 and 14, and subsequently he visited western South Dakota on October 3. Also, he stopped in Indiana on September 8 as he traveled to the west, and during his return journey eastward he made additional stops in the state between October 10 and 12. In the end, there was talk of Roosevelt's record-breaking effort that surpassed the nation-wide effort of William Jennings Bryan in the 1896 presidential campaign.

Following are the stops in chronological order that Theodore Roosevelt made during his whistle-stop tour to Michigan, Indiana, Illinois, and Wisconsin between September 6 and 10, 1900:

Thursday, September 6, 1900
   Detroit, Michigan
Friday, September 7, 1900
   Bay City
   Saginaw
   Owosso
   Lansing
   Jackson

Eaton Rapids
Charlotte
Hastings
Grand Rapids
Saturday, September 8, 1900
  Holland
  Allegan
  Kalamazoo
  Benton Harbor
  Niles
  South Bend, Indiana
  Hammond
Sunday, September 9, 1900
  Chicago, Illinois (no campaign events)
Monday, September 10, 1900
  La Crosse, Wisconsin

Though the visits to St. Paul on July 17 and the Labor Day trip to Chicago on September 3 involved train travel westward from New York, it is a fair claim that Roosevelt's first stop on the western campaign tour was in Detroit on September 6. As the Roosevelt special railcar traveled a short distance through Canada on the trip to Michigan's metropolitan center, a welcoming committee of 150 from Detroit met the train at Essex, Ontario, and presented the vice presidential candidate with a "magnificent floral shield."[16]

Upon arrival at the station in Detroit, Roosevelt was greeted by "large numbers of citizens" and he "was soon shaking hands with both hands at once." In short order, a procession with a band formed and the entire assemblage "marched around City Hall to the Hotel Cadillac."[17] Greeters were decked out for the occasion: "From every man's coat lapel hung a miniature Rough Rider hat swinging on a red ribbon. There were also large numbers of photograph buttons, illuminated badges and other insignia all over the coats of these persons."[18] Lunch was with dignitaries at the Detroit Club, and then the candidate was afforded a few hours rest at his hotel.

In the evening, an early reception began the activities, followed by a large rally at the Detroit Light Guard Armory. It was reportedly "all the governor's most ardent partisans could have desired in point of attendance and enthusiasm."

Only two downside comments found their way into the newspaper wire stories. Russell Alger, formerly secretary of war and the official Roosevelt had openly criticized in 1898 for not bringing home the troops from Cuba expeditiously, was a prominent Michigan Republican who was said to have snubbed Roosevelt by skipping the rally. Also, journalists reported that while three thousand shook the candidate's hand at the reception, at least "half of them were women."[19] This was considered a negative in those days prior to women's suffrage in most states.

What could be simply termed *Roosevelt rhetoric* was flying in Detroit. He railed: "The Kansas City [Democratic] platform commits our opponents to a policy which means material disaster and moral disgrace. . . . The nation that accepts such moral principles cannot live. It will rot to death in the loathsome stew of its own corruption."[20]

Further, and seemingly unmindful of audiences he would face within a few days, he charged forward with these words: "The men who are making speeches on the unrighteousness of our expanding in the Philippines might with as much justification incite the Sioux and the Apache tribes to outbreak against us on the ground that we have no right to retain South Dakota or Arizona. . . . Stand with us now against the men who would bring such abuse and misery upon our country and support us as we uphold . . . the honor of the American flag in the face of all the peoples of the earth."[21]

Roosevelt spoke to those assembled at the Detroit armory for about one hour. By most newspaper reports, his address was enthusiastically received, and he bolstered regional support for the Republican ticket. Following the rally, he returned to the train for a midnight departure.

Friday, September 7, was the second day of the Michigan campaign, and activities began with a stop in Bay City, followed in order by stops in Saginaw, Owosso, Lansing, Jackson, Eaton Rapids, Charlotte, Hastings, and Grand Rapids. At most of the stops, Roosevelt addressed crowds numbering in the hundreds or thousands. In its Sunday edition of September 9, the *New York Times* would report that their state's governor had delivered twenty-one speeches in Michigan and Indiana within two days and that "while in strong health and good spirits the Governor is very much exhausted by his recent labors."[22] Following are highlight from Friday's stops, as reported in newspapers across the nation.

Bay City. "The day was opened by the Bay City meeting at 7 a.m. The Governor was met by a committee and a band. In front was a squad of militiamen in cavalry uniforms. The procession moved up into the city. Many of the houses along the route were decorated. . . . The stand had been built in front of the court house. He spoke to about 8,000 people."[23] The crowd at this event included several members of Michigan's chapter of the Grand Army of the Republic (GAR). Roosevelt was a favorite for many of them, and he used the occasion to speak as a veteran of the recent war to those who fought in the Civil War: "You of Bay City sent your sons to the Spanish war as their fathers before them had gone to the Great War. It was a small war, but it showed the spirit of the people. It showed that they had not forgotten the lesson taught in the great contest of '61 to '65. You did not let us contract in 1865 and we won't contract now."[24]

Saginaw. "At 9 o'clock, the party left [Bay City] for Saginaw. When the Roosevelt train reached Saginaw, a large crowd greeted the vice presidential candidate at the station. A procession escorted the visitors to a stand erected in the center of the city from which Governor Roosevelt spoke five minutes."[25] According to wire service reports, costumed Rough Rider troops escorted Roosevelt at Saginaw, and ten thousand people heard him address the charge of expansionism.[26] During his remarks, the candidate pointed to a banner he spotted in the crowd and said: "The issue of the campaign is contained in that placard: "Let Well Enough Alone." . . . Let the American people have the good sense to keep in office the man under whose administration we have accomplished our present prosperity. . . . We appeal . . . [to] all good Americans to stand with us."[27]

Owosso. "At 11 o'clock the party pulled out [of Saginaw] for Owosso. The Roosevelt special arrived here [Owosso] at noon and a stop of 25 minutes was made. The speakers' stand was only a block from the depot, so practically all of the time was available for speaking."[28] Roosevelt was apparently feeling contentious: "I wish I had an opportunity to talk to you at length on more than one issue. There is this difference between us and our opponents in this campaign. . . . Mr. Bryan not only won't talk on the issues we raise, but he does not even talk of the issues they have raised themselves."[29]

Lansing. "Escorted by the Commercial Travelers' Club of Lansing Roosevelt on arrival here drove to a large tent which had been erected on Michigan Avenue, two blocks from the station and spoke to an enthusiastic audience. . . . At 2 o'clock the party left for Jackson accompanied by an escort from that city."[30] While in Lansing, the candidate said to the crowd: "I do not care how honest and brave a man is, if he is a natural born fool, he is worth nothing on earth. You have got to have common sense. . . .

Government is a difficult thing . . . and common sense enters into every problem from the currency to the Philippines."[31]

Jackson. "At Jackson Mr. Roosevelt met a large number of citizens in the public square, where a stand had been erected, and here he again spoke for ten minutes."[32]

Eaton Rapids, Charlotte, and Hastings. "Good crowds had been assembled. No speaking was done, but a good deal of handshaking was accomplished."[33]

Grand Rapids. The *New-York Tribune* reported: "The demonstration at the Auditorium tonight in point of numbers and enthusiasm surpassed anything that has yet taken place at any meeting held in the present campaign in honor of the vice presidential candidate. Thousands were unable to obtain admittance to the hall, which was crowded to its utmost capacity. . . . When Governor Roosevelt advanced to the stage, the great audience broke into enthusiastic applause."[34] According to coverage by the *Times* in Washington, DC, Roosevelt made two addresses in this city: "The Governor spoke at an overflow meeting in Powers Opera House after making the main speech of the evening."[35] Perhaps the candidate still had in mind his earlier address to the GAR veterans when he said, "In many points there is a curious similarity between this campaign of 1900 and the campaign of 1864, when President Lincoln was re-elected. Not since the close of the Civil War have we ever had an administration which did so much to uphold the honor and interest of America as President McKinley's [administration]."[36]

On the following day, Saturday, September 8, Roosevelt was again in motion from morning to evening, making these Michigan stops: Holland, Allegan, Kalamazoo, Benton Harbor, and Niles. The major stop of the day was in South Bend, Indiana, as the train made its way to Chicago for a day of rest on Sunday. Highlights from the Saturday stops follow.

Holland. When Roosevelt was introduced by the president of a local college, he noted the audience was composed "almost wholly of Hollanders and their descendants."[37] He took the opportunity to recall his own heritage and won the hearts of those who had come out for his morning address: "Roosevelt with a laugh opened his address with 'My fellow-Dutchmen.' This set the crowd cheering, and some of the old settlers yelled Dutch salutes."[38]

Allegan. "The special train then proceeded to Allegan, where the Allegan Rough Rider Club mounted, met Gov. Roosevelt at the station and escorted him over the mile drive to the Court House Square, where a speakers' stand was erected. . . . Fourteen young ladies, wearing Rough Rider hats and carrying flags, threw flowers at Gov. Roosevelt when he finished his speech, and then escorted him back to the train, where all insisted upon shaking his hand."[39]

Kalamazoo. "Governor Roosevelt's special arrived here [Kalamazoo] at noon and a long line of marchers accompanied by bands escorted the governor to the city park."[40] Journalists reported a fifty-minute stop.

Benton Harbor. "There was a great crowd at Benton Harbor, where the Governor left his coach and spoke for ten minutes or more on the financial question and expansion."[41]

Other than a final brief stop at one thirty in Niles, Michigan, on the way to South Bend, Indiana, this busy Saturday morning closed the Michigan portion of Roosevelt's western campaign tour. Already the candidate was feeling the effects of the grueling schedule, and he joked with the newspapermen who were also making the trip that he would "be glad when he crosses the Michigan state line into another state where the Central Committee does not work its candidates so hard."[42]

There was, however, to be no rest for Roosevelt on the evening of September 8, as the Indiana Republican Campaign Committee intended to use the vice presidential candidate's visit to the fullest. Two days prior, the *Indianapolis Journal* reported the status of the expectations: "Indications that a large crowd will be in South Bend on Saturday to give a rousing and enthusiastic welcome to Hon. Theodore Roosevelt continue to multiply. The Indiana towns and cities of Mishawaka, Logansport, Indianapolis, Frankfort, Rochester, Plymouth, Walkerton, North Liberty, Bremen, Knox, Laporte, New Carlisle, Warsaw, Elkhart, Goshen, and others will send people here. . . . Governor Roosevelt will arrive at 5 o'clock in the afternoon on the Michigan Central Railroad. . . . At the South Bend station he will be received by Rough Rider and marching clubs and escorted to the Republican tent, where he . . . will deliver an address."[43]

Predictions of success may even have been understated, as this report of the celebration suggests: "Governor Roosevelt was given a royal greeting on his arrival here at 5 o'clock this afternoon. Over 20,000 people, workingmen and others in Rough Rider uniforms from northern Indiana welcomed the Colonel. It was the most enthusiastic reception he has received on his western trip. . . . To South Bend the day was the greatest in its history so far as crowded streets can tell of immense numbers."[44] Details demonstrate the extent of the preparations: "When the parade started at 4 o'clock there was a small army of riders in the city. South Bend's Rough Riders, commanded by Col. Samuel Leeper, numbered 500. All were fully uniformed and rode big horses. New Carlisle's troop, also uniformed, numbered 250." Also listed in the reports were thirteen other locations that sent Rough Rider troops plus at least fifteen bands and a dozen Republican clubs in the parade.[45]

More than four thousand people crowded into a tent for the speaking. One newspaper proclaimed that "of 12,000 employed in the different factories [of South Bend] 10,000 are for McKinley and Roosevelt."[46] Tired as he was, Roosevelt rose to the occasion, saying to the assembled: "It is the duty of every voter to survey the whole field and then, with the net result in mind, determine whether the present administration shall be continued. It should be enough that this administration is Republican. We know what the McKinley administration is. Who knows what a Bryan administration would be?"[47]

One newspaper contrasted a recent Democratic event: "Just one week ago Bryan was here, but there was no parade, no men or marching clubs to fall in behind the flag. There was a mere handful of people at the depot to meet him, estimated at less than two hundred."[48]

Roosevelt's train pulled away from South Bend at 6:40 p.m., made a brief stop in Hammond, Indiana, for a last campaign appearance, and reached Chicago late in the evening. Roosevelt stayed at the Auditorium Annex where he had spent time during the Labor Day celebration just six days earlier. He and his fellow travelers rested on Sunday, a pattern he intended to keep throughout the next several weeks.

Although Michigan, Indiana, and Illinois were billed as the first stops of the western trip, the real West of 1900 began only when the train crossed the Mississippi River. One campaign stop remained prior to reaching the western states—La Crosse, Wisconsin. In order to meet the schedule, Roosevelt's rest ended Sunday evening: "Between 10 and 11 o'clock he proceeded to the station of the Milwaukee and St. Paul Railway, where he boarded the special car Minnesota, in which he has journeyed from New York and retired for the night. This coach will be attached to the fast mail train . . . at 3 A.M. for La Crosse, Wis. where the Governor is billed to speak tomorrow afternoon."[49]

This was a pivotal stop in Wisconsin, though there would be other visits by Republican leaders to Milwaukee and elsewhere. Roosevelt arrived at 11:00 a.m. and was treated to a parade. He actually spoke twice on Monday, September 10. There was a speech at 2:00 in the afternoon for visitors who arrived on several trains specifically for the candidate's visit. At 8:00 p.m. there was a second, larger gathering where Roosevelt addressed local citizens.[50]

As he had done at previous stops, Roosevelt included references to American Indian tribes in his remarks, obviously not concerned about repercussions at stops further west. He said when discussing the Democratic charge regarding militarism: "We have no larger a proportion of soldiers to the population now than we had one century ago, during the presidency of the elder Adams. In 1870 there was more militarism than now, because militarism was caused by an outbreak of the Sioux, the Comanches, and the Arapahos. There is no more danger from the soldiers now than there was then."[51]

He asked forcefully for the votes of his listeners: "For the sake of yourself and for the sake of your wives and families and for the well-being of our people, I appeal to you for the re-election of President McKinley."[52]

With the cheers of the voters of Wisconsin ringing in his ears, Roosevelt left that same evening for an even more exhausting week in the Dakotas. In his mind and in the minds of those he would visit next, he was headed for home.

CHAPTER 7

SOUTH DAKOTA

As the waiting father welcomed home the prodigal son, the people of South Dakota opened their arms to Governor Theodore Roosevelt of New York when he visited during his campaign for the vice presidency in September 1900. Roosevelt had, after all, spent the middle years of the 1880s as a resident of Dakota Territory. "People knew that the man who could come from a luxurious New York home and adapt himself almost in a day to the rough life of the cowboy of the plains . . . was made of the right stuff," crowed South Dakota's *Aberdeen Daily News*.[1]

After the planning and negotiating, the missteps and recoveries, and the trek across half the nation on a state-by-state whistle-stop tour, Roosevelt and his companions reached the eastern border of South Dakota on September 11, 1900. By the time he exited the state on September 14, he had appeared in twenty-seven of the state's communities located east of the Missouri River. Nearly three weeks later as he toured Nebraska, he would make a short detour into western South Dakota for two additional stops at towns in the Black Hills.

Though South Dakota's four electoral votes may have shifted away from their support of Democrats in 1896 to the Republican column without a Roosevelt campaign visit[2]—McKinley won a solid 57 percent of the ninety-six thousand popular votes in this 1900 election[3]—the vice presidential candidate doggedly traveled hundreds of miles by rail and maintained a rigorous appearance and speaking schedule over the four days of whistle stops, setting a pattern that would accelerate over the days and weeks spent on this campaign tour through the West, the Midwest, and the states bordering the Old South.

In one small community after another, Roosevelt staged responses to attacks made against the president by the Democratic candidate, William Jennings Bryan of neighboring Nebraska, and by the powerful US senator from South Dakota, Richard F. Pettigrew, a converted Silver Republican,[4] who believed the Republican president to be "weak, insincere, deceitful, the tool of men who seek to control the money of the world, a bidder for the smiles and favors of the rich, and a whitewasher of infamy in high places."[5]

Journalists from the Associated Press, the Scripps and McRae Press Association, and from six major newspapers in New York, Chicago, and Minneapolis traveled with Roosevelt, and their reports carried his messages to a nationwide audience.[6] These newspapermen came to be known as Camp No. 2 of the Roosevelt Rough Writers.[7]

South Dakota's major newspapers gushed praise for Roosevelt before, during, and after his visit. He was "the brilliant scholar,"[8] the "most representative American alive today,"[9] the "popular hero of the United States,"[10] the "man of the hour [and] an out and out statesman whom the politicians cannot corrupt,"[11] the "gallant Rough Rider,"[12] and the "idol and hero of the ranges."[13] Most newspaper reports and opinion pieces took the position that Governor Roosevelt was destined to become the next vice president of the United States. (Two notable exceptions were the *Vermillion Plain Talk* and the *Yankton Press and Dakotan,* both of which reported negatively on the visits and even ridiculed Roosevelt and his record.)

Roosevelt met or exceeded all expectations. His speeches were filled with patriotism and references to his western adventures. He was clear in his message that the president had set the nation on a course ensuring prosperity at home and respect abroad. For instance, at Mitchell he spoke to a crowd of four thousand urging the reelection of the president for "the sake of preserving the national prosperity . . . and to start fair in the race for national greatness."[14]

Phrases used by the newspaper representatives reporting on the celebrations could hardly have been more laudatory. His was a "triumphant tour of South Dakota."[15] His "first day in South Dakota was a hummer."[16] The candidate received "a real frontier welcome."[17] Indeed, the newspaper with the largest circulation in the state, the *Daily Argus-Leader* of Sioux Falls, headlined its front-page story on Roosevelt's visit to the city with classical phraseology, making the grand declaration, "*Veni! Vidi! Vici!*"[18]

Insofar as one could cover in four days the entire eastern half of South Dakota using the nineteenth-century rail system, Roosevelt and his small supporting cast undertook to do so. This troupe traveled by special train,[19] and a railcar, the *Minnesota,* usually reserved for the private use of railroad officials, was placed at the governor's disposal so that he might travel comfortably and properly entertain visits by dignitaries and calling committees.[20] Aside from the New York governor, the most prominent of those in the traveling party through South Dakota were Governor Leslie M. Shaw of Iowa, US senator Knute Nelson of Minnesota, and Colonel Melvin Grigsby (see chapter 1).

The day-by-day itinerary was ambitious but the schedule generally held throughout the trip. Following is the agenda of Roosevelt's vice presidential campaign trip to South Dakota, with those stops that were added en route marked as unscheduled. (For most of the states visited on this tour, this level of detail as to the precise times of arrivals and departures is not available. In those instances where there is information on times or duration of stops, it is shown in the chapter-by-chapter lists.)

Tuesday, September 11, 1900
    Flandreau 8:00 a.m. to 8:30 a.m.
    Egan Unscheduled
    Madison 9:50 a.m. to 10:20 a.m.
    Dell Rapids Unscheduled
    Sioux Falls 12:30 p.m. to 3:30 p.m.
    Canton 4:00 p.m. to 4:15 p.m.
    Hawarden and Akron, Iowa Unscheduled
    Elk Point 5:45 p.m. to 5:55 p.m.
    Vermillion 6:25 p.m. to 6:35 p.m.
    Yankton 7:25 p.m. to 11:00 p.m.
Wednesday, September 12, 1900
    Chamberlain 8:00 a.m. to 9:00 a.m.
    Kimball Unscheduled
    Plankinton 9:45 a.m. to 9:55 a.m.
    Mitchell 11:45 a.m. to 12:45 p.m.
    Woonsocket 1:30 p.m. to 1:40 p.m.
    Wolsey 2:15 p.m. to 2:25 p.m.
    Huron 2:40 p.m. to 4:40 p.m.
    De Smet 5:45 p.m. to 6:10 p.m.
    Brookings 7:30 p.m. and overnight
Thursday, September 13, 1900
    Castlewood 9:00 a.m. to 9:10 a.m.
    Watertown 9:40 a.m. to 11:00 a.m.
    Clark 12:00 noon to 1:00 p.m.
    Redfield 2:15 p.m. to 3:00 p.m.
    Faulkton 4:00 p.m. to 5:00 p.m.

Aberdeen 7:15 p.m. and overnight
Friday, September 14, 1900
    Webster 8:00 a.m. to (not recorded)
    Summit Unscheduled
    Milbank 9:45 a.m. to 10:15 a.m.
    Wilmot Unscheduled
    Sisseton 11:30 a.m. to 12:00 noon

As Roosevelt negotiated the details of his campaign tour with party leaders, he consistently stated a preference to make one or two major stops in each state where he would address large crowds. In this model, he would rely upon newspapers to carry his message to the remainder of each state's population. However, state committees preferred multiple stops to heighten the excitement by showing off the Republican celebrity in as many places as possible.

Eventually, party leadership selected a strategy that combined the two approaches, thus significantly elevating the level of effort expected of Roosevelt. The pattern in this chapter and those that follow recognizes that both proposed approaches affected the scheduling and differentiates between major and other stops. South Dakota being the first of the true western states, several stops were planned as pivotal—the one in the state's largest city and those made on each of the three evenings—and these four stops are designated as major: Sioux Falls, Yankton, Brookings, and Aberdeen.

Major Stops in South Dakota

Sioux Falls.   Tuesday, September 11, 1900, dawned as "Roosevelt Day" in Sioux Falls.[21] Throughout the morning stops, Roosevelt and his traveling companions encountered damp and disagreeable weather. However, by late morning the skies cleared and a stiff wind dried the streets of Sioux Falls. This same wind later proved raw enough that Governor Roosevelt chose to deliver his principal address inside the auditorium, while others spoke from an outdoor speakers' stand constructed at Ninth Street and Minnesota Avenue.

When the train arrived, steam whistles blew across the city. Giant stars and stripes decorated the main streets. Stretched across Ninth Street was a huge banner with the legend, "1900 McKinley and Roosevelt Four More Years of Prosperity 1904." Cheering crowds lined a parade route; they waved handkerchiefs, flags, hats, and canes as the dignitaries passed in carriages escorted by the Lennox and Rock Rapids bands, more than thirty-five marching clubs, and a company of mounted cowboys. So crowded was the city that those arriving after 10:00 a.m. by horse-drawn means were unable to stable or hitch their horses anywhere near the site of the 12:30 p.m. celebration.

Roosevelt spoke to the enthusiastic crowd in the auditorium for thirty minutes, telling them that one must have a patriotic spirit, basic honesty, courage, and good sense, and concluding that the candidates on the Republican ticket had these characteristics in full measure. He answered directly the charges of South Dakota's US senator Richard F. Pettigrew, a resident of Sioux Falls, who had charged the president with imperialism in his conduct of foreign affairs. Pettigrew had become a so-called Silver Republican in 1896 and was heavily involved with the Progressive Party movement in 1900.

Moving to the outside venue, Roosevelt delivered a shorter speech to a larger crowd in a voice already strained by overuse on the campaign tour. He said of the McKinley and Roosevelt ticket: "From the Atlantic to the Pacific we are going to roll up majorities that will bury once for all the party that stands opposed to the material prosperity of the country at home and to the honor of the flag abroad."[22]

Yankton.   This community was the last stop on Tuesday, September 11.[23] Here the parade included more than one hundred mounted horsemen in Rough Rider attire, detachments of Civil War and Spanish War veterans, several Republican clubs, and American Indians who had painted their faces and clad themselves in blankets and feathers. Dozens of marchers held lighted Roman candles and shot rockets. Mile-long lines of onlookers filled both sides of the parade route, and they were holding Chinese lanterns with pictures of McKinley and Roosevelt and torches for the affair that began at 7:25 in the evening. Accounts estimated a crowd of six to eight thousand people gathered around the speakers' stand at Walnut and Third.

As the local newspaper that had chosen to support the Democratic ticket in 1900, the *Yankton Press and Dakotan*[24] reported the visit of New York's governor much less generously than all other published accounts. Under the headline "Roosevelted" and the subhead "A Meeting Which Was Scarcely up to Republican Expectations," the candidate's tour of the state was labeled, "Maverick Hunting through South Dakota." The article reported less than three hundred people in Yankton's parade and a crowd of thirty-five hundred or fewer. Acknowledging the cheers, Roosevelt "bowed his thanks in one sweeping obeisance, the political decay in his famous teeth appearing to good advantage, and his Rough Rider hat crushed in his right hand." Of his voice, the account said that it sounded "as though its owner disliked his job."

Two incidents threatened to mar the Yankton event. The horses pulling Governor Roosevelt's carriage bolted just as he was stepping out at the speakers' stand, but several young men, described in the account distributed by the Associated Press as "stalwart," seized and stopped the frightened animals. During the speeches, there was a fire alarm blamed by most newspaper reports on Democrats in the crowd. Again, the *Yankton Press and Dakotan* disagreed with all other sources and reported that there had indeed been a rubbish fire in the rear of the Singer Sewing Machine Company store.[25] Regardless of which account is accurate, all reports agree that the incident did not create a panic. Later, several individuals made a disturbance by shouting slogans in support of William Jennings Bryan.

Brookings. In its story on preparations for the visit of the Roosevelt train to Brookings, the *Daily Argus-Leader*[26] reported arrangements for "a monster torchlight parade."[27] This being the evening stop on Wednesday, the entire day for residents and regional visitors to Brookings was given over to receptions and numerous speeches from specially constructed street stands. Estimates of the crowd size ranged up to eight thousand. One report indicated that the number of farmers in Brookings from the countryside was at its maximum because the weather was sunny, but muddy conditions prevented work in the fields.

As the train approached the stockyards, whistles blew and cheers erupted. The South Dakota State College artillery "belched forth in thunderous tones" and rockets and Roman candles "shot athwart the sky."[28] Torches lit Main Street. The Brookings Cornet Band led the parade that included other bands and drum corps, several Republican clubs, and the Rough Rider Club of White, South Dakota, a unit claiming more than one hundred members.

Three thousand of those in attendance heard the speeches in a large tent erected on the courthouse square. Within the "monster tent"[29] was the municipal bandstand that had been converted into an extravagantly decorated speakers' platform. The Brookings Quartet entertained the crowd with campaign songs. Roosevelt spoke for thirty minutes and retired to his railroad car for a rest immediately after his speech because of what the *Brookings Weekly Register* described as a "very severe strain for several days."[30]

His speech was variously reported as "a magnificent half hour address on expansion"[31] and "short and mainly on topics already presented by him."[32] By the time the evening's speeches concluded, the crowd had spent nearly four hours inside the large tent.

Aberdeen.   Thursday's final event—and the last major stop in South Dakota—occurred in Aberdeen.[33] Judging from the volume of newspaper coverage, it seems that this event eclipsed all others in the anticipatory excitement, the marketing by local merchants, the extravagance of street decorations, the length of the parade, and the sheer numbers of torches and fireworks. So detailed were the plans that one citizen, C. F. Holmes, and a corps of assistants were assigned to tend horses at the Athletic Park to ensure that there would be no confusion of property or hard feelings. The weather surely added to the success of the event, as it was perhaps the finest evening of the South Dakota stops.

Newspaper accounts estimated that six to ten thousand people attended the Aberdeen event, including six hundred Russian immigrants from a colony forty miles to the northwest. They saw colonnade-style decorations with columns set every twenty feet from the depot running a distance of several blocks to a local auditorium known as the Grain Palace where the speakers' stand with national colors and special arc lights was located. Along the length of the parade route there were column-to-column festoons with Venetian masts at all intersections sporting colorful banners on their crossarms. Decorations graced all building fronts.

Just before a special train carrying visitors from communities to the south was to arrive, Aberdeen's chief of police received a telegram informing him that the gang of Chicago pickpockets who had first appeared at an earlier stop (see information on Huron later in this chapter) was on its way to the city by rail. The thieves were clever enough to leave the train as it stopped for a crossing, and the Aberdeen police searched the visitors' train in vain. They did arrest one fellow judged to have a suspicious look, but he escaped through a back door in the washroom at the police station. The *Aberdeen Daily News* carried a warning to the citizenry to guard their pockets and to carry as little cash as possible.[34]

When the Roosevelt train arrived, the dignitaries were taken to the speakers' stand where they reviewed the parade. It included seven hundred torchbearers, one hundred horsemen, and a long line of Rough Riders. The entire procession was six blocks in length with marchers moving six to ten abreast. Many wore locally produced Roosevelt campaign buttons that had been advertised for sale ahead of the event by a local jeweler, D. C. Callett.

Citizens of Scandinavian heritage were especially interested in Senator Knute Nelson, and they mustered at the Commercial House Hotel prior to the parade to form a special escort for him. He sent word ahead that he would like to meet with them in the Grain Palace following the speeches.

Fireworks for the event were spectacular, according to the *Aberdeen Daily News*: "At a signal the fireworks brigade turned itself loose and the scene was one which baffles all attempts at description. Hundreds of men in columns instantaneously lighted mammoth Roman candles. . . . The crowds went wild with delight. . . . Grecian candles were lighted along the entire length of the colonnade and the scene was only less dazzling than had been that of a moment before when the fireworks were being set off."[35]

After acknowledging the displays and cheers, Roosevelt addressed the crowd on the subjects of trusts and labor. He accused certain members of the Democratic Party, particularly his recent opponents in New York, of publicly denouncing trusts while secretly buying into them. He assured his South Dakota listeners that the McKinley administration would act firmly but sensibly in these matters. He used a regionally related metaphor to make his point: "Four years ago we were not bothered by trusts prospering because nothing prospered. Now you know that a good year for the farmers and a good year for wheat is also a good year for weeds, and the farmer, of course, will try to get rid of the weeds; but he is not very wise if he grows angry and plows everything under because he does not like the weeds."[36]

On the following day, Aberdeen was justifiably proud of itself for the size and quality of the celebration. In the local newspaper was this report: "Governor Roosevelt said that ever since he entered the state he was told the climax to his reception would be witnessed at Aberdeen and for that reason he expected something grand here, but the reality entirely eclipsed his ideas of what could possibly be done. All members of the party left with the impression that Aberdeen was by a good deal the best city they had visited during their trip."[37]

Highlights from Other South Dakota Stops

Roosevelt's other twenty-three stops in South Dakota were of shorter duration and received less press coverage than the four catalogued as major.

Following are descriptions of noteworthy events that occurred at some of these other stops.

Flandreau.   At this first stop in the state, a local reporter seemed surprised by the fact that "the governor appears much as the newspaper-cuts and cartoonists represent him."[38]

Egan.   During an unscheduled stop at Egan, a "grizzled and bent old veteran" grabbed Roosevelt's hand and said, "My son was with you."[39]

Madison.   In Madison the New York governor told the crowd that he felt at home in South Dakota and "would enjoy it now to be able to take a day off and go out shooting chickens."[40]

Dell Rapids.   At Dell Rapids W. A. Boyd, the only South Dakotan to serve in the Rough Riders under Colonel Roosevelt and to make the charge up San Juan Hill, met the traveling party, and Roosevelt complimented him lavishly in front of his mother and sister, as well as the other hometown folks.[41]

Canton and Elk Point.   Canton had muddy conditions that reportedly kept farmers from using the roads to attend the celebration.[42] Between the Canton and Elk Point stops, the train paused briefly in its sixty-miles-per-hour rush down the tracks to add unscheduled stops in two Iowa communities, Hawarden and Akron, as a courtesy to Governor Shaw.[43]

Vermillion.   This was one community where the enthusiasm for Roosevelt's visit was tempered by loyalties to other political parties. Though the *Mitchell Daily Republican*[44], the *Minneapolis Tribune*[45], and the *Daily Argus-Leader*[46] reported a substantial and enthusiastic crowd, the local newspaper, the *Vermillion Plain Talk,* ran this headline, "Teddy Was Here," and this subhead, "And Was Met by About Four Hundred of Our Citizens. The Teddy Enthusiasm Seemed to be at a Low Ebb."[47]

Owing to a dispute between Vermillion native Andrew Lee, who was serving as South Dakota's governor, and Melvin Grigsby, one of the dignitaries in the Roosevelt party, there was tension in the air. The *Vermillion Plain Talk* reported: "After the crowd had listened to the unpleasant remarks of Grigsby, Teddy stepped up and made his little spiel. His face looked to any unbiased spectator like an italicized question mark, which implied "What a big hero I am?" When he had finished, Charley Burke, chief hand-clapper, woke the people some and Teddy was given a dismal cheer."[48]

Chamberlain.   Wednesday, September 12, began for Roosevelt and his party in Chamberlain, which differed from other stops in smaller communities in that unique features of its celebration brought it disproportionately extensive media attention.[49] As this is a town located on the southward run of the Missouri River, those planning the celebration recognized that the largest possible crowd would include visitors who lived west of the river. Thus there was an announcement of a special offer: "Arrangements have been made with the Pontoon Bridge Co. so that every person crossing from the west side between the hours of 4:00 p.m. Tuesday September 11th and 8:00 a.m. Wednesday September 12th will receive a free return ticket over the bridge."[50]

Young American Indian men from the Chamberlain area marched as a brass band, and a group of young American Indian women rode in a wagon in the procession. Also in the parade were the Chamberlain Juvenile Band and more than one hundred mounted cowboys, some of whom had served in Grigsby's Spanish War troop.

Up to 2,500 people gathered near the speakers' stand to listen to Roosevelt's campaign speech, but he was so taken with the cowboys attending the rally at the westernmost stop in this phase of the South Dakota campaign that he spent most of his fifteen minutes talking directly to this group about his experiences on the open range. At one point, according to the *Chicago Tribune*, Roosevelt "sprang over the railing, circulated among the whirling, excited bronchos [*sic*], and shook hands with their riders."[51] When the train pulled out, the cowboys galloped alongside for one-half mile, shouting, waving their hats, and discharging their sidearms. According to the *New York Times*, "Gov. Roosevelt enjoyed the exhibition immensely."[52]

Mitchell.   Merchants throughout Mitchell sold khaki Rough Rider hats and decorated their stores with national colors.[53] Flags festooned the streets, and McKinley and Roosevelt banners hung along the route from the depot to a local auditorium known as the Corn Palace, where an outdoor speakers' stand had been constructed. Four thousand watched a parade that included a juvenile band and several Rough Rider clubs attired in matching costumes. More than one hundred horses were in the procession. Members of the Mitchell Rough Rider Club had met during evening hours near the community waterworks to drill in preparation for the event.

Roosevelt spoke for approximately thirty minutes, answering in more detail Bryan's charges against McKinley that he was guilty of imperialism, particularly in the acquisition of the Philippines and the US action in opposition to Filipino leader Emilio Aguinaldo. He likened McKinley's action to Jefferson's purchase of the territory that included the Dakotas. "Mr. Bryan says that President McKinley bought the Philippinos [*sic*] at $2.50 per head," Roosevelt said. "In that case, President Jefferson bought inhabitants, white, black, and red, of the lands then purchased at a more exorbitant price." He asked the crowd, "Can you point out any essential difference?" Then he answered his own query, "There is not a particle."[54]

Huron.   At Huron the parade included many of the same elements—bands, Republican clubs, and mounted Rough Riders—but for the first time there is mention of a few dozen young women mounted on horses wearing khaki Rough Rider hats and national color sashes.[55] American flags, bunting, and decorative draperies adorned the community's streets. Four thousand people crowded around the speakers' stand, and the Roosevelt entourage was treated to a tour of the town following the speeches.

Following the Huron stop, it was revealed in news reports that a gang of professional pickpockets from Chicago had worked the crowd. Stealing amounts at this stop between five and fifty dollars from several individuals, this group of criminals would earn more notoriety at several additional stops along the tracks.

De Smet.   On Wednesday, the people of De Smet made a day of it with baseball games before the campaign train arrived and a community dance after it departed.[56]

Redfield.   On Thursday, Redfield turned out a crowd estimated at two thousand, and a child, Ruth Prior, whose deceased father had once tutored a young Theodore Roosevelt, gave the governor a bouquet.[57] Senator Nelson and Governor Shaw remained in Redfield while Roosevelt journeyed on the train to Faulkton and then returned through Redfield on the way to Aberdeen.[58]

Watertown.   After a brief stop in Castlewood on Thursday morning, September 13, the traveling party reached Watertown where three hundred mounted Rough Riders greeted the train.[59] Estimates of three thousand were given for the size of the crowd gathered at the depot. Roosevelt led a large parade through decorated streets. His rather lengthy speech addressed, once again, questions related to militarism and imperialism, and he complimented Watertown's citizens for constructing a soldier's monument honoring the South Dakota volunteers.[60]

Clark.   During the noon hour, the Roosevelt party visited Clark, where elaborate preparations had been made to host "the largest number of people ever assembled in Clark County" who would come "irrespective of party to see and hear the hero of San Juan Hill."[61] Citizens of the county were said to be "known for the appreciation of deeds of patriotic valor" and the "ladies of this section" were particularly reported to be "deeply interested in the reception of these celebrities." Roosevelt was held by the people of Clark "to be one of the best men the nation has ever had an opportunity to honor." One aside about Clark's population was reported prior to the event: "Our Scandinavian citizens are particularly pleased because of the fact that Senator Knute Nelson, the most popular and gifted Scandinavian in the United States, is to be here at this time."[62]

According to reports, three thousand people gathered for the event, and hundreds of farm wagons lined the streets. A company of one hundred fifty costumed Rough Riders, accompanied by seventy-five women mounted on horses, escorted the party of dignitaries to the specially constructed speakers' stand, where the celebration culminated.

Webster.   Those planning the Webster event expected a crowd of five thousand, but reports following the visit set the number at eight hundred enthusiastic people.[63] In Webster, Roosevelt noted that the Democratic presidential candidate had quoted Republican Abraham Lincoln, and he said, "If Bryan lives, as I hope he will, for 35 years, I have not the least doubt that he will be quoting McKinley at that time with the same approval."[64]

Milbank.   This community's salute of guns was noteworthy enough to earn a place in newspaper accounts.[65]

Sisseton.   For the final South Dakota stop, Sisseton, the rain was falling just as it had for Roosevelt's first stop in Flandreau four days earlier. Expectations had been for five hundred American Indians on horseback wearing Rough Rider costumes and for a crowd of six thousand.[66] It was said the residents of Sisseton had spent eight hundred dollars to create the celebration.[67] Newspaper stories following the event reported one hundred horsemen and two thousand people,[68] and the weather forced the speeches from the trackside speakers' stand into the opera house.[69] Appealing to the spirit of western sturdiness right to the last, Roosevelt said to the drenched audience of people who had awaited his arrival in a downpour, "Men who would stand in rain and wind will be all right in November."[70]

Conclusion

Roosevelt circled the southeast and then northeast quadrants of the state over his four days of campaigning through the eastern half of South Dakota. This was a lengthy stay for the area covered as compared to his visits to states later on the tour. His relative pace was less breakneck than it would become, and, as a result, his visits to some of the smaller communities were longer than those to towns of a similar or even larger sizes in the later states. This suggests two conclusions: (1) plans continued to evolve as Roosevelt traveled; and (2) state committees had a strong role in planning both the number and duration of the stops. South Dakota is also noteworthy as the place where many of the references and images that would fill Roosevelt's speeches during the remaining days and weeks of the tour were mentioned for the first time.

This observation on Roosevelt's 1900 campaign in South Dakota was offered by the reporter from the *Chicago Tribune:* "One wonders riding across the still reaches of prairie landmarked here and there by a little box-shaped house, where all the people who gather at the stations live. The long rides they must make, leaving their plows idle in the furrows, tell better than words of the warm feeling they foster for Governor Roosevelt."[71]

Arthur Link observed, "Roosevelt knew that his greatest resource was the affection of the American people, and he cultivated it assiduously."[72] Clearly, the editorialist for the *Yankton Weekly Gazette* in 1900 felt that affection: "[Roosevelt] is a brother to the western man and even though it is only by adoption . . . a mysterious affinity has been created from one to the other and certainly the blue blood of the liberty-loving, God-fearing plainsman flows warm in his veins."[73]

CHAPTER 8

NORTH DAKOTA

Manly adventure enticed Theodore Roosevelt into the wilderness through-out his life. Whether hunting and ranching in the American West as a young man or exploring the African plains and the Amazon rain forest in his mid-dle and later years, he admired and emulated the likes of Richard Francis Burton and Henry Morton Stanley.

Roosevelt's childhood interest in traveling the world grew from his fascination with natural history and extended trips with his parents. His autobiography tells of multiple European visits during those years and of a journey up the Nile and another through the Holy Land when he was four-teen years of age.[1]

In his account of his early life, Roosevelt admitted to being a weak and sickly boy "with no natural bodily prowess," and he reported that encoun-ters with bullies led his father to encourage his pursuit of boxing, horseback riding, and hunting.[2] He wrote that he willingly shared his story not for the sake of "more happily constituted men," but to "show [that] the average man can profit."[3] At some point, this eastern urbanite became quite expe-rienced in the outdoor pursuits of nineteenth-century adventurers. Late in his life he would readily share such observations as "the lion is the most dangerous [game]" and "rhinoceros are truculent, blustering beasts."[4]

Roosevelt's conversion to a love of the vigorous life was already complete by his middle twenties when he traveled to the badlands of the Dakota Ter-ritory for a buffalo hunt in September 1883. Two weeks after his arrival he purchased a small ranch property and commissioned the building of an improved cabin. When both his mother and his first wife died at home in New York on the same day five months later, he moved to the Dakota Ter-ritory to deal with his grief. Shortly thereafter, he expanded his operations with the purchase of a larger ranch.[5]

His cowboy adventures in these years provided a lifetime of tales for him and his biographers.[6] As we saw in South Dakota and shall see even more sharply in this narrative of his whistle stops in North Dakota, his western experiences could be campaign tools that in the right settings were as valuable as his heroic actions in the war with Spain.

During the middle 1880s, Roosevelt frequently traveled back and forth between his home in New York City and his ranch in what soon became the state of North Dakota. He had on-site partners for the day-to-day management of the ranching property that was located north of Medora in the badlands near the Little Missouri River. After several reversals in his cattle business, Roosevelt abandoned those operations, visited the area infrequently and only for hunting, and eventually sold his ranch in the late 1890s.[7] Selling surely tugged at the strings of his heart because he was giving up what he had earlier described as "great free ranches, with their barbarous, picturesque, and fascinating surroundings [that] mark a primitive stage of existence." It was a place, he said, that he had "felt the charm of the life and exulted in its abounding vigor and its bold restless freedom."[8]

Stephen E. Ambrose described well the dynamic of Roosevelt's western experiences: "Although he was more a tourist and outside investor in the West than a permanent resident, Roosevelt and the West is one of America's great stories. His sojourns in the Dakotas, Montana, and Wyoming had a powerful influence on his outlook and politics. Most of all, his time in the West brought him great joy."[9]

While Roosevelt's years of living and working in the West contributed to his persona and were a satisfaction to him, the effect on his image was not always positive in the East. During his mayoral campaign, for instance, he was derisively introduced as "the Cowboy Candidate," and he found it necessary to blunt the implied criticism by responding, "As the cowboy vote is rather light in this city I will have to appeal to the Republicans."[10] Evidently, Roosevelt's cowboy history led some easterners to assume he was possessed of an odd eccentricity. Most famous among these remarks is that of Mark Hanna, who is reputed to have said when McKinley died: "Look now, that damned cowboy is President of the United States."[11]

What gives voters hesitancy in one section of the nation can encourage and enliven them in another, and that was certainly true of Roosevelt's cowboy history for citizens in North Dakota. During August 1900, when plans were laid for the candidate's western campaign trip, the *Bismarck Weekly Tribune* printed the reminiscences of A. T. Packard, who had been editor of the *Bad Lands Cowboy* during the 1880s: "You cannot pay a higher compliment to Theodore Roosevelt than to say that he won the friendship of every cowboy in the Bad Lands. There isn't on earth a more independent, self-thinking lot of men than these same cow-punchers. They have the faculty of shucking a man out of his crust and looking his real character squarely in the face. If they like him it is a pretty safe guess the man will pass muster anywhere."[12]

Westerners were quite aware, however, that Roosevelt was not a natural-born son of the region, and they enjoyed amusing anecdotes about his sometimes awkward cowboy ways. The same piece from A. T. Packard that offered high compliments also chuckled over a story of Roosevelt's shouts to hardened cowboys when the cattle stampeded. Reportedly, they were confused by his command: "Hasten quickly forward yonder!" There was also the tale of Roosevelt's efforts to ride an untamed horse that had earned the name "Devil." Real cowboys liked to say that when Devil bucked, Roosevelt "ascended to take a look at Wyoming."[13]

On Friday, September 14, 1900, morning came early for Roosevelt and his fellow travelers after their late night in Aberdeen, South Dakota. The campaign special made three unscheduled and two scheduled stops before leaving the state and crossing into Minnesota. One humorous incident was reported from a brief stop in South Dakota: "Seth Bullock, Deadwood, who is with him, stood in front of him at Webster, where he made his first speech of the day. He listened attentively for a few moments, and then exclaimed: "Say, governor, you talk like a Winchester shoots, spat, spat, spat, and no interference."[14]

Roosevelt's timetable specified that the final appearance in South Dakota at Sisseton would conclude at noon. This would leave time for a few brief stops on the way to the next major appearance in Fargo, North Dakota, scheduled for 6:00 p.m.

Still in tow and headed toward the Northern Pacific tracks across North Dakota were Roosevelt's car, named *Minnesota* and loaned to the campaign by the general manager of the Northern Pacific Company, as well as a private dining car and a sleeping car both supplied by the Chicago, Milwaukee, and St. Paul Railway for the newspaper correspondents. According to one report, the Roosevelt train had "three yellow and three black cars," looking as it traveled as if it "were a fiery dragon."[15] Initially, there were three stops planned for the afternoon journey to Fargo. Veering to the southeast from Sisseton would allow a stop in Ortonville, Minnesota. Then the intention was for the train to turn northward and enter North Dakota, stopping briefly in Wahpeton and Abercrombie before running the final leg.

According to the *Minneapolis Tribune,* the afternoon did not pass quite that smoothly. At Ortonville, the train had to be reversed using a turntable that malfunctioned and causing a long delay. Roosevelt and other speakers addressed a sizable crowd while the train was being turned, but a heavy rain drenched both the speakers and the attendees with everyone standing "in mud to the ankles." Roosevelt accepted shelter in the home of a local supporter, pending departure. To further complicate the schedule, Roosevelt agreed, with little notice, to stop at Wheaton, Minnesota, as an expression of support for the legislative candidacy of Henry Nelson, son of US senator Knute Nelson, one of the dignitaries traveling with the campaign party. Five hundred citizens in Wheaton heard a ten-minute address by the vice presidential candidate.[16] Between Ortonville and Wheaton, another brief stop was added in Graceville.[17]

So as not to disappoint anyone expecting to see him, Roosevelt stopped as planned, though well behind schedule, at Wahpeton and Abercrombie in southeastern North Dakota. There were but three hundred thousand people in North Dakota in 1900 spread over a vast area with no urban population centers, so small communities were important to winning the electoral votes in the state.

Principal among towns on the Northern Pacific line were Fargo and Bismarck; their populations were 10,000 and 5,500 respectively.[18] These became the major stops for Roosevelt's train tour through North Dakota, and eighteen other communities were on the agenda or added on the spur of the moment for handshaking or short speeches. Unlike South Dakota, campaigning in North Dakota by train required no loops or side trips; rather, the principal rail line ran east to west, a border-to-border trip of more than 350 miles.

Here is the wonderful description of the first day in North Dakota that ran in the *Sun* for readers in New York City interested in their governor's progress: "A slate-grey thunderstorm came up out of the southwest today and soaked Gov. Roosevelt's audiences with rain, chilled their bodies to the bone, and brought a rain that roared in their ears until they could hardly hear what he said. But that idle curiosity which, the Hon. Richard Franklin Pettigrew says, causes the people of these northwest states to gather by thousands whenever they know Theodore Roosevelt is to speak, or even at bleak shed stations where they know that he is not to speak and where they know that his train is not to stop, has proved itself stronger than wind and rain and lightning. . . . Despite the rain his hearers shouted as much appreciation of the things he said as they have on the sunniest and fairest of days."[19]

Newspapers across the nation carried a wire-service story dated that same day from Canton, Ohio, with a report on McKinley's activities. It must have given Roosevelt at least a moment's pause as he raced hither and yon campaigning in the rain for the Republican ticket he shared with the president. The story read, in part: "A quiet and restful day at the McKinley home closed with an informal dinner, at which the guests were long-time friends of the family. . . . During the day Mr. McKinley paid the town district a visit by walking down unattended and looking over some improvements being made in his block. He stopped to greet acquaintances on the street. . . . There were a large number of social callers, but no one on a political mission."[20]

Meanwhile, Roosevelt plowed forward with the western campaign. Following is the order of his recorded stops in Minnesota and North Dakota:

Friday, September 14, 1900
   Ortonville, Minnesota
   Graceville
   Wheaton
   Wahpeton, North Dakota
   Abercrombie
   Fargo
Saturday, September 15, 1900
   Mapleton
   Casselton
   Buffalo/Wheatland
   Tower City
   Valley City
   Sanborn
   Jamestown
   Dawson
   Steele
   Sterling
   Bismarck
Sunday, September 16, 1900
   Mandan
   New Salem
   Hebron
   Richardton
   Dickinson
   Medora

Major Stops in North Dakota

Fargo.   By the time Roosevelt's train reached Fargo on Friday, September 14, it was 8:00 p.m. and the evening's planned events were two hours late.[21] Originally, the agenda was for a 6:00 p.m. arrival, and it included: a parade with fireworks, bands, and Rough Rider clubs; dinner with dignitaries at the Waldorf Hotel; a speech to a large crowd from the hotel balcony; a reception to top off the evening. However, heavy and steady rains throughout the day coupled with the tardiness of the candidate required several alterations.

Rain had fallen all day, and it was the latest downpour in a season that was proving disastrous for farmers. As the *St. Paul Globe* reported on the Roosevelt stop in Fargo, it also ran a sidebar story on the disastrous fall weather: "Heavy rain has fallen all over the valley, and grain which was ready to thresh is again soaked through. Every rain now destroys great quantities of grain and the outlook in many localities is hopeless. Great damage by wind is reported."[22] Therefore, Roosevelt would address North Dakota crowds that included many who were fearful for their financial futures. Although he was generally good at picking up local nuances for his speeches, journalists recorded no efforts by Roosevelt at any of his North Dakota stops to address this issue. His themes in the state included his western identity, prosperity under McKinley, and the charges of militarism by the Democrats.

In the end, the schedule in Fargo changed to offer two meetings where Roosevelt and others spoke. The larger gathering was at the Opera House and the other moved into the Armory. "Col. Roosevelt was whirled away to the Opera House and some of the other speakers went to the Armory. There were people packed suffocation-tight into these two buildings. Twice as many more tramped the streets, disgusted, threatening to 'hold up Teddy at the train and make him speak.' He sent word that he would say something from the platform of the Minnesota before he went to bed."[23]

Coverage in the local newspaper, the *Fargo Forum*, spoke of "a royal welcome" and bragged that "immense audiences displayed unusual enthusiasm." Citizens arrived all day by special trains from several communities in eastern North Dakota, but "instead of the throng that was expected only about half faced the weather and made the trip." Assurances were offered, however, "that those who did come were enthusiastic for three times the number." Indeed, the journalist reported that Roosevelt "was welcomed with fitting ceremony and with a Rough Rider heartiness that was refreshing."[24]

Apparently a few hundred costumed Rough Riders kept their vigil in the rain and escorted Roosevelt from the train to the event site. Inexplicably, the doors to the Opera House and the Armory stayed locked until 7:00 p.m., and people were forced to wait in the rain "to secure an advantageous seat." When the audiences were seated and became restless, event organizers offered a kazoo band performing "patriotic airs" and a musical group from Casselton, North Dakota, playing songs such as "Hot Time."[25]

Finally, the special guests arrived, and everyone settled in for the speeches. Roosevelt spoke first at the Opera House, and later he delivered another address at the Armory. It was not a short evening. Despite the late start, the candidate gave a lengthy speech on each stage, and others spoke as well, including Senator Knute Nelson of Minnesota, who spent an hour and a half discussing the topic of sound money.

Roosevelt was welcomed to the speakers' podium by "the wildest demonstration that has been extended to a candidate in North Dakota in many years, if ever."[26] In turn, Roosevelt played his trump card, addressing the Opera House crowd as "Fellow Citizens of North Dakota" and saying to the Armory audience, "I have a right to claim citizenship with you since years ago I lived with you, and by the way, I was an officeholder; I was deputy sheriff."[27] He had, indeed, served that role for a brief time during his ranching years.

At both venues Roosevelt spoke primarily on the issues of expansionism and militarism. Though located squarely in territory originally controlled by the Sioux nation, he continued undeterred with his American Indian references, saying, "The progress made by the Indian toward civilization is a good indication of what can be done." He also asked, "Where would North Dakota have been now if Sitting Bull had been treated as a citizen of the original 13 states or a New Englander?"[28] At the end of his second speech of the evening, Roosevelt asked North Dakotans to stand by the flag and for the country's honor.

Citizens of Fargo and surrounding communities apparently left satisfied, despite the rain, the late hour, and the diminished festivities. The *Fargo Forum* concluded its lengthy feature on the event by pointing readers to "the eminent qualifications" of the man who "will be selected as the next Vice President of the United States."[29]

Only one negative report appeared, that being a rather lengthy sidebar on several pickpockets who were active in Fargo, just as they had been at some Roosevelt events in South Dakota. In this case, even North Dakota's lieutenant governor, J. M. Devine, lost his wallet containing money and railroad passes. Though multiple pickpockets worked the crowd, the only arrest occurred when a journalist caught a man in the act and held him for the police.[30]

On Saturday morning, September 15, the vice presidential candidate and his entourage—and presumably the pickpocket corps—left Fargo for a day of stops along the Northern Pacific route. The trip that began with a 7:00 a.m. departure would end in Bismarck, the site of the state's second major Roosevelt event. Before the scheduled 6:30 p.m. arrival in North Dakota's capital city, there were visits planned for eight small communities, with three offering speeches by the New York governor. At the places not being treated to a Roosevelt speech, handshaking and waving were on the agenda. (Highlights of the stops on the journey between Fargo and Bismarck are described in the following section.)

Crossing the state where he spent so many happy days as a young adult proved nostalgic for Roosevelt. The *Minneapolis Tribune*'s report on Friday's events included this moment: "Gov. Roosevelt finding that his train was in North Dakota breathed the ozone and threw out his chest and exclaimed: 'I am coming at last to what I have always called "my country." By tomorrow night I'll be on the edge of it. Sunday we will pass through Medora where I once was. I do hope one of the old timers, some of them I used to know, come to the train there. I want to see them and I want the friends with me to see what manner of men they are.'"[31] As the train set out from Fargo, Roosevelt was surely eager for the two-day immersion experience that was ahead of him.

Bismarck.   Throughout the state, there would be the encounters with old friends that the candidate sought. When he reached Bismarck, for instance, he saw Frank Conyer, who had been a Rough Rider with him in Cuba. Conyer was a North Dakotan by birth and the family farm was near Bismarck, but he had moved to Texas. So meaningful were the Rough Rider bonds that Conyer had traveled from his home in Texas to renew the relationship with Roosevelt, and he combined a visit with his father at the home place. Reportedly there was a joyful reunion, one of several Roosevelt experienced in North Dakota.[32]

Saturday morning's *Bismarck Daily Tribune* proclaimed, "Ready for Teddy," across the top of its front page.[33] Ready and excited described the citizens of Bismarck and the surrounding region. Five days earlier, the same local newspaper had assured everyone that "Governor Roosevelt is an eastern man, but his tastes and sympathies partake largely of western flavor."[34]

When the train arrived at the station in Bismarck, a street demonstration commenced, complete with a parade and fireworks. Flags and bunting decorated the streets. "Cheer after cheer went up to which the governor responded with bows."[35] Dinner was at the home of a local judge.

Reunions continued, as "he met many of his old cowboy friends at the station and in the town, among them some who had been with him on his ranches."[36] One of those along the parade route was Joseph Ferris, who had managed Roosevelt's ranch. The candidate was so pleased to see him that he reached out of the carriage in which he was riding and pulled his old friend aboard.[37]

Those who had planned the celebration were surely pleased that the weather cleared in time for the events after days of rain and chilly temperatures. As a result, the crowd at the station was "immense," according to the *Bismarck Daily Tribune,* and Roosevelt's "carriage was surrounded by another crowd so dense that it was with difficulty the horses could be started."[38]

One reported anecdote demonstrates just how dear Roosevelt held his western experiences. Despite the long trip to reach Bismarck and the evening ahead that would require his full energies, Roosevelt went riding after dinner. The story was as follows: "Down the road a hundred miles or so, Governor Roosevelt asked Senator Hansbrough that a saddle horse be provided for him at Bismarck, as he wanted a horseback ride after he reached the capital city. Mayor Patterson's saddle horse, a western animal such as the governor is accustomed to, was ready for his use, and Governor Roosevelt took a ride in the evening before the beginning of the addresses."[39]

Bismarck's auditorium was called the Atheneum, and it "was packed to the doors" in the evening to hear the speakers. "At 8 o'clock it seemed as though no more could be accommodated, and yet the crowds continued to pour in until Governor Roosevelt and the guests of honor made an appearance at about half past eight. . . . Every seat and all possible standing room were taken. The number of persons present in the Atheneum was from 1,200 to 1,500, and there were hundreds more who were unable to secure entrance."[40] Members of the audience were rapt in their attention to the three speakers. As Roosevelt and others were escorted to the hall, there were once again fireworks along the way.

Mayor Patterson introduced North Dakota's Senator Hansbrough who, in turn, introduced Roosevelt. The candidate began by assuring the crowd that he felt "at home with his old western friends," and he told the story of his earlier encounter with a cowboy whose name he remembered was

George and that he had ridden for "the Bar Open A brand." He continued knotting his local ties by claiming that his western experiences played a role in his decision to raise a regiment for the war with Spain. Stretching further the connection of North Dakota to the Rough Riders and acknowledging the importance of this episode in his life, Roosevelt said, "So you see, you are responsible, possibly, for the fact that I am a candidate for Vice President of the United States."[41]

Encouraged by the positive responses of the audience, Roosevelt rhetoric took flight, as he said, "I am not an orator, and I want to speak to you as neighbor to neighbor." (This may have been a slap at Bryan who had been popularly known as the "Boy Orator of the Platte" since his stirring speech at the 1896 Democratic convention.) Speaking as a neighbor, Roosevelt addressed the Republican position on trusts and large corporations. He said: "[As governor] I was no more against corporations than I was against red-headed men. I am going to do justice to red-headed men. If he is a bad man I will cinch him. If he is a good man I will stand by him. If a corporation does its duty and acts squarely it is all right, and I will stand up for it. . . . If you simply go into a general denunciation with a whoop and a hurrah and promise the millennium you will be hampered by the fact that you can't keep your word."[42]

After opining that "a ton of oratory and promises on the stump is not worth a pound of fulfillment off the stump," Roosevelt took up the topic of militarism. He pointed out the Republican candidate for lieutenant governor who was seated on the stage and who had been a Spanish War soldier, and he said that he saw "no signs of alarm on the part of the audience because this ogre of militarism is present." He went on to compare those attacking McKinley for militarism to Lincoln's critics from forty years earlier. There were no reported references to the history between federal troops and American Indian tribes in Bismarck as there had been at several other locations.

According to the local journalist: "Governor Roosevelt's address was clean, logical and effective, devoid of any appeal to prejudice or passion. He was loudly and continuously applauded at its close."[43]

Highlights from Other Stops in North Dakota

This selection comes from the *Bismarck Daily Tribune,* and it represents the support Roosevelt encountered at all of his stops in North Dakota: "The popularity of Governor Roosevelt in the West has been attested by the numbers who have heard him speak at the cities and towns included in his itinerary. . . . The same popularity with which he was greeted as a ranchman and hunter a number of years ago has marked his tour through the West as a campaigner and candidate for the second highest office within the gift of the American people. . . . Energy, rectitude in office, a determination to perform official duties without fear and favor . . . have brought [him] to the very forefront in American politics. . . . North Dakota claims him as an adopted son."[44]

Following are a few highlights from the shorter stops at smaller locations on the trip through North Dakota:[45]

Jamestown. Just outside of Jamestown, two young boys built a mound of dirt, planted a US flag on it, and waved a banner to greet Roosevelt's passing train. While in Jamestown, the traveling party left the train, and Roosevelt spoke at the Opera House for a few minutes.

Dawson. At this small community, there was a short stop for greeting people. An elderly fellow approached the candidate, saying he had never seen an Eastern man. When he shook hands with Roosevelt, the elderly gentleman said, "You'll do."

Steele. There was a fifteen-minute stop at Steele with brief remarks from Roosevelt.

Mandan. Members of a Congregational church along with their pastor met the train at Mandan.

New Salem. Two Lutheran clergymen and their congregants met Roosevelt at New Salem. A journalist traveling with the candidate reported that a large crowd awaited the train at an early hour; indeed, he said, that everyone in town must have been present.

Hebron. Roosevelt spotted an old friend in the crowd—"Indian Agent Richards," along with "several of his wards from Elbowoods." The wire service report of the stop says that the "manager of the train presented the Indians with Republican campaign buttons, of which they were highly proud."

Richardton. Though smaller than many stops on the campaign tour, Richardton reportedly provided a "rousing reception."

Dickinson.   Episcopal, Methodist, and Presbyterian clergymen and their members met the train at Dickinson. The stop at this community was of one-hour duration to allow the passage of a heavy freight train. Fourteen years earlier, Roosevelt had made a Fourth-of-July address at Dickinson, and it was the rail-stop where he shipped his cattle during his ranching years. The people of Dickinson had not forgotten Roosevelt: "Many of the old western friends of Governor Roosevelt were in the crowd and right pleased were they to see that the governor had forgotten none of them. Many he called by name and referred to some past incident, proving his wonderful memory for names and incidents."

Medora.   Roosevelt could not have been happier when the train reached his North Dakota home community, Medora, because a scheduled passenger train was approaching and the campaign special was forced to make a two-hour stop. It gave Roosevelt a chance to see many old friends and mount a horse for a gallop in the hills outside the town.

According to his rules for the trip, Roosevelt made no speeches on Sunday, September 16, and the train was not "allowed to pass through any village during the hour in which religious services are in progress." Yet at other times, he was very active at stops along the way in greeting citizens and conversing with them.

Conclusion

As the train traveled through the North Dakota Badlands, Roosevelt had lunch with the traveling journalists in the dining car to share tales of his years in the Dakota Territory. In keeping with the theme of the luncheon, the group dined on elk steaks. It was also reported that Joseph Ferris, who had traveled to Bismarck to greet his old friend Theodore Roosevelt, decided to accept an invitation and made the train trip from Bismarck to Miles City, Montana. As they crossed the Badlands, they recalled that the two had been together in that very area eighteen years earlier when Roosevelt killed his first buffalo.

Then there was this wistful moment: Roosevelt's train was moving westward toward the last stop in North Dakota's Badlands, and he was keeping watch from his car's rear platform, his pulpit in hundreds of small towns. "His arms rested on a brake handle, his chin on a wrist, and his gaze on the prairie that rolled gently to all horizons. At some point, he asked a porter to ward off visitors, and he shut the platform door, remaining outside alone. A member of his campaign staff came looking for him and found the porter standing before the door blocking the way. . . . For at least an hour, Roosevelt was left to solitude, to the West, and to whatever memories he found there."[46]

Marketing Roosevelt's popular image as an easterner who survived western cowboy experiences and went on to become an American hero at the head of the Rough Riders was not a hard sell in North Dakota. That it was tremendously appealing elsewhere will be seen at stops all along the western campaign trip. However, the power of the image was clearly understood by one of Roosevelt's contemporaries who was a shrewd marketer in his own right. At the same time the campaign train was rolling through North Dakota's small communities, Buffalo Bill Cody was promoting his Wild West shows in newspaper advertisements across the nation, promising "an assemblage of the mounted soldiers of the world and Rough Riders of the east and west, including rugged Rough Riders who rode with Roosevelt." During that part of the program, the feature was "the realistic dramatic representation of the charge up San Juan Hill."[47]

CHAPTER 9

MONTANA AND IDAHO

To the twenty-first century ear, there are surprises in Roosevelt's messages to his audiences at South and North Dakota stops. When we read laudatory remarks on the suppression of American Indian leaders and the forceful annexation of tribal lands less than a decade after the killing of Sitting Bull and the massacre at Wounded Knee, it is jarring. However, in the context of nineteenth-century American life, the schedule of visits for the next phase of Roosevelt's trip may have actually seemed more dumbfounding. Why would Republican leaders waste the time of their campaign celebrity in an area where there was seemingly no reasonable chance for success?

Neighborly though the westerners of the Dakotas had been to their old friend Theodore Roosevelt, when his train crossed into Montana, he must have felt at least a little apprehensive. South Dakota's presidential vote in 1896 had tipped ever so slightly to William Jennings Bryan—the second closest margin in the nation—and North Dakota had been solidly in William McKinley's camp. Across the border and down the tracks were Montana, Idaho, Utah, Wyoming, and Colorado. In four of the five, the average outcome of voters favoring Bryan in 1896 was nearly 82 percent. (Wyoming tilted toward Bryan with 52 percent of the votes.) Among the forty-five states comprising the Union in that election year, only two gave Bryan higher percentages, and they were located in the solid, Democratic South. These were South Carolina and Mississippi, with 85 and 91 percent respectively.

Perhaps Roosevelt's history in the West gave the Republican committees in these next four states some hope for incremental gains. Ultimately there were surprisingly good results, as the average percentage of those voting for Bryan in 1900 fell to 54 percent in Colorado, Idaho, and Montana, and the states of Utah and Wyoming moved into the Republican column. By 1904, all five states gave a majority to Theodore Roosevelt in his run for the presidency.

As Roosevelt steamed onward in the campaign of 1900, we can guess that he supposed the Dakotas belonged to him and McKinley. And why not? He had just enjoyed several days marked by the cheers of pro-Republican crowds, visits with admirers from his ranching days, and enthusiastic expressions of support, such as this poem written for him by a journalist with the *Bismarck Tribune*:

Ridin' 'cross the continent, our Teddy's on a tear;
He's got sage brush in his haversack an' cactus in his hair.
He's out a-brandin' mavericks that's running on the range;
He'll bring 'em into camp or y' may 'low it's mighty strange.
Y' can hear the boys a-shoutin',
Y' can see the cloud of dust.
Y' can hear the cry a-goin' up "To Washington or bust."
So clear th' way for Teddy, he is bound to fetch up there,
For th' round-up wagon's started, and our Teddy's on a tear.[1]

Given the reactions of the folks across the central tier of northern states and through the Dakotas, one wonders whether Roosevelt had changed his mind since sending his letters to Hanna and other party leaders in the summer pleading to "appear in [each] state and make one speech which can be read throughout it, and then go on." Perhaps he would no longer "make the most emphatic protest against the plan for me to speak all day long in the open air from the tail end of the car."[2] Apparently, his evolving feelings were mixed. He wrote to his younger sister, Corinne, from the train: "I have had a very hard trip, but the last ten days I have rather enjoyed. . . . I have had a half dozen first-class horseback rides." But not all was upbeat: "Otherwise I do nothing but fester in the car and elbow to and from stagings where I address my audiences."[3]

Montana and Idaho would test any change of heart about campaign strategy Roosevelt was feeling, and farther down the line, Utah, Wyoming, and, particularly, Colorado would surely give rise to doubts. These were the mining states, and the sentiment was strong for the bimetallism plank of the Democrats' platform and against the gold standard position of the Republicans' statement. Mine owners and unionized miners exercised authority—generally in countervailing measure—in the region Roosevelt was entering, and the radicalizing influence of the Western Federation of Miners was respected or despised depending on where one sat at the table. In the last decade of the nineteenth century, this was not likely to be a welcoming place for any Republican from the East suspected to favor big business. Roosevelt's reception in Montana and Idaho could be a bellwether.

Following is a list of the twenty-five reported stops, in order, made by the vice presidential candidate as he traveled through Montana and Idaho:

Sunday, September 16, 1900
   Glendive, Montana
   Miles City
   Forsyth
   Billings (overnight)
Monday, September 17, 1900
   Billings (event)
   Columbus
   Big Timber
   Livingston
   Bozeman
   Manhattan
   Logan
   Townsend
   Winston
   Helena
Tuesday, September 18, 1900
   Clancy
   Basin
   Boulder
   Butte
Wednesday, September 19, 1900
   Dillon
   Lima
   St. Anthony, Idaho
   Rexburg
   Market Lake
   Idaho Falls
   Blackfoot
   Pocatello

Vast stretches of flat prairies and rolling hills greeted any traveler in the region where Roosevelt was campaigning in September 1900. Between South and North Dakota there were just over 145,000 square miles populated by less than 725,000 people. Empty space stretched in Montana and Idaho to 230,000 square miles with only 400,000 residents. Distances were greater, communities were generally smaller, and, because of the politics, popular interest threatened to be significantly diminished. Roosevelt forged ahead.

He and his entourage overnighted in Billings on Sunday; Helena, the state capital, on Monday; and Butte on Tuesday. These became the major stops in Montana for Roosevelt. There were 3,200 residents in Billings; 10,800 in Helena; and 30,500 in Butte.[4] Through the census of 1890, Helena had been the largest city in Montana, but a growing demand for copper and expanded mining operations swelled the size of Butte in a very short time, illustrating the importance of this industry to the state. The major stop for Roosevelt in Idaho would be in Pocatello, a community of just over 4,000 people. Although the state's capital city of Boise was larger by half, its location near the western border and off the track for the next major stop in Salt Lake City meant that it would not host a visit by Roosevelt and his party.

Major Stops in Montana and Idaho

Billings. It was Sunday morning, September 16, when the Roosevelt train pulled out of Bismarck, North Dakota, on an all-day run for Billings, Montana, a trip of about 425 miles. On the way, the candidate observed his Sunday rule and made no speeches, but he paused in several communities for greeting and handshaking nonetheless. There were six reported visits in North Dakota—other slowdowns or stops may have gone unremarked by journalists—and at least three Montana towns enjoyed time with Roosevelt prior to his overnight stop in Billings. The train's two-hour layover in the North Dakota Badlands also stretched the long day of travel. Arrival at the destination city was late enough that the festivities, including an address, were scheduled for Monday morning.

As with most of the major stops in these rural western states, the crowd in Billings included not only that community's citizens, but also many folks from the surrounding region, who had come on excursion trains for the political rally. One of the most delightful accounts of a Roosevelt stop during the western tour was written by a visitor to Billings and printed a few days after the event in his hometown newspaper, the *Red Lodge Picket*: "The city of Billings on Monday belonged exclusively to Hon. Theodore Roosevelt, Governor of the state of New York, better known as 'Teddy,' and to the Republican Rough Riders of Carbon County. . . . The Rough Riders who reached Billings on the early morning excursion train were responsible for nine-tenths of the hearty cheers. . . . The freely expressed opinion of those who went from here was to the effect that political missionaries should be sent to Billings to teach them how to welcome a distinguished visitor."

Having claimed credit for the day's energy and enthusiasm, the writer from Red Lodge in Carbon County, whose name is lost to history, provided this account of the journey to Billings: "Before the light of day had come to Red Lodge on Monday morning the handsomely uniformed members of the Red Lodge Republican Rough Rider Club began making their way to the depot. The Finn Band, also in uniform, their name being temporarily changed to that of the 'Rough Rider Band,' marched from their hall toward the station. . . . When in sight of the depot, they heeded the warning whistle of the engine, broke ranks and sprinted for the train. . . . The start was made at about 5 o'clock. . . . At every station the number of passengers was augmented. The band was not backward with its music and late sleepers in houses along the track had their morning dreams made happy by the sweet music. . . . The train pulled into Billings at about 7:30."

Here, then, is how this eyewitness reported his encounter with the Republican vice presidential nominee who had traveled more than two thousand miles by rail for this visit: "Gov. Roosevelt's private car had come in about 1 o'clock in the morning, but the speech did not occur until about 8. At that time the Rough Riders and the Finn Band were pressed into service to escort Teddy from his private car to the speakers' stand. . . . The Carbon County boys had all been provided with flags and the great Rough Rider's passage down this patriotic pathway was a perfect ovation with the shouts of hundreds rending the air. . . . Governor Roosevelt spoke for three quarters of an hour. . . . The funniest thing was the rising inflection Teddy gave on the word 'expanded,' while he smiled the grotesque smile which has been a picnic for the cartoon artists all over the country. . . . He handled the entire question of imperialism in a masterful, convincing manner. . . . It was 9:23 when the special pulled out of the city. Shortly after that the Carbon County delegation boarded the regular Rocky Fork train for home well pleased with the day."[5]

As the visitor from Red Lodge, Montana, recounted, the Roosevelt event in Billings began at 8:00 a.m. after the candidate and his party overnighted in the community, sleeping in the railcars on a siding near the station. Local citizens treated the distinguished visitors to a reception and parade before everyone gathered at the public square for speeches.[6] Sources estimated the size of the crowd at two to three thousand.[7] One puzzling anecdote was reported by the *Sun* to its readers in New York City: "At the early morning meeting in Billings, Senator W. V. Allen [Populist from Nebraska] was on the platform. Senator Carter [Republican from Montana] discovered him in the audience and issued a cordial invitation to him to come up. . . . Senator Allen came up and sat there, looking rather foolish all the time, but taking the joking of his friends very cheerfully."[8] Why Allen had traveled more than seven hundred miles from his home in Madison, Nebraska, and was in attendance at the Roosevelt rally in Billings was unexplained.

Roosevelt stuck to the script in Billings, addressing imperialism rather than matters more targeted toward local citizens. Indeed, the *St. Paul Globe* commented that the aforementioned Senator (Thomas H.) Carter had "not been at all anxious to have the silver issue introduced in the speeches in Montana."[9]

"In this great state of Montana," Roosevelt said, "I don't have to discuss expansion. You've expanded. . . . Here we stand not merely in the middle of the continent; you have got beyond that. You front rather toward the Pacific than toward the Atlantic, and we intend that this country shall assume an even greater and more preponderant weight to the ocean of the West than to the ocean of the East."[10]

Focusing specifically on the questions Democrats were raising regarding US military actions in the Philippines, Roosevelt again defaulted to comparisons with earlier conflicts involving American Indians: "It is not a quarter of a century since the greater part of this, your marvellous state, was roamed by Indians wilder than many of the tribes that we have now to deal with in the Philippines. It would have been criminal folly . . . for our people to have refused to push westward upon any theory that you had to apply for the consent of the governed who were the Indians, the original inhabitants of the state, before the whites could come here."[11]

He continued, mentioning to his hearers in Billings the Democratic nominee by name: "If we turn those islands over to the different tribes who will fight for the mastery among themselves, if we did what Mr. Bryan proposes to do, give them into the hands of a syndicate of Chinese half-breeds, with Aguinaldo at their head, to work their wicked will upon the weak inhabitants of the islands, we would have such anarchy and confusion that it would inevitably happen that some stronger power would step in to do the work that we would have shown ourselves too weak and too unworthy to perform."[12]

By 9:30 a.m. Roosevelt and his party were back on the train and headed toward the next nine visits in Montana that would conclude with the state's second major stop in the capital city, Helena. A musical group known as the Alice Band spent the day riding on the campaign special and entertaining at stops along the way.[13] This was a group of miners from the Alice Gold and Silver Mining Company headquartered at Walkerville, Montana, and the musicians dressed as Rough Riders for the occasion. Surely, this unique addition of a local band for the trip through the heart of mining country was intended as a strategy demonstrating support for Roosevelt by a visible group of mine employees.

Journalists traveling on the campaign special recognized occasional tension in the air, as in this summary of Monday's journey by the reporter from the *Sun:* "Gov. Roosevelt today carried his campaign well into the foothills of the Rocky Mountains. Starting at Billings, the center of the sheep grazing district of Montana, he crossed the mountains to Bozeman, in the Gallatin Valley, and ran up to Helena. . . . He has found a community or two which feels that the crime of '73 is yet to be avenged."[14] This last reference was a Montana colloquialism for the congressional adoption of the gold standard in the so-called Fourth Coinage Act of 1873.

There were also many gratifying incidents along the way. This account of other, more positive moments on Monday, September 17, was provided by the same journalist: "The train dashed through two or three sidehill mining towns. The women and children were all at the doors of the cabins and dugouts. All of them waved their aprons, but in the door of the most miserable hovel of all, a gray-headed woman stood with a flag longer than she was tall and shook it out at the train with the wildest abandon. The train windows fluttered with flags and handkerchiefs in answer to her greeting."[15]

Helena.   Roosevelt's special train arrived at Montana's second major stop, Helena, at 8:00 p.m. on Monday. As with several of the previous major stops on the western campaign trip, two large meetings were necessary to accommodate as many potential voters as possible. On this evening, the entire crowd was served by a celebratory procession through the community, and for those who could gain access, there were opportunities to hear speeches at an auditorium and an opera house. The correspondent for the *Omaha Daily Bee* estimated the crowd at the auditorium to be four thousand, and he reported that the two venues could not serve all who wished to hear Roosevelt speak.[16]

While the lighting for the procession was unquestionably dramatic, the smell, smoky air pollution, and loud noises must have proven disturbing for many of the onlookers: "Helena's battery of the Montana National Guard

saluted Gov. Roosevelt with 17 guns. Bonfires made of six and eight tar bar-
rels burned on the corner of every vacant lot. . . . Once into the city the procession was lighted by a glow of red fire that made the tall buildings stand
out as if by daylight. . . . The McKinley and Roosevelt Club of Helena which
has 1,000 members was in line. . . . Strings of dynamite crackers, yards long,
banged and rattled from every telegraph pole. Bands played discordantly up
and down the whole line."[17]

At the auditorium, Roosevelt was forced to shout so that the thousands
in attendance could hear. He took Bryan to task for a remark about idle
American soldiers, using the example of his old friend, General Leonard
Wood, as one who offered service to those in need. These words are from
the vice presidential candidate's remarks in Helena: "In a recent speech at
Chicago, Mr. Bryan is represented to have spoken as follows: 'Can 100,000
soldiers in a country like this take charge and change the form of government? . . . If 100,000 soldiers are permitted to walk about in idleness,
where one soldier would do, what are we coming to?' . . . Idleness. Was
Leonard Wood idle when for the first time in 300 years he cleaned a Spanish city? Was he idle when he fed and clothed and schooled the children of
the reconcentrado?"[18] Roosevelt's reference was to concentration camps or
reservations where the Cuban people who had opposed the Spanish occupation had been held. Many adults had died, orphaning hundreds of children. General Wood, who was a physician by training, had led efforts to
provide humanitarian aid, following the American invasion of Cuba in the
Spanish War.[19]

After two long, late days, the weary travelers got something of a break
on Tuesday: "Governor Roosevelt is having a rest today. At breakfast time
this morning his special train pulled out of here [Helena] and until nearly
six o'clock this evening, the Rough Rider will have little to do but watch
Rocky Mountain scenery, as his train steams over the divide to Butte. At
that point he will pass the night."[20] Eleven o'clock was departure time, and
there were three stops prior to the evening's major event in Butte. While
such a schedule might have challenged some, to those on the western campaign tour, it likely seemed almost restful, and the distance traveled for the
day was less than seventy miles.

Butte.   Once the train reached Butte around 4:00 p.m., campaign activity began in earnest. While the candidate and his entourage had crossed
the Continental Divide at midday, peaking at 6,000 feet, by late afternoon
they were 1,200 feet underground in Butte's West Colusa Copper Mine,

visiting the miners in an attempt to communicate with a constituency generally inclined to favor Bryan and Stevenson over McKinley and Roosevelt. According to the *Salt Lake Herald*, "[T]hey deposited their outside clothing, donned the outfit of the miners, and were lowered to the bottom of the shaft. Stops were made at the 300-foot level and the 400-foot level. A journey was taken on reaching the bottom far into the interior of the mine, where there were air drills at work picking the mineral from the sides of the rocky arch."[21]

This act of reaching across the political divide to laborers in Montana was newsworthy throughout a nation that was witnessing a strike by Pennsylvania coal miners at the same moment that Roosevelt was descending into a copper mine in the West. Wire service reports took the story everywhere. For example, the *Morning Astorian* in Oregon opined, "Governor Roosevelt may be said to have invaded the enemy's country today."[22] Meanwhile, the first page of the *San Francisco Call* featured two renderings by an artist depicting Roosevelt's act. The first imaged him carrying a smoking torchlight and wearing a Rough Rider hat and miner's coat. The second showed him standing by underground tracks and shaking hands with miners while a horse drawing an ore cart waited to pass.[23] Whether there was immediate political gain in Montana as a result of the visit is uncertain, but there is no question that this nineteenth-century equivalent of today's photo-op caught additional attention across the nation for Roosevelt and the Republican campaign.

According to some sources, Roosevelt and his party received "a hearty reception" at the station, and during the mile-long carriage ride to the Butte Hotel, there was a "flattering demonstration." These sources spoke of streets lined with people, an appearance by the candidate on the hotel balcony, long sessions of handshaking, and demands for an early speech that he politely declined.[24] However, the *Bismarck Daily Tribune* printed quite another version of events, saying that "the sentiment of the crowd . . . was antagonistic to Roosevelt and the campaign committee felt correspondingly glum about Montana."[25] Given the political polarization in the mining states, perhaps it is not surprising that assessments of the visit varied so dramatically.

Regardless of local attitudes and how they affected perceptions of the visit to Butte, the events proceeded on schedule. Tuesday evening's rally and speech-making occurred at Columbia Gardens, a recreational park five miles outside the city where there was a building described by journalists as "immense."[26] That structure was completely filled, and many stood to hear Roosevelt speak for forty-five minutes. He began with stories from his years in the Dakotas and eastern Montana.

Following his warm-up, classic Roosevelt rhetoric filled the hall. He called for an amelioration of tension through conversations and goodwill. He said: "I have spoken to you, gentlemen, about preaching the gospel of hate. The foulest wrong that can be done to our citizenship is done by the man who preaches that gospel. Whether he preaches to the employee to see to it that the protection of his own interests is against the interests of the employer or whether he seeks to combine politics and set the employees against their employers, it matters not which, it is wrong. . . . The only way to permanently secure well-being in this country is to secure conditions that will assure the well-being of all. Something can be done by legislation; much can be done by the association of individuals."[27]

While this message was clearly Roosevelt's attempt to address issues vexing the citizens of the region, most folks likely were dissatisfied regardless of their politics. Management would have wanted the strong support of the Republican candidate; labor would have hoped for encouragement from this man of the people. All in all, the editorial assessment that Roosevelt missed the mark in Butte was probably more accurate than not. His train pulled out of Butte at 2:00 a.m. on the tracks of the Union Pacific line with the next major stop scheduled for Pocatello, Idaho, Wednesday's ultimate destination. During the day there would be two additional stops in Montana and five stops in Idaho prior to Pocatello.

Pocatello. It was 6:00 p.m. when Roosevelt's train arrived at Pocatello, and the initial activity mirrored previous stops—railcars moved onto a siding near the station, candidate introduced from the rear platform of the train to an enthusiastic crowd, and, other than polite thanks, the candidate put off speaking until the evening meetings. Those later gatherings drew approximately three thousand people in Pocatello, as Roosevelt addressed one group at 8:00 p.m. in Pavilion Hall and the other afterward in Lewis Hall. Each venue was so filled that many were forced to stand outside hoping to catch a few words.[28]

Utah was the next state down the tracks for the Roosevelt special, so journalists from Salt Lake City began their coverage in Idaho. This unusual description of the vice presidential candidate was written by the correspondent for the *Deseret Evening News* following the Pocatello visit: "Col. Roosevelt is of medium height and build, looking even rather short of stature in the presence of the taller men who were with him on the platform. His swarthy complexion told of the sunburn which has had its effect upon him. His features show him to be a man of force, and he has a brainy head—a fact readily recognizable even to those not familiar with his career. He is not what would be called a handsome man, but will pass muster with the majority, and attract attention in a crowd as a natural leader of men. He is a forceful, yet not such a fiery speaker as some accounts would lead one to believe; and withal he is a very interesting, convincing talker."[29]

In his addresses at Pocatello, Roosevelt once again picked up the issue of expansion, hoping it might win western votes for the Republican ticket. He said, "Expansion has been the law of our national growth. . . . Now is this giant of the West, those who have conquered the frontier, to sit down idly with folded hands and say, 'Our fathers worked, we rest . . . our fathers conquered the West, but we are a feeble folk and we cannot hold the Philippines?' Are we to sit down and do that? . . . We must go and play our part among the nations of the world."[30]

As he continued to look for just the right pitch to win attention from all sides in the contentious mining communities, Roosevelt extended the theme of seeking peaceful coexistence, ignoring that it had not worked well for him at Butte. These words are from his Pocatello address: "Four years ago, I am informed that the amount of wages paid the wage workers here was much less than they are receiving now. I learn that you had some 600 men employed four years ago, whereas you have 800 employed now. . . . Four years ago the average wages of these men was $60 a month, whereas they now get an average of $85 a month. . . . All I ask is that in your effort to cut down the trusts, you do not also cut down the wage worker. You should not vote so as to bring ruin upon the wage worker's wife and children. . . . Do not injure yourselves in your endeavor to get at the men you would like to get at, for I think we can get at them if we go honestly, rationally, and quietly about it. . . . Nobody ever gained anything by going into hysterics."[31] It was a pointedly moralistic end to his Montana and Idaho sojourn and demonstrated a default position for Theodore Roosevelt in this region that challenged him to craft a politically appealing message.

Highlights from Other Stops in Montana and Idaho

After leaving North Dakota, Roosevelt's first stop in Montana was at the small community of Glendive about 2:00 p.m. on Sunday, September 16. Around 6:00 p.m., the special train stopped in Miles City for one hour and then proceeded toward the first major stop in Billings. Following are highlights and anecdotes from several other stops in small communities in Montana and Idaho, as reported by the journalists traveling with the candidate:

Columbus, Montana. "Gov. Roosevelt spoke from the rear platform of the car. He said in part: 'When Dewey sailed into Manila Bay and destroyed the Spanish fleet, who cared whether he came from Vermont or any other state? When Hobson faced almost a certain death in Santiago Bay, who cared that he came from Alabama? . . . The only point is that they have acted like Americans. . . . All of us take pride in deeds of valor done by any."[32]

Big Timber, Montana. "Gov. Roosevelt spoke in a wool warehouse near the track. The warehouse was well filled. . . . Just as the governor was boarding the train a citizen elbowed his way through the crowd, and getting near the governor said: 'Gov. Roosevelt, how about the currency and the tariff questions?' The governor replied: 'I stand squarely on the Republican platform. I am in favor of a gold standard and a protective tariff. Is that clear enough?'"[33] Though the report indicates that Roosevelt's response brought applause, it is unlikely to have been universally popular in this silver mining region.

One journalist from New York City reported that the wool warehouse was piled high because growers were storing the commodity in anticipation of a McKinley reelection and higher prices for their goods. He also noted that there were many Democrats in attendance at the meeting in Big Timber because the Democratic county convention had been in session and adjourned to allow the delegates to see Roosevelt. In the report, this journalist noted that "there was a good deal of opposition to the adjournment, but the men who wanted to go carried the day."[34]

Bozeman, Montana. "[This community] is populated for the most part by Confederate soldiers and their descendants who left Missouri when it became too hot for them. . . . Gov. Roosevelt did not know anything about this when he began to say that he had fought under General Joe Wheeler and found that he had raised the people to a height of enthusiasm."[35] Wheeler was the Confederate general who subsequently served in the US House of Representatives, volunteered for the Spanish War, and was commissioned a major general by President McKinley.

Clancy, Montana. In his remarks at this small community, Roosevelt touted the value of the campaign trip he was taking: "More and more during this tour it has been impressed upon me that every candidate for a national office should have an opportunity of growing acquainted, by travel if not by residence, with the great areas and with the people of your country that will in the end dominate the affairs of this government."[36]

As the Roosevelt special traveled from Helena and toward Butte later on Tuesday, there was this encounter: "An incident of the journey was the meeting of two special trains filled with delegates and visitors bound for Helena to attend the Democratic state convention to be held at that place tomorrow. Greetings were exchanged by the occupants of the two trains in passing. Cries for Bryan came from across the track and shouts for McKinley and Roosevelt were answered back."[37]

St. Anthony, Idaho.   Expanding demands for metals and new farming methods had caused explosive development in some communities in Montana and Idaho. One observer from the Roosevelt train wrote: "On its journey the train today passed through the famous Valley of St. Anthony, which in the period of five years has sprung from a dry, barren waste to a land blossoming like a garden, with smiling fields of grain. In its valley are also large herds of cattle and sheep."[38] Roosevelt spoke at the opera house, addressing those who had experienced this rapid growth: "A great nation must do its great work. When it stops doing its work it is because it has stopped doing things that make it a great nation. . . . We have taken Hawaii; we have taken the Philippines. It is not a question of expanding now, but it is a question whether we are going to contract."

Rexburg, Idaho.   An incident at the outset of the program—once again, at the local opera house—won over the audience: "[Roosevelt announced that] he had heard there was a volunteer veteran in the audience, but whom he had not seen. Instantly half the people were on their feet pointing to a blushing young man near the platform, who after many and urgent appeals to him by his neighbors rose to shake hands with Gov. Roosevelt. The incident broke the calm with which farmers of this part of the country always come into the meetings, and the rest of the Governor's speech was turbulently approved."[39]

According to one report, most of the people of Rexburg were members of the Mormon Church.[40] Roosevelt said to this audience: "Your forefathers came here to make the wilderness blossom like the roses and as I came along this morning I saw the rising sun throw its light not against the sage brush, but against the green alfalfa fields that have been irrigated, and I saw the houses you have built here, because you have expanded."[41]

Yet another incident at Rexburg was engaging enough that it was reported by the traveling journalist representing the *Sun*. He wrote: "A man who is not thoroughly in sympathy with the objects of Col. Roosevelt's campaign pilgrimage was moved to scorn by the number of women that there were at the meeting. There were almost as many women as men. 'There might be something in this Idaho campaign,' he said, 'if the women who came to the meetings could vote.' A member of the Reception Committee said, 'Young man, you are now in the State of Idaho. Women vote in this state for all elected officers from Presidential electors down.' The wise man subsided."[42]

Visiting St. Anthony and Rexburg had required that the Roosevelt special travel a forty-mile spur, and returning to the main line meant retracing the trip in reverse. This put what was normally the rear platform of Roosevelt's car at the head of the train, and he stood outside for this entire segment of the trip watching the jackrabbits flushed by the movement and noise.[43]

Market Lake, Idaho. "Not long after sunrise, a gathering of 40 or 50 farmers crowded around the platform and demanded a speech or at least a chance to say good morning to Gov. Roosevelt. He was called from his breakfast but hardly had an opportunity to shake hands with three or four of them when the engineer, who, like Yuba Bill, 'had his orders,' pulled out. Engineer Ingling cannot be accused of not having the affairs of this campaign at heart. He is a Republican candidate for the legislature."[44]

Idaho Falls, Idaho. "During a short stop before making the trip up the Snake River Valley, a quarter of a carload of fruit and flowers was loaded on the train. There were great masses of white and purple asters that were hung about the dining car and the special cars until the sides of them were covered. Branches of peach trees have been festooned over the doors, and a lower berth in each car has been filled with boxes of apples, pears, peaches, and grapes. On the dining tables in the Minnesota is a great double armful of magnificent roses."[45]

Blackfoot, Idaho. "The visit to Blackfoot, which is in the middle of the Indian reservation, was colored by the presence of a great number of blanketed Indians who had come into town to spend the $70 each they had just received from the government in part payment for two-thirds of their reservation, which they are to give up to the government next spring."[46]

Roosevelt spoke in the courthouse square in Blackfoot. He said, in part: "I lived in parts of the West where it was middling rough and where a man would occasionally escape a licking if he accepted a kicking. He could get peace on those terms, but it was not a permanent peace. When it was discovered that he took a kicking easily, other people took a part in the exercise. . . . When the men of our nation cease to give aid and comfort to our enemies, peace will come to the Philippines."[47]

Then there was this incident: "The governor made the talk a basis for a little lecture in the public square at Blackfoot on the foolishness of the Democratic Party. . . . While he was in the midst of his talk his attention was attracted by a little tow-headed girl who had worked through the lines of old soldiers and was holding up her hand. . . . 'What is it, little girl?' he asked. 'Please, sir,' she said, half crying with excitement, 'Won't you please help my father get a job?' . . . 'I will do the best I can,' said the governor. . . . 'What is your father's name?"[48] According to the report, Roosevelt wrote down the name and subsequently sent a letter to the civil service office in Washington, DC, inquiring about opportunities for the man.

This opinion ran in the *Salt Lake Herald:* "The fact is that the Roosevelt meeting was a dismal failure here [Blackfoot]. There was no audience to speak of. No more than 400, and the candidate for vice president said nothing of present issues. . . The people hoped for a discussion of the imperialistic tendencies of McKinley's administration. Governor Roosevelt paid a tribute to the valor of the brave volunteers from Idaho and elsewhere who fought and died in the Philippines to free those people from Spanish misrule, but did not attempt to explain why this great republic should succeed Spain in enslaving these people. And Mr. Roosevelt did the Democrats service at Blackfoot. His silence on the silver question was as marked as it was painful."[49]

Conclusion

Yet another editorial in the *Salt Lake Herald* may have addressed what many on the campaign special were feeling after a few days in Montana and Idaho. The piece was entitled, "Suggestions for Roosevelt," and it read, in part: "Now that Governor Roosevelt has seen the silver men of the mountain states, a majority of whom will support Bryan . . . he ought to have seen a new light. . . . In his eastern speeches the Governor has declared repeatedly that silver at 16 to 1 is synonymous with dishonesty and repudiation. It would gratify numerous believers in bimetallism hereabout if Mr. Roosevelt would discuss this subject freely and fully, because it is the one issue nearest to the western voters' interests. . . . The governor has been reticent on the money question since he got into the Rocky Mountains, but he may be assured whatever he has to say about it here will be considered most attentively. . . . He may know more about the Democrats of the West than when he left New York by the time he has seen the thousands of them who will go to hear him."[50]

CHAPTER 10

UTAH AND WYOMING

"Even Republicans are getting tired of Teddy Roosevelt." So said an opinion piece in Kansas's *Barton County Democrat* on September 21, 1900, a day on which Roosevelt was enjoying the attention and adulation of thousands in Salt Lake City, Utah.[1] Two-sided coins are the currency of political campaigns; controversy swirls around contests that provide unique, public opportunities to air strong sentiments or even misbehave. Several examples emerged during the few days it took Roosevelt to roll through Utah and Wyoming on his western whistle-stop tour.

Example 1. On Wednesday afternoon, September 19, 1900, Herbert Manning Wells, the Republican governor of Utah, and his secretary of state, James C. Hammond, crossed into Idaho to meet the Roosevelt train and escort the governor of New York. Their intention was to ride the candidate's special into Utah, make the first few stops with him in the state, and then introduce him to voters in Salt Lake City. The evening of their departure, the president of the state senate, Aquila Nebeker, a Democrat from Rich County, became aware that Utah's constitution had a provision that the person occupying his position was the de facto acting governor whenever the elected chief executive left the state's soil. According to the *Deseret Evening News*, "State Senator Nebeker lost no time but immediately proceeded to exercise the prerogatives of the office. This he did in a manner most startling."[2]

What Senator Nebeker did was to announce the appointment of Judge Orlando W. Powers to fill Utah's vacant seat in the United States Senate, an opening that had been much debated in the legislature with no resolution. Additionally, he removed a key member of the governor's staff in an attempt to blunt resistance to the appointment of Powers, and he filled the staff position with an individual less likely to protest. Finally, he drafted a proclamation on the appointment and took it to the secretary of state's office to have the official seal affixed. When the clerk refused his request, Nebeker entered the vault, took possession of the seal, and placed it upon the document himself.[3]

Though many citizens reportedly believed the act was a practical joke and Governor Wells initially described it as "a highly accentuated burlesque political proceeding,"[4] Nebeker maintained that he was quite serious. Judge Powers told journalists he intended to present his credentials in Washington and to fight for the seat. Apparently, the two were convincing enough that Governor Wells and others felt compelled to abandon their plan to escort Roosevelt. As reported by the *Sun* in its story on the campaign stop in Ogden: "To their great disgust, Apostles John Henry Smith and Reed Smoot and a number of others, including the Governor and the Chief Justice, were obliged to hurry on to Salt Lake to see what they could do with the obstreperous Lieutenant Governor [*sic*] who had appointed a United States Senator in their absence."[5]

After two days of high drama, Powers issued a statement to the press saying that while he believed the acting governor had been within his constitutional authority to make the appointment, he felt that precedent in the United States Senate would prevent his being seated. Though he had earlier given up his position as presidential elector on the Democratic ticket to prevent a conflict of interest with the Senate appointment, he took back that privilege and said that he could do more for his party by exercising that responsibility. He declared, "I shall not accept the appointment." In addition, he termed Nebeker's actions "a compliment."[6]

Whether Nebeker and Powers were serious about the appointment is not knowable from a vantage point more than a century removed. Also uncertain is whether this might have been a trick by two clever Democrats to steal at least some of the spotlight from the Republicans as their national celebrity came to town. If so, it worked famously, as newspapers across the nation featured the story prominently for the few days that Roosevelt visited Utah. The *Salt Lake Herald*, decidedly not Republican in its editorial positions, crowed: "He [Nebeker] is the first Democratic governor the state of Utah has ever had and the man from Rich in a few short hours gave a good example of what a genuine Democratic governor could do for the state."[7] Exactly what that might have been was left undefined.

Example 2. When Roosevelt reached Logan, Utah, he was escorted to the local Mormon tabernacle for a rally, though one of the commonly understood principles of Mormonism is that the church is spiritual and not political or secular. However, in 1896 the tabernacle in Logan had been used for a meeting in support of William Jennings Bryan when he visited the community. This caused controversy, as the *Sun* reported: "There were intimations from all parts of the Mormon communion that never again must a tabernacle be desecrated by devotion to a partisan secular cause. Today the use of the tabernacle by the Republicans for a Roosevelt meeting was the result of strong representation to the central body that the only way the stain upon the good name of the church which had been left there by its use for a Democratic meeting could be removed was by neutralizing the effect of that first meeting by using it for the advancement of a Republican cause."

This same journalist asked a church leader about the situation, and the man gave this answer: "The church is not in politics . . . but this year most of the influential churchmen are Republicans in sentiment." This led the reporter to write: "In those two words, 'this year,' is the keynote of the whole Utah situation, in the opinion of men, who, though not themselves Mormons, have been associated with them long enough to know more of the inner workings of the sect than even some of the lesser members. 'This year' the President of the Church, in assigning elders, has in a majority of cases replaced Democratic elders with those who have been identified with the Republican Party." Two rumors were considered in the story and dismissed, though, of course, he chose to put them in print. The first was that the Republicans had been temporarily out of favor with Mormons in 1896 because they took a stand against seating a Mormon congressman who practiced polygamy. The second was that church leaders had experienced a revelation from God supportive of the McKinley-Roosevelt ticket.[8]

Example 3.   One anecdote from the campaign trail began with an encounter between Roosevelt and a war veteran, and it became a point-counterpoint tiff between two journalists. Here is how the newspaperman traveling with the candidate's entourage told the story: "The Governor saw a man in a soldier's hat and leggings leaning against the corner of the platform and, looking at him earnestly, Col. Roosevelt left the Governor of Utah for a moment and went over to the man. 'Were you in the Utah battery?' he asked. 'Yes,' was the answer. The Governor grasped his hand and leaned over and said something to him in a tone that [this reporter] who was not four feet away could not hear, and passed on. A moment later, the reporter heard a woman say: 'Look at the boy; he is crying.' It was true. The artilleryman, whose battery flag bears the record of 14 battles, was looking straight out over the lake, biting his lip and his eyes were full of tears."[9] Stories filed by this journalist with his New York City newspaper were generally supportive of Roosevelt.

When an editorialist for a newspaper in Washington, DC, usually favoring Democratic causes, saw the story, he wrote: "Think of Roosevelt . . . marching slap up to the place where the man stood leaning against the platform singularly arrayed in the uniform of the Utah battery some two years after the Spanish War! We presume that this shows the preservative effect of the Mormon climate upon old clothes. . . . What could have been the words that the vice presidential candidate almost silently hissed into the ear of the gaping gunner? Alas, we do not know, but they could have not been very satisfactory, for they made the poor fellow weep. . . . Was it for the dramatic glad hand and a muttered 'See you later' that the heroic artilleryman—a hack driver in real life—had been approached by the Republican State Committee, induced to rig himself out in khaki from the local costumer's shop, and made to stand for an hour in a conspicuous place, waiting for his cue? Surely he was justified in looking for something more tangible, a 20-dollar note, for instance, as the minimum. . . . All he got was a cowboy grip and murmured assurance that the committee would make it all right after the meeting. So the artilleryman's eyes were full of tears."[10]

Example 4. State by state, community by community, and even event by event, the assessments that followed Roosevelt's visits were as varied as the political leanings of those who formulated and wrote them. For instance, R. D. Redfern, a member of the Republican National Committee, was quoted in the *Deseret Evening News,* a Republican newspaper in Salt Lake City: "The reception in Salt Lake was the grandest ovation received since leaving Wisconsin."[11] Meanwhile, the editorialist for the Democratic newspaper in the community, the *Salt Lake Herald,* wrote: "Democrats who had been fearing the possible effect of Governor Roosevelt's descent on Utah, were quite well satisfied last night that no harm had been done to their party or their cause. . . . They looked in on the great but unenthusiastic audience at the theatre, and they went home and slept soundly."[12]

In the same vein, could the following two assessments really refer to the size of the crowd at the same event? The comment in one publication was: "The size of the crowd at Saltair may be judged by the statement, which nobody will dispute, that there were not enough people to cover half of the dancing floor."[13] The estimate in another publication was: "Seats for 2,000 had been placed there. They were all filled long before [Roosevelt] came out . . . and many people were standing about the sides of the room."[14]

As with the media, so too could Roosevelt exhibit the skill of interpreting and tailoring his message. At Laramie he said to a typically western audience: "I do not appeal to you primarily as Republicans. I appeal to you as Americans."[15] However, at Salt Lake City, Roosevelt said to an overwhelmingly Mormon audience: "I will not appeal to you as Republicans; I will not appeal to you as Democrats; I will not appeal to you as Americans, but I will appeal to you as Christian men and women."[16] One week earlier, Roosevelt had written to his oldest child, Alice Lee, these words: "I do not believe in lying on the stump or off the stump."[17] Directing his appeals for political support in such a targeted fashion apparently did not fit for him in the category of deception, but it clearly demonstrated his well-developed ability to manage the message in the interest of his audience.

Roosevelt was politically astute to play to the Mormon character of the crowds in Utah. When the vice presidential campaign came to the state in September 1900, there were slightly more than 275,000 people living in Utah and more than two-thirds of them were Mormons, members of the Church of Jesus Christ of Latter-Day Saints.[18]

Just as Roosevelt was avoiding the silver question in the western mining states, so he was ready and willing to play to the religiosity of the people. At one of the events on the shores of the Great Salt Lake, the organizing committee had invited to the platform "not only the Mormon dignitaries . . . but also Bishop Ileff of the Methodist Episcopal Church, a great leader of gentiles, and Fathers Cushlaban and Larkin of the Roman Catholic Church. There were also Presbyterian and Episcopalian ministers in the audience."[19] Roosevelt's campaign recognized and responded to the cultural environment, addressing even the small details. In answer to a local reporter's question, for instance, the candidate referred to "Utah's best crop," meaning the children of the many large Mormon families. Roosevelt was also happy to share the news that his family included six children.[20]

There were but thirteen campaign stops at communities in Utah and Wyoming. Four were in Utah, and nine were in Wyoming. Most included speeches by the candidate; many provided interesting and unique anecdotes for journalists traveling on the special train or otherwise covering the campaign in these states. Each state had one major stop in the categories as we have considered them: Salt Lake City in Utah and Cheyenne in Wyoming. The former gave Roosevelt one of his most event-filled days of the entire western tour. The latter was more like the larger stops in other states.

Roosevelt's train left Pocatello, Idaho, headed south, the predominant direction of travel since the stop in Butte, Montana, two days earlier. Soon the train would turn eastward to begin the long journey home, a destination the candidate would reach only after hundreds of additional stops and speeches. What Roosevelt wrote earlier on the tour to Adelbert Moot, a prominent attorney in Buffalo, New York, continued to be true: "Wherever the train stops or wherever there is any size town at all, the people do come in and [are] waiting perhaps to the number of 2,000 to 3,000, and it seems exceedingly hard to hurt their feelings when they [are] acting partly at least in a spirit of loyalty to me. The West likes me, and I shall have to do some speaking in the Rocky Mountain and trans-Missouri states."[21]

What follows is the itinerary of Theodore Roosevelt's recorded stops during his 1900 vice presidential campaign in Utah and Wyoming:

Thursday, September 20
    Cache Junction, Utah (stopped at 9:30 a.m. for a few minutes)
    Logan
    Brigham City
    Ogden
Friday, September 21
    Salt Lake City
Saturday, September 22
    Evanston, Wyoming
    Green River
    Rock Springs
Sunday, September 23
    (The campaign special spent Sunday pulled onto O'Neill Siding; Roosevelt and his entourage were guests on Bill Daley's Ranch.)
Monday, September 24
    Rawlins
    Hanna
    Medicine Bow
    Laramie
    Tie Siding
    Cheyenne

Major Stops in Utah and Wyoming

Salt Lake City. Roosevelt's campaign train arrived as scheduled in Salt Lake City at 10:30 a.m. on Friday, September 21, 1900. There must have been a brief pause for a spruce-up just outside the community, because one observer reported, "The special came in all decorated with flags and bunting. The national colors flew from every point on which it was possible to tack them."[22] Estimates had the crowd at the Oregon Short Line Depot at two thousand.

Two daily newspapers served Salt Lake City: the *Deseret Evening News,* which had its story of the arrival on the streets the day it occurred, and the *Salt Lake Herald,* which offered its account on the following morning. The former was Republican in sympathy and the latter was stridently Democratic, and the differences in the reports are entertaining. What follows are the two descriptions of the costumed Rough Riders who met the train. Apparently the troop drew attention because of the rather comic nature of some of its members, but the tone of the prose illustrates the diverse editorial perspectives.

From the *Deseret Evening News:* "For fully half an hour before the arrival of the special from the north, the body of 316 Rough Riders was drawn up in a double line flanking the street. . . . All sorts and conditions of men and mounts were represented in this double line, from the professional city man on a spruce charger to the Simon pure horseman from Sevier Valley bestride a nervous bundle of hair and bones, with a pronounced antipathy to street cars. . . . Costumes of every degree of wild wooliness were also in evidence, including a brand new buckskin suit with elaborate fringes, which was worn with éclat by Dr. Higgins, while county attorney Livingston of Manti cultivated a roseate epidermis by mopping his damp brow at stated intervals with a bandanna of true cowboy hue."[23]

From the *Salt Lake Herald:* "Only 306 mounted men turned out, and very few of these were the genuine article. Nearly all were sheepmen who are more familiar with the 'baa' of a lamb than with the neigh of a horse. . . . One of the genuine cowboys in the line was W. O. Ash. He was thrown from his animal and sustained a broken leg, which he is said to regard as righteous retribution for mingling in such company. . . . There were mounts of every conceivable description, from the Indian cayuse bearing the small boy to the finest of blooded saddlers ridden by athletes. It was apparent even to the casual observer that many of the men in line were not familiar with horses. They fidgeted around considerably while the switch engines ran up and down the tracks and while the bands played airs patriotic and otherwise."[24]

When the train stopped, two bands played a march, "The Red, White, and Blue," and they followed that selection with a piece that had become the campaign's theme, "Hot Time in the Old Town Tonight." Roosevelt and others exited the train and moved to their places in the parade. Local organizers asked the candidate whether he preferred to ride a mount or to be transported in a carriage, and Roosevelt chose the carriage pulled by four white horses, preferring "nothing partaking of the hippodrome." The procession reportedly included the dignitaries from the train, the two bands, the troop of Rough Riders, three hundred other mounted cowboys, thirteen carriages, and two automobiles. Roosevelt was kept busy waving, bowing, and tipping his hat in response to the cheers of the crowd lining both sides of the streets. As the procession passed the Knutsford Hotel, several of the women guests offered a "regal reception" by waving handkerchiefs from the balconies. This caused the cowboys to "put their horses through their best paces." Unfortunately, "two gallant sons of the huge trackless desert landed, horses and all, in a prosaic heap upon the metropolitan pavement amid the chaff of their comrades."[25]

Following the parade, the Roosevelt party stopped at the Alta Club, a gentlemen's club on Temple Street in downtown Salt Lake City. It had been founded several years earlier by wealthy executives and professional men to serve their business and social needs. Many members had ties to the mining industry in the state. This was to be the site for the day's luncheon. An interesting event occurred shortly after arrival at the club: "Governor Roosevelt today used the long lines of the Rocky Mountain Bell Telephone Company, from the Alta Club to Cheyenne, being really the first user of the line not connected with the telephone company or newspaper offices."[26] It was widely reported that this call covered a distance of 550 miles.

As the *New York Times* reported to Governor Roosevelt's home-state constituents: "At the Alta Club . . . 150 mounted cowboys were drawn up in front of the club. The Governor was persuaded to mount a horse and take a gallop. . . . This was done, and the column of horsemen disappeared down the street in the dust. The ride lasted for about an hour."[27]

While this description may have satisfied the readers of the *New York Times*, other folks back home in New York City were treated to a much more colorful report by the traveling journalist from the *Sun*, a rival newspaper: "It was an easy jog till they reached the mesa. . . . Without any warning they began to quicken their pace and one of them passed the Governor. He let out his horse a little. The pace grew hotter yet. . . . The horsemen of Salt Lake City were putting him to the test. . . . They led him over shale and over arroyo . . . racing at the wildest kind of breakneck run. . . . The Governor's horse was worthy of its rider and took him steadily to the front. When at last he pulled up and wheeled, 50 or more of the escort were close behind him. The rest were strung out for a mile or more behind on the plain. . . . When the Governor came back he was aglow."[28]

After his vigorous ride and a luncheon at the Alta Club, Roosevelt continued to romance the Mormon community in Utah and elsewhere with a visit to church officials at the Beehive House. This was an 1850s residence built originally for Brigham Young where several church leaders had their offices and hosted small receptions. Mormon officials had scheduled a special event, a private organ recital at the tabernacle for their guests, and the hosts and visitors walked to that facility. When the planned program of music ended, the visitors asked to hear a few favorite pieces, and their requests were accommodated, including Roosevelt's preference, "The Star-Spangled Banner." As this selection played to conclude the concert, "Governor Roosevelt sprang to his feet. He stood at attention with his slouch hat held across his left breast until the anthem was finished. All the others followed his example." After the concert, Roosevelt was heard to say, "I have had many pleasant surprises on this trip, but this is the pleasantest of them all."[29]

Though the day had begun early and the morning and early afternoon were filled with activities, the principal elements of the agenda were still to come. "Governor Roosevelt, accompanied by many of the leading Republicans of the state, went out to Saltair at 2:30 this afternoon in accordance with the program."[30] Saltair was a huge pavilion on the southern shore of the Great Salt Lake jointly owned by the Mormon Church and the Salt Lake and Los Angeles Railroad. It was built in 1893 as a pier, and it rested on two thousand pylons. It served the recreational and social needs of the community and was informally known as Utah's equivalent of Coney Island in New York.[31] Roosevelt and his party traveled the twenty-two miles to the facility on one of the excursion trains scheduled for the campaign event.

Again, physical exertion became part of the day's activities: "The Governor had never been at the Great Salt Lake before and he said he would like mighty well to see what a swim in it was like. He was led at once to the bathing houses, and with a number of his eastern friends put on a bathing suit and started to wade out to the islands in the middle of the lake. They looked very near. They were four miles and more away. The visitors went out a few hundred yards and had fun trying to sink. When the Governor returned a lot of young women were ready for him with cameras. The Governor, being surrounded by other men, the camera fiends could not place him."[32] Another journalist reported that the swimmers were chilled: "Fifteen minutes was enough of this sort of thing. The bathers, including the guest of honor, wore a purple tinge when they came out, but a brisk rubdown in the dressing room restored them."[33]

When the time for Roosevelt's speech arrived, he was greeted by the large crowd that had made the trip for this event, even though there would be another opportunity to hear the candidate in the city that same evening. As to regional issues, Roosevelt said: "Much remains to be done [in Utah], and the national government, should in my judgment, do its part, for here in the West the next great stride must be taken by means of irrigation. It is eminently wise and proper that the national government should do its part in creating proper storage reservoirs and proper means for distributing it, and by that means the products of this country will be tripled and quadrupled."[34]

As to issues of the national campaign, Roosevelt told the audience at Saltair of a recent remark by William Jennings Bryan and then responded sharply to it: "The other day Mr. Bryan, in his speech at Chicago, is reported as having said that it boded ill for the republic to have 100,000 soldiers walking about in idleness. This morning I took lunch as a guest of some of your citizens, among whom were three men who wore the uniform of the United States Army and all of whom were with me at Santiago, the eldest of whom, a lieutenant colonel walks with a cane because on the second day of the siege, when walking about in idleness, a shrapnel struck him, and he will walk lame for the balance of his life in consequence. . . . Do you not think that the courage of these men and their patient endurance of suffering and hardship in what they have done in upholding the flag should entitle them to a better reward than some slander or sneer about their walking about in idleness?"[35]

Bryan's comment about the idleness of US troops in the Philippines and the potential for mischief would serve Roosevelt well. He played off the remark for several days on his western tour.

Following the afternoon on the shores of the Great Salt Lake, Roosevelt and his entourage commuted back into the city for an evening meeting at the Salt Lake Theater. The look was festive: "The building was appropriately decorated for the occasion with flags and red, white, and blue streamers and bunting, while suspended from the balconies were several mottoes which bore such inscriptions as: 'Prosperity at home; prestige abroad.'"[36] More people than expected turned out for the event: "The State Assembly room was selected, but it was not large enough to contain those who sought admission. The seats were filled, the three large galleries were filled, the stage was filled, and all the standing room was occupied to such an extent that members of the National Committee and even members of the reception committee and of the press could not obtain admittance."[37] Enthusiasm for Roosevelt was evident: "Salt Lake turned out in a surging multitude at night and made a greeting for him such as Salt Lake folks say they have never known their self-contained people to give to any man before."[38]

Not surprisingly, the local newspapers were again at odds regarding the reception given the candidate. The journalist for the *Salt Lake Herald* sniped: "At the theatre Governor Roosevelt was warmly greeted at the beginning but sparsely applauded. He seemed to feel the scantiness of the enthusiasm, for he cut his speech short and hurried back to his private car. In none of his speeches did he allude to the silver question."[39] The *Deseret Evening News* saw things quite differently: "With the exception of an animated debate between a little knot of politicians down in the parquet, which terminated in the ejectment of the prime offender, and divers audible ejaculations on the part of a bibulous character in the second gallery, the meeting passed off with a vim, the crowd was heartily in accord with the occasion and applauded loudly and frequently."[40]

As he had done at Saltair, Roosevelt localized his remarks with regional references, even as he addressed the national concerns of the party platform. He used a story from his ranching days to make a point he thought westerners would appreciate: "I don't have to explain to at least a portion of this audience what a maverick is. . . . One week [at the Little Missouri Ranch] I hired a new man, and he and I were out on the range. As we came in we struck a maverick, and he got a rope, tied him down, and branded him. And I said, 'Put on the Thistle brand.' He said: 'That's all right, boss, I know my business.' In a minute or two I said: 'But you are putting on my brand.' He said: 'Yes, I always put on the boss's brand.'" Roosevelt went on to explain that he fired the man because "if you will steal for me, you will steal from me." He was criticizing the Democrats for promoting policies that he said would help some at the expense of others. Roosevelt sharpened his message with these words: "In the east, they cannot prosper unless the West prospers, nor the West have its share of prosperity unless it comes to the East also."[41]

Recognizing that there had been heavy involvement by a military unit from Utah in the Philippines, Roosevelt responded directly to the

Democrats' charge of imperialism against the McKinley administration. He said: "They [the Filipinos] shall have such liberty as they have never known under Spain's rule and such a measure of liberty as they could never know under the rule of the tyrannical and bloodthirsty oligarchy of their own people. They shall have liberty, but they shall have it under the American flag."[42] Apparently, the implicit irony of these words did not occur to Roosevelt.

By most reports, Roosevelt's visit to Salt Lake City was successful. Even the *New York Times* termed it, "decidedly interesting."[43] The *Wichita Daily Eagle* took a similar thought further: "From a standpoint of human interest, Governor Roosevelt's visit to Salt Lake City was the most interesting, both from a political and social point of view, of any that he has yet made on his long tour."[44]

One final anecdote from Salt Lake City offered evidence that the pickpocket issue was still with the campaign. The *Salt Lake Herald* reported the incident as news, but the writer could not resist giving it a Democratic twist: "S. T. Williams' share in the Roosevelt demonstration cost him an even $70, and he is mourning greatly thereat. Mr. Williams is sure the thief was a Republican because the money was all in gold while some silver he had in his pocket at the same time was not touched."[45]

Cheyenne. This community was the major stop for the Roosevelt campaign in Wyoming, the second smallest state in population of those in the Union in 1900. There were fourteen thousand people living in Cheyenne when Roosevelt arrived, comprising 15 percent of the state's total population of just over ninety-five thousand. Cheyenne was (and remains) the capital city of Wyoming. It was an important center for the railroad industry in the western states.

When the vice presidential candidate's train pulled into town at 6:45 on the evening of Monday, September 24, 1900, there was a celebration waiting, but a hard rain was falling on the festivities. "The Roman candles shot their missiles only a few feet before the rain drowned them, but the booming of the 17-gun salute and the cheering of the soaking, steaming crowd could not be stopped by any rain."[46] Roosevelt did not hesitate to step off the train and onto the street to greet supporters with smiles and handshakes. In turn, there was an impromptu procession led by the Douglas Band that escorted the visitors to their hotel.

With eyes and ears always open to engaging incidents, Lindsay Denison, the journalist traveling for the *Sun* from New York City reported what happened next: "When the Governor walked up to the door of the Inter-Ocean Hotel, he was confronted by a St. Bernard dog nearly as big as the Governor himself. The dog urbanely put out a paw as big as a loaf of bread. Before the Governor could catch his breath the dog rose and ushered him into the hotel corridor. The dog was Senator Warren's dog and is said to know a heap about Wyoming politics." US senator Francis E. Warren was important to Roosevelt because he was the state's leading Republican powerbroker. He had demonstrated support for the McKinley and Roosevelt ticket by riding the campaign special across the state, and he was scheduled to introduce the candidate at an evening event. Unquestionably, Roosevelt would have observed whatever tradition was expected when encountering the St. Bernard.[47]

Perhaps it was the weather, the long day of speaking, the miles traveled, or some other factor, but the coverage accorded by the national press to the major stop in Cheyenne, Wyoming, was not as extensive as some other places on the western tour. The *San Francisco Call* told the story succinctly in this report: "Preparations on quite an extensive scale were made for the reception of Governor Roosevelt and his party at this place tonight. . . . Excursion trains from various parts of the state brought in quite a number of visitors. Two evening meetings were arranged, one at Turner Hall and the other at the opera house. Both places were crowded and both audiences were addressed by Governor Roosevelt. Expansion, militarism, and imperialism were the points touched upon by Governor Roosevelt in his remarks tonight."[48]

Local journalists provided much richer details. Running across the top of page one in the *Wyoming Tribune* was the longest one-line headline that could fit: "The Magic City of the Plains Greets the Hero of San Juan and the Next Vice President of the United States—Theodore Roosevelt." In addition to the scanty information wired across the country, this coverage reported that the meeting halls were "a blaze of light and color, the decorations being the most magnificent and costly ever used in the city." Also, the declaration that led the story revealed a strongly favorable opinion in the community: "Teddy has come and gone, but behind him he has left an impression not vague and indistinct, but far-reaching and with the illimitable power of the waves of the sea, which, sweeping on with constantly increasing momentum and force, sway and rock all that lies within their course; and, dashing against the rock-bound coast, destroys not the substance but moulds to its form."[49]

Though he spoke at length, Roosevelt broke no new thematic ground in the two Cheyenne speeches. He reached out to the local folks in his introduction: "You more than any other people of our country—the men of the West, the men of the Great Plains and the Rockies—embody those characteristics which we are proud to call distinctly American." Later in his remarks, he treated the Democratic charge of militarism with humor, telling his audience that there was only 86 percent of one soldier per one thousand people in the United States and that Wyoming's share allowed them about two ounces of concern per soldier. He said, "You would think I am jesting over it. So I am, because it is an issue that is not fit to be met save with a jest."[50]

Roosevelt's evening appeared to be a positive experience for both the candidate and the local citizenry, however not everyone was happy. The *Sun*'s reporter was obviously frustrated and looking toward a long night, as he filed his story by telegraph late in the evening. He included this less-than-newsworthy information: "The Colorado Committee headed by Senator Wolcott and supplemented by Senator Henry Cabot Lodge of Massachusetts is expected along about midnight and the Douglas band which came from Douglas, 132 miles, to add to the clamor of the occasion says that it is not going to bed until they come. Nobody will get any sleep until that band goes to bed."[51]

Highlights from Other Stops in Utah and Wyoming

Between the states of Utah and Wyoming there were thirteen reported campaign stops by the Roosevelt special. Two of those were major stops. What follows is information reported by media from the other communities visited by the vice presidential candidate. It is noted that, in addition to the thirteen campaign stops, there were two other stops identified with place names in media reports. As the train entered Utah, there was a brief stop at Cache Junction for two purposes: first, the train was ahead of schedule and paused to ensure a timely arrival at Logan; second, Utah's governor moved from another car on the train to the Roosevelt car so that he could visit with the candidate and appear with him at subsequent stops. There was also a layover in Wyoming at a location known as the O'Neill Siding to allow a visit on Sunday, September 23, 1900, at the Bill Daley Ranch. Media coverage of that unique visit is also reviewed in the following section.

Logan, Utah. "The first [campaign] stop made by the Roosevelt special train was at Logan at 11 o'clock where a pause of an hour and twenty minutes was made and where quite a demonstration had been prepared. Governor Roosevelt made a brief speech here in the Mormon tabernacle to an exclusively Mormon audience composed largely of women, many of them voters. The tabernacle, which seats about 1,200 people when filled to its normal capacity, was crowded, all standing room being taken. Prior to the speech-making there was a street parade and a reception at the chief hotel."[52]

As the wire service reporters sent the story, so it was printed by most newspapers in the nation. The previous report is an example. However, one journalist added details and perspectives not available elsewhere. He wrote: "The meeting in the Cache Stake Tabernacle at Logan was a queer experience for all of the easterners. . . . The tabernacle, which is built as any other church in a town of the same size would be built, was full of people. The main room of the building was up a flight of stairs. Over the altar was the legend in gilt letters, 'Holiness to the Lord.' On the platform were crayon portraits of Presidents Grant, Lincoln, and McKinley. These were draped with American flags. . . . When the Governor was introduced, the Mormons stood up in the pews and roared out their greetings. The women waved their handkerchiefs and the men waved their hands. . . . When the Governor was through they rose and cheered again."[53]

Roosevelt's train actually arrived in Logan at 10:30 a.m., and at 11:00 the event at the Tabernacle began. A crowd complete with a brass band ushered the candidate and his party to waiting carriages, and they toured the community, stopping briefly to view the campus of the local agricultural college. At the meeting in the tabernacle, Roosevelt told the audience that it was his first visit to Utah and that it was "a privilege to address the people, and the children of the people, who stretched their hands across the continent and redeemed the wilderness of the West." He expressed his pride in the children of Utah and said, "Blessed are they whose seed shall inherit the earth." He also honored "the pioneers who established this community . . . not by seeking easy times, but by facing the rough work." During the main body of his address, the candidate focused on expansion, as he had done in Montana and Idaho. His message was that success for America and for individuals requires a balance of legislation and personal effort.[54]

After the campaign special left Logan, a reported incident reveals why there are so few personal quotations by Roosevelt apart from his speeches on the western tour. One journalist wrote of another: "A pleasant surprise came to the Governor as the train was creeping along the edge of the Bear River canyon. He was confronted by a reporter of a Salt Lake newspaper who had been a trooper in his regiment . . . [who] wanted an interview.

Every time he started to ask a question, the Governor would remember some incident of the Santiago campaign. The train was fairly into Brigham before the reporter got the first intimation of fact that the Governor is not giving interviews for publication."[55]

Brigham City, Utah. "The next meeting was at Brigham, the scene of many of the bloody scenes of the fights between Mormons and Gentiles before the days when intellectual and political weapons superseded physical strife."[56] This journalist was recalling the battles between the Mormon community and the larger society, particularly the conflicts with federal troops that occurred in the late 1850s, known as the Utah War or Buchanan's Blunder. However, there was no remaining conflict with the federal government when the vice presidential candidate came to town on Thursday, September 20, 1900. Indeed, it was a positive visit: "The opera house here was too small for the assemblage gathered to meet Col. Roosevelt, so an adjournment was taken to where the bandstand had been erected. There the large crowd of nearly the whole town and visitors from neighboring places gathered in an outdoor meeting." Roosevelt addressed "trusts, the country's finances, and imperialism."[57]

One additional and interesting anecdote from Brigham City illustrated both the warmth of the reception and one means of provisioning the journey: "The several and separate refrigerators of the various campaign cars were stocked with game birds of all sorts at Brigham by former Assistant Postmaster General Heath, who has been on a hunting trip in this vicinity and was waiting for a train in Brigham station."[58]

Ogden, Utah. It was 6:00 p.m. when the Roosevelt special pulled into Ogden, a city of sixteen thousand people in 1900. The size of the community and the celebration it hosted would likely have made it a major stop in most other western states, but in Utah at the turn of the twentieth century, this community was clearly overshadowed by Salt Lake City. However, the folks at Ogden greeted the Republican candidate enthusiastically with music and cheers, and they ushered him through streets lined with well-wishers and the curious to a reception at the Reed Hotel. One report says that the procession included "a long line of Ogden businessmen," in addition to the typical carriages and mounted men in Rough Rider attire. The principal meeting was scheduled for 8:00 p.m. at the Ogden Opera House. According to a Utah journalist, "Ogden was in gala attire, and all seemed as a holiday."[59]

From the *Sun:* "The Ogden meeting began before the red glow of the sunset had left the sides of the Wahsatch Mountains which almost overhang the city. Large quantities of gunpowder, far beyond the municipal regulations, had been imported for the occasion. It was set off at various unexpected places as the procession of Rough Riders escorted the Governor around through the town. The meeting was in the opera house which was filled to suffocation with a crowd that yelled until the church meeting at Logan seemed like a veritable Quaker meeting."[60]

E. H. Allison, a local citizen of Ogden, chaired the meeting at the opera house. When he introduced the honored guest for the evening, he enthused: "He [Roosevelt] is the greatest governor of the greatest state in the greatest republic the world ever saw." Roosevelt rose to cheers and said that he "felt that he could ask westerners not to let the West go wrong in November, but to see that it was on the right side." He proclaimed that Republicans had kept their promises from the election of 1896 and that prophesies of gloom from the Democrats had proven false. Furthermore, he charged that the Democrats chose imperialism and militarism as key issues to scare the American people.

When Roosevelt spoke of the righteousness of US actions in the Philippines, a man in the crowd shouted, "Hurrah for Bryan!" Roosevelt responded, "Don't forget Aguinaldo, too!" He was referring to Emilio Aguinaldo, the leader of opposition forces fighting American troops in the Philippines. Ogdenites cheered for Roosevelt's quick response.

On the issue of self-determination, Roosevelt picked up and slightly altered a theme he had used elsewhere, saying that an Indian tribe could not be controlled like a New England town meeting. "Savages and semi-savages must be dealt with practically, and be educated up to the standard of freemen." He differentiated between "civilized Indians" and "blanket Indians," pointing to those who served during the Spanish War in Cuba as examples of the former. According to the report, "prolonged cheers followed Governor Roosevelt's address."[61]

Roosevelt's party overnighted in Ogden, sleeping on the train, as they commonly did throughout the trip. Before the party left for Salt Lake City on Friday morning, another encounter occurred that was reported as a human-interest feature from the western tour. "The Governor rose early, as he always does when he is feeling well, and climbed out on the ground to take a look at the mountains. He found Bill Ingling, the engineer, fooling around the engine and administering to it lovingly with an oil can. Ingling is the Pocatello candidate for the Legislature on the Republican ticket. . . .

Ingling shifted his oil can into his left hand and they grasped hands heartily. They walked around the engine together and back again and up and down the length of the train. They walked slowly, the Governor gesticulating . . . and sometimes halting and grabbing Ingling's arm to turn him around so that he could shoot his meaning straight into the other man's eye. . . . For nearly half an hour the two walked.

"[Ingling and Roosevelt] were so much wrapped up in each other that they failed to see the people who were coming out of the railroad restaurant and out of the round-house over in the meadows and out of the freight warehouses to look at them. . . . [Finally] they woke to the fact that they were figures of public interest. . . . [Ingling] said that the Governor was the sort of man the railroad men looked upon as their representative. . . . The Governor said that he was mighty glad to be liked by people whom he himself liked. . . . Then Ingling, with the Governor's permission and thanks, gave him many suggestions as to subjects to which his time might be most profitably directed in his meetings with western workingmen."[62]

Several journalists reported the meeting between the candidate and the engineer who was an aspiring politician. One wrote, "Enterprising newspaper artists with their 'Kodaks' caught pictures of the two men in earnest conversation."[63] (The first Brownie camera by Eastman Kodak was released in February 1900 and sold for one dollar.)

Evanston, Green River, and Rock Springs, Wyoming. Despite an overwhelming sentiment for Democrats and a militant attitude toward Republicans in 1896, these small communities warmly greeted Roosevelt and his companions just four years later. In all three towns, the Republican candidate "found audiences as big as the buildings in which he spoke could hold." These crowds were dominated by railroaders and coal miners, groups in western Montana with a contentious labor history. Fifteen years earlier, there had been a riot of miners in Rock Springs and up to four hundred Chinese laborers were killed. Actions by the federal government and the mine companies forced peace, and by 1900 Rock Springs took cautious pride in its diversity. More recently, the troubled national economy during Cleveland's second term had meant half-time work for many of the region's railroaders, but the recovery during McKinley's first term had brought prosperity and opportunities for overtime hours. Roosevelt's welcome generally resulted from cultural changes in a historically troubled region, as much or more than from the New York governor's popularity.[64]

O'Neill Siding.   Midway between Saturday's final stop in Rock Springs and Monday's first stop in Rawlins was the Sunday layover point for the campaign train, a place commonly called Bill Daley's Ranch. This is one journalist's report on the unique experience: "The Roosevelt special has been all day on a temporary siding near an unfinished piece of the Northern Pacific track, 18 miles from a telegraph instrument. Mr. Daley, commonly called Bill in this country, has [the party] as his guests. . . . Mr. Daley has a ranch which is ten miles wide and 40 miles long. . . . He has a cook who can fix up venison, antelope, and sage hens as nobody else in this wide land can. By way of an appetizer for the wonderful dinner at the ranch the Governor went for a 25-mile ride on Sheriff McDaniels's horse. . . . The deer and the game that made up the dinner were all killed within the limits of the ranch. Bill Daley promised the Governor a real ranch dinner and kept his word. . . . They sat down hungry and they rose up with the utmost deliberation and sought places for slumber."[65] It was reported several years later that Mr. Daley was hosted at the White House by President Roosevelt, who said to First Lady Edith, 'This is the gentleman you have heard me speak of and at whose home in Wyoming I had the grandest dinner I ever sat down to.'"[66]

Rawlins, Utah.   Roosevelt's train left the siding near Bill Daley's Ranch at 8:00 a.m. on Monday and reached Rawlins one hour later. The candidate treated the crowd at the opera house to a speech of forty-five minutes, acknowledging "unquestionable evils connected with our great, extraordinary, complex, and wonderful industrial system." However, he also urged his hearers to "be careful not to kill the patient in cutting out the disease."[67] Why Rawlins was the site Roosevelt chose for the following declaration on the money question after days of ignoring the issue is uncertain. However, he boldly declared: "We ask your support now for President McKinley because he stands on a platform that squarely declares for the gold standard. . . . We believe that only by carrying out the promise of that platform can the present prosperity of the country be maintained and increased."[68] Perhaps it was explained best by the journalist for the *Sun,* who wrote simply: "Wyoming was never much of a silver state."[69]

Hanna, Wyoming.   From a wire service report: "The Roosevelt special made a short stop at Hanna today and Governor Roosevelt spoke a few minutes to the people. Three hundred miners, besides the women, came out to listen to the speech. When this place was named, Mark Hanna was a director in the Pacific Coal Company, whose mines are here. Governor Roosevelt reminded his hearers of the times four and six years ago when it was difficult for miner to get work, and asked them to compare those times with the present, when all were employed, and all obtaining good wages, and asked if they wanted to change back again to the hard times."[70]

Medicine Bow, Wyoming.   From the *Sun:* "A member of the First California Volunteers came smashing through the audience as the train drew out of Medicine Bow, knocking folks right and left. High in the air he held a cigar-shaped package to Roosevelt. It was tightly wrapped in gold foil. 'I got that in Manila,' shouted the soldier, as the train rolled away and left him nearly breathless. 'I have been saving it for you ever since I heard you were coming out here.' The Governor . . . never smokes himself, so he told [colleagues] that the one who made the best speech at Cheyenne tonight should have the cigars."[71]

Laramie, Wyoming.   From a wire service report: "Laramie was reached at about half past 2 o'clock today, and here two speeches were made to permit all who wished to see and hear Governor Roosevelt speak. The day meeting aroused a good deal of interest here. Governor Roosevelt said, in part: '. . . There are two interests in this campaign. One is the interest of our material well-being. . . . The other is the even more important side, the question of national greatness. . . . If throughout our history we had had to deal with timid souls who feared danger, and who feared to risk, who feared to go forward when the nation went forward, you would not have been here . . . It would have been folly and weakness for this nation to have halted in its westward growth because of some fancied scruples as to our right to introduce the spirit of civilization into these waste places of the earth."[72]

Tie Siding, Wyoming.   From Lindsay Denison: "On Sherman Pass the Union Pacific is changing its grade so that it will be cut down 1,000 feet. The magnitude of the undertaking may be understood from the fact that in order to carry on the work, night and day, two electric plants costing $40,000 each have been erected. At Tie Siding, the central point for the workmen, a short stop was made and Col. Roosevelt had just time to exchange greetings with the railroad men. They were as demonstrative as railroad men all along the line have been."[73]

Conclusion

One Rough Writer offered up the summary statement that best represents the days in Wyoming. He wrote: "The whole vote of the state is about 20,000. The Democratic majority in 1896 was but a few hundred. . . . There are enough railroad graders employed along the lines of the Union Pacific Railroad alone to swing the state to one party or the other. . . . In a state whose whole voting population would not by any means overcrowd Madison Square Garden, a meeting of 20 voters is one that the politicians regard with the utmost respect and concern. . . . Such meetings as those along the route of the Roosevelt special for the last few days have never been known in the state. After each stop the local politicians make their way through the train to their car, slapping one another on the back and feeling good all over."[74]

CHAPTER 11

COLORADO

Colorado's Republican Campaign Committee planned stops for the Roosevelt special on either side of a north-to-south axis through the state, and nearly all of them included speeches by the candidate. Over the three-day period, September 25 to 27, 1900, there were reported visits to twenty-five communities large and small. Three of the stops—Denver, Cripple Creek, and Pueblo—were intended to be major according to the categories used in the previous chapters, and each of these had three meetings scheduled, all with Roosevelt addresses. Some of the other stops had quite large events as well, and one of the communities in this latter category became significant, overshadowing all others in terms of the attention it garnered from media, party leaders, and the public.

Roosevelt was heckled and assaulted in Victor, Colorado, in a situation that threatened to escalate into even more dangerous violence. This narrative begins with a recounting of the Victor incident because it quickly became the defining stop of the Colorado days on Roosevelt's western vice presidential campaign tour. Generally speaking, the crowds that greeted the candidate everywhere along the route were warm, courteous, and often enthusiastic in their support. Victor was so different from these norms that what happened there was both shocking and disturbing to everyone, except seemingly to Roosevelt himself, who appeared almost energized by the violence.

Following are listed by date and in order the reported stops of Theodore Roosevelt's vice presidential campaign by train through Colorado. (Note that one source also mentioned a location called Colorado Creek, but that site has not been found by the author and may have been an error by a single newspaper in typesetting the wire report.) Two of the locations—Gillett and Independence—exist today only as ghost towns, and the Independence herein mentioned is the site in Teller County, as opposed to another site by that name in Pitkin County, Colorado.

Tuesday, September 25, 1900
  Eaton
  Greeley
  Fort Collins
  Loveland
  Berthoud
  Longmont
  Niwot
  Boulder
  Denver
  (Roosevelt and a few from his party overnighted twelve miles
  outside Denver on September 25 at Wolhurst, the estate of Senator
  Edward O. Wolcott.)
Wednesday, September 26, 1900
  Castle Rock
  Colorado Springs
  Colorado City
  Manitou Springs
  Divide
  Gillett
  Independence (Teller County)
  Victor
  Cripple Creek
Thursday, September 27, 1900
  Leadville
  Granite
  Buena Vista
  Salida
  Canon City
  Florence
  Pueblo

Violence at the Victor Stop

Two clues indicate that what occurred at Victor was predicted by some. A journalist for the *San Francisco Call* wrote on the day following the incident: "Warnings of Colorado politicians and railroad men that it was not without the bounds of possibility that there might be rough conduct when

Roosevelt reached the Cripple Creek region were laughed at by the people who have been through the trip with him. The Governor himself laughed at them. The air has been full of such stories ever since the Governor reached Montana."[1] Also after the incident, the headline writer for the *Arizona Republican* wrote: "What Was Feared Happened."[2] It is not at all clear, however, why the Colorado Republican Campaign Committee planned stops for Roosevelt in the Cripple Creek District, particularly in Victor, given the highly charged atmosphere.

Though Victor, Colorado, is a community of fewer than four hundred people today, when Roosevelt visited in 1900 it was a bustling mining camp of five thousand. Gold had brought thousands streaming into the region known as the Cripple Creek district, and the area had been a hotbed of labor unrest for several years. The United Mine Workers and the Western Federation of Miners were historically at odds over preferred labor representation, and the strife between oppressive mine owners and militant union members often meant physical confrontation. Hundreds of law-enforcement officers and even the military had been called into the region in the past, and at times some of those in uniform had enforced the will of the owners rather than attempt to bring peace or a fair settlement to the conflicts.

According to the miners' own accounts, the cost of housing, fuel for heating, water, clothing, and food—all provided by the mining companies— outstripped monthly wages and kept the laborers in a state approximating slavery. Work was hard, days were long, and conditions were dangerous.[3] Thus, the ground was fertile for radical social attitudes and actions. Theodore Roosevelt, a wealthy easterner with an Ivy League pedigree, who also represented the political party perceived to favor big business, was an obvious target for the miners' frustration and rage.

Apparently, rumors and legends abounded about the intensity of political feeling in Victor. One source said that there were only twenty-seven votes for McKinley in the community in the previous presidential election. Another reported: "Victor is a town where McKinley polled four votes in '96 and where an angry committee went through the town with a bucket of tar and a feather pillow trying to find out who cast those four votes."[4]

Roosevelt stopped at Victor on the afternoon of Wednesday, September 26, 1900. The next day's front-page headlines shouted the story to citizens around the nation. In Akron, readers saw: "Rough Rider had a Rough Time." In Salt Lake City, the message was: "Roosevelt is Mobbed at Victor, Colorado." In San Francisco, voters read the charge: "Friends of Bryan

Make Assault on Roosevelt." And in Marietta, Ohio, one word summed the story: "Vicious."[5]

As can occur even today, when newsworthy events are fast-moving and involve a large number of people, journalists struggle to find knowledge-able sources and to report with precision. Though all newspapers on September 27 shared the general outlines of the story from Victor, there were some differences in the details. The following account is as accurate as the varied reports allow.[6]

Victor began like most stops for the Roosevelt special: there were brass bands and a troop of costumed Rough Riders at the station, and most onlookers were excited to meet the train. A cheer erupted when Roosevelt appeared, and because the schedule allowed only twenty-five minutes, he moved quickly toward the meeting at the Armory Hall. In so doing, he left his escort behind at the depot.

Armory Hall was not well lighted, and it was difficult for all in the audience to see the speakers. The facility was described as "packed to the doors" with 2,500 people—both Republicans and Democrats—occupying seats and standing. A McKinley and Roosevelt Club had formed in the community, and it was numerically and vocally well-represented in the hall.

When Colorado's senator Edward O. Wolcott, who was never a favorite of the labor community, rose to introduce Roosevelt, the simmering anger in the hall began to boil. Sources suggest that curiosity imposed an uneasy silence as the Republican candidate opened his mouth to speak, but as soon as he said, "Fellow countrymen," shouts for Bryan broke loose. Roosevelt continued to speak into the chorus of frequent interruptions—even responding sarcastically to some of the heckling—until he concluded his remarks.

At that point, there was a rather strange occurrence. As reported by the *Indianapolis Journal:* "While Governor Roosevelt was speaking in the hall, and the interruptions, hoots, and shouts for Bryan were frequent, a tall, brown-faced man arose, walked to the platform, faced the audience, raised his hand for silence, and said: 'Four years ago I voted for Bryan. I have been a champion of silver for a long time. I believe in the doctrine, but I tell you now I am done with it all. This year I vote for McKinley and have done with you cowards and curs.' There was not a hiss, jeer, or shout in derision. The man, in reply to the Governor's question, said his name was Foulke, that he lived at Victor, and then left the hall."[7]

Emotions were running high. Some of the Republican dignitaries visiting the community with Roosevelt had brought their spouses, and these women became sufficiently alarmed that they too left the hall at that point. No sooner had they exited than a mob bent on rougher behavior forced its way into the building. Lieutenant Sherman Bell of the First Volunteer Cavalry and General Irving Hall, two military officers who were present, organized the effort to return Roosevelt to the train, surrounding him with members of the costumed Rough Rider troop that had formed his escort from the depot.

Two women in the group of those determined to disrupt the event carried Bryan banners to the head of the group surrounding Roosevelt, and marched as though leading the candidate back to the train. Other men and women also carried banners and taunted the Roosevelt party. Still others began tossing rotten eggs and fruit and throwing stones. Members of the Roosevelt troop retaliated by grabbing at the banners, and a costumed Rough Rider succeeded in pulling a banner away from one of the women leading the march. The mischief makers then swung the two-by-four planks on which the banners were mounted, and one of the men drove a pole straight into the crowd surrounding Roosevelt, striking the candidate in his chest. Roosevelt lunged forward to defend himself, but members of his group pulled him away and knocked down his assailant. Some among the attackers helped the man regain his feet and escape before he could be identified or captured.

By several estimates, there were now as many as 1,500 persons in the streets, and there were small and large fights breaking out everywhere. The protectors hustled Roosevelt onto the train, even as the rotten food and stones pelted his private car. Senator Wolcott was standing on the ground outside the car shouting insults and threats at the assailants, until he, too, was forced onto the train.

Roosevelt refused to stay inside in the relative safety of the car but insisted on standing on the rear platform to watch events unfolding. Stones hit the car near him, and Lieutenant Sherman Bell stepped in front of Roosevelt to protect him. "Come away, Colonel, come away," he begged, but Roosevelt responded, "Stand aside, sir. I am your colonel, sir." Then Roosevelt reportedly leaned over the rail, waved his arms, and "laughed like a boy on a toboggan ride." As the train pulled away, Roosevelt's supporters could be heard cheering his bravery. He said later to a reporter: "This is bully, this is magnificent. Why, it's the best time I've had since I started. Wouldn't have missed it for anything."[8]

In the aftermath, journalists noted that no police had been in evidence and deemed it remarkable that no gun play had been part of the incident.

Residents of Victor said that the ruffians were not people from the community. Leaders of both parties tried to blame what happened on each other. The governor of Colorado stated that Senator Wolcott, not Theodore Roosevelt, was the target. William Jennings Bryan wrote that no legitimate political organization would do such a thing. Mark Hanna said, "If there is anybody in the East or the West who knows how to take care of himself and to back up his opinions, it is our candidate for vice president."[9]

Rumors developed very quickly that Victor's rioters would travel the six miles to Cripple Creek and disrupt the evening events there as well. Additional deputies were sworn and stationed at the Cripple Creek depot, but nothing approaching the nature of the Victor riot occurred.

Armed guards also accompanied the Roosevelt special as it traveled back through Victor after the evening events in Cripple Creek. Again, there were no additional threats or demonstrations. In fact, the *St. Louis Republic* subsequently criticized the candidate for this response: "Governor Roosevelt committed a serious mistake when he allowed the loading of a case of Winchester rifles on his train for use in arming his Rough Rider guard on the return trip through Victor. Firing upon political opponents, no matter how demonstrative, by a candidate's party would be an unheard-of procedure in an American political campaign." On the other hand, the *Marietta (OH) Daily Leader* wrote: "Governor Roosevelt showed that he is made of the genuine stuff when attacked by a mob of drunken hoodlums at Victor, Colorado, Wednesday night. He stood the fire like the gallant soldier that he is, and never flinched even when assaulted by the mob."

Two related reports of violence that came shortly after the Victor incident filled the nation's newspapers. William Bell, South Dakota's only original Rough Rider, was arrested for shooting the editor of the Flandreau, South Dakota, newspaper because he criticized Bell's speech during the Roosevelt stop in that community. Also, the editor of the *Victor Daily Record* was assaulted for referring to the women among the rioters as "dissolute." A miner entered the newspaper office, claimed his wife was insulted, and proceeded to hit the editor on the top of his head as he sat in his chair.[10]

Finally, the Victor incident brought national recognition of a sort for one man. Daniel M. Sullivan, postmaster from Cripple Creek, was credited in some of the newspaper accounts as the man who sent Roosevelt's assailant sprawling onto the ground. Later in the week, the National Association of First-Class Postmasters, who were meeting in a convention in Peoria, Illinois, sent a telegram honoring Mr. Sullivan for his heroics.[11]

Major Stops in Colorado

Of the three major stops in Colorado for the Roosevelt whistle-stop campaign—Denver on Tuesday, Cripple Creek on Wednesday, and Pueblo on Thursday—only the first occurred prior to the Victor incident and thus avoided both the rumors of additional demonstrations and the worry about responding if violence erupted. Denver also escaped the media speculation about what might happen and the later interpretation of events through the filter of what did happen at Victor. The radical labor elements showed themselves elsewhere, but they did not muster the numbers or the intensity of the behavior in that one small community located in the Cripple Creek district.

Before the assault on the candidate late Wednesday afternoon, the visits in Colorado were much like those already behind the travelers. For these reasons, the Roosevelt sojourn in the state can be categorized not only as major and other, but also as pre-Victor and post-Victor. Journalists seemed to think that the violent incident partway through the run of stops added to the interest and attendance at those that fell post-Victor.

Colorado's Republican Campaign Committee was certainly as ambitious as any state planning group to date in terms of working the candidate to his maximum capacity. Stops were relatively close together, and there were several scheduled each day. Virtually all stops included a speech by Roosevelt on the program agenda, and at most places there was a parade or procession to a speaking site away from the depot. Each of the three major stops went beyond the expectations in previous states by including three large meetings and consequently three candidate speeches during the evening hours. Roosevelt spent his days in Colorado rushing from one small or medium-sized community to another and his evenings shuffling between auditoriums.

Denver.   Colorado's largest city set the tone in terms of the schedule for the state's major stops. Roosevelt had made his first eight community visits in the state before pulling into Denver at 5:00 p.m. When he arrived at the city's Union Station, there were one hundred veterans of the Spanish War awaiting him. They were uniformed and mounted, and their mission was to escort him through the crowds to the Brown Palace Hotel for a brief reception with local dignitaries. However, there was a problem for those managing the evening's events in Denver. Heavy rain was drenching the city, and the schedule included both a festive parade and an outdoor speech on the grounds of the state capitol.[12]

From the *Sun*: "As far up and down as one could see through the rain there was only a densely packed bobbing multitude under rain-wet umbrellas and hats. . . . The rain increased so steadily that more than 2,000 men appeared at the county committee headquarters and clamored for torches with which to march."[13] Members of the county committee made a decision. There would be no parade, and the rally planned for the capitol grounds would be moved into a third auditorium facility. Furthermore, they recruited the men seeking torches to move around the city informing people of the changes in the schedule. Thus, the new plan was to hustle Roosevelt to the reception and then to proceed with three indoor meetings. As one journalist said, "There was no dampening the ardor of the Republicans of Denver."[14]

Everything seemed to go according to plan B. Roosevelt's first speaking stop was at Coliseum Hall, where 3,700 people were overflowing the facility. Next he visited Windsor Hall, the indoor location substituted for the capitol grounds. While specific attendance figures were not reported, it is likely a crowd filled this venue to capacity because the outdoor meeting had been the largest on the original schedule. Finally, Roosevelt was taken to the Broadway Theater where 3,000 people awaited his late arrival. Even given the inclement weather, large crowds could not have been a surprise; Denver was the largest city Roosevelt had visited since he left Chicago. By the time he finished the third event of the evening, the candidate had addressed more than 20,000 Coloradans with a total of eleven speeches on this one day.

Roosevelt's themes and illustrations were familiar during the meetings in Denver: controlling the trusts would require firm but sensible actions, labor's needs cannot be ignored, and national expansion is honorable and should be expected. "During his address [at Coliseum Hall] Governor Roosevelt declared that there was no more excuse for the breaking of a promise made upon the stump than the breaking of one made in private life. It was just as bad, he said, for the people to demand promises impossible of fulfillment as for the candidate to make them."[15] The latter statement was an interesting addition to a theme he had used frequently when talking about the Democratic candidates.

One element of his final speech of the evening at the Broadway Theater was unique to Denver because it was a response to correspondence that had come his way from someone whose name his audience would recognize. Roosevelt said: "I have just received a letter purporting to be from the

Governor of your state, written upon official paper, requesting me, somewhat at length, to state my position on the currency question, and asking why I should not state it in Denver, as well as in Chicago and Milwaukee. I will suggest to the Governor that hereafter he will do well to read the letters of acceptance of candidates. If he had read my letter, which was published in Denver exactly as in New York or Milwaukee, he would have found his questions already answered. I am for a protective tariff, the gold standard, expansion, and the honor of the flag."[16]

Colorado's governor, Charles Spalding Thomas, was a Democrat, and he was legitimately challenging Roosevelt's silence in the mining states on the issue of gold versus silver. Roosevelt's response in Denver may not have laid the matter to rest, but it was certainly an entertaining answer.

After the three evening meetings at Colorado's only major, pre-Victor stop, Roosevelt and a few others from his party traveled twelve miles outside Denver to Wolhurst, the country estate of Senator Edward O. Wolcott. In the 1890s, the Wolcotts had built the Tudor-style home on four hundred acres as a country retreat, and they continued to expand it for entertaining until it encompassed twenty-five rooms at the time Theodore Roosevelt visited in 1900. That same year, the Wolcotts divorced and the senator's sister, Anna Wolcott, headmistress of the exclusive Wolcott School for Girls in Denver, served as hostess at Wolhurst.[18]

Wolcott was born in Massachusetts, earned a Yale baccalaureate degree, graduated from Harvard Law School, and moved to Colorado to practice as an attorney. He had chaired McKinley's Commission on International Bimetallism, a group that toured Europe but effected no change in the administration's unyielding attitude on the gold standard.[19] That Wolcott was despised by miners who slaved twelve or more hours each day to live in debt and squalid conditions was not at all surprising.

Cripple Creek. After passing a peaceful Tuesday night at Wolhurst, Roosevelt, Wolcott, and the senator's other guests returned to Denver and left on the train at 9:15 a.m. for another busy day of campaigning. Once again, the plan for Wednesday was ambitious, including meetings at eight stops during the day and a major stop in the evening with three assemblies and speeches. The first seven of the daytime visits turned out in hindsight to fit the category pre-Victor stops, while the eighth was Victor itself. Cripple Creek was the scheduled major stop for Wednesday evening.

Because the Victor incident filled the headlines and front pages of newspapers across the United States on Thursday, September 27, 1900, the space given to the major stop in Cripple Creek was minimal or nonexistent. Indeed, the coverage actually given to Roosevelt's visit in Cripple Creek generally focused on the threat that what happened in the community's smaller neighbor, Victor, would spill over during the three evening meetings. This was the coverage, for instance, in the *San Francisco Call:* "The rioters [from Victor] threatened to follow the train to Cripple Creek and make the Governor sorry he ever came into Colorado. Sixty special policemen were waiting for them at Cripple Creek. . . . [They] surrounded Roosevelt as he stepped from the train. The mob looked them over, contented itself with noise and that a long way off."[20] Other newspapers had even less. In Ohio's *Marietta Daily Leader,* readers learned only that "Roosevelt spoke at three meetings in Cripple Creek this evening, all of which were indoors and large, orderly, and appreciative."[21]

It is regrettable that the Victor incident effectively pushed the stop in Cripple Creek out of the nation's newspapers because this Colorado community was one of the most culturally, demographically, and economically interesting stops on the entire western campaign tour. Gold mining had swollen the population of Cripple Creek in 1900 to 10,000 people within the city limits and more than 50,000 in the region known as the Cripple Creek district. According to one source, there were 150 saloons, 41 assay offices, and 91 lawyers in town when Roosevelt visited. Also, gold production peaked in 1900 at nearly 900,000 ounces.[22] Labor unrest was reshaping the social order. How Roosevelt was received and what he had to say in Cripple Creek was lost to voters across the country because of the Victor incident.

Roosevelt left Cripple Creek asleep in his private railcar at 11:00 p.m. on Wednesday evening. On the train were the guards armed specifically to ensure safe passage through Victor, six miles down the line. There were no additional incidents, and the campaign special rolled quietly toward appointments on the third and final day in Colorado.

Pueblo.   Thursday must have seemed almost leisurely with six stops during the day prior to the major stop in the evening at Pueblo. Victor continued to dominate coverage of the rest of the Colorado tour, with most journalists reflecting on the incident or reporting reactions to it by politicians or pundits. The *Sun* revealed to New Yorkers that their governor had suffered more than was first known: "It developed today that Gov. Roosevelt had not got off from the rioters as easily as was thought yesterday. In the fight somebody kicked him on the knee. He considered the matter so slight that he did not mention it and nobody else noticed it. Today, however, there was a swelling over the kneecap that hurt him a good deal and required some attention."[23]

Because Victor continued to occupy the minds of reporters and editors, Pueblo shared the fate of Cripple Creek—that is, it did not receive the attention normally accorded to a major stop by national media during the western campaign tour. What did find its way into the journalists' stories was mostly positive. The *New-York Tribune* said simply that there were three evening meetings in Pueblo, and Roosevelt addressed large audiences at all of them.[24] The *Indianapolis Journal* added the details that a large crowd met the train, and a committee escorted the candidate to Royal Park where a procession formed for a march through the streets.[25] Finally, the *Sun* offered more information: "The reception in Pueblo tonight was very much like that which Gov. Roosevelt found in Denver, except that it was not marred by rain. The streets were arched with festoons of electric lights, most of the buildings were decorated with flags, and all Pueblo seemed to be on the streets cheering or in the three halls whooping up the speeches."[26]

There was one negative story reported as a follow-up to the stop in Pueblo that demonstrated not everything had turned toward the positive in the post-Victor visits. From the *Indianapolis Journal*: "Governor Theodore Roosevelt narrowly escaped a mobbing at this city [Pueblo] tonight. The confession of an Italian, named Igo Ferrio, is all that saved him from a rough time. Two hundred Hungarians and Italians here, employed in the smelting works and avowed Anarchists, were prepared to rotten egg him. They also intended to rush his escort with stones and eggs and drive him to his car for safety. During the last two days these foreigners—there is not an American in the crowd concerned—formed a secret organization, whose purpose was to mob Governor Roosevelt. . . . The mayor and chief of police are both Democrats, but they acted with promptness. . . . Six of the ringleaders were under arrest and the others were notified of stern measures. . . . The effect of this was salutary. . . . [However] it is impossible for [Roosevelt] to appear on the streets without insult being offered."[27]

Highlights from Other Stops in Colorado

Aside from the stops already considered—majors in Denver, Cripple Creek, and Pueblo, and the incident in Victor—there were twenty-one other stops in Colorado. Not all had anecdotes or political pronouncements deemed sufficiently newsworthy by journalists to recount them in their stories. Nearly all stops included remarks by Roosevelt. Again, the Victor incident colored those stops that followed it, and the media reports reflected that change.

These are the highlights from the nonmajor stops in Colorado as reported by the nation's newspapers. They are listed in the order in which they occurred. Those prior to Leadville were pre-Victor; the remainder fall into the post-Victor category.

Eaton.   "Governor Theodore Roosevelt was welcomed here today by a large concourse of citizens. The school children of the town were in evidence, each carrying a small American flag. . . . [Roosevelt] said in part: 'I am particularly glad to see these children here. I am an expert in children. I have several myself.'"[28]

Greeley.   "At Greeley, the great potato-raising town, there was the first opportunity to see how enthusiastic the Colorado Republicans are over the outlook for the coming election. . . . There were 400 people from Denver in the Greeley station yard. They had come out from Denver with the famous Cook Fife and Drum Corps simply to make sure that the Governor of New York should know that he had arrived in Colorado. . . . For 40 minutes there was such a meeting as it was worth the while of those Denver people to have come 60 miles to see. The meeting was in Lincoln Park and the speakers stood on a high band stand about which more than 3,000 enthusiastic men and women were assembled. It should be remembered that Colorado is again one of the states in which women vote. . . . The eagerness of [Roosevelt's] audience to seize every point had its immediate effect on him and his ordinary vim was perceptibly heightened."[29] Roosevelt said: "If there ever existed two phantoms that are put forward to frighten political children they are imperialism and militarism."[30]

Longmont.   According to news reports, Longmont gave only thirty-nine votes to McKinley in 1896, but in 1900 the sole political organization in town was the McKinley and Roosevelt Club with nine hundred members.[31]

Boulder.   "At Boulder a large out-of-doors meeting was held near the station, situated in a picturesque valley, the sharp peaks of the nearby Rocky Mountains, cloud capped and solemn, surrounding the city. At the conclusion of his short address Governor Roosevelt was pulled from the platform by the students forming the football team of the state university, which is situated here, and carried into his car on their shoulders over the heads of the people."[32] After leaving Roosevelt at the train, the players hustled back to their practice field, and when the candidate's special rolled by, they kicked a football into the side of his car to get his attention.

Colorado Springs. Citizens celebrated Roosevelt's arrival, and the local businesses were decorated with bunting for a procession. The candidate gave two short speeches in Colorado Springs, the first at the Temple Theater and the second at the opera house. Both auditoriums were crowded. He stayed in the community from noon until just after 1:00 p.m. One source said that "the entire population appeared to see the New York Governor and shake his hand."[33]

Leadville. This stop occurred at 11:00 a.m. on the day following the Victor incident. Reactions affected both the behavior of local citizens and the journalists' emphases in their stories. For instance, the reporter for the *Sun* noted the presence of Democrats at the outset of his account of events in Leadville: "A committee of Leadville Democrats came down to the train when it arrived and conveyed their assurances to Gov. Roosevelt that he would be treated as the guest of the city and not as a politician while he was with them. The Republicans came down with a coach drawn by four white horses and covered with American flags, a mounted escort of 40 men, a foot escort of 200 Civil War veterans of Northern and Southern armies and Spanish war veterans and three bands and drum corps. There were over 3,000 people about the stand in the public square. The governor was to speak from a platform erected six inches from the floor of the stand. He could not see the whole of the crowd from that platform and mounted the reporters' table instead. He was cheered again and again until he departed from his argument for expansion. For the rest of the Republican platform there was respectful attention."[34]

It is also interesting to note that this New York City newspaper, the *Sun*, typically ran daily reports on Roosevelt's western tour on page three, or even on page five. However, the narrative on the Victor incident appeared on page one, as did the reports from Colorado stops on the following day. Clearly, interest in the vice presidential campaign was elevated by the threat of violence, and it is also likely that the actions of the radical miners brought not only additional attention, but also sympathy to the Republican cause. Even in Colorado, evidence demonstrated these effects: "The attitude of the people of Leadville was set forth by their newspaper, the *Herald-Dem-ocrat*, which until this morning has been throwing all its influence to the Democratic ticket. Today it told the whole story of the Victor outrage truth-fully in its news columns and on its editorial page printed an article headed 'Colorado's Burning Shame.' At the top and bottom of the article were deep black mourning leads."[35]

Salida.   "It was at Salida that an attempt was made to break up the Roos-evelt meeting on Thursday. Salida is a division point on the Denver & Rio Grande and has a large repair shop. . . . [Roosevelt] had just begun to speak when a gang of 50 boys, who wore Bryan caps and sat in a room of the depot, began to yell and shout for the candidate whose name was on their caps. There was no police officer around, and the boys only yelled the louder when ordered to desist by Senator Wolcott. One of them said a local Democrat fitted them out with the caps and paid them to create the disturbance."[36]

Canon City.   Journalists writing about the stop at Canon City reported that most of those attending the Roosevelt event were farmers and fruit growers who had little vested interest in questions of silver versus gold. Perhaps that is why Roosevelt chose this place to comment on the violence he had experienced. He said: "Anarchy is the handmaid of tyranny. If ever we grow to substitute lawless mob violence for the orderly liberty that we enjoy under the law . . . then we will indeed be within a measurable distance of losing our liberty."[37]

Commenting further, he railed: "There has been some talk as to what the paramount issue is in this campaign. I will tell you, and I have made up my mind within 48 hours. . . . The paramount issue is to keep the orderly liberty that has made us what we are. . . . The worst thing this country can have is the man sitting at home exciting other men who are ignorant to deeds of violence, and whether exciting of violence be by a politician or the editor of a newspaper, the effect is the same."[38]

On this final point, Roosevelt may have had in mind an incident that had occurred earlier during the Canon City stop. According to reports by jour-nalists accompanying the candidate, the correspondent for the *Rocky Moun-tain News* attempted to influence stories on the Victor incident in favor of the miners, and he personally wrote a published story that Senator Wolcott was behind the riot. This correspondent was riding the campaign train as a guest for the trip through Colorado. When his perspectives and actions became known, he was invited to leave the special train at Canon City.[39]

Florence. "An ovation in the way of reception was inaugurated along the banks of the Arkansas [River] at Florence. A hundred or more charges of dynamite were fired back at a distance of a mile or more from the track as the train entered the town. Every blast shook the cars on their trucks and made every soul aboard jump."[40]

Conclusion

Those scheduling the Roosevelt campaign tour from the Republican Party's national headquarters may not have understood the potential for violent behavior that existed at some of the planned stops in Colorado, but the members of the state campaign committee could and should have known the threat. It was apparent that the history of radical union activity, the ongoing and oppressive treatment of labor by management, and the emotions generated in mining communities by the currency issue made for a combustible political situation. Violence was predictable, and the only questions were in which communities it would occur and how physically threatening it would become.

What is apparent in hindsight is that the Victor incident worked to the advantage of the McKinley and Roosevelt ticket, though it was certainly intended to do otherwise. That firearms never appeared in the hands of the demonstrators surely indicated that serious bodily harm or assassination was not the goal. Rather, the plan was likely to send a forceful political message that would somehow benefit Bryan and Stevenson. Instead, sentiment flowed in the opposite direction and any rage the rioters hoped to catalyze was blunted by the shock and repulsion felt by most of the public. Roosevelt not only survived the attack both physically and politically, but he also had an opportunity to burnish his shiny image as a manly hero.

CHAPTER 12

KANSAS AND NEBRASKA

Unremitting sameness was likely an observation that crossed Theodore Roosevelt's mind as his train rolled through the Great Plains, but for him the thought had little to do with the view outside his window. He surely wrestled with questions that he could voice to no one. For instance, how can I tolerate more crowds? How much adulation and overblown enthusiasm can I endure? How often can I appear to enjoy the ridiculous spectacle of middle-aged, heavyset men in mismatched military costumes? How fresh can my message be when identical themes and images are delivered multiple times each day, week after week? How can I be sure my rhetoric is on target when I try to humanize myself by using local references?

As his attention wandered: How could I have guessed there was this much yardage of red, white, and blue bunting in the entire world? How much more time—days, hours, minutes, and seconds—until I return to home and family? How many more warm handshakes, toothy smiles, and feigned looks of genuine interest must I give before the merciful conclusion of the western campaign?

Undoubtedly, such thoughts vexed the Republican vice presidential candidate as they would any individual, yet he was looking at a schedule for Kansas and Nebraska with nearly six dozen stops over the next few days. Physical exhaustion was a given; mental and emotional fatigue were threats he must guard against to avoid misstatements and inappropriate responses to unwarranted criticisms or ignorant questions. Roosevelt had to wonder, for example, whether his sarcasm from the podium in Victor, Colorado, escalated the rage. Thankfully, there was one day of rest planned for Kansas City halfway through the coming week. He wrote from the train to his sister: "I do nothing but fester in the car."[1]

Though he was surrounded by traveling companions and a steady flow of admirers, supporters, critics, and journalists, Roosevelt must have felt alone in his total commitment to the campaign. Certainly the other three candidates leading the Republican and Democratic national tickets were speaking here and there. Yet only Bryan was regularly traveling and appealing to voters, and he was less avid than Roosevelt. On the day the Republican vice presidential candidate entered Kansas to make seventeen speeches at fourteen of his twenty-nine stops planned for the state, William Jennings Bryan visited South Dakota with major speeches in Mitchell and Aberdeen. Adlai Stevenson announced appearances for fifteen days in October.

William McKinley, on the other hand, took a morning drive with his wife to enjoy the weather near his Ohio home. In the afternoon, the president received the US ambassador to Peru for a chat and later shook hands on his front sidewalk with a few ladies from the Daughters of Rebekah who stopped by after their district meeting.[2]

Theodore Roosevelt made sixty-nine reported stops during his campaign tour of Kansas and Nebraska between Friday, September 28, and Thursday, October 4, 1900. Two of the stops on October 3 were in the Black Hills of western South Dakota, where the train made a quick northern detour to honor an invitation from Roosevelt's friend, Seth Bullock. Twenty-nine communities in Kansas, running generally west to east, were on the tour.[3] Included on the Nebraska schedule were thirty-eight towns and cities in that state and the two communities in South Dakota.

Unlike most other western states where routes generally cut a single path in one direction, Roosevelt and his party traveled two circuits in Nebraska, each stretching from the eastern border nearly to the western boundary of the state.[4] On October 1 and 2 there was an east-to-west-to-east southern circuit; on October 3 and 4 there was a matching round trip on a central-outbound and northern-inbound circuit. Why so much attention was given to rural Nebraska is not certain, but a likely explanation is that the Republicans wanted a visible statement of strength in the home state of William Jennings Bryan.

Also important to note regarding the strategic planning that went into the Roosevelt western whistle-stop tour is that population patterns in 1900 were quite different than they have become in twenty-first-century America. When McKinley and Bryan faced off for the presidency, there were more people—and, thus, more voters—in Kansas and Nebraska combined than there were cumulatively in the previous seven states visited by Roosevelt. Most significantly, eighteen electoral votes were available to the winner of Kansas and Nebraska. During the two-circuit Nebraska visit, Roosevelt managed stops in forty-four of ninety counties, passing through all six of the state's congressional districts.[5]

Following is a list in order of the reported stops in Kansas, Nebraska, and western South Dakota:

Friday, September 28, 1900
    Jennings, Kansas
    Norton
    Prairie View
    Phillipsburg
    Smith Center
    Mankato
    Belleville
    Clyde
    Clay Center
    Junction City
    Abilene
    Salina
    Lindsborg
    Hutchinson
Saturday, September 29, 1900
    El Dorado
    Eureka
    Yates Center
    Iola
    Chanute
    Cherryvale
    Parsons
    Cherokee
    Weir
    Pittsburg
    Pleasanton
    Paola
    Olathe
    Fort Scott
    Armourdale (suburban Kansas City, KS)
    Kansas City, MO
Sunday, September 30, 1900
    Kansas City (No campaign events)

Monday, October 1, and Tuesday, October 2, 1900 (Southern Nebraska
  east-to-west-to-east circuit)
  Falls City, Nebraska
  Auburn
  Tecumseh
  Beatrice
  Wilber
  Crete
  Fairmont
  Minden
  Holdredge
  McCook
  North Platte
  Lexington
  Kearney
  Grand Island
  Aurora
  York
  Seward
  Lincoln
  Ashland
  Plattsmouth
Wednesday, October 3, and Thursday, October 4, 1900 (central/
  northern Nebraska east-to-west-to-east circuit)
  Broken Arrow
  Seneca
  Hyannis
  Alliance
  Crawford
  Chadron
  Lead, South Dakota
  Deadwood
  Valentine, Nebraska
  Ainsworth
  Bassett
  Atkinson
  O'Neill
  Clearwater
  Neligh

Norfolk
West Point
Fremont
Blair
Omaha

Some stops were relatively large in terms of attendance, but most were brief to allow the inclusion of so many communities. For purposes of reviewing the campaign tour through Kansas, Nebraska, and western South Dakota, only two of the stops are catalogued as major—namely, those in Kansas City and Omaha. In Kansas City, there were two large events scaled to include crowds of a size unmatched in most other states. In Omaha, the demand for seating was also large, but because the venues were more modest in size, there were four events scheduled for one evening.

Strictly speaking, the second event of the Kansas City stop was not in the state of Kansas. Convention Hall had been the site of the Democratic National Convention during the summer of 1900, and its location was the corner of Thirteenth and Central in Kansas City, Missouri. Also, the Midland Hotel where Roosevelt was a registered guest during his day of rest on Sunday, September 30, 1900, was in Kansas City, Missouri, at the corner of Fifteenth and Walnut.

Following are sections on the major and other stops in Kansas and Nebraska, with a brief jaunt into the Black Hills of South Dakota and a tiptoe across the western border of Missouri. Most of the narrative is presented in a similar fashion to previous chapters. However, information on the two circuits through Nebraska relies verbatim on the journal of a regional newspaper correspondent who made the trip, took extensive notes on every stop, and provided a detailed account that ran in several of the state's weekly newspapers. It is a resource unique to one state on Roosevelt's western tour, and an abbreviated but still-comprehensive version in this text tells the story of the thirty-seven Nebraska communities catalogued as other stops. This gentleman obviously took seriously a newspaper's responsibility to provide the first draft of history, and he accepted the implications of his job title *journalist*.

Major Stops in Kansas and Nebraska

According to reports immediately following Roosevelt's whistle stops in Kansas and Nebraska, the candidate was seen and heard by 175,000

Kansans and 330,000 Nebraskans.[6] Many of those who saw and cheered Roosevelt were in the metropolitan centers on the states' eastern borders, Kansas City and Omaha. Roosevelt visited the former as his farewell to Kansas on Saturday, September 29, and the latter as his concluding stop in Nebraska on Thursday, October 4, 1900. Both came at the end of long days of campaigning, and each taxed the candidate's endurance to the limit. Indeed, to the third of four crowds during the evening in Omaha, Roosevelt's fatigue and annoyance spilled over briefly. He complained as he took the podium: "I am sorry that I am a little late but I have been handled as a mere article of convenience by the committee and we have done our best to keep all appointments."[7]

Kansas City. This urban center that spans into Missouri where the real heart of the city beats is accounted here as the conclusion of Roosevelt's Kansas tour because it came at the end of two days in that state that included visits to twenty-eight other communities. As soon as he arrived in the early evening, the candidate and his party were escorted by a costumed regiment of Rough Riders to "Shawnee Park in Armourdale, Kansas City, Kansas, where an immense open-air meeting was held." Following this event, Roosevelt was taken to Convention Hall in Kansas City, Missouri, where a capacity crowd had sat through preliminary speeches since 7:00 p.m. His scheduled arrival at nine o'clock stretched to 10:10 p.m. before he entered the hall.[8]

At the first of the two events at Shawnee Park there was a disruption: "On [Roosevelt] being introduced to the vast assembly an organized effort was made by a large number of men and boys to prevent his making a speech. Cries and interruptions were frequent during the first few moments. Each interruption was followed with hard hits from the speaker, until quiet was restored and the greater part of the speech was listened to in respectful silence."[9] Apparently the attempt to disrupt the Armourdale gathering surprised most observers who were witnessing a large and enthusiastic crowd: "Nobody expected any such demonstration as was seen at Armourdale on the Kansas side. Bryan is a great drawer of crowds but never did he have here or in Armourdale such audiences as waited for Gov. Roosevelt."[10]

As soon as Roosevelt's speech at the open-air event concluded, he left the podium to others and proceeded to the Missouri side of the city for the evening's second meeting at Convention Hall. Because this facility had served the Democrats as the site of their national nominating convention barely three months earlier, there was a certain satisfaction for Roosevelt as he faced a full house with a crowd variously estimated between 22,000 and

25,000. "Although the people had been waiting . . . their enthusiasm was undiminished and their patience unexhausted. When Governor Roosevelt mounted the platform he was greeted with a storm of applause which lasted for at least 20 minutes. Order being at last restored, the governor proceeded with his address, which continued for three-quarters of an hour."[11]

Speaking at Convention Hall, Roosevelt addressed the list of issues that were his standard fare on the tour, including the trust question. His language varied somewhat here and was interesting: "I did not go at them [in New York] in a Socialist or Anarchist spirit, but I went at them with the spirit of doing justice to them and exacting justice from them. . . . As a consequence of legislation . . . by which we have got a proper return from the corporations for what they got from the state, we now have in [New York] the lowest tax rate we have had for the last 40 years. . . . Now I ask you and I think I have a right to ask you, to compare what has been done by us with what has been promised and prophesied and has not been done by our antagonists. 'By their fruits shall ye know them,' and I ask you to look at the actual Democratic thistles, and not take into account the imaginary figs they have promised to pluck from these thistles."[12]

Reactions to the Roosevelt visit in Kansas City were reportedly very positive: "In Kansas City there were 25,000 wildly noisy people before him in the Convention Hall. It has been the biggest and noisiest day of the whole trip."[13] And there was this assessment: "The Republicans of Kansas City are jubilant over the success of the two meetings here last night."[14] Even the showman Buffalo Bill Cody, who understood crowd response better than most, was amazed. When he was interviewed after the rallies in Kansas City, he said: "Look at the way they are receiving Roosevelt. They have gone wild over him wherever I have struck his trail. He is the greatest magnetizer this country holds today."[15]

Sunday offered a welcome break in campaigning for the candidate and his entourage. He stayed over Saturday night at the Midland Hotel in Kansas City, Missouri, and he used the hotel as his base of operations on Sunday. He attended a church service, took a horseback ride through the countryside, lunched with a senator, and visited with the city's most important newspaper editor. Each of these elements illustrated that a candidate running for national office may take time billed as a day off, but choices and actions related to campaigning never really allow rest.

Even Roosevelt's visit to a worship service demonstrated this point. "As soon as the Governor learned that he was to be in Kansas City over Sunday he asked friends here to find a Dutch Reformed church which he could reach conveniently. He was informed that there was such a church in the city and made up his mind to go there today. On his arrival here last night, however, he found a letter from the Rev. Dr. George, in which it was suggested that inasmuch as the Dutch church was without a pastor just now, it would be better for the Governor to go to the church which most nearly approached it and he invited the Governor to the Westminster Church. The letter appealed to the Governor as being very sensible and he decided to accept the invitation. He began to prepare for bed when a very young minister came to his room and told the Governor, with visible agitation, that there were some doubts about the orthodoxy of the Westminster Church, which is independent. The minister assured the Governor that the church of which he had the honor to be the shepherd would be glad to have him worship under its roof. The Governor said that if he went to church at all he would probably go to Dr. George's. He rather inclines to independence, anyway."[16]

Exactly how many votes the Republican ticket gained or lost by this decision is uncertain. Roosevelt's keen sense of media relations must have warned him that he did not want to become embroiled in a church controversy by snubbing an established congregation.

There was evidently some public knowledge that Roosevelt would visit the Westminster Church because one journalist reported the Lincoln and Fremont Club, a Republican organization, chose to attend the same service. This story also recorded that "it was old men's day in the church . . . and Dr. George's sermon was one of hope and encouragement for old men."[17] Roosevelt reportedly returned to the hotel appreciative of the positive message.

So, the day went. Because a few hundred people were ready to join the candidate on his horseback ride from the hotel and would push "a pace that would not become the Sabbath day," Roosevelt took a carriage to the country club and rode in the country alone. However, as there were several supporters eager to have the honor of loaning him a mount from their stables, he changed horses three times during the ride.[18]

Roosevelt lunched with US senator Albert J. Beveridge of Indiana, a friend and strong supporter of the party platform, who was in Kansas City to meet with the candidate about the upcoming tour of Indiana scheduled for ten days hence. Since Roosevelt could not ignore the media for so much as a day, he spent the afternoon at the home of W. H. Nelson, editor of the *Kansas City Star,* the regional newspaper for eastern Kansas and western Missouri. Finally, as one journalist wrote: "In the evening he entered his private car, Minnesota, much refreshed by the day's rest."[19] One wonders whether Roosevelt had reckoned with how brutal would be his four-day schedule in Nebraska. If so, he might have been more serious about taking a full day of refreshment and rest.

Omaha.   By the time he reached Omaha, the second major stop of the Kansas and Nebraska tours, Roosevelt had visited thirty-nine additional communities since Kansas City, just four days earlier. He had traveled from the east side to the west side of Nebraska twice and taken a side trip into western South Dakota. Nearly all stops had included speeches, and he had seen tens of thousands of people spread across the state's 77,000 square miles. When he reached Omaha on the evening of Thursday, October 4, 1900, he still had four rallies and four speeches ahead of him before retiring for the night. He was visibly exhausted, standing on the brink of what the *Omaha Daily Bee* termed "four hours of continuous cheering."[20]

Roosevelt's special train pulled into Omaha's Webster Street Station about thirty minutes behind schedule. As soon as he emerged from his car, the 30,000 at the station and 100,000 lining surrounding blocks began to cheer,[21] and he was ushered to a carriage for a winding parade through the downtown. "Electrical illuminations . . . and thousands of cheering men and women welcomed the distinguished guest as he rode at the head of a procession of horsemen, torch-bearers, flambeaux wielders, and plain marchers that required nearly a half hour to pass a given point. Everywhere were throngs of eager spectators anxious to greet the famous Rough Rider." As the parade passed any given point, spectators rushed away to find seats or places to stand at one or another of the speaking venues. At one point in the parade, Roosevelt became aware that a member of his original troop of Rough Riders, Jesse D. Langdon, was on a horse following the carriage. "The tired look vanished from the candidate's face," wrote one journalist, "and he beamed with real pleasure. He gripped the trooper's hand hard."

Scheduled first among the evening's four rallies was one on Capitol Avenue in a tent erected for the occasion. Six thousand people jammed into the temporary structure, where the president of the local McKinley and Roosevelt Club, H. H. Baldridge, praised the candidate with these words: "Fortunate is the party which calls to its leadership its highest and best type of manhood, that type which stands for something and means something. . . . [Roosevelt] stands for all that is best and highest in American politics and statecraft. . . . If his culture, his attainments in letters, his urbanity are of the East, his boldness, dash, and heroism are of the West, and we are proud of it."

Audience members at the tent reportedly stood on their chairs cheering and waving. When Roosevelt was introduced, a group of twenty Harvard men in the crowd stood and gave the college yell for their fellow alumnus (BA, 1880). Roosevelt still had humor to share. He said: "It is a little bit difficult to know what issue to discuss, because our opponents change the paramount issue so often. But I am perfectly willing to meet them on any issue if they will only stay long enough on it." The crowd laughed obligingly.

Later in his speech, Roosevelt obviously recognized his geographic separation from the mining states, because he brashly said for the first time at a major event in several days: "Take the question of free silver. . . . There is no doubt how we stand. We stand on the gold standard, and we stand on it on the Atlantic seaboard and in the Rocky Mountains anywhere. We are fortunate in having issues which don't wear thin in any part of the country." The rest of his forty-five-minute speech was filled with themes and illustrations that had been his stock-in-trade for the western tour.

Creighton Hall was the second venue. Here a standing-room-only crowd of one thousand had gathered. "The stage and gallery were hung with monster flags and the entire wall at the right of the proscenium arch was spanned by a mammoth portrait of the Rough Rider painted on cloth." At 8:30 the stage party entered and a "colored quartet opened the meeting with a couple of sentimental melodies." Several speakers occupied the platform before Roosevelt arrived. One local dignitary, C. J. Greene, particularly entertained the crowd with this remark that found its way into the newspaper coverage: "The best that is said of Bryan is that he cannot do much harm, but like the man who ordered the remains of a deceased female relative embalmed, cremated, and interred, we do not want to take any chances."

When finally the candidate arrived, people again stood on their chairs and cheered. Styling an extravagant introduction was apparently a local custom, and at this venue Roosevelt was introduced with these words: "[He is] the tenderfoot whose spirit brought him to the West to be the prince of Rough Riders, and from the Hudson to the Yellowstone, from the Rio Grande to San Juan, no name so thrills the hearts of Americans as that of Roosevelt."

At Creighton Hall, "Governor Roosevelt spoke for only about 12 minutes, while the perspiration streamed down his cheeks. He said that Nebraska is not only a vigorous state, but it exacts vigor from its guests." This was certainly a quick jab at the nearly impossible schedule the committee had planned for Omaha, and he left immediately after speaking and shaking a few hands on the platform for the ride to the third event, this one scheduled for the Bohemian Turner Hall.

As Roosevelt entered the next event and went toward the stage, the Bohemian Turners' Band played "America," and the capacity crowd of one thousand stood and "voiced its admiration for fully five minutes." Prior to Roosevelt's arrival and during some of the preliminary speeches, some "hoodlums in the gallery persisted in disturbing the speaker by hisses and shouts." As Roosevelt began to speak, the hecklers again interrupted, but they were "finally taken from the hall by policemen."

For the final event of the evening "Governor Roosevelt was scheduled to speak at the Boyd Opera House at 10:30, and the company now playing an engagement there timed its performance so as to close at that hour. It seemed that the regular theater-going crowd had filled the playhouse. The assurance of having a good seat from which to see and hear the hero of Santiago had attracted large numbers, but when the ushers threw open the doors to admit the advance guard of the Roosevelt column, a good 500 were added to the big audience, bringing the total up to 2,000, the full capacity of the house. . . . At 10:30 sharp the drop curtain was rung up and a column of prominent citizens, headed by Governor Roosevelt . . . filed across the stage and took seats. Instinctively the audience arose to its feet to cheer the lion of the evening. . . . Governor Roosevelt's talk was brief, and he was frequently interrupted by cheers."

Mercifully, the evening ended for Roosevelt when he finished his remarks at the Boyd Opera House and returned to his railcar at the Webster Street Depot. The campaign special was turned over to the Illinois Central Railroad Company, and the Roosevelt train pulled eastward out of Omaha at midnight bound for the next day's stops in Iowa.

Highlights from Other Stops in Kansas, Nebraska, and Western South Dakota

When reviewing the national newspaper coverage of the Kansas and Nebraska segments of Roosevelt's western tour, there is a noticeable paucity of space given to the stops generally, but particularly those that occurred in the smaller communities. Perhaps the space occupied by the Victor incident and its aftermath in Colorado meant that a backlog of routine news had accumulated, or it might simply signal fatigue with the sameness of the trip stop by stop. It might also be that the sheer number of stops in Kansas and

Nebraska discouraged coverage of all of them by those newspapers published in other areas of the United States. Suffice it to say that several of the stops are known only from their inclusion in lists of visits between the larger towns.

That anticipation of Roosevelt's visits remained high for the citizens of Kansas and Nebraska is attested by the size of the crowds not only in Kansas City and Omaha, but also in the smaller and mid-sized towns where figures are available. In Wichita, for instance, a community of 25,000 people in 1900 that was near but not on Roosevelt's route, this item ran in the *Wichita Daily Eagle* while the train was making its way through Colorado: "Last evening the Wichita Eagle swung to the breeze a big Republican banner, the only net banner which Wichita has ever indulged in. The banner is a monster, containing large portraits of McKinley and Roosevelt, a big eagle with the lettering, 'Daily Eagle,' and above it all: 'Four more years of prosperity.' It is a handsome thing and so big that it took ten or twelve men half the afternoon to swing it up above and clear of telephone, telegraph, and trolley wires across Douglas Avenue."[22]

Friday, September 28, 1900, the first day of the trip through Kansas, was apparently successful, as the *New York Times* reported that "meetings have been larger and the interest greater than at any other time during the trip west of the Mississippi River."[23] However, there was a persistent problem because of the number of stops, the expectations that Roosevelt would speak everywhere, and the size of the crowds: "The train failed to run on schedule time, and thousands of people were kept in the open air at different places along the road for hours awaiting its arrival."[24] This was an occasional problem elsewhere on the western tour, though stops and events seemed generally to run close to the scheduled time.

What follows are the reported highlights from a few of the twenty-eight stops other than Kansas City in the state of Kansas:

Jennings. The only widely available information from the visit to Jennings is that it was the first stop for Roosevelt in Kansas and that he spoke to a small crowd from the rear platform of his railcar.[25]

Norton. This visit occurred at 8:00 a.m. and was the second stop of the day. Roosevelt "left the train, was escorted to a platform in the open air and made a brief speech. . . . There was a large number of Hollanders in the crowd, and the Governor saluted his hearers in opening his remarks with a few words of their mother tongue."[26]

Prairie View.   Dutch settlements were a significant element of the population in western Kansas,[27] and this gave Roosevelt several chances to refer to his own family heritage. To the people of Prairie View, he said: "I am told that there is here a settlement from the land from which my ancestors came. Is it true? (Cries of 'Yes, yes.') If you will let a Dutchman give a word of advice, I will give it. Out in the land from which my ancestors came they kept the flood out by dikes. As you know, Holland has been won from the sea. They put the dikes up to keep the waters out. Putting the dikes up does not make the land prosperous unless the land is cultivated. The only way it can be cultivated is to keep the water out. During the last four years in this country we have been putting up a big dike to keep Bryanism out. I hope no one is going to be foolish enough to break down the dikes."[28]

Clyde.   "Here there was a shout and a rush for the rear platform where Governor Roosevelt stood. A short speech was made, and when the train was moving off a rush was made to shake hands and several women and children were trampled on and injured in the rush."[29]

Junction City.   "When the train arrived at Junction City a great surprise awaited the Governor. Drawn up in line on their horses were Buffalo Bill's soldiers and Indians in costume and a large crowd of people. A dozen or more of the soldiers were found to have been members of the Roosevelt regiment in Cuba. Cannon and Gatling guns belched forth a salute to the incoming train. When the train stopped Buffalo Bill in the picturesque dress of a pioneer frontiersman appeared at the rear of the coach and was warmly greeted by the Governor."[30]

William "Buffalo Bill" Cody was never shy, and he took the podium saying, in part: "Ladies and gentlemen, Gov. Roosevelt is the American Cyclone, and I don't wonder that some have taken to their cellars. The Wild West is not here to make political speeches. The ticket Gov. Roosevelt represents is already elected, and all they have got to do is to show down and take the pot."[31] He continued with lengthy remarks. Eventually, the train moved away in an attempt to stay close to the schedule, and Buffalo Bill's speech was cut short.[32]

Hutchinson.   This town of nine thousand was the fourteenth and final stop of the first day in Kansas. Not only had the train made several stops, but the trip was a journey of 490 miles as well. Thus, Roosevelt and his party reached Hutchinson at 10:30 p.m., two and a half hours behind schedule.

The event included a reception and a speech at an auditorium in the community. After a warm social, Roosevelt cut his address short and retired for the night.

One journalist reported that crowds had to brave thick, sticky mud to attend the Friday events in Kansas because there had been rain for several days. There was also a problem for the train: "When the Union Pacific engineer was trying to cut down the time that had been lost during the afternoon, the train struck several miles of track under which the earth had softened so that the train rolled and bounded over it as though it were a ship in a heavy sea. Typewriters fell and men in the private cars were tossed out of their chairs."[33]

However, as the train reached eastern Kansas on Saturday, the tracks were underlaid with a sound gravel bed, and the engineer was able to add speed. The same journalist wrote: "It was great to see the knots of hundreds of people at some of the stations throw themselves against the walls of the station and even drop down on the platform to save themselves from the rush of the hustling flyer. A storm of gravel as big as the end of your finger beat on the rear windows of the Minnesota [Roosevelt's car] for miles and miles."[34]

Eureka. Eldorado was the first stop on the second day in Kansas. Then at Eureka, Roosevelt recalled that the Kansas delegation had been the first to visit at the Republican National Convention, urging his candidacy. He said from his car's rear platform: "I have a certain peculiar right to come before you, for it was Kansas more than any other state that insisted on my nomination for vice president, so that you are responsible in a large measure for my being here."[35]

Also at Eureka, "25 or 30 women came forward in a body from the crowd that stood on the edge of the mud pools alongside of the track. . . . They marched right into the mess, and it came up to their shoe-tops, and they insisted on shaking hands with the Governor as soon as he stopped talking. The Governor told them that he was sorry that they were getting mussed up. . . . One of the women called: 'It wasn't politics that made us come to see you; it was because we liked your picture.'"[36]

Though no stop for Roosevelt is reported at the small community of Neal just east of Eureka, this interesting anecdote survives: "The special train passed a big freight train on a siding at Neal. The engineer of the freight leaned far out of his cab and touched the Governor's shoulder as he passed. When the Governor turned, the engineer waved his hand and shouted: 'Kansas is sure for you.'"[37]

Yates Center.   Roosevelt's train stopped for only five minutes at Yates Center, and the candidate stepped out of his car just to say hello. However, a journalist observed this interaction: "'I'm sorry you are going to get beat,' said one of two women who came up to the car at Yates Center. The other woman who was the daughter of the first one laughed. 'I'm glad you're not going to be beat,' she said. The three, mother, daughter, and the Governor had a good laugh. The Governor said he was glad at any rate that the rising generation looked on the brighter side of life."[38]

Iola.   This stop produced a story with local color. General Frederick Funston gained national prominence during the Philippine conflict that had become much a part of presidential politics in the 1900 election. Funston won both the Congressional Medal of Honor and a battlefield promotion to brigadier general because of his bravery. Roosevelt noted that this courageous man was the product of Iola. Moments later, a heckler in the crowd listening to Roosevelt shouted for Bryan, and there were demands to have him excluded. Roosevelt said: "No, let him shout for Bryan and Aguinaldo until he is black in the face, but for heaven's sake do not let him mention General Funston in connection with either."[39]

Cherryvale.   At this stop, Roosevelt mounted a speakers' stand to scold the Democrats for "invoking the doctrine of the Declaration of Independence as applied to the Tagalog bandits on the other side of the world, while they fail to apply that doctrine to fellow countrymen of ours whose skins are dark in North Carolina and Alabama."[40]

Fort Scott.   This was the final stop prior to Kansas City. Here Roosevelt stayed longer than anticipated, speaking for three-quarters of an hour. He became "more than ordinarily impassioned." He shook his fist as he said, "I feel as if I am approaching a crusade. I do not feel as if this is an ordinary political contest. I feel that I have a right to appeal to the manhood of every American citizen as we appealed to it in the dark days of the civil war."

At this point begins the coverage of the other, nonmajor stops in Nebraska. As described previously, what follows is the journal narrative prepared for publication in a number of weekly or semiweekly newspapers in Nebraska—for example, the *Custer County Republican,* the *Nebraska Advertiser* (Nemaha City), and the *North Platte Semi-Weekly Tribune.* This rather lengthy journal of Roosevelt's trip ran in the editions printed during the week of October 14, 1900, and it was carried as one feature rather than published serially. The piece was, unfortunately, presented without attribution. It was apparently prepared by a correspondent who joined the Roosevelt train for the journey through this one state, as selected journalists had done in other states.[41]

Most of the quotations from Roosevelt's speeches and a few anecdotes are eliminated from the text in the interest of abbreviating slightly. Otherwise, the piece is verbatim, as it offers a unique perspective of the Roosevelt trip through the eyes of a western newspaperman. Though it was written in a straightforward and subdued Midwestern style, it was headlined, "Sets Nebraska Wild."[42]

This is the feature as it ran on page three of the *Custer County Republican* of Broken Bow, Nebraska, on October 18, 1900:

"Never in its history has Nebraska turned out and extended a more cordial greeting to a public man than it accorded to Theodore Roosevelt. . . . All along the line thousands of people turned out to hear him, the tour closing with a demonstration in Omaha in which fully 150,000 people participated and which was clearly the largest political demonstration ever held in Nebraska.

"All told fully 330,000 people turned out, or approximately one-fourth of the entire population of the state. This is a record which stands alone . . . in the history of Nebraska.

"The enthusiasm and attention accorded would indicate that Nebraska is, not only strongly imbued with patriotism, but that it is going to pin its faith to Republicanism and prosperity.

"The Roosevelt special entered the state at FALLS CITY, where 1,200 people awaited its coming. There were 1,500 at AUBURN, 2,000 at TECUMSEH, 15,000 at BEATRICE, 1,200 at WILBER, 2,000 at CRETE, 3,000 at FAIRMONT, 5,000 at MINDEN, 5,000 at HOLDREGE, 15,000 at MCCOOK, 5,000 at NORTH PLATTE, 2,500 at LEXINGTON, 10,000 at KEARNEY, 10,000 at GRAND ISLAND, 2,000 at AURORA, 5,000 at YORK, 2,000 at SEWARD, and 40,000 at LINCOLN with a parade three miles long.

"At ASHLAND the crowd numbered fully 5,000 and its enthusiasm was unbounded. A conspicuous feature of the gathering was two uniformed ladies' marching clubs. Rough Rider uniforms were noticeable everywhere.

"PLATTSMOUTH concluded the second day's tour and at that place 12,000 enthusiastic admirers turned out and accorded Governor Roosevelt a welcome that would have been a credit to a metropolitan city. He spoke at length to the multitude on national issues and his words met with many generous responses.

"During the night the train proceeded to BROKEN BOW. . . . That station, though reached before the breakfast hour, was the scene of much enthusiasm . . . 2,000 voices.

"The train stopped for water at SENECA and Governor Roosevelt alighted and shook hands with a large number of school children. 'Let the little ones all come,' he said to the school master. . . . An elderly lady with two towheaded youngsters stepped up and informed him that her two grandchildren had kept her awake all night for fear they would miss seeing him. Placing his hand upon the shoulders bent with age [he said], 'That's all right, Grandma, don't disappoint the children. It may not appear much to you, but the slightest disappointment in youth sometimes turns the course of a whole life.'

"HYANNIS greeted him with 1,000 enthusiasts. . . . ALLIANCE announced the arrival of the Roosevelt special by the blowing of whistles and firing of bombs. There were 3,000 people at the depot and when the gallant Rough Rider emerged from the car a deafening cheer was given. After acknowledging the salute Governor Roosevelt turned to where 75 Rough Riders sat on prancing steeds and answered their clarion cheers with bows and smiles. 'Every time I see you, boys,' he said, 'I think of San Juan Hill. . . .'

"CRAWFORD was reached promptly on time, and 2,000 enthusiasts were out in force and extended a royal greeting. Governor Roosevelt spoke of the cattle industry and quoted figures to show that all grades of cattle are selling at prices 40 percent higher than four years ago.

"The stop of moment was at CHADRON, where 3,000 people were at the depot, among them being a large sprinkling of cowboys dressed as Rough Riders. Governor Roosevelt was greeted with rousing cheers. He had made his way to the speakers' stand and had just commenced speaking when he was interrupted by Senator J. H. Van Dusen, who in a brief and appropriate speech presented him with a set of spurs.

"'Boys,' said Governor Roosevelt, after returning thanks to the donors, 'If I were 20 miles north of here, where I used to do a little punching myself, they would insist on me putting these things on. And (with a significant look at the cowboy section of the audience) don't you coax me too much.' This was a bit of pleasantry that greatly pleased the cowboys, and when Governor Roosevelt spoke of them as 'comrades of the cow country' . . . their ecstatic admiration was awakened almost beyond control. . . ."

(Note: it was at this point in the trip that the Roosevelt special steamed northward for two stops in western South Dakota. The journal narrative on the Nebraska stops continues in the following.)

"Returning from the Black Hills country the train made its first stop at VALENTINE, where upward of 1,000 people and a club of Rough Riders greeted it. . . . 'Boys,' [Roosevelt] said, addressing the cowboys, 'you were roping cattle four years ago when they were hardly worth catching. . . . Today you are getting good prices for all your stock, and I do not hesitate to say that credit for this is due the Republican Party.'

"At AINSWORTH fully 3,000 people cheered as the train stopped at the depot, the engine panting as if fatigued from its fast flight. An escort of 40 Rough Riders was on hand and a stand was provided near the depot. Among the decorations was a flag carried in the Lincoln and Hamilton [*sic*—this should have been Hamlin] campaign 40 years ago. Governor Roosevelt in opening his address referred to it with some display of feeling. The proceedings at this point were interrupted by an admirer of Bryan, who seemed to have just been in executive session with a canteen, but it amounted to nothing more than a slight interruption, and after the disciple of Bryan and Baccus had been led away everything passed off smoothly. . . .

"At BASSETT a crowd of 1,200 met the special at the depot, and Governor Roosevelt was roundly cheered as he emerged from the car. . . . He compared Bryan's predictions with existing conditions, and the manner in which he dissected the philosophy of the 'boy orator' elicited marked attention and repeated applause. . . .

"While the engine was taking water at ATKINSON Governor Roosevelt alighted and shook hands with a number of school children. . . . 'You are the coming guardians of this great nation,' he said. . . .

"At O'NEILL 5,000 people were on hand and unbounded enthusiasm prevailed. It was at this place that Governor Roosevelt castigated Governor Poynter for the latter's unpatriotic reference to American soldiers as $15-a-month hirelings. . . . [Roosevelt said,] 'I am sorry that the governor of your state should entertain such sentiment I would like to have had him with me at El Cana or San Juan Hill and let him see what stuff the American soldier is made of. . . . I look upon such unpatriotic sentiment with keen regret. . . . They were American boys, possibly some of them came from homes among you, and they were not "hirelings," but patriots upholding the cause of humanity and the honor of the nation. . . . [It is] a blight on the patriotism of all the people of this state for Governor Poynter to speak of them as "hirelings" while the mould is yet damp on hundreds of their graves.'

"A brief halt was made at CLEARWATER. . . . There were 3,000 enthusiastic people at NELIGH. . . . NORFOLK turned out and gave Governor

Roosevelt one of the most enthusiastic receptions of the trip. More than 12,000 people turned out, and there was an escort of 300 Rough Riders. . . . Just as the train was leaving Norfolk, George Brooks, a well-known business man of that place, presented Governor Roosevelt with a mess of brook trout. . . .

"WEST POINT gave Governor Roosevelt a rousing reception. Fully 2,500 people were on hand to receive him . . . [and give him] rapturous applause. Like at many other places, the town was profusely decorated, and suspended across the street was a banner with 'Teddy' painted on it in large letters, then a large red rose and a velt in emerald green. . . .

"FREMONT met all expectations. There were 15,000 people on hand . . . and nearly all the business houses displayed lithographs of the distinguished guest. . . . There was a monster parade with banners, bands of music, and Rough Riders; in fact, the demonstration would have been a credit to a city five times its size. . . .

"Night had spread its mantle over the city of BLAIR when the train reached that point. The reception at Blair was a surprise to everyone in the party. No less than 15,000 people were at the depot. In every direction you looked there were people, torches, and men on horseback attired in the regalia of the Rough Rider."

This concludes the journal narrative on the other, nonmajor stops in a Nebraska.

Lead and Deadwood, South Dakota.   Roosevelt also visited two communities in the Black Hills of western South Dakota between the stops at Chadron and Valentine, Nebraska. The train steamed northward for visits to Lead and Deadwood, old haunts for Roosevelt during his days in the Dakota Territory and home to the well-known (and well-heeled) Old West cowboy Seth Bullock.

While visiting South Dakota earlier on this campaign tour, Roosevelt had traveled no farther west than the Missouri River that runs north to south through the middle of the state. The stops in Lead and Deadwood, two quintessential western South Dakota towns, appealed to voters of that region and satisfied Roosevelt's personal desire to honor an invitation from Bullock, a longtime friend.

Though the people of Rapid City, the largest community in the region, were disappointed to be overlooked, the *Rapid City Journal* reported that well-wishers built a bonfire near the tracks and exchanged waves with Roosevelt as his train passed.[43]

Conclusion

Kansas and Nebraska were two of the states pivotal to success in the presidential election of 1900. Between them were eighteen electoral votes, a significant block as contrasted to many of the other western states. This was Bryan's home country, and he had won both states in 1896. However, his margins were thin, and there was perceived vulnerability for Roosevelt and the Republicans to exploit.

Both state campaign committees planned ambitious schedules for the vice presidential candidate's visit. Time was short, expectations were high, and Roosevelt responded nearly to the point of complete exhaustion. Supporters, potential voters, and the merely curious turned out by the tens of thousands to see this high-profile celebrity who was visiting their communities. He entertained them and won their hearts. In November, he also won a majority of their votes.

CHAPTER 13

IOWA, ILLINOIS, AND MISSOURI

Theodore Roosevelt's campaign special entered Iowa on Friday, October 5, taking the campaign to the heart of the Midwest, traveling generally eastward but looping north to south for five days with Chicago and St. Louis as the anchor cities. That visiting seventy communities, making as many speeches, and greeting an estimated half a million people over the past week in Kansas and Nebraska had taken its toll on the candidate was neither a secret Roosevelt was able to protect nor a reality journalists could ignore.

What follows are three reports on the issue of Roosevelt's exhaustion that ran on October 6, 1900, in San Francisco, New York City, and Rock Island, Illinois. This was the day the story broke and appeared in many publications. First is the account from the *San Francisco Call*; it represents one of the wire stories that carried the news to many readers across the nation. Second is the report from the *Sun*, a leading New York City newspaper long remembered for its 1897 editorial, "Yes, Virginia, There Is a Santa Claus." This journalist, who covered Roosevelt's western tour in depth, obviously liked the candidate and wrote engaging stories about him each day. Third is the story from the *Rock Island Argus*, a Democratic-leaning newspaper from the city in Illinois where Roosevelt spoke at the end of his long day traveling through Iowa. Seeing these three accounts together offers a rare opportunity to see how journalists' opinions affect language choices and shape the news they report.

From the *San Francisco Call*: "[Roosevelt] is beginning to feel the effects of the arduous work undertaken by him at the request of the Republican managers. . . . Since he began his itinerary through the northwestern states, [he] has been speaking from ten to twenty times each day, closing the day's labor usually with a night meeting. Many of these meetings have been in the open air requiring extra exertion on his part. He has now been on this journey for more than 30 days, and though strong beyond the powers of most men to endure, he is beginning to show signs of distress and a failing voice. He has been worked unmercifully by the state committees of the different states through which he has passed. Beyond this he has had to endure unlimited handshaking, interviews without number, and much pulling and hauling by the eager but inconsiderate mob which has swarmed around him in all the cities of any considerable size which he has visited. If some relief is not afforded his physical powers, he may be unable to last to the end of the campaign. It has even now been suggested that all his eastern engagements be postponed for one week. This matter will be determined by the national committee on the arrival of Governor Roosevelt in Chicago Saturday night."[1]

From the *Sun:* "When [Roosevelt] left Detroit on September 6, he looked forward to one speech each night in some large city and to an afternoon speech or two where conditions seemed to call for it. . . . Then he entered the strongholds of Populism and saw that frequent stops and direct appeals to the people from him would do a great deal more good than the wide publication in the newspapers of a few speeches made at big towns and cities, and so he undertook the work laid down for him by the state committees. The task became greater and greater until the Kansans in their zeal . . . required of him 36 speeches in two days on an itinerary covering more than 1,000 miles of dusty, throat-irritating traveling. . . . Today his voice is painfully husky and it is quite clear that there is now imminent danger that the number of speeches he is expected to make in Illinois and Iowa may have to be curtailed, and it is even possible that a whole day's engagements may have to be canceled to give him a chance to renew his strength of voice."[2]

From the *Rock Island Argus:* "The excitement is over. . . . Gov. Roosevelt last night completed 13,000 miles of his campaign tour. He has talked to more than 500,000 people and has shaken hands with 30,000. When he fought his way out of the crowd at Waterloo, IA, at 4 o'clock yesterday afternoon, he rushed into his stateroom, locked the door, and went to bed. He is nearly played out. He regards the change of program which will keep him speechmaking in Illinois today, instead of permitting him to go to Chicago and rest, as an imposition. He is angry and almost sick. The routine speeches have tired him less than the task of talking to local committeemen and politicians in competition with locomotive whistles, the rattle of the train, and all the other noises of campaign travel. His coat is torn from the tugging and jostling of the crowds. His right hand and arm are swollen and sore. His voice is almost gone."[3]

Though the story of Roosevelt's near-total exhaustion ran in newspapers across the nation on October 6, it turned out to be a story without legs, and the issue was rarely mentioned beyond that day of intense scrutiny. Here and there a sentence would say that Roosevelt was tired or, conversely, that he was rested and energetic, but the extensive focus on his level of fatigue was a one-day phenomenon. Perhaps he looked overly tired or sounded particularly hoarse on October 5. Maybe he discussed his feelings with a journalist and got unexpected ink from a casual conversation. Whatever the case, there was no further mention of negotiations to shorten the trip, reduce the number of stops, or cancel speeches. Roosevelt and his party moved on with the schedule of events.

Following is a list of the reported stops in order made by the Roosevelt campaign special in Iowa, Illinois, and Missouri. In the pattern of the previous chapters, four of the stops—Davenport/Rock Island, Chicago, Springfield (IL), and St. Louis—are categorized as major stops. Among the other twenty-one stops in Iowa and Illinois, several had highlights that are mentioned in the second section. (St. Louis was the only stop in Missouri other than the event in Kansas City described in the previous chapter.)

> Friday, October 5, 1900
> >   Fort Dodge, Iowa
> >   Iowa Falls
> >   Waterloo
> >   Cedar Rapids
> >   West Liberty
> >   Davenport
> >   Rock Island, Illinois
> >   (Overnight at Burlington Yard)
> Saturday, October 6, 1900
> >   Sterling
> >   Dixon
> >   Belvidere
> >   DeKalb
> >   Elgin
> >   Chicago
> >   (Overnights on October 6 and 7 at the Auditorium Annex in Chicago)
> Sunday, October 7, 1900
> >   Chicago (no campaign events)

Monday, October 8, 1900
 Joliet
 Streator
 Minonk
 Eureka
 Peoria
 Lincoln
 Mount Pulaski
 Springfield
 Jacksonville
 Litchfield
 East Alton
 East St. Louis
 (Overnight at the Planters' Hotel in St. Louis)
Tuesday, October 9, 1900
 St Louis, Missouri
 (Overnight on the train traveling for a morning departure from
  Chicago)

Iowa and Illinois were considered near-certain electoral successes for the national Republican ticket in the 1900 election, and they were affirmed and rewarded with visits from the Republicans' celebrity, Theodore Roosevelt. Despite an unexpected incident in Chicago (described later)—perhaps prompted by Democratic sympathizers in the Hearst newspaper organization—the trip through these two states went smoothly, and Roosevelt's crowds were enthusiastic.

Missouri, on the other hand, still had sympathies with the Democratic block in the states of the old Confederate South and was likely to go for Bryan. Thus, Roosevelt's mission included a Kansas City stop appended to the Kansas tour and a St. Louis stop at the end of the Illinois tour, but the midwestern state of Missouri was otherwise ignored.

Major Stops in Iowa, Illinois, and Missouri

One community at the end of the Iowa tour, Davenport, hosted a sizable Roosevelt event, and it was paired with a second large event on the same evening just across the river in Rock Island, Illinois, making the two a major stop. These are two of the communities comprising the metropolitan area known as the Quad Cities. Other major stops in Illinois included Chicago and Springfield. St. Louis was the final major stop of these days, coming at the end of the north-to-south Illinois tour. Following are the details of each of these major stops.

Davenport and Rock Island.   Although Davenport and Rock Island are part of the same metropolitan area in the fashion of either Kansas City, Kansas, and Kansas City, Missouri, or East St. Louis, Illinois, and St. Louis, Missouri, there was apparently a competition for preeminence between Davenport and Rock Island not reported in those other locations. On the day following the Roosevelt events, the *Rock Island Argus* reported the shenanigans thusly: "Members of the [Illinois] state transportation committee left town at 2 o'clock yesterday morning to intercept Teddy and his party away out in Iowa before the Davenport committee got in its work, and convince him that he must make it short on the other side of the river. They met the special train at Waterloo, and had things all fixed up when the Davenport committee made its appearance at Cedar Rapids. Davenport had mapped out a nice little program, including a parade from the courthouse to the big tent near Schuetzen Park, but it was nipped in the bud. While all the marching clubs and carriages containing prominent citizens were lined up near the courthouse last night, the train quietly stopped in the lower part of town and the whole show was over before the [citizens of Davenport] knew what had happened. Many of them were denied even a glimpse of the long-looked-for, as he was whirled in a carriage to this side of the river."[4]

Things were apparently not quite as abrupt in Davenport as Rock Island's newspaper reported, but Roosevelt's train did arrive late, and he was taken directly to the tent erected on the west side of the community for his speech. He did not participate in a parade that had been arranged, but he did speak to Davenport's voters for about thirty minutes. One journalist even termed his remarks "the principal address of the day" among those given in Iowa, and he wrote that Roosevelt "spoke along familiar lines."[5]

According to the coverage, however, Roosevelt added a new dimension to the silver question, criticizing the Democrats' unwillingness to discuss it in the East, thus turning attention from the fact that he had mostly ignored the issue in the mining states where the Republican position was widely disapproved. Roosevelt said:

"Distrust any party; distrust any body of men who dare not tell you how they stand on the great questions before the people. Distrust them and especially if they stand one way in one part of the union and another way in another part of the union. We are for the gold standard on the Pacific coast and in the Valley of the Mississippi or anywhere else. We are straight for the gold standard."[6]

Roosevelt also gave voice to the general sentiment of his party leadership regarding Iowa for the fall election. He said: "To tell you the truth, I am not a bit nervous about Iowa's electoral votes. You are going to vote right, because you are built that way."[7]

As soon as Roosevelt concluded his remarks in Davenport, he was spirited away to Rock Island. Events there were also abbreviated because the schedule was dragging: "In spite of the desperate attempt to bring things to a focus at 8 o'clock, it was 9:15 before the tired crowd had the satisfaction of seeing the line of marchers in motion. . . . The original plan had been to have the special car run to this side across the Crescent Bridge and a reception committee waited on the levee. . . . They remained steadfast where they had been sent till a messenger informed them that Teddy had already arrived. . . . The Market Square review had to be abandoned and those who came from a distance and spent a weary day on the streets sustained by the thought of passing in martial array under the critical eye of Teddy, the soldier, had to be contented with bringing up the rear of the procession."[8]

Wire service journalists traveling on the campaign train wrote of a "great street parade" and "immense numbers of people" who witnessed "the Governor's carriage driven for several miles through the shouting populace."[9] However, a local reporter, writing for a Democratic-leaning newspaper, saw things differently: "It was a cheap affair. . . . The imitation Rough Riders naturally felt sheepish in following the real hero. The ward clubs are sadly in need of drilling. . . . A few of the bands that took part deserved to be pinched for disturbing the peace. . . . The girls in the duck suits really looked sweet. It's too bad they cannot vote the whole ticket. . . . If you happen to hear a Republican boasting about the big crowd, do not argue with him, for he has not yet recovered from the intoxication of the occasion."[10]

Roosevelt spoke from a speakers' stand for about twenty minutes. According to the local report, "he crushed his slouch hat up into a roll and showed his teeth to the audience." His remarks were well received and greeted with cheers. Immediately upon concluding his speech, "he was helped into his overcoat and left for his private car."[11]

Overnight was spent on the train parked at the Burlington Yard in the Quad Cities. The next morning, another car bearing Judge Richard Yates, the Republican candidate for governor of Illinois, joined the campaign special for the trip through the state. Roosevelt's train pulled out of the

Burlington Yard at 8:30 a.m., after Judge Yates had made the rounds of the railroad men handing out cigars. As they left, Roosevelt stepped out on the rear platform of his railcar "with his hat wadded up in his hand, and treated the bunch that had assembled to a melting smile."[12]

Chicago.   After a Saturday spent on stops across northern Illinois, Roosevelt and party made it to Chicago where the candidate was scheduled for two rallies. The first was planned for the Coliseum and the second for the First Regiment Armory. It was actually a rather routine evening, except that the pattern of tardiness that had plagued the travelers of late was again a problem. Roosevelt addressed nine thousand cheering supporters at the Coliseum and six thousand at the Armory. Police limited the extent of the crowding at both venues, and thousands were left in the streets unable to gain admittance. Roosevelt was described as "full of fire and vim,"[13] apparently having survived his short-lived bout with exhaustion.

When they shared a balcony reviewing the Chicago Labor Day parade, Roosevelt and William Jennings Bryan were all smiles and handshakes. However, that was early September, and now Election Day 1900 was looming in less than one month. Roosevelt was at his oratorical best, as he leveled accusations at Bryan and the Democrats: "This year our opponents rest their hope of success upon exciting envy and hatred in one class of our citizens against other classes. They are striving to stir up the forces of social ill-will and therefore of social disorder."[14]

Roosevelt could not have known how prophetic his words would seem the very next day. He stayed overnight in Chicago, taking a room at the Auditorium Annex where he had overnighted during the Labor Day observance. As had been his pattern, he intended for Sunday to be mostly recreational, a sort of working day of rest; that is, he might have meetings or a small campaign-related dinner, but there would be no large public events. Also, he would include relaxing activities that he enjoyed as time permitted.

On Sunday morning, Roosevelt went to church with his colleague, Curtis Guild Jr. The two were fellow Harvard alumni and friends, and Guild had made the entire journey, serving as an alternative speaker, usually while crowds awaited the candidate or when Roosevelt had to rush away for a second, third, or fourth event during an evening. Guild had also fought in the war with Spain, and he would become the governor of Massachusetts in 1906. He was known as an outstanding speaker.

Roosevelt chose to attend a 9:00 a.m. worship service at the Trinity Dutch Reformed Church, a congregation he favored whenever he was in

Chicago. It was located on Marshall Avenue near Polk Street and served a small, blue-collar constituency. Pastor Peter Moerdyke greeted the pair when they arrived, and then he proceeded with the service, preaching a message focused on the heroes of the Bible.

After the concluding benediction, Moerdyke asked Roosevelt whether he might offer a word of greeting to the congregants, but the candidate declined, offering instead that on his next visit he would preach a lay sermon on the text from James 1:22, "Be ye doers of the word and not hearers only." Roosevelt did agree to shake hands with those in attendance.[15]

On the way into the sanctuary, Roosevelt and Guild had encountered a newsboy reclining on the sidewalk in a position that required them to step around him. When the pastor, Roosevelt, and the other worshipers emerged after the service, that youngster and as many as thirty other boys and young men were waiting outside the church. This mob began shouting vile epithets, curses, and accusations that Roosevelt was a coward for having shot a Spanish soldier in the back.

Following a moment of shock and inaction, Roosevelt's fury overtook him and he started toward the boys shaking his fist and shouting for them to be quiet in the presence of the congregation's women and children. Recognizing that the situation could escalate, Guild grabbed Roosevelt by the arm, told him sternly to back off, and physically forced him into the carriage. As the two men drove away, the unruly rioters ran alongside the vehicle, shouting insults and throwing clods of mud.

Later in the day, Guild told journalists that the boys were wearing hats with *Chicago American* printed on them and many were carrying copies of that newspaper. Roosevelt's campaign was charging the Hearst organization with inciting the incident.

William Randolph Hearst and his chain of newspapers were perfect foils for the Republicans' demagoguery. He was powerful and well known. He was willing to take sharply political positions. And best of all, he was unapologetically Democratic and supportive of William Jennings Bryan. To make an accusation of creating social disorder stick to him, or at least to those close to him, was the best opportunity presented to the Republican campaign leadership since the chance to take the high ground above the bimetallists after the Victor incident. The message was inescapable: if Hearst was behind this unseemly demonstration, surely the Democratic Party was nearby, lurking in the shadows. Given his personality, Roosevelt's outrage was unquestionably genuine. Given the reality of politics, the Republicans' outrage was just as certainly calculated.

To cool off, Roosevelt and Guild went for a drive in the early afternoon, but then the candidate and Senator Hanna, in his role as party chair, spent the rest of the day together planning strategy. In the evening, there was a dinner for all national managers of the Republican campaign at the Chicago Club. Breaking his rule that he would not speak on a Sunday, Roosevelt served as the keynoter for the event, reporting to the guests on his western trip and sharing his thoughts on the likelihood of Republican success in the election. After overnighting in Chicago, Roosevelt and his party left bright and early at 7:15 on Monday morning bound for stops in downstate Illinois and St. Louis, Missouri.[16]

Springfield.   In typical fashion for the Roosevelt campaign tour, the morning of October 8 was a blur of activity with reported visits to seven Illinois communities before reaching the major stop of the day at Springfield, the state's capital city. Again, the crowds were large for the celebration that had been designated Roosevelt Day. According to news reports, the curious had come from as far as fifty miles, and there were thirty-five thousand visitors, effectively doubling the size of the town for the day.[17]

At noon, two and a half hours prior to the planned arrival of the campaign special, a parade began with six thousand men in line, and the streets were lined with the thousands of onlookers there to see the costumes, the music, and the entertaining tomfoolery. Most of those viewing the parade had undoubtedly jockeyed for positions favorable to viewing hours earlier and intended to stay put for a look at Roosevelt as his carriage conveyed him to the grounds of the state capitol for the rally. About twenty thousand could actually gain access to the venue where the speeches would occur, so many would see only the parade before making the long trip home late in the afternoon.

When the train arrived on the Illinois Central tracks at the Union Station, it was predictably late, and the Roosevelt party was driven quickly to the rally site. There were, after all, three stops with speeches scheduled after departing Springfield. Mounted men in Rough Rider attire lined the route of travel to ensure unimpeded passage to the Illinois capitol, so the view of Roosevelt afforded to many must have been disappointing.[18]

Despite the press of the schedule and stops to come, Roosevelt tailored his remarks to the moment: "At Springfield the governor refrained from discussing finance, trusts, and such topics, devoting himself exclusively to the life achievements of Abraham Lincoln."[19]

Reviewing Lincoln's contributions, Roosevelt aimed a lesson at his opponents: "[Abraham Lincoln] sacrificed himself in death that his people should know not only liberty, but the union that symbolized order as well. . . . Lincoln came to prominence by his great debate with Douglas, when they were opposed to one another, but when the honor of the flag was at stake Douglas turned and upheld the hands of his rival. So we have a right to appeal to the Democrats today to put patriotism above partisanship."[20]

During his twenty-minute speech, Roosevelt even found a way to relate the contemporary Republican position on the Philippines to a passage from the Gettysburg Address. He said: "On the platform with me is a veteran of the Civil War whose son now serves in the Philippines. Lincoln's words at Gettysburg were spoken of the army in which his father served, when he said, speaking of that army, 'Let us see to it that their lives shall not have been spent in vain.' So we have a right now to say on behalf of the comrades of that man's son in the Philippines, who there gave up their lives for the honor of the flag, 'Let us see to it that their lives have not been spent vain.'"[21]

Following his speech, Roosevelt and his traveling party hurried back to the train, leaving the podium to Illinois politicians. There were still communities to visit, speeches to give, and one hundred miles to travel before the day ended after a rally in East St. Louis, Illinois.

St. Louis.　Tuesday's campaign focus was St. Louis, Missouri, the fourth-largest city in the United States at the turn of the twentieth century. Though Missouri was not a likely electoral victory for the Republicans in 1900, the size of St. Louis and its prominence among the urban centers of the day made it a must-visit stop on a trip billed as a western campaign tour. St. Louis may have adopted the nickname "Gateway to the West" later in its history, but this city on the Mississippi River had been seen in that light at least since May of 1804 when Lewis and Clark left from there on the corps of discovery expedition.

When Roosevelt finished his speech in East St. Louis late Monday evening, his train crossed the railroad bridge into St. Louis and pulled into Union Station. He was escorted to the Planters' Hotel by L. P. Philpott, a veteran of the Rough Riders in Cuba, who was serving as grand marshal of the St. Louis event. Because of his long day on Monday and his late arrival, Roosevelt breakfasted late on Tuesday and spent the morning resting and receiving prominent St. Louisans who called to pay their respects. At 12:30 p.m. he was taken to the Merchants' Exchange for a reception and a brief speech to the business leaders of the community. In the afternoon, Roosevelt passed his time with a horseback ride through the streets of St. Louis, turning down the carriage ride that was offered to him.[22]

Apparently, the din of manufacturing was in the background during the speech at the Merchants' Exchange because Roosevelt used it as a clever reference: "In this building the hum of industry never ceases, and so I will have to talk against it. I am usually talking for it!" His message was targeted and succinct: "Men of business will not get up if the wage-worker and the farmer go down. . . . Fundamentally, our interests are the same."[23]

Early in the evening, Roosevelt was again feted with a parade, the route of which was illuminated with torches and colored fire. Among the marchers was a mounted regiment of costumed Rough Riders and several thousand citizens who joined on foot or in their carriages. The parade ended at the Coliseum, a vast hall used for conventions and expositions. Crowd size was published at twenty-five thousand, though that was considerably beyond capacity of the facility. Regardless, the large crowd was remarkable for a state expected to vote for Bryan in November. People were waiting when the doors opened at 6:00 p.m., and they sat patiently until the program began at 8:00 p.m. with the singing of "America." Even the local Democratic-leaning newspaper, the *St. Louis Republic,* predicted: "His speech at the Coliseum will be heard with that respectful attention which is due as coming from a man whom all Americans admire."[24]

There was plenty to be heard. Roosevelt spoke for an hour after being introduced by Mayor Henry Ziegenhein of St. Louis. The candidate had entered the hall during the remarks of the evening's second speaker, who had to discontinue his presentation because the cheering would not quiet. Immediately the mayor arose and offered his introduction.

Roosevelt moved quickly to the podium and began his address, which was a rehash of issues, language, and images that were quite familiar by this time to those who had accompanied him on the western tour. At one point, however, his classical education showed itself with this reference from John Bunyan's allegory, *The Pilgrim's Progress:* "If the people of this country want to go back into the slough of despond out of which we have so painfully emerged—if they want to do that, why under the Constitution it is their inalienable right." Perhaps Roosevelt was hit with the thought that not all in his audience were as well read, so he mixed metaphors to finish the thought: "But when they get back there do not let them advance the 'I did not know it was loaded' excuse."[25]

Newspaper stories generally spoke of a crowd that cheered Roosevelt frequently and enthusiastically. However, just as the prior speaker was forced by the crowd to discontinue his address in favor of the vice presidential candidate, so Curtis Guild Jr., who followed Roosevelt to the podium, cut his remarks short because people were leaving the Coliseum to begin the journey home. On the positive side, that gave Roosevelt and his party a chance to return to Union Station from where the special train departed for Chicago, the point of embarkation for the next day's journey into Indiana.

Three sidebar stories in conjunction with the St. Louis visit are worth noting. The first ran under the headline "Attempt to Make Political Capital" in the *Indianapolis Journal*, and it described a politically motivated incident that occurred while Roosevelt was in Missouri: "Requisition papers issued by Gov. Sayers of Texas were served on Governor Roosevelt at the Planters' Hotel today for the extradition of John D. Rockefeller, Henry M. Flagler, and other Standard Oil magnates. The defendants are wanted in Texas for alleged violation of the anti-trust law. Governor Roosevelt said he could not act on the requisition as long as he was out of the State of New York, as he was technically not Governor. He said he would look into the case when he returned to New York."[26]

Second was a story, gleefully reported during the stop in St. Louis, that the commissioner of patents decided a "Teddy's Teeth Puzzle" could not be patented "because Roosevelt is Governor of a great state and vice presidential candidate of a great party." That partisan politics had nothing to do with the decision was the assurance from the commissioner. Rather, he said, it was because the device was so unflattering. "The grinders had so many cavities in them that the filling of them would have made the fortune of a dentist." According to the news story, the game was to guide balls of "quicksilver" (mercury) into the cavities. "Who the inventor is the Commissioner will not say," the journalists reported, "and an effort has been made to keep the matter quiet."[27]

Finally, there was a physical description of Roosevelt in the *St. Louis Republic*, the local Democratic newspaper, offering details on his speaking style and his appearance quite unlike those reported elsewhere: "His enunciation was so distinct that there was no difficulty in following his every utterance. He has a peculiar delivery, which is further accentuated by the peculiar trick of exposing his teeth at frequent intervals and champing them like a horse. This creates the effect of fierceness in his speeches which is absent in the published accounts of them. . . . He is of medium height, with a robust, athletic figure betokening a good constitution. He was dressed quietly in a suit which fit him rather badly. . . . [He treated interruptions] good-naturedly . . . and incidentally showed his teeth again, which of course set the audience yelling."[28]

Highlights from Other Stops in Iowa and Illinois

Friday, October 5, 1900, was the one day given to stops in Iowa. Because of the geography, two days, Saturday, October 6, and Monday, October 8, were allowed for stops in Illinois. The first of the days in Illinois carried Roosevelt and his party from the Quad Cities on the border with Iowa to Chicago; the second day covered communities on the route between Chicago and St. Louis, Missouri. Between the first and second days of stops in Illinois was the Sunday spent as a day of rest in Chicago, the day on which Roosevelt was verbally assaulted outside the church where he worshiped. Following are highlights from selected communities categorized as other stops.

Fort Dodge, Iowa.   "Governor Roosevelt, Senator Dolliver,[29] and the distinguished party accompanying them made their first stop in Iowa at Fort Dodge this morning. Although only 12 hours' notice was given, the train, which arrived from Omaha at 7 o'clock, was met by an immense crowd. The party was taken in carriages to the homes of leading citizens, where they breakfasted. After breakfast, Governor Roosevelt was escorted to the city park, where he made a brief address to a crowd of several hundred. Roosevelt said: 'I wish that I could stay here and speak with you. I say speak with you, because we have come to Iowa not to teach, but to learn. I wish that if Iowa Republicanism is catching, Iowa would bite some of the other states which I know. Iowa is entitled to be called a typical Republican state, because of its high level of material prosperity and its devotion to civic honesty.'"[30] Roosevelt's train left Fort Dodge at 9:00 a.m.

Waterloo, Iowa.   Demonstrating Roosevelt's popularity in rural Iowa, far more people showed up for the stop in Waterloo than were expected. This was the home of US representative David B. Henderson, a ten-term Republican congressman who was serving as speaker of the house. Roosevelt was treated to a driving tour of the city and a luncheon at Henderson's home. Then the vice presidential candidate and other dignitaries went to the city park where a speakers' platform had been erected.[31]

"There were 10,000 or 15,000 people in the public square in front of the stand. . . . Far beyond the limits of the actual audience could be seen the streams of people pouring up and down the streets uneasily, because they knew that they could not hear the speaker comfortably and the best they hoped for was to get a look at Theodore Roosevelt. There could be no better indication of the number of outsiders in town than the signs advertising improvised eating houses. There was hardly a church in the city that did not bear placards two feet high and ten feet long with the words, 'Meals, 25 cents.' Nearly every window had its portrait of one or the other of the Republican candidates."[32] Roosevelt congratulated the Iowans on their honesty, courage, and common sense.

Throughout the western campaign tour, Roosevelt spoke of his dealings with the trusts in New York from the perspective that he had been firm but reasonable in his actions. This represented his party's strategy as well as his personal perspective. In Waterloo, he was again asked by a journalist about the trusts, and rather than his stock answer, Roosevelt said: "We will have to ask that an essay be written by Mr. Croker on that subject, and then if you would like further literature on the trusts we will get Chairman Jones of the Democratic National Committee to write one."[33]

This wonderfully pointed answer would not have been lost on Roosevelt's contemporaries. Richard Croker was the Tammany Hall Democratic boss in New York City and James Jones was an Arkansas senator who headed the Democratic National Committee. Investigations had shown that Croker's wife had received gifts of shares in the so-called Ice Trust to the tune of 250,000 dollars, and Jones's name was associated with a cotton trust. Other powerful Democrats, and even some Republicans, were known to have accepted shares intended to influence policy decisions or legislation. Roosevelt's remark was not only humorous, but it was also an inflammatory accusation of wrongdoing aimed at his opponents.[34]

Cedar Rapids, Iowa.   "It was twilight when the train ran into Cedar Rapids. The meeting there was to be held in a park beside the track. When the train slid out of the grimy railroad yard from between long strings of freight trains and excursion trains, joint evidences of prosperity and the people's appreciation of it, what seemed like an army . . . came swooping across the grass toward the tracks. . . . There were not less than 7,000 of them. . . . Gov. Roosevelt and his colleagues were able to reach the speakers' stand . . . [so they] could be seen from every part of the park. He was so hoarse that he was unable to make his voice audible to more than half the audience."[35]

West Liberty, Iowa. "The special Roosevelt train stopped at West Liberty for the purpose of changing engines sometime after dark today. The fact being known about town a wild and enthusiastic crowd surrounded the train and insisted on the Governor showing himself. Governor Roosevelt appeared on the rear platform of the car and greeted his audience with a few words. A rush was then made to shake hands, and women and children became involved in a whirlpool of humanity which for a time promised disaster to some of the weaker ones. Fortunately the train pulled out in time to prevent accident."[36]

Belvidere, Illinois. After stops in Sterling where there were ten thousand people gathered and Dixon where Roosevelt addressed five thousand, Belvidere was the third stop in Illinois on Saturday, October 6. There the "thoughtful Republicans had erected a platform such that the Governor was able to walk over a sort of gangplank over the heads of the surging and hungry crowds to the speaking platform."[37] Elgin was the stop following Belvidere, and the report recorded a crowd of eight thousand people.

DeKalb, Illinois. "Gov. Roosevelt's Chicago greeting came to him at DeKalb, when a delegation of the Chicago headquarters of the National Committee came out with two special trains. . . . They were waiting on the station platform for the Governor, when an exultant DeKalb committee fairly carried him down the steps of his car. Senator Hanna and the Governor grasped hands with utmost heartiness and grabbed each other by the shoulders to emphasize the pleasure of their meeting. Three hundred Rough Riders from Chicago came along on a second section of Senator Hanna's train; they brought their equipment with them and rode horses furnished for them in DeKalb. . . . Gov. Roosevelt and the Senator rode through the Main Street in a carriage at the head of the procession, which also included nearly 1,000 men and women in white marching uniforms from neighboring towns. . . . Every telegraph pole in DeKalb had been wound with red, white, and blue bunting, and a broad banner of the same sort had been stretched between every two posts. . . . A gentle drizzle had begun by the time the procession started, and it increased into a steady rain. The red in the decorations ran out of the fabric and the streets ran red. . . . At the public square, where the speaking was done from a covered platform, thousands of people stood under a great roof of umbrellas with water swirling about their feet and listened patiently. . . . After the meeting, Mr. Isaac L. Elwood entertained the whole company at his home. . . . [Meanwhile] a party of ladies . . . brought several bushels of carnations and other flowers to the Governor's car and made it literally a bower."[38] After the stop in DeKalb, Roosevelt and his expanded entourage traveled into Chicago, arriving at 5:00 p.m.

Joliet, Illinois. On Monday morning at 7:15, Roosevelt's campaign express pulled out of Chicago headed through downstate Illinois toward St. Louis, Missouri. There would be ten reported stops on Monday, October 8, of which Joliet was the first. "A large crowd, including local Republican organizations, greeted the arrival of the Roosevelt special train here. Cheers were given for Governor Roosevelt . . . as [he] appeared upon the platform. Governor Roosevelt's speech was brief. . . . In the course of his remarks at the courthouse square, Governor Roosevelt said: 'Give Congress the power to deal with trusts. I mean the large corporations. Such evils can be wiped out by cool, resolute common sense. June 4 last, Congress tried to pass a constitutional amendment. The bill was beaten by the Democrats, who said it would take the only issue from this campaign.'"[39] Continuing the attack he launched in Waterloo, Roosevelt was laying the trust issue squarely in the laps of the Democrats.

Streator, Illinois. Here Roosevelt addressed "a dense throng of people."[40] Speaking from a flat car, the candidate referred to the thugs in Chicago. One journalist wrote that there was "a most angry cheer" followed by a man shouting: "We'll square with them for that on Election Day!"[41]

Peoria, Illinois. Roosevelt found himself in the middle of Peoria's annual corn festival when he arrived in this community. Two days prior to the candidate's Monday arrival was the flower parade with prizes for corn-decorated carriages, and the mood in town was festive.[42] Roosevelt and Judge Yates, the Republican gubernatorial candidate, spoke to several thousand people from a speakers' stand in Courthouse Square.

Governor Roosevelt picked up the theme of mob violence, blaming the conduct on his opponents. He said: "Let [the Democrats] remember that men can't incite riot either on the stump or through the columns of the newspapers and hope to escape the responsibility for disorder. When the appeal is made to every foul and evil passion of mankind, when every expedient of mendacity and invective is resorted to by the chiefs of a great party, whether through their platform or on the stump or by some newspaper which is itself a foul plague spot on the body politic, it is well to keep in mind that the responsibility for any disorder or mob violence which follows lies less with the people who make the disturbance and who may have to pay the penalty than with those who, sitting at ease in a place of safety, have done all they could to excite not only the vicious but the well-meaning ignorant to actions which discredit our civilization."[43]

Jacksonville, Illinois.   Serving as the speaking venue in Jacksonville was a large tent erected in the public square. Nearly all newspapers reported some version of this amusing—perhaps embarrassing—anecdote: "The chief feature of the meeting was the racket made by the whistle of the special train. On the invitation of the engineer, Mrs. Richard Yates, wife of the candidate for Governor, rode on the engine from Springfield to Jacksonville. The train made 40 miles in 42 minutes. Just as the train was approaching Jacksonville, the engineer allowed Mrs. Yates to pull the whistle rope. The noise she made pleased her so that she kept the whistle tooting nearly all the time the train was in Jacksonville."[44]

Alton, Illinois.   "On his arrival at Alton Governor Roosevelt was greeted by a large body of citizens and organizations bearing flambeaux. A feature was the presence of 60 marines and 30 former members of the regular army, all of the latter having served under Governor Roosevelt at Santiago."[45] Roosevelt made a short speech because the day was woefully behind schedule.

East Alton, Illinois.   Though not a planned stop, there was a newsworthy moment at the small settlement of East Alton. "William J. Bryan, on his way to Alton, where he made an address last night to 8,000 persons, and Theodore Roosevelt, on his way to East St. Louis, where he spoke later, exchanged mutual greetings at East Alton, a small station near Alton, last night, each calling the other 'Colonel.' Their trains stopped for several minutes on adjoining tracks. The two men saw each other at the same moment and their salutation was most friendly. The party on Bryan's train gave a cheer for Roosevelt and those with Roosevelt cheered Bryan."[46] Obviously, Monday, October 8, was a busy day for hosting in Alton, Illinois.

East St. Louis, Illinois.   Roosevelt's train arrived in East St. Louis at 11:00 p.m., three hours behind its scheduled time. Still there were five thousand people gathered at the speakers' platform in front of the city hall. The candidate was reported to be filled with energy, as he said: "I see before me men who served in the navy and in the regular army near me or under my personal command on the battlefield at Santiago. . . . You are the heirs of the men who fought under Grant and upheld the arms of Lincoln. We hold our heads high because of what those men did. Are you going to leave to your children in their turn a similar heritage of honor?" Then he used a local reference for his case on the health of the economy: "Remember how the glass blowers in this very town have had a raise of 15 percent in their wages and that there is twice as much employment as there was four years ago. And with all this in mind you cannot but realize that it is for your material interest to keep unchanged the policies of President McKinley and that it would be folly unworthy a serious people to trust yourselves to the exploded fallacies of our antagonist."[47]

Conclusion

As he traveled into Iowa and saw in his mind's eye Illinois looming over the horizon, Roosevelt must have felt as though he was in friendly territory and that because he was steaming eastward, this was the homestretch. Still, when he experienced the insulting attack in Chicago, it surely gave him at least a moment's pause regarding the certainty of even those places already numbered in the anticipated Republican electoral total.

Shortly after this threatening incident, he reviewed with party leaders the strategy for the remaining month before the election, and there he came face to face with the reality of his trip. It would take two days to finish Illinois and St. Louis, Missouri. Then, there were admirers, supporters, and, most important, voters awaiting him at stops throughout Indiana, Kentucky, Ohio, West Virginia, and Maryland. In two weeks he would be home at Oyster Bay, New York, for one day before the schedule continued with many more speeches across the length and breadth of his home state.

We cannot know whether he was discouraged or energized at this point, but we do know that he soldiered on. When Monday came to Chicago, Theodore Roosevelt arose early, took his place on the campaign train, and spent the next eighteen hours meeting, greeting, and wooing sixty-five thousand people.

CHAPTER 14

INDIANA

Local and regional newspapers thrived alongside the larger but significantly fewer statewide publications serving the public in 1900 America. Several of those smaller newspapers have proven excellent sources for this narrative of Roosevelt's run for the vice presidency, not the least because they often gave space to nearly verbatim use of the wire stories from the correspondents traveling with the campaign special. Larger-circulation newspapers frequently chose to edit wire reports to a shortened version in favor of other news important or appealing to a broader range of their readers. Five-hundred-word stories could become sixty-word items used to fill columns on one page or another.

Among the most useful sources of information for any review of Roosevelt's campaign is the *Indianapolis Journal*, a publication that regularly printed all or most of the daily reports from A. G. Nevins of the Associated Press, one of the Rough Writers who witnessed the whistle stops firsthand. As a regional newspaper, the *Indianapolis Journal* had a long history, tracing its roots to earlier publications as early as 1825, when Indiana's capital moved from Corydon to Indianapolis.

During the nineteenth century, the newspaper rolled off the presses with a few different names on the banner, but it finally became the *Indianapolis Journal* in 1867 and maintained its existence against competitors with larger circulations until 1904, when it was purchased, absorbed into another newspaper, and lost its identity. At the time of Roosevelt's campaign in 1900, the daily circulation of the *Indianapolis Journal* exceeded twenty-two thousand copies. James Whitcomb Riley had worked briefly as a reporter for the newspaper, and he and others in the Indiana literary community found its pages open to their creative works.

John C. New, the chairman of the Indiana Republican Party, purchased the *Indianapolis Journal* in 1880. New had also served as the US secretary of the treasury in the Grant administration. The newspaper's editorial history had leaned Whig and then Republican, and New naturally embraced that perspective, notably supporting Benjamin Harrison against the incumbent Democrat, Grover Cleveland, in 1888.[1]

While the newspaper's Republican editorial position was not apparent in any significant revisions of the daily reports from the Associated Press, it was certainly expressed by the lengthy, front-page coverage afforded Roosevelt's western tour nearly every day of the trip. Significant amounts of ink and space spent on stop-by-stop reporting of the vice presidential campaign demonstrated the political preference of the publication.

In the weeks leading up to the three days of whistle stops in Indiana, growing excitement was evident in the *Indianapolis Journal*'s newsroom because the frequency of stories detailing the preparations for Roosevelt's visit increased. When the candidate actually reached Indiana, each stop received careful attention in this newspaper. Thus this regional publication provides a valuable and unique resource for a portion of the campaign tour, just as the *Daily Argus-Leader* from Sioux Falls, the *Deseret Evening News* from Salt Lake City, and other regional newspapers served that role elsewhere.

As an example of the rich detail available when a local newspaper takes interest in the story, the following list of Roosevelt's campaign stops in Indiana shows the precise time each was scheduled, a feature missing from most of the agendas in other chapters. Indeed, the coverage in the *Indianapolis Journal* was so thorough that the list could have included both intended arrival and departure times, as well as the railroad lines serving each stop. As would be expected, the actual times varied; for example, the scheduled departure time from Chicago's Polk-Street Depot was 8:35 a.m., but Roosevelt's train arrived there from St. Louis at 8:45. That meant a departure about 9:15, making the schedule more than a half hour late at the outset.[2]

Following is a list of the thirty-six communities reported as the campaign stops of Theodore Roosevelt in Indiana. Twenty-four of these were on the official schedule as the trip began, and twelve were added as time permitted and crowds appeared. Four of the twelve unscheduled stops were actually slowdowns so that Roosevelt could step onto the rear platform of his railcar and greet crowds that had gathered in the station yards.

Wednesday, October 10, 1900
   (Overnighted in Chicago; scheduled to depart for Indiana at
      8:35 a.m.)

Hammond 9:30 a.m.
Rensselaer (unscheduled)
Monon (unscheduled)
Lafayette 12:35 p.m.
Frankfort 2:40
Logansport 4:00
Peru 4:39
Wabash 5:23
Huntington 6:09
Fort Wayne 7:10 (Departed 11:00 p.m.)
(Overnighted on the train as it traveled and then stopped on a
    siding outside Marion)
Thursday, October 11, 1900
Marion 1:40 a.m. (Departed 8:30 a.m.)
Fairmount 8:50
Summitville (unscheduled)
Alexandria 9:25
Anderson 10:05
Muncie 11:00
Winchester 12:10 p.m.
Richmond 1:20
Cambridge City (unscheduled)
Knightstown (unscheduled)
Greenfield (unscheduled)
Indianapolis 4:00
(Overnighted in Indianapolis; departed the city at 9:10 a.m.)
Friday, October 12, 1900
Plainfield 9:30 a.m.
Greencastle 10:20
Brazil 11:10
Terre Haute 12:00 noon
Lewis (unscheduled)
Linton 2:40 p.m.
Bee Hunter (unscheduled)
Marco (unscheduled; slow roll-through greeting)
Sandborn (unscheduled; slow roll-through greeting)
Edwardsport (unscheduled; slow roll-through greeting)
Bicknell (unscheduled; slow roll-through greeting)
Vincennes 4:00

Princeton 5:00
Evansville 6:15
(Overnighted in Evansville)

As Theodore Roosevelt and his campaign party steamed east toward Fort Wayne and then southwest to visit Indianapolis and Evansville, William McKinley continued to keep a leisurely schedule. As his running mate entered Indiana, the president was in Washington, DC, having traveled there the day before from his home in Canton, Ohio. He intended to stay at the White House until October 29, when he and Mrs. McKinley would return to Canton to await the election results.

McKinley was said to be "absolutely confident of his reelection." Also, it was reported that his political advisers were certain of success "to such a degree that today's meeting of the Cabinet was somewhat in the nature of a political jollification." This was the first time the cabinet had met for months because, in the pattern of the day, most officials abandoned the nation's capital during the summer to return to whatever cities they considered home. News reports of the meeting indicated that rather than attending to the nation's business, the cabinet spent "considerable time . . . reviewing the political situation."[3] It was about as close as McKinley got to engaging in the late stages of his reelection campaign.

While the president bedded down in the White House and led symbolic sessions of the cabinet, Roosevelt overnighted in the *Minnesota*, his private railcar, as the campaign special traveled nonstop from St. Louis to Chicago. No sooner had the train arrived at 8:45 a.m. on Wednesday, October 10, than it departed Chicago for Hammond, Indiana, a community within the Chicago metropolitan complex.[4] For this segment of the trip, the campaign party was hosted by US senator Charles W. Fairbanks of Indiana, who would join President Theodore Roosevelt on the 1904 Republican ticket as the vice presidential candidate.[5]

Though Senator Fairbanks was the symbolic host of the Indiana whistle-stop tour, the working manager of the trip was Harry S. New, a member of the Republican National Executive Committee.[6] In 1916, he would be elected to the United States Senate from Indiana, and in 1923 President Warren G. Harding would appoint him postmaster general of the United States.

Harry Stewart New was also the forty-one-year-old son of John C. New and his wife, Melissa, of Indianapolis. As mentioned previously, John owned the *Indianapolis Journal*, perhaps the state's leading Republican voice. When the newspaper owner's son accompanies the biggest political celebrity of the day on a tour of the publication's home state, access and attention to detail in the stories are remarkable.

Just as the small-town correspondent who rode the Roosevelt train through Nebraska provided a unique journalistic account edited and used in chapter 12, so this chapter's narrative reviewing the vice presidential campaign in Indiana will rely heavily upon edited clips from this urban newspaper's reporting. Harry S. New not only rode the train, but he also sat with Roosevelt in the carriages that conveyed the pair through parades. New frequently preceded or followed Roosevelt on the speakers' stands.

Coverage of Roosevelt's Indiana stops dominated space in the *Indianapolis Journal* for three days, October 11 to 13, 1900 (Thursday through Saturday). Each front page had at least two headlined stories relating to the trip, and each story stretched to multiple pages. All stops, even the smallest, received attention. This unique situation offers an opportunity not available in any other state—namely, the chance to observe insider coverage in detail by a newspaper that became the quasi-official Republican publication for a few days. During that time, it was not just a newspaper with a certain editorial position; it effectively became a Republican broadside.

Although the *Indianapolis Journal* had faithfully printed Associated Press wire stories to the point that Roosevelt entered Indiana, the in-state stories were all written by the newspaper's own correspondents. Even as the reports became much longer, they also included opinion materials that colored the news reports to promote both the Republican ticket and the party's platform. Additionally, details with regional significance were regularly included—for example, the names of all members of local planning and reception committees, the full lists of parade participants, and the like—to maximize the positive effects of the stories. Volunteers got recognition.

Editing the materials for this narrative was necessary to address the problem of excessive length and to eliminate the worst of the shameless promotion. However, each of the thirty-six stops is mentioned in the following, and the material is presented in chronological order, rather than taking the pattern of other chapters where major stops are profiled first and other stops are presented through highlights.

Keeping faith with the information from other states, the major stops in Indiana are identified. They were Fort Wayne, Indianapolis, and Evansville, and the volume of material related to those visits in the narrative will make that case. Nowhere else—with the possible exception of South Dakota—is there so much available information that allows nearly minute-by-minute precision in tracking the progress of the trip. All materials are quoted from reports in the *Indianapolis Journal* that ran during the three days of coverage. Only an occasional transitional phrase or sentence is inserted to smooth the editing, and the format by stop conforms to elsewhere in this study.

These are the reports from the whistle stops of Theodore Roosevelt in Indiana during his vice presidential campaign in October 1900:

Hammond. "The first stop made by the Roosevelt train in Indiana today was at Hammond, the Monon special arriving there a little after 10 o'clock, more than a half hour behind schedule time. . . . A committee of Hammond citizens . . . went to Chicago early in the morning to meet Governor Roosevelt. On the way to Hammond the train was greeted with a crowd of people at the Hedgewich car works and they cheered as the train passed. . . . When the train drew into Hammond and stopped at the Hohman-Street crossing, Governor Roosevelt was greeted by cheers from thousands of patriotic Indianians. It was estimated that 5,000 people were waiting for the arrival of the train. . . . A company of mounted Rough Riders . . . escorted Governor Roosevelt in a carriage to Central Park, a block or two distant. A cordon of Rough Riders on foot formed about the carriage and kept the crowd back. Governor Roosevelt spoke from a prettily decorated stand. . . . The Governor's speech was brief. He contrasted the good times of today with the souphouse period that prevailed a few years ago. His remarks were received with enthusiasm."[7]

Rensselaer. "The special train was not scheduled to stop at Rensselaer, but a big crowd had gathered there, and a short stop was made. . . . There were between 2,000 and 3,000 people at the station, among them many school children, who cheered the vice presidential candidate. As the train left, the people clung to the Governor's car in an effort to grasp his hand."[8]

Monon. "There was a large crowd at Monon, and it was decided to stop the train there for a few minutes. . . . Governor Roosevelt spoke ten or fifteen minutes and was in a fine humor for making a good speech. He said in part: 'Our opponents are stronger on oratory than they are on action. We have read in the good book that "Ephraim feedeth the winds." There is no possible objection to that so long as Ephraim enjoys it, but there is no call for our sharing the fare.'"[9]

Lafayette. "It was after 1 o'clock when the booming of cannon at Lafayette announced that the train had arrived there. The special stopped at the

Salem Street crossing, where carriages were waiting. Governor Roosevelt spoke from the steps of the Lincoln Club, about six blocks away. . . . It has been many a day since Lafayette saw a like political event. The crowd in the streets was estimated all the way from 15,000 to 20,000. There was a procession of mounted Rough Riders, 1,000 strong, and they all took off their hats to Governor Roosevelt as he passed. A feature of the parade was a stalwart young man, wearing a coonskin cap and riding a young bull. . . . The Purdue College boys were out, and when Governor Roosevelt appeared at the Lincoln Club they gave him many an enthusiastic 'Rah! Rah!' Along the line of march there were tasteful decorations."[10]

Frankfort. "The train reached Frankfort over the LE&W [Lake Erie and Western Railroad] several minutes late and Governor Roosevelt was greeted by a large crowd of people. . . . He spoke from a gaily decorated stand in the courthouse yard. . . . There was some confusion at Frankfort in getting the party away, the arrangements not being as perfect there as at some of the other places. Governor Roosevelt only spoke a few minutes. . . . As the train left Frankfort the Landis Drum and Bugle Corps of 25 pieces from Delphi got on and rode to Logansport. . . . The train left Frankfort at 3:30, over the Vandalia, 25 minutes behind time."[11]

Logansport. "Ten thousand or 12,000 people greeted the train at Logansport and Governor Roosevelt was escorted to a stand near the railway station, where he made a short speech. . . . Logansport had a big time all day. Shortly after dinner, there was a parade of 300 Rough Riders and numerous other organizations. There were several hundred factory men from Kokomo in the parade. . . . The train left Logansport at 4:00 o'clock in the midst of the greatest enthusiasm."[12]

Peru. "Peru gave the Roosevelt party a genuine ovation and one that must have delighted the Governor. When the train arrived there at 5 o'clock a crowd of from 10,000 to 12,000 people was gathered at the depot. The speakers' stand was within a short distance of the depot. . . . As the train pulled out the band played 'The Star-Spangled Banner,' while the people waved flags and cheered."[13]

Wabash. "The next stop was at Wabash, the train arriving there a few minutes before 6 o'clock. Although it was growing dark, the crowd had patiently awaited the appearance of the train. Wabash had an all-day rally and at one time the crowd numbered 20,000 people. As late as it was, when the train arrived, there was still a crowd of from 10,000 to 15,000 people."[14]

Huntington. "Huntington also gave Governor Roosevelt an ovation with its large band of mounted Rough Riders and other mounted clubs. It was dark when the train reached Huntington and the marching clubs made a demonstration with red fire and rockets. Governor Roosevelt reviewed them from a stand near the station and spoke very briefly to the great crowd. He spoke more particularly of Indiana and paid the state some high compliments. It was ten minutes to 7 o'clock when the train started for Fort Wayne."[15]

Fort Wayne. "The Roosevelt special train arrived here tonight about 7:30 o'clock, and found a great crowd waiting and cheering. The line of march of the parading clubs lay in the direction of Princess Rink, and was at least a mile in length. All along the way the streets were thronged with a cheering, surging mass of humanity. . . . The Rough Riders were in evidence. . . . Here and there great rockets shot skyward . . . and the streets at times were brilliant with pyrotechnics.

"One unfortunate incident occurred to mar the success of tonight's event. Two stones were thrown at the carriage in which Governor Roosevelt rode with Col. Curtis Guild, Joseph B. Kealing, and Harry S. New. The stones were thrown while the parade was on, and as the carriage was about passing the courthouse on Calhoun Street. The first stone struck the lamp reflector on the side of the carriage. The other struck Governor Roosevelt in the side, and, rebounding, hit Col. Curtis Guild in the mouth. The stone was evidently thrown by some miscreant on his own account, and the visitors do not feel that the incident should in any way reflect on the city of Fort Wayne.

[There were] "three big meetings, including one in the Princess Rink, the largest hall in this city, where the Governor spoke to more than 5,000 people, who cheered him enthusiastically and sincerely. The hero of San Juan Hill invaded the stronghold of Democracy and conquered. . . . Governor Roosevelt was introduced by a young man who fought with him in Cuba— A. T. Kehoe."

At the rink, Roosevelt responded to his opponent's recent charges against the administration: "I notice that Mr. Bryan's own organ in Indiana, the *Indianapolis Sentinel,* reports him as having said last night at Macomb, Ill, that the real object for permanently increasing the army is to intimidate the labor element when it presents just complaints. The idea is to erect forts near the large cities and with the forces located in them, meet all the demands of labor. I earnestly hope that the *Sentinel* has misquoted Mr. Bryan. . . . The increase in the army has been made necessary by the war in the Philippines. . . . There was no idea of erecting forts near the large cities and never has been, save where they are to be used for defense against a foreign foe. . . . Mr. Bryan must know that the army would be reduced if the insurrection in the Philippines, to which he and his party associates have given aid and comfort, were put down. . . . There is no true patriot in the country who ought not to be indignant and yet there is no man of good sense who ought not to laugh at [Bryan's] effort to persuade 75,000,000 people or any fraction thereof that 65,000 regular troops . . . could under any conceivable circumstances be a menace to this country.

"Besides the big meeting in the rink, two overflow meetings were held, one in a tent nearby, and the other in Library Hall on Calhoun Street. Both of these places were crowded. . . . Governor Roosevelt visited both the overflow meetings and made brief remarks. . . . The Republicans of Fort Wayne are delighted with the success of their meetings. . . . It is said this is the greatest crowd Fort Wayne has had since the visit of the late James G. Blaine.

"The Roosevelt special train left about 11 o'clock tonight for Marion."[16]

Marion. "Governor Roosevelt's second day's campaigning in Indiana began at Marion yesterday about 8 o'clock a.m. The morning was an ideal one and there was an immense crowd waiting for the special train which lay the greater part of the night on a switch near the Malleable Iron Works, about two miles out of the city. The special train arrived at Marion between 1 and 2 o'clock yesterday morning and pulled out into the country to give the people on board an opportunity to have a quiet night's rest from the fatigue of the day before. Governor Roosevelt awoke very early and looked out on a field of corn. During the morning someone remarked that although the Governor slept in the midst of a cornfield, his voice was not husky. At 7 o'clock the people on the train were awakened by the sounds of campaign horns and the noise of cheering that came across the fields from the city. About 8 o'clock the train moved into the city and stopped at the Adams Street Crossing.

"Marion was in gay attire in honor of Governor Roosevelt's visit. . . . [There was a] crowd of 25,000. . . . The fact that the hour of the Marion meeting was very early caused the Republican leaders to look on the big assemblage as somewhat phenomenal. There was a street parade which was led by a company of several hundred veterans from the soldiers' home. Governor Roosevelt spoke from a stand in the courthouse yard. . . . There was a company of mounted Rough Riders in the procession and they saluted the Governor and fairly split the air with their enthusiastic shouting of the following: 'We ride, we shout, we yell right out; We make our presence felt; We are all for Teddy, Rough and Ready; Theodore Roosevelt.' . . . Hundreds of dainty handkerchiefs fluttered along the line of march, which showed that the women were as enthusiastic as the men."[17]

Fairmount. "The train left Marion about 8:30 o'clock and the next stop was at Fairmount. The committee there had a platform erected within a few feet of the railway track and Governor Roosevelt had to go but a few steps."[18]

Summitville. "The train was not scheduled to stop at Summitville, but there was a crowd at the station and the special stopped long enough for Governor Roosevelt to shake the hand of a number of people."[19]

Alexandria. "The next stop was at Alexandria, which was reached about 9:25. Here there was a crowd of from 8,000 to 10,000 people. The train was saluted by the firing of cannon and great cheering. It was a great outpouring of the people of the gas belt. . . . So great was the desire of the crowd to hear him speak that many men and boys climbed to the top of the Governor's car, within hearing distance of the platform, which had been erected about 200 feet away. . . . As the train started from Alexandria a number of women pushed forward with children in their arms. They held the little ones up for the Governor to see them. 'Good,' said he with a smile, 'I have six of those at home; I'm an expert at that.' The crowd cheered and the Governor threw kisses at the children as the train left."[20]

Anderson. "The train reached Anderson a few minutes before 10 o'clock. . . . A stop of three-quarters of an hour was made at Anderson. The speaking was held in a field about 300 feet southwest of the Big Four Depot. A crowd of 15,000 greeted Governor Roosevelt. Charles L. Henry presided at the stand, and did his talking through a megaphone, so that he could be plainly heard. . . . As Governor Roosevelt was stepping out of his carriage, C. C. Williams, a Rough Rider living near Pendleton, dashed up on a horse. He carried an immense flag, and as he drew near the stand he threw his Rough Rider hat to the ground. Still holding the flag he reached low over his horse and picked up the hat. . . . 'By George!' [Roosevelt] exclaimed, 'that man is a rider.' . . . [Roosevelt] picked out Williams from a group of horsemen who dashed up. 'I'd like to know your name,' he said, and Williams introduced himself. Williams has made application to be inspector in the rural mail delivery service. . . . A significant feature of the street demonstration in Anderson was the large number of workingmen's organizations in line. Nearly every establishment was represented. The faces of the men looked bright and contented, and they did not appear to want a change of administration. . . . An organization of Rough Riders had a banner that read: 'Beef tongue, 18 cents a pound; pork tongue, 16 cents a pound; Bryan tongue, $300.' [Roosevelt looked at the banners and said:] 'You understand all the questions—I can see that.'"[21]

Muncie. "One of the biggest ovations of the day was tendered Governor Roosevelt at Muncie, the train arriving there about 11:30 o'clock a.m. Twenty-five thousand or 30,000 people filled the streets and cheered the Governor as he passed. There was a street parade which covered two or three of the principal streets of the city. . . . The industries of Muncie were especially represented. . . . Many of the residences were beautifully decorated. Everywhere the people cheered for McKinley and Roosevelt. . . . Governor Roosevelt did not speak in Muncie, but the parade lasted for more than a half hour. . . . Pretty girls in Rough Rider hats waved their handkerchiefs as the line of carriages passed. Here and there, drawn up at the sidewalks, were wagons containing young girls dressed in white. . . . Yellow was the favorite color of the day in Muncie. Everywhere there were fluttering badges of yellow silk that indicated the loyalty and patriotism of the wearers. There was a demonstration in honor of Perry S. Heath, assistant postmaster general, given by many of his fellow-townsmen, and especially by the employees of the Muncie post office, who cheered as he passed in a carriage. . . . There were a few Bryan cheers. . . . At the station, as the train was about leaving, a broad-shouldered young man, with a sneer on his face, shouted several times for Bryan. 'That man is on the stone pile half of his time,' remarked a Muncie citizen who heard him."[22]

Winchester. "The train left Muncie for Winchester about noon. . . . It was a generous greeting that Governor Roosevelt receive at Winchester. . . . The crowd was estimated at 10,000 to 15,000 people The place was bright in attractive decorations and the people were enthusiastic. A parade that was an hour and three-quarters in passing a given point, it was said, had just taken place and the Republicans were feeling jubilant. . . . Governor Roosevelt spoke from a stand almost within the shadow of the soldiers' monument that stands in the courthouse yard. He was introduced by Senator Fairbanks.

"The Republicans . . . said that last week, when Bryan was in Winchester, the three Summers brothers, who are engaged in the blacksmithing business, were Democrats. Yesterday they were in line with the Republican organizations with a wagon fitted out with a blacksmith shop. They had a horse on the wagon and a man in the act of shoeing the horse. Their attitude was explained by Republicans on the theory that Bryan, in his speech last week, failed to tell them anything that was satisfying enough to keep them in the party."[23]

Richmond. "In beautiful Glen Miller Park at Richmond, Governor Roosevelt spoke to thousands of people. He was received warmly when the train arrived at the park. The party took carriages and was driven to the stand half a mile distant. It was on a sloping hillside and gave the Governor an opportunity to see the people and be seen by them. There was a sea of faces in front of him and back of him. It was difficult to estimate the number of people in the park when the Governor began speaking. Citizens of Richmond said that Colonel Roosevelt's visit had drawn out the biggest crowd the city ever had. It was estimated that between 30,000 and 40,000 people were in the streets at one time during the day. There was a fine parade about 11:30 o'clock a.m. [prior to Roosevelt's arrival], which was led by the Republican Bugle and Drum Corps. There were 300 Rough Riders in line, besides numerous other marching clubs. . . . The train left Richmond about 2:30 o'clock with the people cheering and shaking hands with the Governor."[24]

Cambridge City. "At Cambridge City a short stop was made, but there was no speech-making—only handshaking."[25]

Knightstown. "A minute's stop was made at Knightstown, where a crowd had gathered on the platform. In the crowd were children from the Soldiers' and Sailors' Orphans' Home and a number of veterans."[26]

Greenfield. "At Greenfield the special train stopped a few minutes to allow a regular train the main track. No speech was made there, although there were a good many people on the platform."[27]

Indianapolis. "Governor Roosevelt's visit to Indianapolis yesterday will go down as an epoch in the history of Indiana politics. It was a triumphant close to his second day in Indiana. . . . It was expected that he would be greeted with the record-breaking crowd of the campaign, and he was. It was about the biggest crowd ever seen in Indianapolis. . . . Everybody wore a Roosevelt badge and everybody tried to outdo his neighbor in shouting his praise. . . . Superintendent Zion said he had never experienced such a busy day and the attaches of the Union Station were of opinion that over 30,000 people passed through the gates during the day and evening. Part of this immense crowd came in on special trains while all the regular trains on every road and from every direction were loaded and carried many extra cars.[28]

"The special train bearing Governor Roosevelt and party arrived in Indianapolis about 18 minutes after 4 o'clock. . . . The train stopped at Southeastern Avenue, according to programme, and the distinguished party alighted. . . . Several hundred people greeted the train. . . . A long line of carriages were waiting, and everybody on the train was invited to ride downtown. . . . There was no attempt at a parade. . . . On both sides of Southeastern Avenue there were people to greet the Governor . . . and from Noble Street to the Courthouse, Washington Street was thronged. . . . [Roosevelt] was kept busy doffing his gray slouch hat, which he is wearing almost constantly these days. . . . The windows of the buildings were filled with heads. Handkerchiefs were waved in profusion.

"A salute of cannon was fired and immediately the crowd became stilled in a hush of expectancy. All eyes watched with eager gaze the window in the county clerk's office through which the Governor would have to descend to the speakers' stand as if their hopes of eternal salvation depended upon the man who should soon confront them. Colonel Roosevelt's appearance on the speakers' stand in the courthouse yard was the signal for one of the grandest ovations ever accorded to a candidate. . . . There was not an available inch of ground that was not occupied. . . . A conservative estimate of the crowd that encompassed the speakers' stand places it at 20,000. . . . Pretty girls decorated with Roosevelt badges were thicker than bees in a hive. . . . The air was full of patriotic music from dozens of bands and drum corps and the thousands of people were adorned with McKinley and Roosevelt buttons and badges. . . . They all yelled for prosperity and the Republican ticket.

[When Roosevelt appeared] "the ovation tendered the Governor was so enthusiastic and accompanied by such a powerful forward movement of the crowd to get a nearer view of the great man, that there was danger of the speakers' stand being demolished. . . . The Governor was followed onto the stand by Harry S. New, national committeeman from Indiana, [and several others]. Mr. New presented to the audience Captain William E. English, as a Democrat of the old school, who could not stand with his party in its present disorganized state, and as one of Colonel Roosevelt's comrades at the memorable battle of San Juan Hill. . . . [English introduced Roosevelt, ending with these words:] 'I take the very greatest pleasure in presenting to you a statesman in peace, a hero in war, and the best beloved among his comrades, among the soldiers of the Republic, Theodore Roosevelt.'

"The free and easy position assumed by the gallant Rough Rider—leaning carelessly against the post supporting the platform at his left, with his right foot elevated to the railing in front of him—increased the heartiness of the ovation given him. The crowd saw that the man before them was not of the fastidious, supercilious class so detested by right-thinking people, but a plain, common man—a brother in every sense of the word. It seemed as though they would never have done with their welcome so that he might begin his address. The Governor finally contrived to secure something like quiet by a commanding wave of his hand, and commenced his eloquent speech.

[Roosevelt said, in part:] "I want no better campaign argument than can be made out of the speeches of Mr. Bryan himself four years ago. If you read the Old Testament you will find that false prophets had a bad time in those days, but nowadays they nominate them for President on the Democratic ticket. . . . Bryan's book is called 'The First Battle' . . . and if you will turn to page 526 you will see the speeches he made here in Indianapolis four years ago, and as generally happened he could not resist prophesying, and when the inspiration came to him he said this: 'Gold is arrogant and tyrannical, and it deserts any nation in time of war.' We have had the Spanish War since, and gold stayed with us. . . . We are for the gold standard here, and in New York, and in Denver—everywhere. [Applause. A voice: 'In Victor.'] . . . [Roosevelt responded:] 'Yes, in Victor. Once more, we are for the cause of law and order—or orderly liberty under the law—everywhere.'"

Roosevelt continued, again quoting from Bryan's book: "This you will find on page 532 of the book. I would not dare to quote it except at first hand. It is addressed to traveling men. He was describing the misery that would come to all our people if they had the gold standard, and he said this: 'Only a few of our people will be able to wear shoes under the gold standard.' And then he goes on: 'As it is with shoes so it is with clothing.' Gentlemen, this crowd is packed too close for me to see if they are barefooted, but they seem well clad. Now, think of that! . . . It is really a little difficult to argue seriously when propositions like that are advanced. . . . [Bryan] said that the farmer would lose the market for his crops, and he has had a greater market than ever before. He said that failures in the business world would increase, and they have been but one-tenth as numerous. He said that the saving deposits would go down, and they have gone up 25 percent. He said that mortgages would go up, but they went down 40 percent. Now if you are dealing in private life with a storekeeper or anyone else, and he misleads you, the first time it is his fault, and the next time it is your fault."

After the late afternoon rally, there was an evening parade. "The crowd on the streets of this city last evening was estimated at between 100,000 and 125,000. . . . Marching clubs galore . . . carried banners, transparencies, and flags, all of which were seen in the parade in the evening."

Roosevelt's party overnighted at Indianapolis. In the morning, this small event occurred, before comrades parted. "When Captain English and Governor Roosevelt met this morning, Mr. English presented the Governor with a pretty little keepsake, a button bearing on its face the insignia of the Society of Santiago. Governor Roosevelt had remarked the first day of the Indiana trip that he had forgotten to wear his button, and Captain English, having two, divided with the Governor."[29]

Plainfield.   "Governor Roosevelt began the work of his last day in Indiana at Plainfield early this morning. In that peaceful little Quaker city the vice presidential candidate spoke to a big crowd of people just after the arrival of the train, shortly after 9 o'clock a.m. . . . The stand from which he spoke at Plainfield had been erected at the railway station, only a few steps from the train. . . . Roosevelt said: 'I understand that this community is composed largely of members of the Society of Friends, who stand for social and industrial virtue in a way that entitles them to the respect of all people. . . . I am glad to address the members of the society that stood by President McKinley and gave their influence toward international arbitration at the peace conference at The Hague. . . . We have not advanced far enough to be able to settle all our difficulties peaceably by arbitration, but in every case we should avoid appeal to arms where possible, for we, as a party, are pledged to peaceful settlement until war becomes a last resort.'"[30]

Greencastle.   "The next stop was at Greencastle, which was reached about 10:20 o'clock. . . . There was a large turnout of farmers, and they were enthusiastic. It was said the crowd was one of the largest Greencastle has ever held, and that it was almost three times as large as the crowd which greeted Bryan last week. Prior to Governor Roosevelt's arrival there was a parade in honor of the day, in which were many gaily decorated wagons from the out townships. Many of the wagons were occupied by pretty girls. . . . The Governor said in part: 'Judging from the cheering I hear, evidently they play football in this neighborhood, and I want to assure you that, from what I have seen in Indiana, on the 6th of November next, I think the score will be about 16 to 0.'"[31]

Brazil. "At Greencastle a committee from Brazil boarded the train to meet Governor Roosevelt. . . . There was an immense crowd in Brazil to see the Governor—perhaps 8,000 people—who were very enthusiastic, and cheered the procession of carriages all along the line of march to the speakers' stand. Although a strong Democratic city, Brazil did the honors very handsomely. The miners were out by the hundreds, and Governor Roosevelt in his remarks paid especial attention to them." In Brazil a group of veterans carried a banner that read: "We voted for Lincoln—We will vote for McKinley."[32]

Terre Haute. "Governor Roosevelt's ovation at Terre Haute today was a most remarkable one. . . . Terre Haute Republicans never do things by halves, and the arrangements . . . were complete in every detail. The Governor spoke to an immense crowd at the Republican Tabernacle, Walnut and Eighth Streets, and enthusiasm was unbounded. . . . Before his speech and immediately after the arrival of the train, there was a street parade, the line of march being a mile and a half in length. . . . A stay of an hour and a half was made at Terre Haute, and during that time the town was exceedingly lively. The fact that a street fair was in progress in the city, of course, helped swell the crowd, but the Republicans make due allowance for this in estimating the multitude. It was one of the greatest political rallies ever held in Vigo County and Republicans feel proud of the demonstration. . . . [During his speech at Terre Haute, Roosevelt said:] 'A ton of oratory does not count as much as an ounce of action.' [Someone from the crowd shouted:] 'How about it if you get well paid for it?' [Roosevelt's response was:] 'From a personal and financial standpoint I will not discuss that because I don't know the price paid to campaign orators on the other side. The only worth of a prophecy is its fulfillment.'"[33]

Lewis. "The special train left Terre Haute at 1:30 o'clock and made a stop at Lewis, about 16 miles south on the line of the Southern Indiana Railroad.

Several hundred people gathered at the station. Governor Roosevelt spoke from a platform within a few feet of the station that was erected for William Jennings Bryan. When the Bryan train stopped at Lewis it was raining and the presidential candidate declined to alight, but spoke from the platform of his car. The Democrats, not feeling at all complimented, presented the platform to the Republicans on the agreement that Governor Roosevelt would occupy it. The Governor made his speech there and was well received."[34]

Linton.   "The next stop was at Linton, one of the most important mining towns in southern Indiana. . . . The crowd there was estimated at 20,000. The reception Governor Roosevelt received there was one of the most flattering of the day. . . . It was with the greatest difficulty that Governor Roosevelt and the men accompanying him made their way back to the train, so eager was the crowd to see more of the soldier and orator. Today was a great day all around for Linton. There was a big parade in the morning in which nearly 1,000 Rough Riders turned out. There were glee clubs of young men and women [and] a big drum corps. . . . Badges [in Linton] read 'Prosperity at home; Prestige abroad.' The mines at Linton were closed for the day. . . . Harry S. New, of the national executive committee, wired Henry C. Payne, of the national committee: 'Teddy's last day in Indiana equals the other two. . . . The greatest meeting of the day was at Linton; nearly all miners. The crowd . . . was the most enthusiastic of the trip. We are all right here, and don't you forget it.'"[35]

Bee Hunter.   "At Bee Hunter the train was transferred to the Indianapolis & Vincennes Road, and no more stops were made until Vincennes was reached about 4:40 o'clock. At Marco, Sandborn, Edwardsport, and Bickness, however, people were gathered on the platforms. The train slackened its speed while passing these places to give the people an opportunity of seeing Governor Roosevelt."[36]

Vincennes.   "The county fair is in progress at Vincennes this week, and a great number of the people were in town. From 10,000 to 12,000 were waiting for the train. . . . The Governor said in part: 'Speaking here in Vincennes I am inevitably reminded of the first expansion of the United States. It was a 121 years ago that George Rogers Clark and his troop of riflemen, joined by some of the old French Creole inhabitants, forced the British garrison to surrender, and added what is a portion of the State of Indiana to the

American Union. And, gentlemen, they did it without asking the consent of the inhabitants and much against the will of the British garrison. . . . We spread then because our forefathers were men and fitted to do a man's work. . . . Mr. Bryan has just learned, 35 years after the rest of us, that Abraham Lincoln was right in 1864. If he lives as long as I hope he will, for I wish him well in private life, I have no doubt in 1935 he will realize that McKinley was entirely right in 1900.'"[37]

Princeton. "The train left Vincennes after a stop of 20 minutes for Princeton, the next stop. . . . The train drew into Princeton a few minutes after 5 o'clock. A crowd of perhaps 10,000 people was cheering and waiting for Governor Roosevelt to appear. . . . As the Governor walked toward the stand where he was to speak, these words on a banner met his eye: 'Welcome, Roosevelt; this is not Colorado.' Princeton had an all-day rally. . . . One of the banners carried by the railway men's club said: 'We are satisfied—McKinley told the truth.'"[38]

Evansville. "Evansville streets were crowded with cheering thousands tonight, and the two meetings held after the street demonstration were big affairs. Governor Roosevelt spoke at both, first in Evans Hall and later in the Grand Opera House. Both places were packed with crowds that gave the Governor a hearty welcome. . . . The Grand Opera House meeting was held under the auspices of the Lincoln League of Vanderburg County. . . . Governor Roosevelt was warmly received when he entered the opera House." [Roosevelt spoke briefly. Also on the program was Colonel Charles L. Jewett, who said] "that after he had seen the ovations given Governor Roosevelt in Indiana it seemed to him like hitting a man when he was down to criticize Bryan."

The day before Roosevelt was in Evansville, W. J. Bryan made a speech at Nashville, Michigan, in which he posed ten questions for the Republican Party regarding trusts, militarism, and imperialism in the Philippines. Roosevelt began his last major speech in Indiana answering the questions one by one, using material that had been the basis for his speeches all along the whistle-stop route. Significantly, Bryan asked nothing about gold versus silver. Then, Roosevelt turned the tables on Bryan and asked him to answer another set of questions: Will he pay the obligations of the nation in gold or silver? Will he decline to accept the electoral votes of North Carolina because they are obtained without the consent of the governed (i.e., African American citizens)? Will he denounce Democrats in Congress who voted against federal authority over trusts?[39]

Conclusion

Having relied upon the *Indianapolis Journal* regarding the events of Roosevelt's whistle-stop tour through Indiana, it seems only right to give the publication the final word: "From Lake Michigan to the Ohio River the trip has been a triumphant one, each city visited seeming to try to outdo the other in enthusiasm and hospitality. If there has been any doubt in the minds of Indiana Republicans as to the result in this state, it has been dissipated in the last three days. . . . Governor Roosevelt's view of the situation in Indiana may be given in the comment he made today, after addressing a big crowd. [He said:] 'I don't need to ask these people how they are going to vote; I see it in their faces.'"[40]

After the stop in Evansville, responsibility for hosting the next segment of the campaign tour was turned over to a new committee from the next state down the tracks. The train left at 6:00 a.m. on Saturday, October 13, 1900, for Henderson, Kentucky.[41]

CHAPTER 15

KENTUCKY

No calmer than the boiling waters of Colorado politics, Kentucky was bubbling with controversy when Theodore Roosevelt's campaign train entered the state on Saturday, October 13, 1900, with eighteen whistle stops on the schedule. Just nine months earlier, in the aftermath of a disputed election, the Democratic gubernatorial candidate, William J. Goebel, was shot in Frankfort, the state capital. Then, as he lay dying, he was declared the winning candidate and sworn into office. He signed one gubernatorial proclamation and succumbed, becoming the only sitting governor assassinated in the history of the United States.[1]

Everyone in Kentucky was reasonably certain that the dispute behind the governor's murder was related to vote manipulations in the close gubernatorial election. Also assumed was that political enemies, opponents from big business, or both were behind the shooting. Goebel himself was no stranger to arguments and violence; five years earlier he had shot a man in what was eventually declared by the court to be self-defense. Many were convinced the incident was actually an illegal duel between two antagonists in a struggle over corporate reforms.

Goebel's political career began in 1887 with election by fewer than one hundred votes to an unexpired term in the Kentucky state senate. He was a Democrat in a majority Democratic state legislature, and he was known for taking political positions against some of Kentucky's strongest business interests. When a Republican was elected governor in 1895 and McKinley carried the state by a margin of less than three hundred votes in 1896, Goebel pushed election reform legislation through the legislature and overrode the Republican governor's veto.

After a lengthy and heated nominating convention in the summer of 1899, Kentucky's Democratic Party selected Goebel as its gubernatorial candidate. William Jennings Bryan, whom Goebel had supported in his first bid for the presidency, traveled to Kentucky to speak for the Democratic candidate during the gubernatorial campaign, and at several of his whistle stops, Roosevelt referred in his remarks to Bryan's participation in the tainted election.

Goebel lost to the incumbent Republican governor by slightly over two thousand votes in the bitter statewide election. However, that proved to be only the first outcome of the election of 1899. As there were disputed ballots, the Democratic-controlled legislature stepped into the fray under the authority of the state's constitution. The controversial ballots were examined by a contest committee of eleven legislators chosen by lot; however, this supposedly random process had yielded a membership in which nine of the eleven happened to be Democrats. Needless to say, when the committee took action, sufficient Republican votes were lost to give Goebel the election.

This was the hostile backdrop as Goebel was assassinated and the newly elected Democratic lieutenant governor was sworn in as the governor. For a time, the Republican governor refused to yield his position. Irvin S. Cobb, the well-known Kentucky author, happened to be on-site as a journalist when the assassination occurred and in the melee was himself fired upon by a policeman. He reported: "Immediately after Goebel's death two sets of state officials functioned in Kentucky."[2]

Eventually, the previous governor, fearing either for his safety or his potential entanglement in the assassination investigation, fled the state to live out his life in Indiana. Of course, outraged arguments between Democrats and Republicans were ongoing as Roosevelt and his traveling companions steamed into Kentucky, and once again they brought party politics to public meeting halls and speakers' stands.

Campaign advisors must have strongly encouraged the candidate to focus his speeches on the issues of the national election, but it was not in Roosevelt's nature to avoid controversy. As the reports on his various stops in Kentucky that follow in this chapter show, Roosevelt beat the drum loudly, openly blaming the state's Democrats for denying citizens their right to vote. He could hardly have been more outspoken or provocative, and at some of his stops, the predictable reaction occurred. Perhaps he was weary of the constant sandpapering by Democrats over his failure to address the gold-versus-silver issue in the western mining states.

There were warnings of demonstrations and possible violence that Roosevelt chose to ignore. For example, this story ran in the media on the day after the campaign left Kentucky: "The Chairman of the Republican State Committee, Leslie Combs, had received dispatches from Covington informing him that leaders there were apprehensive that an organized effort would be made to break up the meeting. Mr. Combs hurriedly transmitted his information to Governor Roosevelt, whereat the latter smiled broadly, and he assured the chairman there could be no possible danger of serious interruption of his tour in Kentucky. To insure absolute tranquillity and to provide against any display of hostility, Chief of Police Pugh and the sheriff of this county doubled their forces."[3]

These were no idle threats that were sloughed off by Roosevelt. Covington was the hometown of the assassinated governor, William Goebel, and Chief Pugh, reportedly himself a Goebel partisan,[4] was sufficiently alarmed to stiffen the protection. Yet the vice presidential candidate offered assurances of safety to those around him, and he proceeded with a public event in hostile territory where he brazenly condemned election fraud before a crowd that included friends and neighbors of the man who had benefited, then died violently. Roosevelt's boldness in Kentucky—some might say his recklessness—was astonishing.

How bad was it? Professor Marianne Walker of the University of Kentucky summed it up quite pointedly. Of this period in the state's past, she wrote: "In the last days of the nineteenth century, Kentucky was the most violent state in the union. New York reported a few more murders, but that's mainly because in some parts of Kentucky such records were not kept. Kentuckians fought, dueled, and killed all the time, over family grudges, property, railroads, turnpikes, insults, and especially politics."[5]

As would be expected, Kentucky Democrats were not going to sit by while a bombastic Theodore Roosevelt besmirched their integrity and carved up their party's platform. Many small towns were served by newspapers with Democratic sympathies, and they attacked from before Roosevelt's arrival until after his departure.

Some of the Democrats' anti-Roosevelt pieces are mentioned in the following, but one was particularly effective and was likely based on propaganda available from national Democratic sources. One day following the candidate's departure, the *Hopkinsville Kentuckian* ran a series of quotations from Roosevelt's earlier publications and conversations; the tactic was, of course, to discredit him on the basis that his campaign statements were often the opposite of his personal positions.[6] Hopkinsville was one of the Kentucky whistle stops, but these points were clearly intended for much wider exposure.

Example one was aimed at Roosevelt's campaign position that the nation dare not hesitate to maintain and use a strong military. "On page

295 of the September, 1896, *Review of Reviews,* Theodore Roosevelt made the following statement: 'The men who object to what they style government by injunction are, as regards to essential principles of government, in hearty sympathy with their remote ancestors who lived in caves, fought one another with stone headed axes, and ate the mammoth and woolly Rhinoceros. . . . They are not in sympathy with men of good minds and sound civic morality.'"

Example two intended to show Roosevelt's courting of the blue-collar vote as hypocritical opportunism. "In the *Century Magazine* for February 1888, an article appeared from the pen of Col. Roosevelt entitled 'Ranch Life in the Far West.' On page 502 appears the following: 'When drunk on the villainous whiskey of the frontier towns, the cowboys and Rough Riders cut mad antics, riding their horses into the saloons [and] firing their pistols . . . but they are much better fellows and pleasanter companions than the small farmers or agricultural laborers; nor are the mechanics of a great city to be mentioned in the same breath with them.'"

Example three addressed the candidate's professed argument against imperialism. "In 1898 C. P. Putnam's Sons issued from their press a book by Mr. Roosevelt entitled *American Ideals and other Essays.* . . . [He wrote:] 'The only hope for a colony that wishes to attain full moral and mental growth, is to become an independent state. . . . But if the colony is in a region where the colonizing has to do its work by means of other inferior races, its condition is much worse. From the standpoint of the race, little or nothing has been gained by the English conquest of Jamaica.'"

Example four demonstrated that the vice presidential nominee had not always approved of the nation's presence in the Philippines or thought so highly of his running mate as his campaign speeches suggested. "On the third day of last April, President David Star Jordan of Leland Stanford University said in an interview when asked which view of the issue of imperialism, McKinley's or Bryan's, was gaining most among people: 'Let me quote you Roosevelt on that. He said to me last week, "Jordan, I wish to God we were off the Philippines and had them off our hands." I am free to quote Roosevelt because I consider him in many respects one of the greatest men in the Republican Party.' When asked 'How do you like McKinley?' President Jordan said: 'Let me quote you Roosevelt again. He said to me: "McKinley has about as much backbone as a toy chocolate man that you can see on the confectioner's stand. He is a terrible disappointment."'"

Still another dynamic in the coverage of the campaign's three days in Kentucky was provided by one of the traveling correspondents, a so-called

Rough Writer, who viewed the internecine squabbling among Kentuckians with a decidedly jaundiced eye. The reporter for the *Sun,* a New York City newspaper, wrote this about the crowds that attended the Roosevelt events: "They have been as inattentive and as careless of the rights of the speaker as the Governor's party has been told that Kentucky country audiences always are. They find once they are gathered together that the instinct of sociability overcomes all others in the country Kentuckians' breasts. The women want to compare babies and tell one another their troubles and the men have equally engrossing subjects to engross them. But for argument and subtle differentiations between civic righteousness and civic dishonor the Kentuckian of the type that Gov. Roosevelt has addressed today cares nothing. He will seize gratefully at a chance to yell like an Indian for any oratorical outburst of language that voices the sentiments that he has announced his intention of supporting at the polls, but he does not want to be argued with. He will not be argued with. He would rather fight."[7]

Likewise, the same East Coast correspondent sniped about what he clearly felt was halfhearted support for Roosevelt on the part of local leadership. He wrote this sarcastic narrative poking fun at a man he obviously considered ineffective, at best: "After [a contentious] meeting, Chairman Combs of the Republican Campaign Committee, who had been in charge of the Kentucky trip, came to the Governor with this almost apologetic explanation: 'If it hadn't been,' he said, 'that I saw, sir, that the rudeness of that villain, sir, was stirring you to more effective oratory, the longer it continued, I would have stepped to the front of the platform, sir, and would have asked that inasmuch as the police did not seem disposed to prevent the shameless behavior of the scoundrel that I wished that some Republican would undertake to do what the police had left undone. Why, sir, Gov. Roosevelt, sir, he would have been knocked on the head in two minutes, sir. But inasmuch as he seemed to be aiding our cause, I permitted him to persist.'"[8]

Thus, the tour of Kentucky may be fairly characterized as a prize fight of eighteen rounds, one for each planned stop. Notably, there were no reported stops in addition to those scheduled with but one exception, that being the Sunday repose at a farm near a rail siding at Spring Station. These are the nineteen reported stops of Theodore Roosevelt's campaign for the vice presidency in Kentucky:

Saturday, October 13, 1900 (Kentucky)
    Henderson 8:00 a.m.
    Madisonville 9:15

Hopkinsville 10:45
Guthrie 11:45
Russellville 12:45 p.m.
Bowling Green 1:45
Munfordsville 3:15
Elizabethtown 4:20
Louisville 8:00 p.m.
Sunday, October 14, 1900
Spring Station (Roosevelt train on a side track from early Sunday
    morning until Monday departure; travelers spent Sunday at the
    nearby farm of A. J. Alexander; located eighteen miles north of
    Lexington)
Monday, October 15, 1900 (Kentucky)
Lexington 8:00 a.m.
Winchester 8:45
Mt. Sterling 9:30
Morehead 10:45
Ashland 1:00 p.m.
Greenup 2:26
Vanceburg 3:40
Maysville 4:45
Covington 8:00

Two Kentucky communities visited by the Roosevelt campaign were the
major stops for the state. These were Louisville and Covington. Other communities on the route hosted sizable events and some became for the candidate or his opponents venues for important statements, but Louisville
and Covington proved to be the pivotal stops, garnering much of the media
coverage. Anti-Roosevelt and anti-Republican sentiment was obvious and
fairly organized across the state, but Roosevelt again proved his mettle and
faced down his enemies. Following is a review of the major stops in Kentucky and then selected highlights from other communities visited.

Major Stops in Kentucky

Louisville.   Roosevelt's train reached this city of more than 200,000 people
in the early evening hours of Saturday, October 13. Louisville was, at the
turn of the twentieth century, one of the twenty largest cities in the nation,

and it was then, as it is now, an important center of transportation and commerce. There was a large crowd at the station to greet the Republican vice presidential candidate, and the first event on the agenda was dinner with the state's Republican elite at the Galt House, a classic and historic downtown hotel that had hosted many visiting luminaries for decades. When the dinner ended, Roosevelt was escorted to the auditorium for an eight o'clock rally where more than ten thousand people filled the same space that another capacity crowd had occupied to hear William Jennings Bryan exactly one week earlier.[9] Kentucky was alive with political awareness, and those that gathered to hear Theodore Roosevelt were described by the *New-York Tribune* as an "admiring, curious, [and] surging mob."[10] He did not disappoint his audience.

After a typically laudatory introduction, Roosevelt attacked the Democratic candidate for president directly and without mincing words. He charged: "Mr. Bryan has shown some uncertainty as to what was the paramount issue in this campaign, and it has changed a little. He has not stood pat on it. I can tell you what the paramount issue is: it is Bryanism, and Bryanism means different things in different states, but it means something bad everywhere."

Low-hanging fruit on the Kentucky tree was the recent upheaval connected with charges and counter-charges of voter fraud that ended with Governor-elect Goebel's assassination. Continuing with his allegations that Bryanism was wrongheaded, even evil, Roosevelt said: "There are certain men who are sufficiently unfortunate to have their names typify social phrases of which we are not proud. Mr. Altgeld has risen to that eminence. In Illinois it means Altgeldism; in South Dakota it means Pettigrewism and in my own state Crokerism, and here it means Goebelism." Though the accounts do not record the mid-speech audience reactions, this must have brought the Republicans to their feet and given any curious Democrats in the crowd a shot of adrenaline.

Roosevelt was not finished with William Jennings Bryan. He wanted to be sure the Kentuckians in the auditorium and those who would read about this event in the state's leading city knew that the man at the top of the Democrats' ticket was mired in the scandal. He continued: "Here Mr. Bryan comes to the aid of those who commit the capital crime against a republic of suppressing or altering the votes of the majority of the freemen of this state. . . . Mr. Bryan is immensely concerned for the right of self-government for a Tagal bandit on the other side of the earth, and yet Mr. Bryan comes down into Kentucky to champion the party of fraud, to champion those who have disfranchised the majority of the inhabitants of this state and who have seated a governor who was not elected."

Lest anyone in the crowd mistake where the locus of honor resided, Roosevelt made it clear: "We have a right to appeal to every man, Republican, Democrat, Populist, whatsoever he be, provided he is an honest man. . . . A free man has the right to cast his vote as he pleases and to have it counted as cast. That is not a party question. If in this election the impossible should occur and the majority of the people should cast their votes for Mr. Bryan, though I should feel that they had inflicted the greatest wrong it was in the power of mankind to inflict upon the commonwealth, I would strain every resource that there is in the state before I would let a single vote that was cast for Mr. Bryan be counted for anyone else. That should be the attitude of every man fit to call himself an American citizen."[11]

After the meeting in the auditorium and the rousing denunciation of Bryan and his support of political shenanigans in Kentucky, Roosevelt stepped outside the building and addressed an overflow crowd described to be "as large as that which had filled the structure."[12] Then, when the rallies had ended, the traveling party returned to the train and left Louisville bound for the clandestine destination where they would spend Sunday in relative seclusion. "Before leaving Louisville, word was given out that the train would proceed at once to Lexington, but a secret order directed that it stop over Sunday in the country to enable the governor to recover from the fatigue caused by his unusually hard work of the last few days."[13] (More about Roosevelt's Sunday stop is in the next section of this chapter.)

Covington.   As soon as Roosevelt's train arrived at Covington at 6:30 p.m. on Monday, October 15, the candidate was escorted to the home of prominent Republican attorney Richard Pretlow Ernst, a man who would eventually serve the state as a United States Senator (1921 to 1927). According to a 1904 biography of Ernst, he was prominent and powerful enough in Covington to become the first Republican since the Civil War—more than a quarter century earlier—to be elected president of the city council.[14] Covington was slightly larger in 1900 than it is today with a population at the turn of the twentieth century of 43,000 people; then, as now, its economy was closely linked with the greater Cincinnati metropolitan area. Its political interests, however, were centered in Kentucky.

As reported earlier in this chapter, there had been warnings that Covington would be a site for anti-Roosevelt and anti-Republican demonstrations, and those threats were taken seriously enough that law enforcement was strengthened by temporarily adding personnel to the force that would protect the candidate. Exactly how contentious the situation became is not clear. One journalist wrote: "All such precautions proved to have been unnecessary, for beyond isolated instances of good-natured badinage and the tooting of a few tin horns the meeting was as peaceable as a matinee."[15] However, another newspaperman traveling with the campaign party saw it differently: "Gov. Roosevelt was again and again interrupted by Bryan shouters on the outside of the crowd. There was so much of a disposition on the part of the Bryanites to be ugly that the committee at the conclusion of his speech had him leave the platform quietly and enter a hack out of sight of the audience."[16]

Regardless of the threats and whatever shouts and other interruptions occurred, Roosevelt stepped up to the podium on the decorated speakers' stand in Courthouse Square for the 8:00 p.m. rally. He was facing "one of the largest crowds that has ever assembled in this city to listen to a candidate for public office," and the grounds were "congested with men and women anxious to hear him."[17] It must have been a nightmare scenario for those charged with security at this large, outdoor event.

Roosevelt addressed standard campaign themes for part of his speech. He said about the Philippines, for instance: "The simple truth is, as Mr. Bryan perfectly well knows, that every intelligent man foresaw that there would be trouble in the Philippines. . . . The only thing that could have avoided trouble in the Philippines was the policy of scuttle, the policy of craven ignoble flying and shirking of duty. To stay there and establish a stable government, as proposed by Mr. Bryan, is a policy which would cause just as much trouble with Aguinaldo's followers as any other, because they are fighting simply to found a cruel and oppressive oligarchy. The only way to secure permanent peace and civil and individual liberty for the great bulk of the inhabitants of the Philippines was to do precisely what we have done: take them over as a necessary incident of the war with Spain, and then to put down the bodies of armed bandits and introduce a government of law, order, and justice."[18]

However, Roosevelt again played the role of righteous provocateur, as he had in Louisville and elsewhere in the state: "I wish to appeal to you men of Kentucky in the name of civil liberty. . . . More important than anything else is the right of every man to cast his vote as he chooses and to have it counted as cast. We can afford to differ on questions of policy, but we cannot afford to differ on the fundamental rights of American citizenship. In the State of Kentucky every man is in honor bound to stand up and see that there is no condoning of the offenses of those who violate the will of the people. There should be favoritism for none and discrimination against none. . . . [Bryan] has not answered the questions why he supports in Kentucky a faction of the Bryanized Democracy which seeks to deprive, and has deprived, white men as well as black, ex-Confederate, as well as ex-Union soldiers, Gold Democrats and Silver Democrats, as well as Republicans, of their rights to cast their vote as they wish, and to have them counted as cast."[19]

Covington was the last of the stops in Kentucky. Republicans were aglow with Roosevelt's affirmation of their position. Democrats were outraged that he gave no quarter in his commentary on the political disputes. Thus, the Republicans' campaigner in chief left behind a state stewing over his remarks, not only at the two major stops in Louisville and Covington, but also at several of the other communities he and his party visited.

Highlights from Other Stops in Kentucky

At stop after stop, Roosevelt hammered the theme of his Kentucky tour—namely, that by their actions, Democrats had denied the basic principle of the Republic entitling every man to a vote and that William Jennings Bryan was complicit in that subterfuge. News reports from the various communities on the tour left no doubt that the Republican vice presidential candidate's remarks on Kentucky politics were direct, decisive, and clear in their accusations.

Henderson. "Governor Roosevelt began his campaign in Kentucky at 8 o'clock [Saturday morning, October 13] with an address at this city. Despite the early hour, there was a large crowd at the station to greet the Governor. . . . He said in part: 'I believe emphatically in a square deal for every man, and that he be allowed to have his vote counted as it was cast. I believe it in New York, and I believe it in Kentucky, and I believe this is less a party contest than a crusade for freedom. I have stood on the platform with Northern men and Southern men, with men who have worn the blue and men who have worn the gray, and all agree that liberty stands as the basis of American citizenship. If the people are wise they will pursue the course which has brought material prosperity, but greater than material prosperity is freedom."[20]

Journalists supportive of the opposing party's ticket were eager to find anecdotes that proved Roosevelt was having no impact. The *Times* reported this incident to its readers in Washington, DC: "A Democratic newspaper man came aboard the Roosevelt train at Henderson with a report that Frank Rogers of Frankfort, who is to Kentucky what Bun the Button Man is to New York, said that he had not sold a single McKinley or Yerkes button this year."[21] John W. Yerkes was the Republican candidate for governor. He was defeated, and not long thereafter he was appointed by President McKinley to be the federal commissioner of internal revenue.[22]

Madisonville. "Severe hoarseness is interfering seriously with Governor Roosevelt. He caught cold at Evansville last night and strained his voice in speaking there. At Madisonville he made a brief address, but could speak scarcely above a whisper. He said in part: 'We may differ as to the policies and the nation still go ahead, but when once a considerable body of our people cease to understand that it is the right of every man to cast his vote as he wishes and to have that vote counted as cast, self-government itself is in danger. We cannot, my countrymen, long go on as a republic if that right is denied.'"[23]

Hopkinsville. "At Hopkinsville Governor Roosevelt had an enthusiastic greeting. There was a parade from the train to the Town Hall, where he made a few remarks and then yielded to Colonel Curtis Guild, Jr. who was followed by Frank B. Posey. In speaking here Governor Roosevelt said: 'Mr. Bryan is exceedingly worried for fear there may be an infringement of the doctrine of the Declaration of Independence in the Philippines. . . . Let him stop being jealous about that, and let him explain how it was that he came into this state to uphold fraud and dishonor. It is a good thing to set one's own house in order before you attend overmuch to that of someone else on the other side of the globe.'"[24]

Elizabethtown. "At this place the Governor suffered the first indignity thrust upon him in the state. . . . The Republicans had done all in their power to make the candidate's stop there a pleasant one. No sooner had the governor mounted the platform, with other members of his party, than an attempt was made to break up the meeting. Small boys carried Bryan banners in the outskirts of the crowd, and empty coal wagons were driven at full speed through the square. The steam whistle on a mill close by was blown loudly, and half a hundred men or more shouted, 'Hurrah for Bryan!' when the Governor began speaking."[25]

Such antics, of course, made Roosevelt all the more determined to speak his mind, and though his hoarseness had caused him to shorten his remarks at previous stops, he took the podium and shouted as loudly as he could to be heard. Even as the demonstrators protested and the steam whistle shrieked, Roosevelt said: "I call your attention to the attitude of Mr. Bryan's friends on the subject of law and order." Then he waved his hand to the crowd and continued: "It is natural that the men who have tried to deprive Kentucky of a free ballot should be opposed to free speech. It is not extraordinary that the men who have stolen the Governorship and who seek to steal it again should not dare hear the truth of history, but should seek to gag an American citizen before he had uttered one word of his opinions in a political controversy."[26]

Despite encouragement from some in his party to stand down and allow others to give his throat relief, Roosevelt stood at the podium and delivered his full message for the entire fifteen minutes allowed for speaking at the Elizabethtown stop. Cheering by supporters in the crowd drowned out the protestors, and when a reporter asked later about the demonstration, Roosevelt said: "Just a put up job to break up the meeting, but I guess I got back at them."[27]

There was also a sidebar story to the reports from Elizabethtown of an exchange of telegrams between the Republican National Committee in Chicago and the candidate. The committee informed Roosevelt that a handbill was circulating with the claim he had said in two earlier speeches that supporters of Bryanism and striking laborers should be shot. Roosevelt wired this response for publication: "Both statements are absolute lies, without one particle of foundation of any sort, character, or description. I never said anything remotely resembling either statement. . . . I would suggest a suit for criminal libel. . . . They are slanderous lies which would only be circulated by scoundrels."[28]

Spring Station. This location was chosen as the appropriate site for Theodore Roosevelt to spend his Sunday resting halfway through the tour of Kentucky, and the farm of A. J. Alexander hosted the vice presidential candidate. This 3,300 acre farm had a distinguished history of breeding championship thoroughbreds for racing in the United States and Europe. One journalist wrote: "Here since early this morning, 18 miles from Lexington, in a country of colonels, beautiful women, blooded horses, the greatest stock farms in the world, and hospitality of superlative degree, Governor Roosevelt's special train has rested on a Louisville & Nashville side track. . . . Not 50 persons in Kentucky save those residing here know where Governor Roosevelt is resting."[29]

Though few details leaked about activities during the day of rest—unlike other Sunday stops on the western campaign trip—the results were reported: "The rest brought about the desired physical brightening. The governor's voice has almost entirely lost its huskiness, and he says he feels as well as on the first day of the campaign."[30] Roosevelt was ready to go when the train pulled away from the siding in Spring Station bright and early on Monday morning.

Lexington.   Even though it was an early rally at the beginning of the work week, the reception for Roosevelt in Lexington was uniformly reported as large and enthusiastic.[31] As far away as El Paso, Texas, readers of the Associated Press report learned: "Horseless Rough Riders in uniform and 200 strong acted as an escort to Cheapside, Courthouse Square. There 10,000 people filled all available space and climbed telegraph poles to get a view of the stand."[32] It was "one of the largest demonstrations of the day. . . . Apparently everybody in Lexington was at the railway station or at the speakers' stand, or in front of the courthouse. The expression of enthusiasm was limited only by the crowd's ability and facilities for making noise, and when the Governor spoke he was given the closest attention."[33]

Roosevelt continued with his Kentucky theme: "Last year you elected a Legislature to choose a senator and saw a Legislature that had not been elected choose a different senator. . . . We will never see our government fall unless we connive at and condone the outrages upon the ballot, that corruption of the franchise which puts in power against the will of the people those who sit in office, and deprives the office of the men honestly entitled to sit there. . . . Party leaders who cheat for your interests, if it agrees with their interests, will cheat you as they have cheated foes before."[34]

Winchester.   "At Winchester, where the Roosevelt train arrived at 9:30 a.m., was another big crowd and a procession. The latter feature was provided, notwithstanding that the speakers' platform was only 600 feet from the train. When Governor Roosevelt stepped out on the platform he was greeted with cheers of applause. The Governor's voice is in excellent condition and his speeches have been interrupted repeatedly with cheers."[35]

Mt. Sterling.   Roosevelt's train continued eastward from Lexington headed for an intersection with the Ohio River before turning northwest toward the second major stop in Covington. It was a long loop, and the stops during the day were necessarily brief. The difference in Republican reports and

Democratic coverage is clearly illustrated by newspapers with stories on the visit to Mt. Sterling. Maintaining its solid support, the *Indianapolis Journal* reported: "At Mt. Sterling, a mountain town, another demonstration of generous degree and proportion was provided and the Governor spoke to an enthusiastic crowd."[36]

Those who favored Bryan would have preferred reading the coverage of the *Mt. Sterling Advocate*: "Terrible Teddy, the intellectual ex-cowboy, has come and gone. His coming had been extensively advertised, and, consequently, with this extra attraction, combined with the usual Court Day crowd, a large number of people were in the city. Possibly 5,000 people were in hearing of the distinguished gentleman, which he faced from a platform erected in front of the Court House wall. It was half past ten when he arrived. He was briefly introduced by Major Wood, and spoke about ten minutes, saying among other things, that Bryanism and Goebelism represented everything that stood for dishonor and cowardice abroad. He did not say anything about shooting that fleeing Spaniard in the back, anything about a half drunken cowboy being as good as a farmer or mechanic, or anything about the Ninth and Tenth regiments of colored troops saving his regiment from annihilation at San Juan. He appealed to the good people to support him and his ticket and thereby save the country from destruction."[37]

Ashland.   "The meeting was in a grove of oak trees on a hill back of the town. There was a space of several acres in the middle of the grove that was quite clear of trees. Two stands had been erected, one of them for the speakers and the other for the glee club which was 50 strong and sang with a great volume of harmony. There was also a brass band that was powerful, even if the wind instruments were somewhat wheezy. In the open space 2,000 or more people were gathered. There was a considerable number of mountaineers, among them long, unkempt, wild-eyed fellows who roved uneasily up and down through the audience, greeting one another in uncomplimentary terms and in tones that had no reference to the fact that speaking was going on from the stand. Most of the people in the audience wore McKinley badges, but many of [the mountaineers] had on Bryan insignia."[38]

Greenup.   "Today at Greenup, a quarrelsomely drunken Democrat insisted upon breaking up the meeting by roaring Bryan's name in the face of the orator of the day. Gov. Roosevelt ignored the man once or twice until he saw a movement among the Republicans about him that boded ill for the peace of the occasion. Then he asked the drunken man why he forgot to cheer for Aguinaldo. The question put the Republicans on the platform in a good humor and turned the edge of their resentment, but the man below let out another whoop for Bryan. 'The man who interrupts a public meeting,' said Gov. Roosevelt, 'is usually a coward. He generally proves that he is a coward by getting behind somebody when his interruptions are noticed. You will always find the coward behind the lines.' The interrupter was rapidly making for the rear. 'There is only one thing that tends to excuse a man for such conduct,' said the Governor, continuing, 'and that is intoxication.' In the roar of applause and laughter that followed the man who had drawn down those remarks upon himself was altogether lost sight of."

Maysville. This Kentucky community with slightly more than six thousand people in 1900 supported a Republican newspaper and a Democratic newspaper. The Republican publication—whose editor introduced Roosevelt—was, naturally, enthusiastic in its report: "It was Teddy's Day! And a bright and beautiful one it was, showing that all nature smiled in unison with the occasion. . . . Colonel Roosevelt's special train did not reach the city until 4:45, but the large crowd was entertained by a speech from Hon. Augustus E. Wilson of Louisville, who, by the way, is a Maysville boy. . . . He held his large audience enraptured for two hours and 45 minutes, and only gave way upon the arrival of Governor Roosevelt's special train, the approach of which was greeted by such an outburst as was perhaps never heard in this city before. . . . As the train stopped opposite the platform, the police cleared a passageway, and Governor Roosevelt was led to the stand and introduced by Editor Davis of *The Ledger*. Within the limits allotted to the Governor it was hardly expected that he should make anything in the nature of a speech, as his schedule gave him less than 15 minutes at this point. . . . He implored [the crowd] to preserve inviolate the sacred right of suffrage accorded to every man. . . . It is safe to say that the presence of Governor Roosevelt, not only in Maysville but throughout Kentucky at large, will have a wonderful influence in moulding opinion. It has given the Republicans new heart, while the Goebelized Democracy is correspondingly depressed."[39]

Not surprisingly, the Democratic publication in Maysville was not as generous. Two days after the event, it continued its coverage with this letter to the editor signed by a reader named George R. Gill: "I am an independent Democrat. I wear no collar. I call no man master. I staid [*sic*] in town Monday for the first time in months to hear the Republican speakers. . . .

The interest centered in Theodore Roosevelt the candidate for Vice President on the Republican ticket. I had seen and heard for 50 years the most of the celebrated orators, preachers, and lecturers in the U.S. I took special pains to hear Teddy, to get near, and to see him. To say that I was disappointed, but feebly expresses the result. I was simply disgusted. He had a grand audience so far as numbers were concerned, but he mistook its character and shot underneath even them. He evidently did not know Kentucky people. The cow and calf story he told had whiskers on it when Methuselah was a baby. Its vulgarity and obscenity were patent. Teddy would make a good second clown in a circus. There were ladies in his audience, but luckily they were of too pure minds to catch the drift of his dirty joke."[40]

Conclusion

Roosevelt's bold determination to denounce Democrats, William Jennings Bryan, and both Bryanism and Goebelism brought particular stridency to his speeches throughout Kentucky. This was an area of the nation beset by a tendency toward violence, and in that regard was a threatening environment for the Republican candidate at least the equal of Colorado. Though some of the traveling journalists poked fun at Roosevelt's hosts in Kentucky, a few reports made it obvious that the Republican planners in the state were aware of the risks and attempted to address them. Roosevelt's efforts were courageous—perhaps foolhardy—but in November Kentucky was not counted in the Republican column.

CHAPTER 16

OHIO, WEST VIRGINIA, AND MARYLAND

Any Republican campaigning for national office in Ohio from the 1880s through the turn of the twentieth century had to deal with a number of significant power brokers. Marcus Hanna was at the top of the list, and William McKinley was, by default, among the elite on the list as well. Another man no one could ignore was Joseph B. Foraker, who was in 1900 a United States senator from Ohio and who had been the state's governor from 1886 to 1890. Though he was one of the leading Republicans on the scene, he was occasionally at odds with Hanna and McKinley, and eventually he would have a serious and public falling out with President Theodore Roosevelt. However, for the election of 1900, relations were sunny. Foraker accompanied Roosevelt to many of his Ohio stops and served as one of the luminaries who shared speakers' stands with the vice presidential candidate.[1]

So critical and well-recognized was the need to maintain a positive relationship between the McKinley forces and Foraker that a meeting between Roosevelt and the Ohio senator in Dayton on Tuesday, October 16, 1900, was celebrated on a campaign item. It is a five-and-a-half-inch long, reddish-tan ribbon meant to be pinned to a lapel with the words "Vice President—Roosevelt and Foraker Meeting; Oct. 16, 1900."[2] This ribbon's existence records for history that the meeting occurred and underlines its importance.

Students of the issues and events of presidential elections in the United States are well-advised to pay attention to the material culture of campaigns, particularly those that occurred during the 1896 to 1920 period, known as "the golden age of the political celluloid."[3] There was, in fact, a tremendous variety in the types of campaign devices used to promote party tickets, generate enthusiasm, highlight issues, or join two or more candidates in the public's mind. Among the types of items distributed during the presidential election of 1900 were such things as buttonhole studs, gold or silver bug pins, metal shell badges, metal tokens, ribbons, political postcards, watches and watch fobs, metal trays, bandanas, handkerchiefs, banners, ceramic and glass items to sit on shelves or hang on walls, lithographed portraits and posters, cigar boxes, dinner pails, dolls, wooden collar and jewelry boxes, torches and lanterns, transparencies, canes, umbrellas, aluminum combs, pencils, flags, figural pipes, clocks, and parade uniforms. Each item carried an image, a slogan, the date of an event, or a pointed reminder of a national or regional issue.

Despite this variety of campaign materials, the single most common type of item in the 1900 campaign was the celluloid button, a device of fairly recent origin at the time. "On December 3, 1893, a patent was granted to a Boston woman, Amanda M. Lougee, for a clothing button with a textile surface covered with a thin sheet of transparent celluloid. Her patent was soon acquired by the Whitehead and Hoag Company of Newark, New Jersey, which on July 22, 1896, secured patent rights to the celluloid button as we know it today: a printed paper disk under celluloid set into a metal collet with one of several types of fastening devices."[4]

Accounts from the stops along Roosevelt's entire western tour mentioned enthusiastic supporters who were wearing buttons or ribbons. Many of those lapel items were produced by merchants for sale; others were distributed by state campaign committees or local Republican clubs to promote the candidates or the planks in the party platform. There were posters in storefronts, signs carried by paraders, and decorations in meeting halls with slogans or pictures. Everywhere there were Rough Rider costumes, made and worn to demonstrate party loyalty and to honor Theodore Roosevelt, the hero of the war with Spain. Despite the hesitancy of Mark Hanna and a few others among the Republican leadership to put Roosevelt on the ticket, there was clearly an understanding of the power of his image in their marketing effort. His face was on millions of buttons, and symbolic Roosevelt attire dressed tens of thousands along his whistle-stop route.[5]

Electronic media have blunted the significance of celluloid buttons in twenty-first century political campaigns, although election committees continue to produce a selection of the lapel devices—perhaps more as nostalgic reminders of an earlier time in American history or simply because voters expect to see them. But the variety and style of the golden age is no longer in evidence. Here is but one example of how it was: "With a total solar eclipse appearing on May 28, 1900, commercial political minds found a way to exploit the astronomical sight for campaign fodder. A variety of buttons depicted Bryan eclipsing McKinley or McKinley eclipsing Bryan, accompanied by such predictions as 'Total Eclipse Nov. 6' or 'Partial Eclipse/

Will Be Total in November.'"[6] So competitive and potentially lucrative was the material aspect of golden-age campaigns that "well over 200 companies were involved in the manufacture of campaign buttons."[7]

Ohio was an important market for button sales at the end of the nineteenth century. Not only was the state home to Senators Hanna and Foraker, two of the fiercest political animals of the period, but also Canton resident William McKinley was the sixth Ohioan to become president of the United States. Political awareness was high, and Republicans were feeling confident of victory in Ohio. As Roosevelt's train entered the state through Cincinnati, button manufacturers and sellers must have felt like retailers of children's toys at Christmas.

Meanwhile, members of the Republican National Committee were ready to open their Ohio gift of twenty-three electoral votes on November 6, and these party leaders were also expecting that the vice presidential candidate's visits would put a bow on the packages of six electoral votes from West Virginia and eight from Maryland. The final five days of Roosevelt's seven-week-long whistle-stop tour were just ahead, including a morning in Washington, DC, for a debriefing at the White House with President McKinley.

Following is a list of the reported stops of Theodore Roosevelt's vice presidential campaign special in Ohio, West Virginia, and Maryland. On the campaign's last day in Kentucky, this notice had appeared in several newspapers across the nation: "Governor Roosevelt announced that he will make only six speeches in Ohio. This removes six towns from the itinerary."[8] Whether journalists misconstrued private conversations as public announcements, opponents made mischief, or the Ohio State Republican Committee begged or demanded that Roosevelt honor the original schedule is unknown. Regardless, he made all planned stops in Ohio, adding a few unscheduled visits, and this announcement ran as his tour of the state was nearing its halfway point: "At noon on Thursday, [Roosevelt] will arrive in Wheeling, West Virginia, having made twenty-seven speeches in Ohio."[9]

As to the information in the following list, note that the published Ohio agenda showed the anticipated length of stops, not scheduled arrival times. West Virginia and Maryland lists were compiled stop by stop from newspaper reports. In all, there were twenty-eight reported stops in Ohio, nineteen reported stops in West Virginia, and one reported stop in Maryland. Between the last reported stop in West Virginia at Hinton and the stop in Baltimore, Roosevelt spent a morning with President William McKinley in Washington, DC. (There were references to "stops along the way" in West

Virginia and "other stops" in Maryland, but the available sources mentioned by name only those listed.)

Tuesday, October 16, 1900
   Cincinnati Ohio (departed at 8:00 a.m.)
   Hamilton (unscheduled)
   Middletown (20 min.)
   Miamisburg (20 min.)
   Dayton (2 hrs.)
   Springfield (50 min.)
   Yellow Springs (unscheduled)
   Xenia (40 min.)
   South Charleston (20 min.)
   London (30 min.)
   Columbus (evening events and overnight)
Wednesday, October 17, 1900
   Delaware (30 min.)
   Marion (20 min.)
   Upper Sandusky (20 min.)
   Carey (10 min.)
   Fostoria (30 min.)
   Bradner (train stop for water)
   Pemberville (20 min.)
   Toledo (2 hrs.)
   Fremont (30 min.)
   Clyde (unscheduled)
   Bellevue (unscheduled)
   Norwalk (30 min.)
   Elyria (30 min.)
   Cleveland (evening events and overnight)
Thursday, October 18, 1900
   Akron (20 min.)
   Canton (20 min.)
   Navarre (unscheduled)
   Scio, West Virginia
   Dillonvale
   Long Run
   Warrenton
   Martin's Ferry

Wheeling
Benwood
Moundsville
New Martinsville
Sistersville
St. Mary's
Waverly
Parkersburg (evening events and overnight)
Friday, October 19, 1900
Ravenswood
Mason City
Point Pleasant
Huntington
Charleston
Hinton (departure 9:45 p.m. for Washington, DC)
Saturday, October 20, 1900
Washington, DC 7:00 a.m. (visit with President McKinley)
Baltimore, Maryland 5:45 p.m. (departure 11:45 p.m. for New York City)

Six community visits in these three states will be reviewed as major stops for the Roosevelt campaign: Dayton, Columbus, and Cleveland in Ohio; Wheeling and Parkersburg in West Virginia; and Baltimore in Maryland. Cincinnati was the entry point for the campaign special, but the lateness of the hour following the event across the Ohio River in Covington, Kentucky, limited what Roosevelt could do in the city. "After the speaking [in Covington], Governor Roosevelt was escorted by the First Voters' Club of Cincinnati to the Grand Hotel, in that city, where an informal reception was held, and where he will remain until tomorrow morning, when he will enter upon his itinerary in Ohio."[10] Roosevelt and his party left at 8:00 a.m. for the tour through Ohio's towns and cities.

Major Stops in Ohio, West Virginia, and Maryland

Dayton, Ohio.   With a population of eighty-five thousand people in 1900 and a signal role in the state's economy, Dayton merited the attention accorded a major stop, but its location on Roosevelt's route between Cincinnati and Columbus meant that national media reports gave the events there somewhat short shrift as compared to those farther up the road. Arrival at 11:00 a.m. on a Tuesday interrupted the workflow in offices, factories, and other places of business for any who desired to join the rally. Still there was a crowd and the good people of Dayton showed enough enthusiasm to draw sarcasm from one of the corps of traveling journalists.

Upon arrival, the crowd made the visitors feel welcome. "It was reserved for Dayton . . . to raise the roof over Republicanism by the quantity and quality of their whoops and howls. . . . There was a conservative sort of a mob at the station. It didn't lift the cars off the tracks or pull the station down. It simply remarked in tones and expressions that had no doubtful meaning that it was glad that Gov. Roosevelt had come."[11] Escorts moved the celebration to the Beckel House Hotel for a public reception. Here the locals became unruly in the eyes of one visiting reporter: "It was meant to be a reception, but it was more like a riot. The lobby of the hotel was impassable two minutes after Gov. Roosevelt arrived. The rush to reach his hand was so impulsive that access to the parlor where he stood was cut off and he simply came out to a railing overlooking the lobby and bowed to the populace. They tried to climb the air to reach him and failing that insisted on a speech, but the Governor shook his head."[12]

After the reception at the hotel, there was a parade reviewed by Roosevelt, and then the dignitaries moved to the fairgrounds where an overflow audience awaited the program inside a huge tent. "The Governor began to speak and the people began pouring into the entrance of the tent who had stayed down town to see the parade. They couldn't get in. They pushed. . . . The police were helpless. . . . The Governor had to stop talking and tell the police what he thought of the way they were handling the crowd. . . . The police closed the entrance of the tent and conditions were better for a while."[13] Apparently, there was no intent to be disorderly or to disrupt; rather, there were more people eager to see Roosevelt than capacity would allow, and those outside had an unyielding determination to push inside until the candidate insisted that the police control the situation.

When things quieted, Roosevelt said: "You have had four of the most prosperous years in your history. Here in Dayton the six largest factories in your city have handed me an abstract of the increase in their business. Their increase in the amount of wages paid during these four years and the increase in business have been about at the rate of 140 percent on the average. . . . Now let the business man and the wage worker compare that with Mr. Bryan's prophecies."[14]

Lindsay Denison, the reporter who made the tour for the *Sun* out of New York City, often had sly and slightly off-center ways to include anecdotes in his stories. He wrote of one moment in the Roosevelt speech: "The Governor inquired, in the most pointed manner, whether anybody had heard if Mr. Bryan had answered the questions asked him at Evansville about the payment of the nation's obligations in gold or silver, and the rest. Nobody in the audience seemed to have heard from Mr. Bryan on these subjects."[15]

By early afternoon, Roosevelt and his companions were ready to continue on their journey from Dayton to Columbus. There were several shorter visits between these major stops.

Columbus, Ohio. Roosevelt's special pulled into Columbus at 7:30 p.m. and an immediate transfer to the Goodale Street Auditorium, where the rally was scheduled, might have been the most logical expectation. However, the planning committee had other ideas: "For two hours the Governor rode in a brilliantly illuminated electric car in a great parade which traversed High and other principal streets of this city. The parade was more than two hours passing a given point and its course was marked by a blaze of colored fire, rockets, firing of cannon, and bursting of bombs."[16]

Columbus was alive with enthusiasm, and the local Republicans were going to make the most of it: "Not once since the great Blaine demonstration in 1886 has this city been so crowded with visitors as it is tonight, the occasion of the appearance here of Governor Roosevelt. Every hotel is full and hundreds of those who came to see or hear the Governor are being cared for at the homes of residents of Columbus. Ten speeches made to large audiences since leaving Cincinnati at 8 o'clock this morning had not impaired the Governor's vocal organs, nor did he show any evidence of fatigue when he was introduced at the Auditorium at 9:30 p.m. An impatient throng had been awaiting him nearly two hours."[17]

Apparently the long wait had not dampened the mood of the seven thousand people who were jammed into a space with a capacity of six thousand. "When he strode across the platform the Governor was greeted with a roar of applause. . . . When Governor Roosevelt rose to speak he was given such an enthusiastic greeting that for five minutes he could not make his voice heard in his endeavor to restore order."[18] His speech to the people of Columbus repeated the themes and used the terms that had been Roosevelt's stock-in-trade since the first week of the long campaign tour.

Roosevelt and his party overnighted in Columbus. They continued with the Ohio tour the following morning.

Cleveland, Ohio.   After another full day of campaigning, the Roosevelt special pulled into Cleveland around 6:00 p.m., looking ahead to a full evening that included three rallies on an agenda with a good bit of marching and parading between events. The meetings occurred in a large tent erected in the Newburg Iron Works district, at the Armory, and outside the Hollenden Hotel. Crowding the thoroughfares were tens of thousands of people who spent the entire evening enjoying streets "glistening with electric lights and decorated pillars." As most every community claimed: "Cleveland does not remember another such night of political parading."[19]

These are some of the details as reported by an Ohio journalist: "This was a day of triumph for Roosevelt in Ohio. Tonight Cleveland gave him a reception rivaling any similar demonstration ever made here. There was an immense parade, consisting of half a score of brass bands and a dozen political organizations. Superior Street, through which the parade passed, was a blaze of electric lights. Thousands of rockets and flambeaux flared. The walks were thronged. Riding in a gorgeously decorated carriage, drawn by four white horses . . . Roosevelt was escorted to a large tent on Marcelline Avenue, in the Newburg Iron Working District, where he addressed a large audience on prosperity."[20]

It was at this first event that things did not go exactly as the Cleveland committee would have preferred. "The Newburg meeting, in the iron workers' district, was thoroughly disorderly. The Bryan element got early into the tent in which the meeting was held and stayed there until the place was filled right up and hundreds of good Republicans were left outside out of hearing. The police did what they could to suppress the disturbers, but were not very successful. There was a persistent hissing of the Governor from the Bryan-packed corners when he appeared. The Governor, however, showed his grit by speaking three times as long as he had intended and meeting every assault on his patience with a cheerful and expansive smile."[21]

As the candidate left the Newburg tent to move to the second rally, a young boy threw a stone that hit Roosevelt in the head. Immediately the group escorting the governor surrounded him and got him to a nearby vehicle. In a later interview, Roosevelt said: "I was not hurt at all. The rock was thrown by one of a number of hoodlums and I saw him throw it. It struck my head but my hat prevented it from wounding me. In the light of the splendid reception Cleveland has given me, the stone-throwing is scarcely worth remembering for a moment."[22]

Again at the Armory, where the crowd size was estimated at twenty thousand, there were attempts to disrupt with hoots and shouts, but in this case, the "groans of disapproval" from the rest of the audience drowned out those determined to cause a problem, and the interruptions ceased. Roosevelt said to the Armory crowd: "I am very glad to have a chance to see you. It seems to me that I have come here not to try to teach you anything, but rather to hear a good message from you, for I shall go back to New York and tell them that I want New York to try well as Ohio is doing. Ohio is going to make the riffle. It is going to be a washout."[23]

Roosevelt's long day and evening ended with yet another rally and brief speech outside the Hollenden Hotel late at night. He had made more than a dozen speeches during the various stops, and all of them, of course, were shouted in a loud voice in those days a decade before amplification systems were available. So serious was the concern for his throat that his personal throat specialist, Dr. Holbrook Curtis, traveled to Columbus from New York City and joined Roosevelt for the rest of the trip through Ohio.

Journalists learned and reported that Dr. Curtis gave the candidate several treatments after finding his voice strained and his throat inflamed. The physician released this statement: "Governor Roosevelt's voice depends upon the avoidance of over-fatigue. If he exercises a little more care than he has in the past, I think he may be able to fulfill his engagements, but I could not guarantee any voice where 25 speeches are made on two consecutive days, with interrupted rest and under great nervous strain. Otherwise Colonel Roosevelt is in superb physical condition."[24]

For Roosevelt, however, the schedule was the schedule, and he was a man determined to do his duty. The campaign special pulled away from Cleveland at 3:00 a.m.

Wheeling, West Virginia. During the morning of Thursday, October 18, 1900, Roosevelt's campaign special made three stops in Ohio and five stops before arriving at Wheeling over the lunch hour. Arrival time was variously reported as 12:00 noon, 12:45 p.m., and 1:15 p.m., with the last of those most likely accurate. When the train pulled into the station, factory whistles blew a greeting and the five thousand people who had gathered shouted their welcome. As an Ohio River city of nearly forty thousand people with good rail service bridging into the neighboring state, Wheeling was an important commercial center that merited attention from the vice presidential candidate.

Few other newspapers across the nation had given nearly the amount of space to wire service stories on Roosevelt's entire trip as the *Wheeling Daily*

Intelligencer. Rivaling the *Indianapolis Journal* (refer to chapter 14), the *Intelligencer* was a Republican-leaning voice with a long history that worked to maintain its legitimacy as a newspaper. John Frew had owned the publication since the 1860s, and this is the assessment by scholars at West Virginia University: "While Frew and his editors expressed strong political opinions, pursued political offices, and benefited from political patronage, they did not abandon the paper's spirit of neutrality, nor compromise its commercial success to advance their personal ambitions and views."[25]

For weeks the *Intelligencer* built local interest in Roosevelt's trip, and for days prior to his stop in Wheeling, the newspaper published every detail of the agenda, including the order of march, the names of committee members, and the minute-by-minute schedule. Quite naturally, the coverage of this outstanding local newspaper is at the heart of the information available on the Wheeling stop.[26]

"When the Roosevelt special pulled in at the Terminal Station . . . an effort was made to disembark from the rear platform, but the crowd surged around in such a press that the local committee decided to execute a flank movement by taking Colonel Roosevelt and his party through the train to the first coach, and there disembark near the waiting carriages. . . . When Teddy's spectacled countenance with its pleased smile and uplifted Rough Rider hat appeared at the car door, the thousands united in one glad cry of welcome. . . . After the carriages had been entered, they were drawn up in line on Eighteenth Street, and the Rough Rider Regiment and other marching clubs passed in review before Colonel Roosevelt. . . . When the last club had passed in review, Governor Roosevelt's and the other carriages fell in line."

Everyone's political sympathies were obvious by their use of campaign devices: "The most remarkable feature of the demonstration was the unanimity of the badges worn by the people on the sidewalks." Also, local merchants used political imagery and participation in this big event to spur sales: "Hannon Bros. presented Governor Roosevelt with a box of their Rough Rider Cigars."

"Colonel Roosevelt's and the other carriages were driven into the track enclosure [at the fairgrounds], and when the 7,000 people in the grandstand and the 13,000 that filled the space in front of that structure caught their first view of the familiar countenance of the candidate, their enthusiasm knew no bounds. The applause continued until Colonel Roosevelt reached the speaking stand. . . . It was 2 o'clock when the Roosevelt party reached the stand, and it was decided to push the exercises with all speed, in order that the special might leave for below [i.e., south in West Virginia] within a few minutes of its scheduled hour, 2:30."

Because the crowd in the grandstand would not be quieted, Roosevelt jumped onto one of the press tables on the stage "and obtained a fair degree of order." He required quiet not just in the service of orderliness, but it was also critical in order that the crowd could hear his remarks. "[Roosevelt] spoke with some difficulty, and his usually strong voice would break slightly, showing that it is in none too good condition."

Anti-Roosevelt circulars had become commonplace, and most were of the variety he had been warring against for the past couple of weeks. In Wheeling, Roosevelt attacked the pamphleteers directly: "Before I make the remarks I have to make I want to call your attention to a circular that has been circulated on these grounds by a lot of scoundrels. It contains what purports to be extracts from speeches I am said to have made. . . . They dare not give the dates of the speeches because there were no such speeches in Chicago or New York or anywhere else. The statements are lies, known to be lies by those who started them and by those who circulated them, and it is characteristic of the party . . . that takes refuge in the foulest and most deliberate mendacity when all other methods fail."[27]

Roosevelt spoke in Wheeling for only a few minutes because of his throat issues and because the schedule for the day was running late. As soon as he concluded his address, Roosevelt and his fellow travelers left for the station, and they pulled out of town at 2:50 p.m.

However, Wheeling was not finished celebrating: "The night demonstration on the streets by the Republican marching clubs of Wheeling, together with many visiting clubs from West Virginia, eastern Ohio, and western Pennsylvania, was a spectacle of magnificence without a parallel in Wheeling's political annals. . . . Altogether by actual count over 2,300 men were in line, and the crowds on the street that enacted the role of spectators numbered 40,000 or 50,000. . . . Fully two-thirds of the crowd wore McKinley and Roosevelt badges."

Parkersburg, West Virginia. Though Parkersburg was a moderate-sized community in 1900 with barely twelve thousand people, newspaper stories reported crowds that exceeded the local population. Trains from communities in southeastern Ohio and western West Virginia brought hundreds, perhaps thousands, into Parkersburg. This coverage of the events ran in Ohio's *Marietta Daily Leader:* "Last night Parkersburg was the scene of one of the largest political demonstrations ever witnessed in the Ohio Valley. There were at least 15,000 people on the streets. . . . Two meetings were held in order to give everybody a chance to hear the noted speakers who were present. The street parade was a mile and a half long, and in many places the police had to use force to get the crowd to give way. . . . At 8:40 eastern time the parade reached the Wigwam which was already filled."[29]

Roosevelt addressed familiar themes at the Wigwam, speaking to an audience of five thousand, and then he hurried to the auditorium for another speech heard by two thousand. For Roosevelt's speeches, the themes and references were familiar, but this charming incident occurred: "A lady near the platform attempted to force her way out and the Governor stopped speaking to help her by asking the crowd to give way. Her child began to cry and one of the men on the platform said, 'Shut the child up.' 'Never mind,' said the Governor, 'I know how it is; I have six of my own.'"[30]

One aspect of the Parkersburg stop would not have been seen as charming by those affected: "A gang of pickpockets boarded the excursion . . . and literally went through the train robbing people right and left of their money. The coaches were all so crowded that it was an easy matter for the thieves to do their nefarious work without fear of detection. . . . An old gentleman from Beverly lost $140. . . . Another man lost a $60 gold watch. . . . Brakeman Fred Congrove, who was collecting tickets, had his overall pocket slit and about 85 cents in change taken."[31] This was the first mention for a couple of weeks of the vexing and recurring problem with pickpockets.

Roosevelt and his party remained overnight at Parkersburg. The campaign special left at 5:00 a.m. for the second day in West Virginia. The next day would bring the final leg of the tour ending at Baltimore, Maryland.

Baltimore, Maryland.   Union Station in Baltimore was the arrival point for the Roosevelt special at 5:45 p.m. on Saturday, October 20, 1900.[32] Two meetings were planned for the Music Hall—one inside and one outside—with events there beginning at 8:30 p.m.[33] Maryland's Republican State Committee had hoped to negotiate a parade and public reception in honor of the candidate, but Roosevelt indicated a preference to rest in his railcar until the rallies. Thus none of the street demonstrations typically part of a major stop were included in the schedule.[34]

As so frequently during the trip, there were rumors that Democrats or other groups might try to disrupt the events in Baltimore. However, the relatively minor interruptions that occurred were either enthusiastic applause for Roosevelt's speech or occasional "cheering and stamping of feet" when Bryan's name was spoken. Resting had been good for the candidate's throat:

"Governor Roosevelt was in fair voice and made his points with his usual vigor and emphasis."[35]

While Roosevelt's remarks generally centered on familiar themes and used oft-repeated illustrations, there was a unique target available and the candidate shot at it several times. US senator George Wellington was a Maryland Republican who had announced at a rally for William Jennings Bryan that he would leave the party over his opposition to McKinley's policies in the Philippines.[36] For Roosevelt, this made Wellington fair game.

Here is how Roosevelt treated the Wellington matter in Baltimore: "I noticed that last night the Honorable Wellington appeared in this hall on behalf of his new allies. From the psychological standpoint and chiefly from that, I have been interested in the mental processes by which Mr. Wellington has just found himself joined to Mr. Bryan. . . . He is trying to believe . . . but his views are of the gold standard; he loves the gold standard, while Mr. Bryan loves free silver. . . . Mr. Wellington is for protection, or was for protection; I do not know how sharply he has turned the corner since. . . . And so they came together. . . . You are always certain, gentlemen, when you follow a bold course to slough off certain men; but we have gained others . . . lifelong Democrats. . . . This is a contest in which Easterner and Westerner, Northerner and Southerner, wherever the man's birthplace might be, whatever his creed, his color or his national origin, is vitally interested, providing only he has the root of Americanism in him."[37]

Not only were there two rallies to serve all who wanted to see and hear Theodore Roosevelt, but there were also other speakers. Roosevelt's colleague, Curtis Guild, spoke, as did another traveling Republican orator from Massachusetts and a local Republican candidate for Congress. When he moved outside, Roosevelt told those present that their prosperity demanded a return to office for McKinley and that a vote to reelect the president was necessary to uphold the honor of the flag. After the festivities, Roosevelt and his party returned to the train and left at 11:45 p.m., bound for New York City and home.[38] Roosevelt's seven-week trip that had been billed as a campaign tour to the western states finally ended in the East at Baltimore, Maryland.

Highlights from Other Stops in Ohio and West Virginia

Hamilton, Ohio. "At this place, 25 miles from Cincinnati, Governor Roosevelt made the first stop today on his tour of Ohio, speaking to a large crowd. . . . A feature of the meeting was the presence on the platform of the mother of Captain Huston of Oklahoma. Captain Huston was an officer in Colonel Roosevelt's regiment in the war with Spain, and on the breaking out of the trouble in the Philippines he went thither, where he died. Governor Roosevelt escorted Mrs. Huston to the platform. 'I recall your noble son,' he said, 'and knew him well as a brave man and soldier.' Her reply was, 'Yes, Governor, I gave my son to my country and would give another if I were blessed with one.' Captain Huston's body is buried here."[39]

Middletown, Ohio.   Here Roosevelt addressed a large audience, and, snippy as always, the correspondent for the *Sun* from New York City couldn't avoid a little condescension: "Middletown has a cannon of which it should be proud. The cannon had more sense than the people of Middletown. They loaded it to burst. The cannon went off 20 feet from the Governor's car and it did not burst. But it wasn't the fault of the people of Middletown that the governor did not have powdered glass all over his dining table. Apparently, too, the people of Middletown were loaded the same way that they had loaded their cannon. None of them blew up, but it seemed as though every yell strained them."[40]

Miamisburg, Ohio.   Roosevelt addressed a large crowd, speaking from the front porch of the Miami Steel Company's headquarters facility.[41]

Springfield, Ohio.   "At Springfield another large crowd greeted the governor. As the train approached the city every factory whistle screamed a salute. The platform was within 100 feet of the train and on it with the governor were all the leading Republicans of this part of the state. Prosperity constituted the burden of the governor's speech, which was applauded loudly. The train stopped there nearly an hour."[42]

South Charleston, Ohio.   "The South Charleston people, when they found how late the meeting was to be [i.e., after dark], ran natural gas pipes up to the top of each of the four posts of the platform. They spurted streams of flame five and six feet long that blew back and forth with the wind. Gov. Roosevelt's voice has become so weakened that Col. Guild had to do almost all the talking at the smaller towns today. At South Charleston Gov. Roosevelt did not talk for more than three minutes."[43]

Delaware, Ohio.   "Delaware is the home of the Ohio State University [*sic*— Ohio Wesleyan College]. It is also the house of a hack driver who made up his mind to distinguish himself when he got the Governor into his carriage. . . . He had heard of Gov. Roosevelt as a Rough Rider. He made up his mind that the Governor should have a ride after his own heart in Delaware. . . . The driver started up the hill at a pace that made the Governor and his companions hold on to their seats and one another with both hands every time that the carriage struck a bump. When the Governor reached Gray Chapel, where he made his speech to 3,000 people, including the students of the university, the driver turned to him with pride and said: 'I guess you never rode much rougher than that, did you? It will be a long time before you forget your visit to Delaware.' . . . It was quite apparent that the man had no idea that the Governor had not passed through one of the most joyous treats of his life."[44]

Fostoria, Ohio.   "Fostoria, the glassmaking town, had arranged for the governor to speak from the balcony of the Hays House. The street was narrow and space was at a great premium. One citizen who fought and struggled on the sidewalk consoled himself audibly with the reflection that he had sold the use of his office window opposite the hotel for $3 for the morning."[45]

Bradner, Ohio.   "The train stopped for water at Bradner, a small town near Toledo. Soon after it started on, Dr. H. Holbrook Curtis and Col. Guild found a small boy on the front platform of the Minnesota crying as though his life was in danger. They took him in and he told them between sniffles that he was Howard Roe, that he was 11 years old, and that Salty Evans and Joe Pike and some other mean fellows had put him on and wouldn't let him get off until it was too late. He was very hoarse, and they learned that he had lost his voice at a political rally last Monday night. On his indignant denials that it was a Democratic meeting they took him up to Gov. Roosevelt, who took solemn counsel with him as to the best treatment for sore throat. Then Ballard and Henry, the servants of the Minnesota, filled his insides and Col. Guild provided him with a ticket from Pemberville back to Bradner. At the last moment, Roe was very grateful. 'Specially,' he said, 'cause it's my birthday.'"[46]

Toledo, Ohio.   "Toledo, the home and bailiwick of the Hon. Sucker Rod Jones,[47] turned out more people to see Gov. Roosevelt than have come out in any other city he has visited, except perhaps Indianapolis. He rode the whole length of the city at the head of a parade. The sidewalks all the way were full of people. The windows of all business buildings and residences were filled with women and girls. The jam on the sidewalks was frequently so great that the outer line of spectators was forced out into the streets and the parade was blocked. . . . Every ward in the city had a uniformed delegation in line. The workingmen wore nice clean overalls and jumpers; the businessmen wore grayer attire. At the very head of the parade, as escort to the Governor, was the famous Toledo Rail Splitters Organization in gorgeous purple and white uniforms that set off their machine-like marching to great advantage. The celebration ended with speech-making and a barbecue at the circus grounds on the outskirts of the city. Gov. Roosevelt made his speech against the opposition of successive brass bands which came up at the rear of the speakers' stand at regular intervals with sections of the procession. . . . The paraders were fed with 40 roasted oxen."[48]

Clyde, Ohio.   "At Clyde the employees of the granite and marble company presented the Governor with a bucket filled with sandwiches, pie, cake, and coffee, and bearing the legend, 'Eight hours and a full dinner pail.'"[49]

Norwalk, Ohio.   "At the Norwalk meeting, [Roosevelt] spoke from a stand which held the Ladies' McKinley Club, 300 strong, waving bright yellow parasols."[50]

Akron, Ohio.   "The train, having left Cleveland at 3 a.m., reached Akron soon after 4 o'clock and was held on a siding. Before 6 o'clock a crowd began to gather and at 7:00 a band came alongside the Governor's car, giving a serenade. . . . When the governor appeared on the platform of his car he was given a rousing chorus of cheers and was introduced while so many trains were passing that for five minutes he could not begin his speech. He appealed to the voters of Akron on the grounds of prosperity and patriotism. At one time the noise made by the engines was so great that the governor said: 'This speech will read like a serial story.'"[51]

"[The train] left Akron at 7:20 a.m. The run to Canton was made in 43 minutes. At each station along the line people congregated to get a flying glimpse of the candidate. The governor stood on the rear platform of the dining car and bowed and smiled as he was whirled through the villages between Akron and Canton."[52]

Canton, Ohio.   This community was a pivotal stop for Roosevelt because it was the home of President William McKinley and thus drew particular interest from the media. McKinley, of course, was in Washington, DC, at this time. While the traveling Rough Writers and other correspondents dutifully reported on the stop, the fullest and most entertaining coverage was provided by the local newspaper. Ironically, it was a Democratic publication in the hometown of a Republican president. The narrative that follows is a shortened version of the slanted story Canton's citizens read on the front page of the *Stark County Democrat.*[53]

"The special train bearing Governor Roosevelt and party arrived in Canton over the Valley at 8:03 a.m. . . . Upon his arrival at Canton the train was surrounded by an immense crowd, anxious to get sight of the gentlemanly cowpuncher, warrior, and politician. . . . Governor Roosevelt saw several camera fiends taking snap shots. He remarked: 'That is worse than Santiago.' The camera snapped, and the governor shook his head, deprecatingly.

"Governor Roosevelt was no sooner in the carriage than the spectators began to surround the vehicle and asked to shake hands with 'Teddy,' as they called him. He shook hands with quite a number in a mechanical sort of manner, at the same time conversing with Judge Day. Only once in a while at the depot did any semblance of a smile unbend his face. An old gentleman raised a curly haired little girl up to the governor's carriage to shake hands. The grim look left his face for a moment while he shook the little tot's hand.

"The governor was dressed in a Rough Rider hat, light gray overcoat, checked cutaway coat and waistcoat, and brown trousers. He wore a lay-down collar and small black string tie. He would be the last man one would pick out as well dressed; in fact his clothes looked anything but fine.

"The reception of the distinguished visitors was a most cordial one. Owing to the brief stop it was not possible to form a parade, so the Republican managers decided to rush the vice presidential candidate and his party from the train to the Tabernacle, and let him put in all of the time here talking. . . . The weather was most delightful and no untoward incident marred the visit.

"The Tabernacle was icy cold. People sat with their top coats turned up and their hats down over their eyes, yearning for some of Roosevelt's hot stuff. Somebody went over to the hall and felt the steam pipes and came back announcing that there really was heat in them. The crowd imagined itself warmer after that. . . . The audience was estimated at not more than 2,200. . . . [The introduction of Roosevelt included these words:] 'He is equally at home whether fighting the grizzly in the West or the Tammany tiger in the east.'

"The first thing Roosevelt did was to show his teeth. He was in good voice. . . . [He said in part:] 'I'm speaking not as a politician, but as a student of history. . . . The president has faced more grave problems, more great dangers to the nation, than any president since Lincoln. . . . I ask you to stamp under your heel the dark, savage flame of distrust. . . . If we treat each man only according to whether he does or does not do his duty as a citizen, there will be no class distinctions. . . . Our opponents seek to have you believe it is a good thing to act on the motto of "some men down," while we want to ask you to act on the motto, "all men up.'"

"Gov. Roosevelt bowed and stepped toward the rear of the stage. Half the audience rose to its feet, cheering. The shouting continued for a couple of minutes, while the governor left by the side door. He had spoken 22 minutes. . . . Roosevelt's train was scheduled to leave Canton at 8:40, but it was delayed until 8:55.

"The trouble with Mr. Roosevelt is that, while in every relation of private life he is a good fellow, an upright and honest gentleman, he has, as regards public matters, a direful and wicked maggot in his brain. He intoxicates himself with his own frantic garrulity until he believes—quite honestly we think—that he has some divine appointment to regenerate and purify the world."

Navarre, Ohio.   "The only stop between Canton and the Ohio River was at Navarre, where a short address was made. In introducing Governor Roosevelt, Governor Nash [of Ohio] said: 'I hope you will be very quiet now, for Governor Roosevelt only made 13 speeches yesterday and his voice is not in the best of condition.' . . . Just at this point, the governor's talk was interrupted by the train pulling out. The crowd cheered heartily."[54]

Martin's Ferry, West Virginia.   One regional newspaper had reported that Roosevelt's busy schedule and the likelihood of a lengthened stop at Canton would prevent a stop at Martin's Ferry. Yet, on the day of the run through the community, the local correspondent wrote: "Today will not only be a big day in the city of Wheeling, but also in Martin's Ferry. . . . Through the persistent efforts of a number of our prominent Republicans, our next vice president, Theodore Roosevelt, will deliver a five-minute address in this city from the rear platform of his special train en route to Wheeling. The train is due at the station on the Wheeling & Lake Erie road at 11:30 this morning. This city is very fortunate in securing the Governor for even a five-minute speech, as many cities triple this size will not be given the opportunity to see him."[55] Someone in this small community wielded greater power in political circles than the regional journalist realized.

Martin's Ferry had its stop at 1:00 p.m. on Thursday, October 18, 1900, and both Theodore Roosevelt and Governor Nash of Ohio appeared on the rear platform of the candidate's railcar. Roosevelt's brief remarks brought an ovation from the five thousand people who cheered him at the station.[56]

Benwood, West Virginia. "Colonel Roosevelt arrived on an Ohio River train at Benwood at 3 o'clock and addressed a crowd of over 2,000 for two minutes from the rear platform of the train. The space about the depot was crowded with people eager to hear the gallant Rough Rider, and the housetops were dotted with humanity. . . . Colonel Roosevelt was vociferously cheered during his brief address and it was with difficulty that he could be heard. As the train pulled out of the station the cheers did not subside until the train passed out of sight."[57]

Moundsville, West Virginia. "The Roosevelt special train was about a half hour late arriving at Moundsville, but the delay seemed to swell the large crowd and add to its enthusiasm. When the train arrived over 3,000 people were assembled and greeted the next vice president with great enthusiasm. Colonel Roosevelt was escorted from the car to a stand, which had been erected a short distance from the depot."[58]

New Martinsville, West Virginia. "The crowd at New Martinsville numbered 2,500. Governor Roosevelt . . . spoke for ten minutes, with frequent applause. . . . He said that he hated to interrupt the hum of prosperity in West Virginia by causing his train to stop even for 15 minutes."[59]

Sistersville, West Virginia. "At Sistersville there was a crowd of 5,000 and short speeches were made by Colonel Roosevelt and Colonel Guild to the accompaniment of tremendous applause."[60]

St. Mary's, West Virginia. "St. Mary's turned out a crowd of 2,000. Hon. W. D. Bynum had held the crowd for an hour and a half with a splendid presentation of the issues, and Colonel Roosevelt's train arrived just in time for the latter to add a characteristic five minute speech that set the crowd wild."[61]

"A crowd of 25 hoodlums collected on the outskirts of the crowd at St. Mary's, another oil town, and undertook to prevent Governor Roosevelt from making himself heard. They were partly successful for a while, despite the Governor's efforts taking shots at them. . . . A crowd of McKinley men took a hand in the matter, and going back to the disturbers, gave them the alternative of keeping quiet or taking a drubbing. It is not necessary to state which alternative was chosen."[62]

Huntington, West Virginia.   "The Roosevelt special train arrived here on time at 12:15 today. The party was met by the reception committee and escorted to the stand at Fifth Avenue and Ninth Street where they, with Governor Roosevelt, reviewed the magnificent parade, which in numbers was the largest ever seen in the city, after which he addressed over 15,000 people."[63] Unlike the miners in the western states, reports suggested that West Virginia's miners welcomed Roosevelt: "At some places in the mining regions there was a liberal use of powder in the cannonading as the special train arrived, and the miners got up all sorts of demonstrations in honor of the vice presidential candidate."[64]

Hinton, West Virginia.   This was the final reported stop in West Virginia. "Governor Roosevelt and party arrived in Hinton at 7:30 o'clock this evening. They were met at the station by a crowd of 3,000, while that many more were seated about the speakers' stand which had been erected in the park awaiting his arrival. . . . Cannons were fired, torpedoes exploded, and at the Chesapeake & Ohio shops nearby, many locomotive whistles were sounded on the arrival of the vice-presidential train. Roosevelt and Colonel Guild made addresses. The party left here at 9:45 by special train for Maryland."[65]

Conclusion

After Hinton, then Baltimore, the campaign tour of western states had concluded for Theodore Roosevelt, Curtis Guild, members of Roosevelt's staff, train company employees, and the Rough Writers. Many of them left Saratoga, New York, from the state's Republican Convention, and headed west on Thursday, September 6. It would now be early on Sunday, October 21, when their feet once again touched the soil of New York. They had visited large cities and small towns as far west as Idaho and Utah, as far north as North Dakota and Montana, as far south as Kentucky, and as far east as West Virginia and Maryland. It had been a remarkable trip—record-setting some said—and the miles, stops, speeches, handshakes, and numbers of citizens who had seen the candidate would be totaled and retotaled (see chapter 18).

There was one other stop of significance wedged between Hinton, West Virginia, and Baltimore, Maryland. Faithful to the last, Theodore Roosevelt stopped by Washington, DC, to report on his trip and its successes to President William McKinley at the White House. Very likely the vice presidential candidate was also looking for his next set of marching orders. When Roosevelt did reach New York and his family, he barely had time to take a breath before setting out again to blanket the Empire State with campaign stops and speeches.

Two of the Rough Writers covered the Washington, DC, stop. Lindsay Denison of the *Sun* wrote: "Gov. Roosevelt will arrive in Washington tomorrow morning [i.e., October 20]. He has engaged rooms at the Arlington."[66] A. G. Nevins of the Associated Press offered additional details: "Gov. Roosevelt arrived here this morning from the West. His special train pulled into the Sixth Street Station soon after 7 o'clock. The Governor went to the hotel for breakfast. Governor Roosevelt called at the White House at 10:30 o'clock this forenoon and was shown to the library, where he was at once joined by the President. The Governor was accompanied by Curtis Guild Jr. They remained with the President for an hour discussing the political situation. Mr. Roosevelt refused to be interviewed, stating that he could not at this time talk politics. At 11:30 this morning he took luncheon with the President, in company with Secretary Long and Lieutenant Commander W. S. Cowles of the Navy."[67]

After a Saturday morning in the nation's capital spent visiting and lunching with the president, Theodore Roosevelt returned to his railcar for the short trip to Baltimore. Surely he was looking beyond that destination to his home just over the horizon.

CHAPTER 17

NEW YORK, NEW JERSEY, AND PENNSYLVANIA

On October 21, 1900, the Sunday on which Theodore Roosevelt returned from his seven-week, vice presidential campaign tour, many newspapers across the nation ran feature stories on the likely outcome of the election. Voting would occur on Tuesday, November 6, and most citizens were, of course, vitally interested in whether William McKinley would return to the White House for another term or be displaced by William Jennings Bryan.

McKinley, the Republican, and Bryan, the Democrat, had run against each other in 1896, and McKinley had won the electoral vote 271 to 176, garnering 51 percent of the popular votes in the process. Reelection of the president seemed reasonably sure from the outset of the campaign—especially in view of an economy that had gone from depression to prosperity during his first term—but there were elements in the political environment that raised nagging doubts. Bryan was a spellbinder who was not afraid to work tirelessly on the campaign, and he enjoyed a solid block of Democratic southern states, as well as a natural constituency among blue-collar workers. Democrats carved issues out of public uneasiness over a conflict in the Philippines, resentment over perceived unfair practices by big business, and a currency issue that lent itself to sloganeering, even though its nuances were complex.

Strengthening the positives for McKinley was the addition of Theodore Roosevelt to the ticket. Garret Hobart, McKinley's first-term vice president, had died in office, and despite the misgivings of many Republican leaders, the young governor of New York was the popular choice to replace him for the second term. Roosevelt had come home from the war with Spain in 1898 a national hero. His life story was well known and compelling. Delegates to the Republican National Convention nominated him unanimously—except for his own vote—and suddenly he was the likely next vice president of the United States. As a bonus, he proved to be an able and willing campaigner who exceeded even William Jennings Bryan in miles traveled, speeches made, and hands shaken. In community after community, state after state, the crowds interested in seeing and hearing Roosevelt were remarkably large and enthusiastic. His detractors were ignored, and his missteps were overlooked. Generally speaking, he was masterful in his manipulation of the media.

Thus it probably surprised few readers when the Sunday edition of the *San Francisco Call* ran this headline on the front page of a special inside section focused on the national election: "Victory Sure for Prosperity." On the second page of the section, another headline made the message even clearer: "Bryan Defeat is Inevitable."[1] Under the front-page headline in a highlight box was this summary of the story that would fill several pages: "President McKinley's re-election is certain. A poll made by *The Call* and *New York Herald* of the principal states shows that McKinley will probably receive 281 electoral votes and Bryan 166, giving the Republican Party's standard-bearer a majority of 115 over the Democratic candidate."

According to the reports that followed, this was as sure and scientific a finding as one could reasonably expect in the late nineteenth century. These newspapers had stationed "men of experience" in pivotal states to gauge "public sentiment on political questions." They worked "absolutely without bias," and they made "a cold-blooded calculation" in order to form "what they considered the strong probabilities." Added to these analyses was "a canvass of major newspapers to ascertain their opinions on probable outcomes." This latter exercise produced "results said to be nearly identical."[2]

Among the conclusions of the experts were that the Republicans would hold all states they carried in 1896 except Kentucky, and that South Dakota, Kansas, Washington, and Wyoming would switch to the Republican column. Except for Washington, Roosevelt's tour had included all these states. West Virginia, Illinois, and Indiana were listed for McKinley, but the analysis acknowledged that these were not being won without struggles. Roosevelt had also visited these battleground states. Even Nebraska, Bryan's home state, was said to be in play, though the *Call* opined "state pride is likely to give the eight electoral votes to Mr. Bryan."[3] Roosevelt had been warmly welcomed at more than three dozen communities in Nebraska.

It was all, of course, informed conjecture, and experienced politicians knew then, as they know now, nothing was certain until the votes were cast, counted, and certified. Theodore Roosevelt had finished his tour of western, midwestern, and border states, and he was finally home with his family and friends, yet his campaigning was, by no means, completed. In fact, he would spend less than twenty-four hours at his home in Oyster Bay before he, once again, boarded a special train to begin an intensive, two-week tour of New York State. He was a nationwide celebrity and the governor of New York, but a landslide victory in his home state was uncertain. "It is not likely that in any eastern state will the plurality for McKinley be as large as in 1896. The plurality of 268,000 in New York will be more than cut in two."[4]

"New York, as the natural strategic point of the campaign, has become the great battleground. Mr. Bryan and his supporters realize that if they do not carry New York State, they will have no chance whatever of getting the election. Therefore the eyes of the country are on the Empire State. . . . Both parties are claiming the state, the Republicans with a much greater show of confidence. . . . In every county the estimates show a decrease more or less marked in the Republican majorities. . . . Generally speaking, the Republican strength is greatest in the eastern and northern parts of the state."[5]

It was not just the poll conducted and reported by the *San Francisco Call* and *New York Herald* that yielded this conclusion. For example, the *St. Paul Globe* reported on the same Sunday, sixteen days prior to the election: "New York State is the center of the political maelstrom. Conditions are rapidly changing, and with the Democratic candidate for president, as well as the Republican candidate for vice president, touring the state next week, estimates may have to be revised. Tonight a non-partisan review of the presidential situation based upon conservative estimates from up the state and from greater New York, gives the state to McKinley by a plurality much less than that of 1896."[6]

Thus the *Globe* reported: "From now on until Election Day, the campaign is to be a strenuous one in this state [New York]. Roosevelt and [Senator Chauncey] Depew, on separate special trains, will race up and down the state, reaching practically every county in it, and Mr. Bryan makes another trip through the Empire State next week. A great reception to Gov. Roosevelt is scheduled at Madison Square Garden next Friday. It will be made to eclipse, if possible, the great demonstration which marked the arrival of Mr. Bryan in New York the other night. The day following, Mr. Bryan is to have another great meeting in the same place, and it will be to the great delight of [Democratic boss] Richard Croker if he can make this meeting outshine not only the first Bryan meeting, but the Roosevelt demonstration as well."[7]

With stakes not unlike those facing competing gladiators and against the backdrop of eroding certainty, Theodore Roosevelt packed his suitcase and mounted his railcar for yet another two weeks of exhausting appearances. He was setting out to carry the Republican standard for what the *Indianapolis Journal* called the "spectacular finish in New York." It was to be political theater at its purest: "It is in the Empire State that the stage effects will be seen at their best. It is here that Bryan will make his last desperate charge, and it is upon the electoral vote of New York that he relies for success."[8]

Commenting further on the signal role of the Democratic boss of Tammany Hall, Richard Croker, and his promise to deliver New York to Bryan, the *Indianapolis Journal* had this note that sounds odd to the twenty-first-century ear: "Croker himself seems to think he will be able to make it good, although it is observed he is not at the present time betting his money that way. That fact possesses great significance in the minds of Mr. Croker's associates and in the minds of the bookmakers who take care of other people's bets on elections. . . . The sporting gentry argue that, if Mr. Croker is really as confident as he professes to be, he would be betting the opposition to a standstill. . . . The collector has been around in this case and a colossal slush fund has been raised and placed at the disposal of Mr. Croker, to be used as he alone may direct. He can put it all into the betting market if he wants to, or devote it entirely to other campaign use."[9]

Two economists from the University North Carolina, Paul Rhode and Koleman Strumpf, have studied the phenomenon of wagering on election outcomes, writing that it was once commonly practiced in the United States: "A large, active, and highly public market for betting on elections existed over much of U.S. history before the Second World War. . . . Although election betting was often illegal, the activity was openly conducted by 'betting commissioners' (essentially bookmakers) and employed standardized contracts that promised a fixed dollar payment if the designated candidate won office. The standard practice was for the betting commissioner to hold the stakes of both parties and charge a five percent commission on the winnings."[10]

According to Rhode and Strumpf: "Although such markets emerged in most major cities, New York was the center of national betting activity. . . . The extent of activity in the presidential betting markets of this time was astonishingly large. . . . Crowds formed in the financial district— on the curb or in the lobby of the New York Stock Exchange—and brokers would call out bid and ask odds as if trading securities."[11] These scholars have calculated that in 2002 dollars, the betting volume in New York for the election of 1900 was 63.9 million dollars.[12] Furthermore, "the market did a remarkable job forecasting elections in an era before scientific polling. In only one case did the candidate clearly favored in the betting a month before Election Day lose."[13]

Given this environment and the predictive power of the betting market, it was highly significant when the *Sun*, a New York City newspaper, included this report in its Sunday edition of October 21: "Men with money to bet on the election of President McKinley had to hunt with a dark lantern and a search warrant yesterday to find anybody who wanted to bet on Bryan. In Wall Street Bryan money had disappeared almost as completely as if it had never been there. All kinds of inducements were offered by McKinley supporters to draw Bryan money into the hands of the stakeholders, but there was nothing doing. In fact, in the last hope of getting a bet down, the men with McKinley money offered luxurious bets. . . . Cooper, Cramp & Beadleston announced that they had $4,000 to bet against $1,000 that McKinley would be elected. The news of this offer was sung through the street, but nobody appeared to have $1,000 which he cared to risk on such a proposition. . . . One customer remarked: 'Looks like it is all over but the shouting.' . . . A professional bettor uptown said: 'There's no use talking about election betting, for there isn't any. You can't find Bryan money. . . . I don't believe that 10 to 1 would draw out any Democratic money. The fact is, the bottom fell clean out of the Bryan campaign a little over a week ago and nobody with any sense is going to take the Democratic end of any betting proposition this fall.'"[14]

Despite this indicator of probable success, Theodore Roosevelt was ready for battle. He surely did not want to be embarrassed in his home state. His sense of duty compelled him to campaign for every vote to the end. While the polling, punditry, and wagering indicated a Republican victory, the New York vote could not be assumed. He would travel the rails and make the case for McKinley, for the Republican platform, and for himself.

In the assessment that New York was a very important toss-up and that last-minute effort was warranted, Roosevelt was not alone. This anecdote from the campaign trail was telling: "When the Governor arrived at the railway station at Elmira this morning there was pointed out to him a private sleeping cot in a private car in which was said to be reposing John G. Woolley, the Prohibition candidate for President. Then pretty soon the special train containing William J. Bryan, the democratic candidate for President, flashed through the station. Mr. Bryan was on his way westward and was not visible, and those in charge of the train did not have it stop at the Elmira Station."[15]

Roosevelt's Stops in New York, New Jersey, and Pennsylvania

Altogether Theodore Roosevelt made ninety-three reported campaign stops in the towns and cities of New York State between October 22 and November 2, 1900. Additionally, he departed on his special train twice from depots in New Jersey, did roll-through greetings in two other New Jersey communities, and stopped in four Pennsylvania villages along his route. One scheduled visit was reported as canceled en route: Little Falls, New York. As the second week of his trip progressed, Roosevelt also made the decision to forgo a planned tour of Long Island communities on Monday, November 5.

This is the broad outline of Roosevelt's planned trip, as it was reported at the outset by the *Evening World* of New York City: "He will whirl up as far as Kingston; then tomorrow he climbs to the apex of the Catskills, descending on the other side of the range into the Susquehanna Valley. Thence he runs up and touches at points along the Mohawk, then away out to Watertown on the east and back to Auburn in Central New York. Striking Syracuse on Thursday night, he comes down the Mohawk and Hudson Valley, reaching New York City on Friday night prepared to talk to many meetings. Saturday following he will rush along the Erie Road, reaching Binghamton that night and remaining over Sunday. The following week will find him at every place of importance in western New York and back in New York City on Saturday, November 3."[16]

These are the reported campaign stops of Theodore Roosevelt in New York, New Jersey, and Pennsylvania between October 22 and November 2, 1900. They are listed in chronological order:

Monday, October 22, 1900
    Weehawken, New Jersey
    West Nyack, New York
    Congers
    Haverstraw
    Cornwall
    Newburg
    Kingston
Tuesday, October 23, 1900
    West Hurley
    Shokan
    Phoenicia
    Pine Hill

Shandaken
Fleischmans
Arkville
Roxbury
Stamford
Bloomville
Davenport Centre
Oneonta
Otsego
Unadilla
Sidney
Norwich
Wednesday, October 24, 1900
Earlville
Cazenovia
Canastota
Oneida
Rome
Herkimer
Utica
Thursday, October 25, 1900
Camden
Watertown
Oswego
Sterling
Weedsport
Auburn
Syracuse
Friday, October 26, 1900
Little Falls (scheduled; later canceled)
Amsterdam
Schenectady
Albany
New York City
Saturday, October 27, 1900
Jersey City, New Jersey
Paterson (roll-through greeting)
Passaic (roll-through greeting)
Suffern, New York

Hillburn
Middletown
Port Jervis
Shohola, Pennsylvania
Lackawaxen
Cochecton, New York
Callicoon
Long Eddy
Hancock
Deposit
Susquehanna, Pennsylvania
Great Bend
Binghamton, New York
Sunday, October 28, 1900
    (Rested in Binghamton; no campaign events)
Monday, October 29, 1900
    Cortland
    Ithaca
    Van Etten
    Elmira
Tuesday, October 30, 1900
    Corning
    Bath
    Wayland
    Livonia
    Avon
    Geneseo
    Canandaigua
    Geneva
    Penn Yan
    Rochester
Wednesday, October 31, 1900
    Brockport
    Holley
    Albion
    Medina
    Lockport
    Niagara Falls
    North Tonawanda

Black Rock
Buffalo
Thursday, November 1, 1900
  Batavia
  Attica
  Warsaw
  Silver Springs
  Ellicottville
  Salamanca
  Little Valley
  Cattaraugus
  Dayton
  Dunkirk
  Jamestown
Friday, November 2, 1900
  Randolph
  Olean
  Friendship
  Cuba
  Wellsville
  Hornellsville
  Addison
  Waverly
  Oswego

As the previous chapters have shown, the whistle-stop tour of states in the West, the Midwest, and on the border of the Old South combined two strategies. The first was Roosevelt's idea that there should be a major stop in each state where he would make a significant public policy or campaign address. The second was the approach preferred by state leaders that there should be many stops in communities large and small. The result was a burdensome schedule for the candidate and his entourage.

New York was different in that Roosevelt was the governor, and he promoted the expectation that he would blanket his home state with visits. From the outset, the coverage was planned over a two-week period and intended to support not only the McKinley and Roosevelt national ticket, but also the gubernatorial candidacy of Benjamin Odell and other statewide and local Republican candidates for various offices. Thus the narrative that follows is organized not by presenting the details of major and then other stops, but with day-by-day summaries as Roosevelt and others were experiencing it—as a countdown to Election Day.

Monday, October 22, 1900—Fifteen Days to the Election

Roosevelt and his traveling party of thirty—staff, Republican leaders, candidates, and newspapermen—departed at 11:00 a.m. on the West Shore Railroad from Weehawken, New Jersey. It was an ambitious plan from the beginning: two weeks, more than two thousand miles, and nearly one hundred stops and speeches. Actually, it was a two-part trip. He would return to New York City on Friday, October 26, for a huge celebration in Madison Square Garden, and then on the next morning he would reboard the campaign special and spend another week touring the farthest western reaches of the state. Game to a fault, as he left the metropolitan area, Roosevelt said to his companions: "We are going to knock them out."[17]

From his initial speeches on his first day, Roosevelt established the message of his New York tour: he would attack Richard Croker, the Democratic boss of New York City, with accusations of trying to control the entire state, and he would tie Bryan to the evil intent of this urban power broker. Clearly, he had also learned from his gubernatorial whistle-stop tour in 1898 that he would be interrupted by his opponents in several locations, and he had apparently decided to go on the offensive. Early on this day, a listener shouted, "Hurrah for Bryan!" Roosevelt fired back, "Why don't you cheer for Aguinaldo [America's opponent in the Philippines]?" And then he declared that it would be a "shame and a disgrace to elect Bryan."[18]

Several hundred people awaited him in West Nyack, some in Rough Rider attire, and there was a band. During his speech, a heckler asked about the trusts, and Roosevelt glared at him before shouting, "How about rot? Intelligent men don't ask such questions, but ignorant chunkers like you do!"[19]

At Congers and Haverstraw, the crowd sizes were again between five hundred and one thousand, and the speeches went well with no interruptions. At the latter location, the crowd included many brick makers from a local factory, and Roosevelt criticized Bryan for trying to turn labor and management against one another.[20] At Cornwall, students from a military college fired a salute, and the candidate took the opportunity to speak of Bryan's foolish arguments about the danger of militarism.[21]

Newburg was the first of several larger stops—it was the hometown of the Republican gubernatorial candidate, Benjamin Odell—and Roosevelt stayed from 1:30 p.m. until 5:00 p.m. Odell was there to meet him, as was Odell's father, the former mayor of the community. Large crowds offered a warm greeting at the station and all along a parade route that ended at a park. Roosevelt spoke twice: once from a platform in front of the courthouse, and a second time to a crowd assembled behind the building. Supporters presented him with a dinner pail symbolically filled with fresh vegetables, and a group of college students gave him a rousing cheer.[22]

Again, Roosevelt responded to an antagonist in harsh terms: "A man present began shouting: 'Three cheers for Bryan!' He repeated this cry again and again until at last Governor Roosevelt turned toward him . . . and said: 'That gentleman has all the symptoms of a Bryanite. He is one of those people who work exclusively with their mouths.' 'Three cheers for Bryan!' shouted back the man. 'That's right,' answered Governor Roosevelt pointing his finger at him. 'You interrupt the meeting because you are a hoodlum. You belong to the disorderly classes which are naturally against us. You object to prosperity because you don't work. Go back to your fellow hoboes and learn to do something useful.' . . . The man by this time was moving away out of the crowd and Governor Roosevelt called out to him: 'I am glad you are going away. I think you will learn hereafter not to monkey with a buzz saw.'"

There was also this report from Newburg: "One of the most effective passages in his speech was where he reminded a colored member of the Grand Army of the Republic present that he, the colored man, could not vote in North Carolina and yet Mr. Bryan would give a vote to brown men in the Philippines who were shooting down soldiers of the United States Army."

This first day ended at Kingston where there were three large meetings planned: one at the Academy of Music, a second at the Kingston Opera House, and a third at the Young Men's Christian Association.[23] The overflow size of the crowds necessitated a fourth meeting out-of-doors.[24] Festivities included a parade along streets brilliantly illuminated, and though he was interrupted by Bryan supporters, Roosevelt dismissed them as "some whom we cannot reach," and he characterized them as men "who think noise is a substitute for thought." Furthermore, he said, "They had better holler now, for they won't holler after the election."[25]

Roosevelt's aggressive behavior was duly noted by Democrats. Richard Croker was quoted as saying: "That wild Governor of ours gets wilder all the time. How would the American people like him as president?"[26] A Democratic newspaper, the *St. Louis Republic*, reported: "Disappointed on every hand, the Rough Rider was nervous and irritable, and when at West Nyack and Newburg, cheers for Bryan were asked for by some of his auditors, Roosevelt fumed and lost all control of himself. He indulged in personalities with several individuals, and even the Governor's best friends do not hesitate to say that they were both shocked and amazed at his indiscretions."[27]

Tuesday, October 23, 1900—Fourteen Days to the Election

Before he finished his travels on Tuesday—two weeks before Election Day—Roosevelt traveled to several communities. Some were Catskill resort towns, and the summer season being well past, a few of the crowds were among the smallest he encountered. At West Hurley there were barely one hundred at the station. One journalist wrote: "The absence of the summer boarders was startlingly apparent. The carriages in which the boarding-house keepers came to the meetings were all of the queer summer-boarder types. There was a suggestion of faded summer-girl frivolity about the head-gear of some of the women."[28] Still, Roosevelt continued to pound away at the message that Boss Croker and the big-city Democrats of Tammany Hall were trying to extend their influence across the state.[29]

So it went along the length and breadth of this region of New York. At Shokan a factory steam whistle kept interrupting the speech, and Roosevelt referred to the hum of industry as evidence of the nation's prosperity under McKinley.[30] At Phoenicia, Roosevelt made the point that Bryan's solutions would destroy the country by telling "Charles Lamb's story of how the Chinese discovered roast pig was good, namely, by finding the pig roasted to death in a house which burned down, but said he did not believe, as the Chinese did for a while, that the way to roast pig was to burn down a house."[31]

Pine Hill hosted "a splendid gathering" with several flags and banners, one of which read, "No 50-Cent Dollars for Us!"[32] While the cheers at Shandaken were welcoming, there was one man who insisted on shouting, "Hurrah for Bryan!" Roosevelt asked, "Why?" And the man said, "Because he gave the poor people ice this summer in New York." Roosevelt replied, "If you believe that, I don't wonder you can hurrah for Bryan or anything else." Someone in the crowd shouted, "Never mind him!" Roosevelt said, "I like him. He amuses and interests me."[33]

Fleischmans had a band in the crowd; Roosevelt told his hearers that the interests of workingmen were the same as those of their employers.[34] When the governor saw a soldier in the crowd at Arkville, he addressed Bryan's charge of militarism, saying, "Think how preposterous the idea is of an army of 100,000 men overawing the nation of 75,000,000. Compare this soldier here with this crowd here, and the Army with the nation."[35]

Cheers for Bryan at Roxbury prompted this Roosevelt response that condensed several points he frequently used in these situations: "When a man says, 'Hurrah for Bryan,' I am inclined to say, 'Why?' Is it because Bryan is supported by Croker; is it because Mr. Bryan proposes to cut in two the nation's debt and pay all debts at 50 cents on the dollar, or do you want to say also, 'Hurrah for Aguinaldo,' and thus give the greatest amount of comfort possible to the yellow man in the Philippines who is shooting down the American soldier?"[36]

Still traveling with Roosevelt after the many weeks of campaigning was Lindsay Denison of the *Sun,* who never failed to entertain with his wry takes on locals. This is his narrative of the Stamford celebration: "A band with four nickel-plated wind instruments sat in a carry-all at Stamford, and as soon as the train stopped [the band] started the strains of 'The Star-Spangled Banner.' They played it to such slow time that it sounded like the death march in 'Saul.' The carry-all went slowly up the hill while the four players did the best they could to keep the instruments at their lips and their eyes on the governor at the same time. . . . There was an audience of 1,000 in the Opera House before the procession reached it. The procession got in somehow, most of it, but there were many left outside. . . . At the end of the meeting the men with the four nickel-plated horns got into their carriage again, and led the long line back down the hill. This time they played 'America.' The committee explained that the few Democrats in the town belonged most of them to the band and that they had refused to blow wind for any Republican candidate."[37]

When Roosevelt reached Oneonta, a prominent Gold Democrat was there to meet him and drive him to the public square to address a crowd of five thousand.[38] Those designated to serve as his official escorts were members of a local campaign club, and they wore Roman helmets and tunics.[39] Some in the crowd at Otsego wore buttons designating them as members of the Grand Army of the Republic, an organization of Civil War veterans. Roosevelt asked for their earnest support for the nation, just as they had given it nearly four decades earlier.[40]

Citizens at Unadilla stood in the rain, and from the speakers' stand Roosevelt could see no faces, only the tops of umbrellas.[41] When yet another individual repeatedly shouted, "Hurrah for Bryan!" at Sidney, Roosevelt initially ignored him, but finally he remarked, "Our friend there is not a sober man."[42]

Norwich was the final stop on Tuesday, and the party reached the community ahead of schedule. This allowed the train to pull onto a siding, while Roosevelt and his party ate dinner. "While the governor was eating, 30 or 40 boys, who, it was learned later, had organized in the village during the day with the knowledge and consent of their Democratic fathers, gathered about the window of the dining car at which the governor was sitting and amused themselves by calling the Governor of the State of New York a horse thief. Beyond remarking that parental discipline seemed to be below par in Norwich, the Governor paid no attention to them."[43]

Rain did not keep the crowds away in Norwich, and two halls filled with New Yorkers eager to see their governor and hear what he had to say. Sensibly, the fireworks and other outdoor elements of the celebration were canceled, but Roosevelt pushed forward sharing what was described as "exhortations in the McKinley doctrine."[44]

It was on this day the Roosevelt campaign announced that the planned tour of Long Island communities scheduled for Monday, November 5, would not occur. The governor would appear at a so-called Sound Money Parade in New York City on Saturday evening, November 3, and then await Election Day with only one other brief address to friends and neighbors in his hometown of Oyster Bay.[45] Whether he was confident, exhausted, or simply ready to end the whistle stops is unclear; perhaps all three explanations played a role in this tactical decision.

Wednesday, October 24, 1900—Thirteen Days to the Election

Roosevelt's day started with a 10:00 a.m. departure from Norwich, and he stopped briefly at Earlville to speak to several hundred persons gathered at the depot.[46] At Cazenovia, Roosevelt met a large crowd that included students from Cazenovia Seminary. He referred to one of his traveling companions to make his point: "This is the summer home of Charles S. Fairchild, once the Democratic Secretary of the Treasury. Mr. Fairchild is with me on this political trip, because he believes in sound money and in orderly liberty."[47] Stops with crowds of a few thousand followed at Canastota and Oneida, and at Rome there were more than six thousand, including many factory workers. Some small boys heckled Roosevelt in Rome, and he told his hearers that Democrats were so afraid of the truth that they sent children to drown it with shouting.[48]

Utica was both an afternoon and an evening stop, with the governor speaking twice after the 3:00 p.m. arrival, leaving for a side trip to Herkimer, and then returning for another event in the evening. He spoke at the Utica Skating Rink to a combined meeting of the Sound Money Democrats and the local Republicans and then to the overflow crowd at an outdoor meeting in the square. Roosevelt's escort was provided by the Conkling Unconditional Club, a group that revered the memory of New York's senator Roscoe Conkling and his faction known as the Stalwart Republicans.[49]

In the Roosevelt introductions at Utica, Senator Chauncey Depew said, "In all the campaigns in which I have been engaged, I have never known one when the vice presidential candidate has accomplished so much for the good cause as Colonel Roosevelt has. He has had hard work each day convincing Democrats, and he has had recreation in having fun with Colonel Bryan." Utica's local Republican chairman voiced what many around the nation were thinking: "I have the honor to present the next Vice President of the United States and one who by the grace of God in 1904 will be the coming President of the United States." In turn, Roosevelt drove home his upstate New York theme: "Mr. Bryan has been in this state as the political guest of Mr. Croker. . . . Mr. Bryan wishes Mr. Croker to aid him in Bryanizing the state, and, in return, he will aid Croker to Crokerize the state. I ask you to aid us in defeating the men who would reduce the state to the level of New York City."[50]

On the way to the Utica station for a brief trip to Herkimer, "a body of 50 Hamilton College students, all with red felt hats, worked out of the crowd and formed a supplementary escort. They gave the Hamilton yell once or twice. . . . Then a Colgate College crowd, somewhat smaller but every bit as noisy, started a cheer on the other side of the street and the two colleges had most of the noises between them all the way to the station."[51] When he returned from Herkimer, the governor spent his evening reviewing a long Sound Money parade from a platform in front of the Butterfield House Hotel.[52]

There was this report from Herkimer: "When Mr. Bryan was at Herkimer the other day he tried to square himself with the workmen in the gun factories there by saying that there was plenty of work for them and their factories in the manufacture of guns for shooting game. Gov. Roosevelt asked the people of Herkimer, which is near Ilion [home of Remington Arms Company], whether Mr. Bryan had suggested the mounting of pop-guns on the decks of our men-of-war and the arming of the police of the great cities with Fourth of July toy pistols."[53]

Thursday, October 25, 1900—Twelve Days to the Election

Fog blanketed the countryside as the train pulled out of Utica at 8:00 a.m., but an hour later in Camden there was sunshine, and the skies were blue. There Roosevelt praised New York attorney general Davies who was a son of the community and a zealous prosecutor of crimes related to trusts.[54] While in Watertown, Roosevelt addressed six thousand persons in front of the Woodruff House. He recalled that the late Democratic Governor Roswell P. Flower had his summer home in Watertown and that Flower had been a fervent advocate of the gold standard. Also, a local Republican asked Roosevelt whether he was afraid when Bryan supporters shouted insults, and the response was: "No, I am among my own folks."[55]

When he reached Oswego, Roosevelt remembered Governor Flower once again, and he recited for his three thousand listeners what Flower said about William Jennings Bryan in 1896: "He is a shifty and unwise man for whom no true Democrat can vote."[56] As he did in many places, Roosevelt spoke both indoors (Richardson Opera House) and outdoors in Oswego. Several thousand heard him accuse Bryan of unwillingness to say exactly what he would do as president, lest it "impair his chance of election."[57]

After brief and uneventful stops in Sterling and Weedsport, Auburn proved challenging: "The entrance of the governor into the Opera House was the signal for a general outpouring of roughs from the saloons on the other side of the street, who hooted and yelled a good deal until he had entered the building. After he had gone, a request was made for an outdoor meeting, and the speakers there had much trouble in making themselves heard. . . . [The speakers finally] turned attention to the people on the sidewalk, ignoring those in the roadway who had disturbers in their midst. Meanwhile, Gov. Roosevelt was having his own troubles inside. He had hardly started his argument when a man with leather lungs in the gallery started a howl for Bryan. . . . [The crowd shouted:] 'Put him out! Make him shut up!' . . . [Roosevelt calmed them and said:] 'He will be quiet enough after I get through with him.'"[58] Despite the conflict in this community, there were fifteen thousand people who watched the Roosevelt procession and attended one of four political rallies with various speakers or heard the governor's address at the Auburn Opera House.[59]

Reports came to Roosevelt in Auburn that disturbances were to be expected at the next and final stop for the day, Syracuse.[60] However the forty thousand that turned out to see the governor were enthusiastic and welcoming, and there were no reported incidents. "*The Sun* reporter interviewed a policeman about the promised disorders. . . . 'Trouble tonight?' He asked. 'No, not on your life. . . . If any man raises his hand to make trouble tonight, he gets his arm broke, that's all. It's going to be like Sunday School tonight.'"[61]

Two meetings—one in the Wieting Opera House and another in Clinton Square—gave nearly fifteen thousand citizens in Syracuse the chance to hear Roosevelt speak. Nearly that many marchers later formed a huge parade, and many of the participants wore uniforms and carried torches. "They began to march before 7 o'clock, and at midnight, they were still marching, simply because it made them feel good."[62]

Friday, October 26, 1900—Eleven Days to the Election

All of the stops on the fifth day of Roosevelt's canvass of upstate New York were secondary to the principal stop in the heart of New York City for the huge Republican rally honoring the governor and formally welcoming him home from his campaign tour to the western states. From Syracuse he would travel more than 275 miles to New York City, stopping to speak along the way, and timeliness was important because crowds numbering in the hundreds of thousands were expected for the evening's events. He had to arrive at his ultimate destination by 5:30 p.m. if the schedule was to proceed as planned. His first decision of the day was to cancel the scheduled stop in Little Falls to save his throat and to buy time down the road.

Amsterdam was next on the schedule with an expected ten-minute stop.[63] Local committee members, however, intending to make the most of the occasion, turned out a crowd at the station, organized an escorted procession with a uniformed battalion and a band, and conveyed the governor to a meeting in the public square quite some distance uptown from the depot.[64] There was an enthusiastic crowd of five thousand in attendance at the outdoor meeting, but one heckler took an approach Roosevelt had not previously encountered and that he chose to ignore: "The Governor had been roasting Mr. Croker along the lines of his recent speeches and occasionally dragging in the name of Mr. Bryan, when the man yelled: 'How about Platt?' 'What's that?' asked the Governor. 'How about Platt?' repeated the man. The Governor glared, then winked and went on talking about Mr. Croker. 'How about Platt?' asked the man for the third time, and failing to get an answer pushed his way out of the crowd."[65] Platt was, of course, the

Republican boss of New York politics and a man with whom Roosevelt had often locked horns. However, in the environment of an election, the governor was unwilling to criticize a fellow Republican or embrace a big-city boss regardless of his party affiliation.

Schenectady was to be the largest of the day's stops prior to New York City with several special features. As Roosevelt arrived, the Workingmen's Republican Club of the General Electrical Works was in formation awaiting the governor's review. This was a welcome statement about the appeal of the Republican Party to the labor community. The eight thousand workers at the General Electric factory could hardly misunderstand management's political preferences, since the facility closed for Roosevelt but remained open when Bryan visited the city one week earlier.[66]

Three large audiences were also ready for Roosevelt speeches, one in the square behind the Schenectady train station, a second at Crescent Park, and a third at the Centre Street Opera House. The governor chose to address only the crowd at the Opera House, leaving the other venues to alternate speakers. Again, he was aware of both the schedule and the condition of his throat.[67] When interruptions began, Roosevelt first treated them in a good-natured fashion, asking for the civility that had been extended to Bryan during his visit.[68] Then the atmosphere of the hall became less cordial: "The shower of interruptions angered the Governor, and he did not attempt to answer any of them. Shaking his fist at the audience, he said: 'Gentlemen, and I hope you are gentlemen, you are getting a fair sample of the Bryanites today. This is what you must expect from the Bryanized and Crokerized democracy. I will willingly answer all your questions, but my time is limited.' 'Well, tell us about San Juan,' came a voice from the central part of the hall: 'Didn't you capture it alone?' The Governor did not answer. He roasted Mr. Croker to the delight of the crowd."[69]

Down the rails in Albany, there was a ten-minute stop to greet friends at the station, then a race to New York City made up a half hour on the schedule and allowed a timely arrival at 5:30 p.m. as the agenda prescribed. Immediately, Roosevelt joined his escort for a procession to the Fifth Avenue Hotel where the city's dignitaries and Republican power brokers were awaiting the governor's arrival at a special dinner in an ornate parlor. However, Roosevelt chose not to join the gathering in his honor, preferring instead to dine quietly with his sister and to see his physician for a throat treatment. Others took the podium, extolling Republican principles, candidates, and Roosevelt, and at 7:47 p.m. the governor appeared for an end-of-event toast to the health of those who attended his dinner.[70] It had to be a strange and socially strained moment, and the Democratic press certainly enjoyed speculating on Roosevelt's behavior.

Still, the evening belonged to governor and vice presidential candidate Theodore Roosevelt. There were lavish displays of fireworks and a parade of 50,000 people viewed by 200,000 or more. Madison Square and Madison Square Garden were filled to overflowing. One hundred thousand supporters jammed the square to hear 142 orators speaking for three hours from thirty-two specially erected and decorated platforms. Roosevelt was the star of the show in the Garden, where a chorus of 5,000 voices serenaded him, and a capacity audience cheered his every word.[71]

Democratic newspapers took a jaundiced view of the proceedings. The *St. Louis Republic* opined: "Roosevelt made his appearance here on Friday night and was cordially greeted by his party friends. His reception, however, paled into insignificance when compared to the grand ovation given to Mr. Bryan last night [Saturday]."[72] On the other hand, Republican newspapers had a completely different interpretation. The *New-York Tribune* reported: "The vast audience which filled Madison Square Garden last night . . . was, in the opinions of many persons, equal in numbers, equal in enthusiasm, and far superior in intelligence to that which greeted Mr. Bryan there ten days previously."[73] (Note that Bryan addressed two gatherings in New York City—one a week and a half prior to the Roosevelt event and the other the night following the governor's visit. Thus, the writers are comparing the Roosevelt celebration to two different Bryan meetings.)

Saturday, October 27, 1900—Ten Days to the Election— and Sunday, October 28, 1900—Nine Days to the Election

Overnight following the Madison Square Garden event, Theodore Roosevelt stayed at the home of his sister and brother-in-law, Mr. and Mrs. Douglas Robinson, on Madison Avenue. "At 8:25 o'clock [Saturday morning] the Governor appeared at the window [of the Robinson home] with one arm about his little son and the other around his wife's waist. The boy patted his father's arm, at which the Governor stooped and kissed him on the forehead. The crowd outside, which was eagerly watching the windows for a sight of the Governor, set up a lusty cheer at this. At 8:30 o'clock the Governor came down the steps carrying two dress suit cases and was followed by Mrs. Roosevelt and the three men who acted as an escort. When the Governor reached the sidewalk he set down his grips and shook hands with Acting Captain Lantry, saying: 'This is my first experience at sleeping with police watching in front of my door. Your men are no doubt tired out with their long vigil, and I thank them very much for the careful manner in which they have discharged their duties.'"[74] Note the nature of his celebrity was such that admirers were surrounding the place of his overnight lodging eagerly awaiting his appearance.

Roosevelt and his party took a ferry to Jersey City, New Jersey, to catch his campaign special, and there, again, a crowd of several hundred met and cheered him enthusiastically, as the train pulled away at 9:30 a.m.[75] During the night, the governor had been awakened at 2:00 a.m. to answer a request from the citizens of Paterson, New Jersey, that he stop to speak as he passed through the city. He demurred, citing the need to stay with the timetable as planned.[76] However, both in Paterson and Passaic the train slowed, and Roosevelt made an effort to greet the crowds from the rear platform. He was said to be in high spirits because it was his forty-second birthday, and because he was quite satisfied with the supportive demonstration of the previous evening.[77]

Mrs. Roosevelt accompanied the governor with the intention of staying on the train until Monday, October 29, to celebrate his birthday with him. Members of the campaign entourage presented him with "a handsome bouquet of American Beauty roses. . . . The flowers adorned the stateroom occupied by Governor Roosevelt and his wife."[78]

Children were waving flags during the brief stop at Suffern, and Roosevelt said, "I appreciate you, the voters of the future, coming here, and I hope you will always guard the flag."[79] At Hillburn, he saw a club of supporters in white sailor suits, and he said that the military was obviously not as unpopular as Mr. Bryan preached.[80] The only conflict in Middletown was at the door, where there was a good bit of fighting between those who were barely in the theater of the Middletown Casino and those who could not gain entry.[81] Down the road in Port Jervis, Roosevelt spoke from the balcony of the Fowler House Hotel, and he told a large crowd of railroad workers "that he hoped the day of soup kitchens as an established institution had been settled for good and all."[82]

There were two stops of less than five minutes each in Pennsylvania— Shohola and Lackawaxen—as the rails traced the border between that state and New York.[83] "At Cochecton [New York] the only incident that marked the short stop made was when a man in the crowd started to cry 'Hurrah for Bryan.' Another man standing nearby slapped him in the mouth with the back of his hand and no further trouble ensued."[84]

Citizens of Callicoon heard the governor say: "I ask you railroad men to compare the amount of work done on this railroad now and four years ago. . . . If you want to go back to those conditions, you can go back by voting for free silver."[85] His topic in Long Eddy (New York) was imperialism, and he addressed a Civil War veteran in the crowd: "You remember they told you in 1861 that you could not coerce a sovereign state, but you did. They told you that you could not establish the rule of the American Republic in the Southern States without the consent of the governed, but you did; and now the Southern States are glad of it. So it will be in the Philippines."[86]

Hancock was known for gracious hotels with Corinthian columns that were decked out in bunting to greet Roosevelt. He stood in their shadow and addressed more than one thousand supporters.[87] Millers straight from their dusty jobs met the governor in Deposit, and some of them were clearly supporters of Bryan. "One of them stood on a folding chair and entertained himself with remarkable opinions as to the personality [of one of the speakers]. When one called Bryan a false prophet, this man shouted, 'Liar,' and leaped into the air in his excess of emotion. When he came down the chair went down under him with a great crash. 'You're all right my friend,' said the speaker, 'but you're on a rotten platform.'"[88]

Following the stop in Deposit, New York, the Roosevelt campaign special cut through the northeastern corner of Pennsylvania. Everyone on the train "assembled in the dining car, and ex-Senator John Laughlin, addressing Governor Roosevelt said to him that since he was out of the State of New York, and therefore without any jurisdiction, some of those present had decided to inflict a speech on him. . . . All remembered that it was the Governor's birthday and rejoiced over his good fortune which they hoped would continue. . . . [They] then presented the Governor with a beautiful pair of gold cuff buttons and a gold scarf pin."[89]

After two additional Pennsylvania stops—Susquehanna and Great Bend—the Roosevelt campaign reached the final stop of the day and of the first week of the New York tour, Binghamton. It was 7:00 p.m., and an entire evening of activity was still ahead. On the positive side, one traveling journalist noted that it was a relatively quiet day in terms of insults from "those who argue or who run for office on the other side" and that the stops had been "less disturbing today than at any time since Gov. Roosevelt entered his own state."[90] Perhaps the presence of Mrs. Roosevelt tamed a few who would otherwise have misbehaved.

First in Binghamton was dinner at the Hotel Bennet, and then the campaign party moved to the Stone Opera House where a capacity crowd awaited Roosevelt. Those unable to squeeze into the main hall attended another meeting in the same facility, a large meeting out in the street, or one of a number of meetings elsewhere in town.[91] In the fashion of these large community celebrations, each venue undoubtedly had its program of speakers. In addition to his main address, Roosevelt spoke at the Odd Fellows' Hall and the Lyceum Theater.[92] He was right on point, if barely understandable, with his New York theme: "Bryanism means, in the sphere of civic honesty, Crokerism; in finance, Pettigrewism; as regards liberty and order, Altgeldism; as regards an honest ballot, Goebelism; and as regards our foreign policy, Aguinaldoism."[93]

Though it had not been the case elsewhere in the country during the Roosevelt tour, the hymn "Onward, Christian Soldiers" seemed to become the unofficial march of the campaign in upstate New York. "Tonight the streets of Binghamton rang with it from one end of the city to the other."[94] Also, there was a unique presentation during the evening: "A Binghamton chair firm, Stickley & Brandt, added its gift to his birthday collection today in the shape of a prosperity chair which was presented to him in the opera house."[95]

Governor and Mrs. Roosevelt decided to stay at a local hotel for two nights, rather than in the railcar.[96] Sunday was passed visiting Binghamton.

Monday, October 29, 1900—Eight Days to the Election

Compared to most of Roosevelt's whirlwind days, Monday was lived at an almost leisurely pace, though it turned out to be stressful because of an incidence of violence at the final stop. Cortland was the first community of the four visited on Monday, and its thriving manufacturers made it a perfect place for the message of prosperity under McKinley. Roosevelt's campaign special arrived at noon. "At a little distance from the train there could be seen the Fair Grounds, filled with hundreds of people and a big skating rink, which held 3,000 persons who desired to hear a speech by the Governor. Governor Roosevelt was escorted to the skating rink. . . . He made an earnest address in the rink. Then the Governor was escorted to the Fair Grounds, where he made another speech. [Roosevelt said in part:] "I am informed that there are 7,000 depositors in your savings banks as compared with 4,000 only four years ago, and that ten mortgages have been cancelled to one that has been taken. That is a sample of what is going on all over the country."[97]

Ithaca gave the governor a ride in a trolley car from the railway station into the heart of the community. Cornell University students played a prominent role in the visit—turning out by the hundreds to join the thousands of local citizens—and providing a noisy cheering section. "The students . . . carried transparencies upon which were inscribed political mottoes. . . . [One said:] 'Prexy is Right on the Philippines.' . . . [Another said:] 'Cornell is for Sound Men and Sound Money.' A little one had the inscription: 'Sibley Wants Four More Years of the Full Dinner Pail.'" In a display that would never be permitted in twenty-first-century America, many of the Cornell students brought revolvers to the rally and repeatedly fired them into the air. Roosevelt was said to have enjoyed the commotion, and he referred to a recent victory of the university's football team in his speech. However, he avoided all mention of Richard Croker, as a courtesy to Croker's son who was in the crowd of Cornell students.[98]

After a brief stop at Van Etten, complete with a short speech, the campaign party arrived at Elmira at 6:00 p.m., expecting what had become a routine evening schedule with a crowd of several thousand, a procession, and two events where Roosevelt would speak to those assembled. Predictably, the governor was whisked from the depot to a local hotel, the Rathbun House, and from there he was to be transported first to the Lyceum Theatre to address 2,500 persons and then to the Tivoli Theatre where another 1,500 would hear his message.[99]

On the short carriage ride from the hotel to the first meeting, the evening took a nasty turn. "For the first time in New York State, Theodore Roosevelt was assaulted on the streets on his way to the place of a political meeting. . . . A crowd of roughs of Elmira, poured out of a dark alley, gathered about the carriage, and applied most insulting epithets to the Governor and threw pictures of Stanchfield [Democratic candidate for governor] in his face and finally began throwing sticks, eggs, and vegetables at the occupants of the carriage. One of the sticks struck the Governor on his hat, but did not harm him. The driver of the carriage then whipped up his horses and drove among some Rough Riders and the mob did not follow the carriage further."[100]

Unfortunately, the thugs were not finished with their rampage. "Two Republican campaign clubs from Elmira . . . were attacked in the line of parade. An attempt was made to wrench their banner . . . and it was torn to pieces. It represented Bryan as favoring a 50-cent dollar. Stones were thrown at the Corning Club, and five of its members . . . were badly hurt. Some of them were cut on the face and others on the back of the head and required the care of surgeons. The club made a charge with their canes and drove their assailants away. After the dispersal of the parade, however, solitary members of the club were attacked on the streets. . . . A squad of policemen guarded them to the train they took for home."[101]

Within the event venues there were no interruptions, and Roosevelt addressed his familiar campaign themes. Afterward, he said of the attack: "It was nasty conduct; the conduct of hoodlums."[102] One member of the governor's staff told a journalist: "The fight at Victor was not half so bad as that here tonight. At Victor no blood was shed, but here blood flowed quite freely."[103]

Tuesday, October 30, 1900—Seven Days to the Election

Folks in Corning were outraged at the treatment their fellow citizens had received at Elmira the night before, and when Roosevelt arrived on a rainy morning, he immediately addressed the situation. He said to the crowd at the rail station: "'It is perfectly evident that Corning has not been daunted by its reception in Elmira last night. It indicates that you have good stuff in you here.' A man in the crowd called out, 'So have you!' Roosevelt said, 'I think that sooner or later our opponents will grow to understand that mob violence is not the way to keep Republicans back.'"[104] He noted that Senator Chauncey Depew, who was also canvassing New York communities on behalf of Republican candidates, had been shouted down by demonstrators at Cobleskill on the previous day. Roosevelt openly blamed it on the Democrats and said: "It is an outrage that any party should so arouse and inflame a spirit like that which was manifested last evening."[105]

Heavy rain continued to fall at the Bath depot where several residents of the State Soldiers' and Sailors' Home were in the crowd. He used their presence to say that the issues of the election were as important to the nation's honor as those during the Civil War. An approaching engineer on a side track blew his train whistle in greeting, and Roosevelt said: "His heart is with us, but I wish he would let me have the show."[106]

Wayland's cement factory was booming, and the governor asked the crowd whether they wanted to close the facility by agreeing to Bryan's tariff proposals.[107] When a drunk standing on a barrel cheered for Bryan and fell off his perch, Roosevelt said: "It is evident that the gentleman isn't, at any rate, a Prohibitionist." And when the governor grasped the railing as he spoke, the rain-soaked drapery stained his hands bright red. Someone in the crowd shouted, "He ain't afraid of blood!" Roosevelt used it as an opportunity to refer to the importance of patriotism.[108]

Two hundred local citizens at Livonia heard Roosevelt criticize the Democrats' role in suppressing African American voting in the southern states: "At the coming election in Porto [sic] Rico next Tuesday, when they vote just as we vote here, one in eight of the inhabitants of that island is registered and can vote. In Mississippi and South Carolina, the voting has been but one in 18 and one in 16 of the population. Now, I would like to have Mr. Bryan answer that if he can. He cannot, and he won't answer it."[109] Voters in Avon, Geneseo, and Canandaigua stood in the rain to hear the governor, and in the last of those places, Roosevelt used it as an illustration: "Prosperity, like this rain, falls on the just and unjust. It is falling here on the just, at this moment, but it is still falling on the unjust, as Mr. Bryan is making a tour of the state also."[110]

At 5:30 the train reached Geneva, and the program on an open stand several blocks from the depot was difficult because of the rain, the incessant blowing of factory whistles, and hecklers shouting from windows through megaphones.[111] Penn Yan offered up a large audience, despite the rain. "On the way to Rochester from Penn Yan, the engine was stalled and nearly tore up the tracks in the effort to make headway. A rumor was spread aboard in the dining car that the Bryanites had greased the tracks, but it was at last found out that the engineer and firemen had become so engrossed in a political discussion that they had let the fire go out and the steam ran down. The train entered Rochester an hour and a half late."[112]

Roosevelt and his party actually reached Rochester for the first time at 2:00 p.m., but after a brief greeting, they made a circuit of several of the small communities previously mentioned. It was after 9:00 when the train returned to Rochester and the evening's events began. Greeters welcomed Roosevelt at the station, and even though a strong rain continued, there were three brass bands and fireworks. "The fireworks did not shoot very far in the rain, but the Rochester folks had bought larger quantities to make up for that contingency."

Another large crowd awaited the governor at the Powers House Hotel, where he went to freshen, before going to Fitzhugh Hall and the Washington Rink for addresses to several thousand people.[113] Roosevelt responded directly to a charge from Croker that young people had few opportunities under the Republican administration. The governor said: "I ask every father here to answer to himself the question whether he would prefer his boy to start in life with the prospect of Bryanism ahead of him or with the prospect of a continuance of present policies. . . . It is a mere axiom that a young man's chances are best in a community where there is general prosperity."[114]

Even as Roosevelt endured exhaustion, as well as verbal and physical attacks, defending McKinley and his policies, the president continued his passive approach to the campaign. It was a strategy not uncommon at the time for incumbents. On this particular day, one week prior to the election, McKinley was at home in Canton, Ohio, where he greeted the principals and teachers of the Canton public schools at the superintendent's residence in the evening. During the day, he and his wife hosted visiting friends for a drive through the countryside. Also, the president reportedly received several telegrams congratulating him on a letter he wrote that was read to a Republican meeting at Alliance, Ohio. It encouraged labor and management to work hand in hand to "secure industrial triumphs as yet unknown."[115]

Wednesday, October 31, 1900—Six Days to the Election

As he boarded the train in Rochester on Wednesday, Roosevelt was wearing a button that read, "Railroad Men's Sound Money Club of Rochester," a group with a membership of eight hundred that turned out in force to greet the campaign party.[116] Rochester had required late-night effort, but it proved to be a welcoming place after the violence of Elmira on the previous evening. The campaign special pulled away from Rochester at 9:30 a.m.[117]

As he traveled from Brockport to Lockport, Roosevelt stopped at Holley, Albion, and Medina. Most of the five communities had large stone quarries, and the governor used the opportunity to talk about questions related to labor, particularly where there were many quarrymen in the crowds. He also criticized Bryan's purported attempts to set workers against management, denouncing it as an un-American strategy.[118] Rain, again, vexed the campaigners, but according to one journalist: "The audiences apparently did not know it. They listened as quietly and shouted their approval as loudly between sentences as though there had been the balmiest of sunshine over them all."[119] One clever remark came from the governor at Medina: "I want to ask, if any of you here has ever seen a single imperialist? I have never found one from the Rocky Mountains to the Atlantic Coast. I have met lots of expansionists. I am one myself."[120] At Lockport, anti-Roosevelt circulars were distributed in the streets, asking why he had signed certain legislation perceived to be unfriendly to labor unions.[121]

When the chairman of the meeting at Niagara Falls introduced Roosevelt to a large crowd in the International Theatre, he said that the governor was a friend of the workingman who was a workingman himself. Roosevelt said: "I do not believe that in this campaign I have been introduced in a manner that pleases me so much, because I do not feel that any American is worth his salt unless he is a workingman."[122] Hundreds heard Roosevelt promote both the national and state Republican tickets at North Tonawanda,[123] and at an added stop in Black Rock, he had an opportunity to speak to a large, enthusiastic group of laborers.[124]

Buffalo was a model stop in terms of enthusiasm, crowd size, and decorum. Roosevelt and his party arrived at 4:15 p.m., and though the local committee had gathered a large, formal reception at his hotel, the governor refused to attend for any purpose other than to offer a brief greeting. He gave the excuse that he needed to rest in anticipation of the evening agenda that would require him to address three large meetings. His rest was a short one, however, because both dinner and a driving tour of the principal streets of Buffalo were included in his activities prior to the later events. Fireworks and cheering crowds were everywhere, as he traveled through the city.[125] (Note: Roosevelt's driving tour included the Pan-American Exposition grounds that were under construction at the time. This would be the site of the McKinley assassination less than one year later.)

Roosevelt spent his evening speaking at three large rallies: the first was an outdoor meeting at the Broadway Market that included many blue-collar laborers; the second was at St. Stephen's Hall, where an ethnic Italian community filled the room; and the third was at the largest indoor venue, City Convention Hall, where twelve thousand assembled. This last meeting began, finally, at 9:30 p.m., and nearly half the crowd had stood for two hours while they awaited Roosevelt and listened to another speaker by the name of Clerk Whipple.[126]

Though the audience was loud, the noise represented enthusiastic cheering, and the disturbances were reportedly "enthusiasts waving flags over their heads, thus obstructing a view of the speaker from those standing behind."[127] Roosevelt systematically addressed Democratic charges that he characterized as "erroneous by intent,"[128] and, at the end of his speech, he thanked the police force for their efforts and the large crowds for their orderliness.[129] Following the events, Roosevelt and his party retired overnight in Buffalo to await their departure at 8:30 the following morning.

Thursday, November 1, 1900—Five Days to the Election

Stops on this day were apparently routine, and Roosevelt's messages must have broken no new ground because journalistic coverage was at a minimum. Either little of a newsworthy character occurred, or the newspapermen were organizing to cover the larger event planned for New York City on Saturday evening, the Sound Money parade.

Batavia, as the first stop, received some attention, as the governor assailed Richard Croker for his recent exhortation to Democrats that if vote totals showed Bryan losing, they should invade election sites and throw out those counting the ballots. Croker was likely making a statement about the depth of his personal confidence in victory for Bryan, saying, in effect, that only voting fraud could bring a different outcome. Roosevelt, of course, chose a less charitable interpretation of Croker's words, and he accused the Democratic boss of "inciting the ignorant, the violent, and the lawless to riot on Election Day." Furthermore, he said, that as governor he would protect Bryan's rights should he win a majority.[130]

Campaign committee members at Dunkirk scheduled three meetings with an address at each by Governor Roosevelt. Laborers from the Brooks Locomotive Works were given time during their day to step outside and join the crowd in front of their factory, where Roosevelt said: "Mr. Bryan said if we were prosperous it was not due to us. Well, I tell you one thing, Mr. Bryan is not responsible for it. . . . He said it was due to Providence. Well, Providence helped us, because it helped us to keep Mr. Bryan out."[131] Both of the other rallies in Dunkirk were indoors—one at the opera house and the other at a smaller hall. Five thousand heard the governor speak while he visited this community.[132]

Lindsay Denison of the *Sun* pulled out all the stops in describing the culminating events of the day: "Jamestown tonight gave Gov. Roosevelt a reception such as he has not had anywhere except in one or two mining towns in the West. The turbulent, noisy crowds have overrun the sidewalks and jostled one another in the middle of the streets. The continuous din of thousands of horns, the explosion of bombs and dynamite firecrackers, and the deep thumping of the bass drums in the bands and drum corps . . . have made such a din that no man can hear himself talk. . . . The Scandinavian blood in the community seems to have found in the occasion the chance to turn loose its love of carnival. For oratory the evening has not been a successful one, because no man can make himself heard against an all-pervading hullabaloo like that in Jamestown tonight. . . . The Roosevelt reception parade of tonight will be the talk of western New York for a long time to come. . . . The pastor of the Swedish Lutheran Church said to a reporter tonight that he had 1,200 people in his congregation. In all that number, he said, he knew but two families in which there was the slightest Bryan feeling."[133]

After the evening's events, Roosevelt was shown and asked about a dispatch from New York City in which he was said to be "in a state of utter collapse." This was the governor's response: "You may say that if a bull moose may be said to be in a state of utter collapse, then the phrase describes my condition exactly."[134]

Friday, November 2, 1900—Four Days to the Election

Roosevelt's final day on the road campaigning for the election of William McKinley and other Republican candidates, as well as his own ascension to the vice presidency, was almost anticlimactic in that it produced little in the way of newsworthy happenings. Perhaps that was to be expected. After thousands of miles traveled and hundreds of speeches given, what more was there to do or say? In one sense, the day offered a capsule picture of the entire trip—several smaller stops, a culminating event with multiple meetings, enthusiastic crowds, a hostile incident, and a candidate very much in control of himself and his message. Little drama remains when events are played out on a stage where a positive outcome is all but assured.

Yet Theodore Roosevelt, the hero of this performance, was determined to work his audience to the end, even as he decided more and more frequently to make ad hoc choices about skipping some nonessential events or canceling stops. He had become one of the most experienced over-the-road campaigners in the Republican Party, and he was no longer willing to work himself to the point of ill health.

Randolph was the first visit on the final whistle-stop day, and the size of the crowd at the station surprised Roosevelt and others in his traveling party. To see one thousand people awaiting the train in the early morning seemed more of a crowd than the village could produce, and the happy assumption for the campaign strategists was that a number of farmers had traveled in from the countryside.[135]

Olean, too, turned out a large and enthusiastic crowd, with onlookers lining the streets to cheer Roosevelt as his carriage rolled across the city to the public square where a speakers' platform had been built for the occasion. The governor spoke of the large Republican plurality usually cast by this area, Cattaraugus County, saying: "I am now passing through a part of the state which can always be depended upon to roll up great majorities for the cause of decent citizenship."[136] Indeed, the people showed themselves to be so eager when the speaking ended that they started running toward the station to accompany Roosevelt right to the door of his railcar. However, the facts that he was traveling by carriage and the distance was a mile and a half to the depot meant that the runners were soon left in the dust. Eventually, he turned a corner, and the people of Olean lost sight of the governor.[137]

Friendship and Cuba hosted visits, as did Wellsville and Hornellsville. At Wellsville, a preliminary speaker was in competition with a screaming baby and finally gave up, announcing: "That child has summed up the whole Bryanite argument."[138] Hornellsville's parade was so long that there was little time for the speeches—one scheduled for a bandstand in the park, and another for the local opera house. When Roosevelt did get the podium, he linked voting Democratic with madness: "If this nation chooses to turn Bedlamite and put in Mr. Bryan and try his policies, we have nobody but ourselves to thank for the disaster that will surely follow."[139]

Newspapermen reported but one negative incident on this day. At Waverly, someone threw a sizable stone at the governor's railcar, breaking a window near where Roosevelt was seated. Though neither he nor others were injured, he referred to the incident at the final stop in Oswego, saying that "so long as the leaders of the Democrats were foolish enough and criminal enough to encourage that sort of political argument, so long was free speech in this country to be dangerously menaced."[140]

Oswego warmly welcomed the governor for his final stop of the hundreds that led him through counties and states across the nation. Here, as in so many places, there were thousands eager to see and greet him. Red fire and torches filled the air with smoke and a sulfur smell, as an escort of local dignitaries, Republican faithful, the curious, and hero worshipers ushered him first to an outdoor speech in the public square, then to a second address at a facility known as Ahwaga Hall (named for the Iroquois word that became the town's name, Oswego), and lastly for the principal speech at the local opera house. Roosevelt played his New York strategy to the end. As reported by one of the traveling journalists: "In closing his speech [Roosevelt] declared that Mr. Bryan, by his appeals to class feeling, and Mr. Croker by the advice to Democrats to take possession of the polls if dissatisfied with the announcement of the result of the count of the ballots, were inciting riot."[141]

Conclusion

At 10:30 p.m. on Friday, November 2, 1900, Theodore Roosevelt boarded his car on his special train to leave Oswego, New York.[142] His weeks as an itinerant were finally behind him.

CHAPTER 18

ELECTION

When Theodore Roosevelt completed his campaign travels on Friday, November 2, 1900, he had been the Republican candidate for the vice presidency for 134 days. Recalling that he spent fifty-eight of those days at his home in Oyster Bay, New York, between June 21 and September 2, it was remarkable that his whistle-stop tours had carried him to twenty-three states plus the District of Columbia and the Oklahoma Territory. Journalists writing for the wire services and the major newspapers reported by community name a total of 480 stops in cities and towns of all sizes, and in most of those places Roosevelt made one or more speeches. (See appendices A and B for a comprehensive list and state-by-state totals.) Some of his addresses were as short as two minutes, many were fifteen or twenty minutes, and occasionally he spoke for forty-five minutes or more.[1]

While the crowds nearly everywhere Roosevelt visited were satisfyingly—even impressively—large, welcoming, and enthusiastic, not every moment would be fondly remembered. Hecklers frequently interrupted his speeches with cheers for opponents, antagonistic questions, insults, or blasts from horns or steam whistles. Depending upon his mood and the situation, Roosevelt ignored, answered, or even shouted back while shaking his fist at the disrupters.

Protestors in at least twenty-two communities tried to intimidate the candidate or his supporters with physical threats or actual violence. (See appendix C for an annotated list.) One radical unionist struck Roosevelt in the chest with a wooden pole, and other opponents hit him at least twice with thrown stones and once with a stick. He endured episodes of vegetables, eggs, and clods of mud hurled his way, and he barely escaped injury when a particularly large stone broke the window near where he was sitting in his private railcar.

On Roosevelt's first day back in the New York metropolitan area (Saturday, November 3), he attended a breakfast at the Lawyers Club and a reception at the Produce Exchange, but both were pale preliminaries to the major event of the day; namely, the McKinley and Roosevelt Business Men's Sound Money Parade, a highly anticipated end-of-campaign statement of support. Some predictions suggested as many as 350,000 New Yorkers and guests might attend the event, but whether that was ever realistic is uncertain. Heavy rain and cold weather made the day unpleasant and surely limited attendance. However the Associated Press put the number of marchers at 87,615 by actual count, and estimates of the total number of attendees watching from the sidewalks were well into the six figures.[2]

Parades were a common feature of campaign events, as the narrative of the previous chapters has shown city by city, and large-scale parading was often a strategy employed as an exclamation point just before Election Day. Attendance for New York's Sound Money parade was compared to the crowd size for a similar event in 1896 by both the Republican newspapers and their Democratic counterparts with nearly opposite conclusions as to the significance (or even the accuracy) of the estimated figures. There were also reports of sound money parades on the campaign's final Saturday in other cities—for example, Pittsburgh, Buffalo, and Cleveland.[3]

Despite the rain and the arguments over whether the participation foretold victory or disappointment, the McKinley and Roosevelt Business Men's Sound Money Parade was a big event. "The great parade of Sound Money took place between 10 a.m. and 6 p.m. Thousands of enthusiastic men marched up Broadway and Fifth Avenue carrying flags and banners. . . . The column took nearly seven hours to pass a given point. . . . Governor Roosevelt, Lieutenant-Governor Woodruff, B. B Odell, Jr., and others reviewed the parade, which was led by General Anson G. McCook, as Grand Marshal."[4] Odell was the Republican candidate to succeed Roosevelt as governor, and McCook was an attorney and businessman who had been a Civil War general and a three-term congressman from New York.

Marchers in this parade comprised one of the Republicans' most valued constituencies—namely, businessmen. These were the very party members who had reportedly threatened to withhold campaign funding if Roosevelt was renominated for governor because his policies and politics were seen as unfriendly to their interests. All of that was forgotten on this day of celebration, and strengthening the likelihood of prosperity was a theme businessmen supported wholeheartedly. As the *New-York Tribune* opined: "It is when the businessmen's parade surges up the avenue that Republican confidence always reaches its highest point. . . . For they are not politicians, or heelers, or hangers on, or ignorant or easily led men—they are substantial men, men whose interest is the country's interest, and who know what their own and the country's interest is."[5]

It was a massive parade: over one hundred bands and thirty-eight divisions of marchers organized by profession. There were ranks of lawyers, bankers, hardware men, coal men, builders, coffee producers, brokers, marketers of paper products, members of the produce and cotton exchanges, and many, many more. Forty minutes were required for the first division—the wholesale dry goods sellers—to pass the reviewing stand. This division alone had sixteen sections of sixteen hundred men each.[6]

Roosevelt, Woodruff, and Odell took their places on the reviewing stand just before 11:00 a.m., the time when the honor guard leading the parade passed. This unit had left the starting point for the marchers shortly after 10:00 a.m., and they reached the "disbanding point" at 11:18 a.m. Thus, each marcher could expect to walk the route in about an hour and a quarter, assuming the procession kept moving. Published estimates for the number of marchers who could pass a given point per hour varied from eight to ten thousand, and the parade was officially declared concluded at 6:06 p.m.[7]

Roosevelt stood on the reviewing stand, waving his hat, shouting words of thanks and encouragement, and, by all reports, thoroughly enjoying himself from the beginning to the end. Colleagues and even some marchers urged that he put his hat on or rest, but he would have none of it. There was no cover over the reviewers, and the governor's clothing was soaked. Yet, he kept the vigil.

"There was no doubt in the mind of anybody who was in a position to look on at all this of the magnetism of the Governor's personality. As each battalion caught sight of him, it was as if an electric current had suddenly been sent through it, and it was set to shouting and dancing. . . . And all the time Teddy . . . was smiling and bowing and waving his hat and recognizing those whom he knew, now and then calling to someone in the line to come over and shake hands, as if nobody had ever paid any attention to him before in his life, and he was quite intoxicated by it."[8]

After more than seven hours, Roosevelt retired from the reviewing stand, and his first act was to send this telegram to President William McKinley in Canton, Ohio: "In spite of the unfavorable weather the sound money parade was an even more magnificent demonstration than four years ago. The aroused civic honesty and business intelligence of the nation are behind you. Theodore Roosevelt."[9]

Then Roosevelt stopped briefly at the home of his sister and brother-in-law for dinner and proceeded to the Thirty-fourth Street ferry. He crossed to Long Island City and took the 8:00 p.m. train to his home in Oyster Bay to await the results of the election that had received his full-time attention since September 2.[10]

Still there was one more event for Roosevelt prior to Election Day on Tuesday, November 6. On Monday evening, the Republican Club of Oyster Bay planned a welcome-home celebration for the governor, and they invited residents of other communities on Long Island. Until barely a week earlier, the campaign schedule had the vice presidential candidate touring Long Island on Monday for yet another round of events and speeches, but Roosevelt canceled that series of stops in favor of one hometown celebration. Local Republicans had erected a circus tent at a site on the outskirts of Oyster Bay known as Tucker's Lot, but the prospect of visitors from all over Long Island prompted organizers to set another tent of similar size adjacent to the first. Capacity had expanded to three thousand, but the interest was so great that more than half the crowd had to be content with the parade and standing in the evening air outside the tents.[11]

Excursion trains arrived one after the other to the village station where a large bonfire welcomed visitors. Five bands led a procession to Tucker's Lot for the celebration. Though it was the eve of Election Day, the *New-York Evening Journal*, William Randolph Hearst's Democratic newspaper, had tacitly conceded victory to the Republican ticket, and the crowd at Oyster Bay likely had read the news. The editor wrote: "Four years ago on election night the *Journal* beat the entire country with the news of William McKinley's election. This year the *Journal* expects history to repeat itself."[12]

Roosevelt was greeted warmly, and he spoke for almost forty-five minutes, touching on various issues of the day. He addressed the crowd as "my good friends and my old neighbors," and he said that he wasn't making a speech so much as he was talking to them as he often did in his home or in their homes. He included this summary statement on his season of campaigning far and wide: "In this campaign I have not only appealed in my speeches to the Republicans but to all who have the honor and integrity of the country at heart. I have appealed to higher motives than partisanship; I have appealed to honor. I have appealed to all whether agreeing or disagreeing with me in politics to stand by their country. I have appealed to the teachings of Jefferson and Jackson and of Lincoln."[13]

Finally, Roosevelt's vice presidential campaign was at an end. He left the tent on Tucker's Lot and boarded his carriage to go home. Nearly the entire crowd surrounded him and walked along with the carriage until it reached the entrance of the drive to Sagamore Hill. As he turned toward home, the people shouted and cheered, calling out, "You're our next vice president!"[14]

Election

Election Day, November 6, 1900, came and went, and though all indicators had pointed to the certainty of victory for the presidential and vice presidential candidates heading the Republican ticket, the November 7th page–one headlines proclaimed the news afresh:

"McKinley and Roosevelt: Standard-Bearers of Prosperity Gain Victory that Forever Crushes out Bryanism" *(San Francisco Call)*

"McKinley and Roosevelt Elected: Republican Pluralities Reduced in Eastern and Middle States" *(Houston Daily Post)*

"Grand Old Party Continues in Power Four Years Longer" *(Wheeling Daily Intelligencer)*

"McKinley has Swept the Country Again" *(Wichita Daily Eagle)*

"Landslide to McKinley" *(Indianapolis Journal)*

"Victory for Party of Hanna" *(Rock Island Argus)*

"William McKinley Again Elected President of the United States" *(St. Louis Republic)*

"McKinley and Roosevelt Elected: New York Gives 120,000 Plurality" *(New-York Tribune)*

On the morning that these headlines ran, President William McKinley and Vice President-elect Theodore Roosevelt exchanged telegrams. Roosevelt wrote: "I congratulate you and I congratulate far more the nation. I feel the most heartfelt gratitude over the results. Theodore Roosevelt." McKinley's response acknowledged that Roosevelt had done the heavy lifting: "I heartily appreciate your kind expressions and congratulate you upon concluding in health one of the most memorable campaigns in our political history. Wm. McKinley."[15]

Of the twenty-three states where Theodore Roosevelt campaigned, eighteen of them gave a plurality of votes to the McKinley ticket. (See appendix D for a state-by-state list of winning percentages.) Illinois, Indiana, Iowa, Maryland, Michigan, Minnesota, New Jersey, New York, North Dakota, Ohio, Pennsylvania, West Virginia, and Wisconsin voted Republican, as they had in 1896. Kansas, Nebraska, South Dakota, Utah, and Wyoming switched from Democratic pluralities to Republican. Colorado, Idaho,

Missouri, and Montana stayed Democratic. And Kentucky moved back into the Democratic column.

Altogether, McKinley received over 7.2 million votes, slightly more than 51.5 percent, and Bryan won nearly 6.4 million votes, approximately 45.5 percent. Third-party candidates received the remainder of the votes, almost 400,000 or 3 percent. As ranked by vote totals greatest to least, these candidates were: John Granville Woolley (Prohibition), Eugene Victor Debs (Social Democrat), Wharton Barker (People's Party or Populist), Joseph Francis Maloney (Socialist-Labor), Seth Hockett Ellis (Union Reform), Jonah Fitz Randolph Leonard (United Christian), and Job Harriman (Social Democrats of the USA).[16]

Of the votes that actually elect the president and vice president of the United States—that is, those cast by the electors of the Electoral College— William McKinley won 292 and William Jennings Bryan won 155. The corresponding numbers in 1896, when the two ran against each other for the first time, had been 271 to 176. Even though some state pluralities shrank, the overall totals for the Republicans' national ticket and the strength of the party's mandate to govern had grown rather significantly.

Despite Mark Hanna's misgivings, adding Theodore Roosevelt to the ticket as the vice presidential candidate had obviously not damaged the party's electability, and the widespread enthusiasm for his candidacy as demonstrated by the large crowds during his campaign tours suggests that his nomination was a good choice. Roosevelt's celebrity encouraged the Republican faithful and likely appealed to both disaffected Democrats and curious voters who were uncommitted or apathetic as the campaign began.

Owing perhaps to the custom of the day, McKinley gave the appearance of a lackluster candidate, while Roosevelt was obviously energized by the rough and tumble of campaigning. It proved to be a pairing of styles that could be described as inspired, though it was not one that key party leaders would necessarily have chosen apart from the manipulations of Republican state bosses Platt and Quay and the demand of the delegates to the Republican National Convention. When McKinley refused to make a vice presidential choice, those who wanted to keep Roosevelt from the ticket had no chance of gaining their preference. It was going to be the Rough Rider, and, in the end, the convention vote was unanimous.

Buffalo Bill Cody tagged Roosevelt the "American Cyclone," during the candidate's whistle stop in Junction City, Kansas. During the western campaign tour, that moniker, hundreds of engaging anecdotes, ceaseless stories of cheering crowds numbering in the thousands or tens of thousands, and a constant drumbeat of Roosevelt's campaign themes crossed the nation's newswires daily because of the journalists who traveled in a railcar, named the *Montana,* coupled with the candidate's own car, the *Minnesota.* Those were the newspapermen of the so-called Camp No. 2 of the Roosevelt Rough Writers.[17]

One regional journalist listed the members of the Rough Writers in the *Deseret Evening News* on September 21, 1900, during Roosevelt's visit to Salt Lake City. They were: H. V. Jones of the *Minneapolis Journal,* A. G. Nevins of the Associated Press, C. H. Carpenter of the Phipps-McRae League of Papers, W. H. Williams of the Western Union Telegraph Company, Lindsay Denison of the *Sun,* John H. Rastery of the *Chicago Record* and *New York Herald,* G. W. Ogden of the *Chicago Tribune,* and H. I. Cleveland of the *Chicago Times-Herald.*[18] In addition, newspapermen representing statewide, regional, or local publications joined the traveling party for one or another segment of the tour.

As he had demonstrated during his 1898 stint in the Spanish War and during his time as governor of New York, Theodore Roosevelt had a gift for understanding and working with the media. Lindsay Denison of the *Sun,* who was consistently the most entertaining among the Rough Writers, wrote that of the original group of journalists, staff, and alternate speakers who started the western tour with Roosevelt on September 6, only three persisted to the conclusion of the New York tour on November 2. Denison wrote proudly, because he was one of the remaining three: "Business affairs, family cares, homesickness, and absolute weariness have caused the rest of the 15 or 20 to drop out and let others take their places." Then he referred to those who made it to the end as "the three survivors." So committed had Denison become after traveling with Roosevelt and hearing him speak for weeks, he wrote in his summary piece on the New York tour of "the restful certainty of Bryan's defeat."[19]

Relaxing in Oyster Bay was the intention of Theodore Roosevelt on the day following the election, and he was said to be "a happy man" in light of the outcome.[20] Congratulations came to him by telegram from Secretary of War Elihu Root, Senator Chauncey Depew, Archbishop John Ireland of St. Paul, and many other friends and dignitaries around the country. Neighbors and local officials stopped by Sagamore Hill to add their well wishes in person. Two Roman Catholic priests from New York City visited Roosevelt at home and caused a minor dustup when they refused to tell journalists gathered in Oyster Bay the nature of their mission. As they boarded the train, one of the priests mumbled that they had been "trying to sell the Governor a horse."[21]

For his part, Hanna was still not a believer. After the election, he reportedly said, "The best we can do is pray fervently for the continued health of the president."[22]

Roosevelt celebrated the president in his official statement. Faithful, as always, to the commander in chief, he wrote: "I deeply rejoice over the result. President McKinley had to face more serious and complicated problems than were faced by any president since Lincoln. . . . I do not see how there could have been any material improvement in the way he has faced and solved each of them. It, therefore, seems to me a perfectly fair test of the way our people are willing to back up a man who has done such difficult and all-important work for the nation. . . . In this contest for true Americanism, the men who believe in it have stood together without regard to locality or place of birth, without regard to creed or race origin, without regard to occupation or anything else excepting the needs of American citizenship in a way that is a splendid omen for the future."[23]

Conclusion

Roosevelt could not have known, of course, how soon that American future of which he wrote on November 7, 1900, would be his to shape. Barely ten months after Election Day, assassination claimed the life of William McKinley, and Theodore Roosevelt was thrust into the presidency. He had reportedly found his short stint as vice president boring and meaningless,[24] and suddenly his days were filled with the sort of leadership opportunities he relished.

Historian David McCullough proposed that Roosevelt, at forty-two years of age, the youngest man ever to hold the office, may have been the best prepared because of the variety of his experiences in both appointed and elected positions, as well as his formative years spent in the culture of the eastern urban elite. "He was a well-to-do, aristocratic, big-city, Harvard-educated Republican with ancestral roots in the Deep South and a passionate following in the West, which taken all together made him something quite new under the sun."[25]

However, this was not the perspective held by all of Roosevelt's contemporaries. For some, he had shown himself to be an individual with ambitious goals for which he was underprepared. Despite the fact that he often beat odds stacked against him, critics saw him as a man who frequently overreached. He had pushed himself physically to overcome a sickly childhood, but he was not an athlete. He had studied the natural world, but he was not a trained naturalist. He had researched and written history, but he was not schooled as a historian. He had bought a ranch and lived the frontier life for a time, but jokes about his eastern ways persisted among the cowboys. He had gone to war, but he was not soldier. He had become a hero whose heroics were questioned and downplayed by opponents. He had even been elected governor of the most important state in the Union, but several in his own political party refused to take him seriously. Whether the self-confidence he appeared to possess was genuine or feigned is uncertain.

What is certain is that the celebrity status he enjoyed upon his return from the Spanish War was real in the minds of millions of people across the United States who knew his name and thought of him as a unique individual possessed of the qualities marking a determined leader. That he was admired had to be clear to him. As he interacted with crowds of dozens, hundreds, thousands, and even tens of thousands, he could not misinterpret their eagerness to see him, to hear him, and to push close enough to him to claim a personal experience they could talk about with their families, their friends, and their neighbors.

In that context, it is possible that for the first time in a very eventful, but relatively young life, the few months that are the subject of this book are the time that Theodore Roosevelt took on the confidence and the maturity that would stand him in good stead for the rest of his years in national leadership. In early 1898, he was uncertain enough of his ability to lead that he preferred to stand aside for Leonard Wood to command the Rough Riders. By September of 1901, he was ready to become the president of the United States. One cannot go to war, wrestle with machine politicians and state legislators, and come to recognize the power of his own popular appeal without being changed.

On the Thursday evening following his election to the vice presidency, the citizens of Oyster Bay gathered at the home of Theodore Roosevelt. Faithful to the last, journalist Lindsay Denison of the *Sun* covered this celebration for the governor, now vice president–elect. He wrote: "That he has grown in the estimation of his fellow townsmen was shown tonight when 3,000 people stood in the streets in a drizzling rain, watching and waiting for more than 100 mounted horsemen to form a line and lead the way to Sagamore Hill. . . . The crowd was larger and more enthusiastic than the one that greeted Col. Roosevelt when he landed fresh from San Juan Hill. . . . The Oyster Bay Band headed the procession and when it arrived Gov. Roosevelt was out on his front porch, smiling and bowing. . . . In a neighborly, heart to heart talk, he said: 'I can't tell you how I appreciate this. I have done a great deal of hard work, but I enjoyed it.'"[26]

APPENDICES

APPENDIX A
Chronological List of Campaign Stops

July 1 to November 2, 1900
(Note: This list includes in chronological order all of Theodore Roosevelt's campaign stops in the summer and fall of 1900, as included in wire-service reports, selected New York City newspapers, and several regional sources. Rarely, an unscheduled and brief stop may have gone unreported by media, and thus is not listed here. Where specific information on the time or duration of some stops is available, those data are included in the chapter narratives.)

Sunday, July 1, 1900
>   Chicago, Illinois
>   Joliet
>   Streator

Monday, July 2, 1900
>   Carrollton, Missouri
>   Kansas City
>   Holliday, Kansas
>   Lawrence
>   Topeka
>   Osage City
>   Emporia
>   Florence
>   Peabody
>   Newton
>   Winfield
>   Arkansas City
>   Newkirk, Oklahoma Territory
>   Guthrie
>   Oklahoma City

Thursday, July 5, 1900
>   Quincy, Illinois
>   Camp Point
>   Augusta
>   Plymouth
>   Macomb

Bushnell
Avon
Abington
Galesburg
Galva
Kewanee
Princeton
Mendota
Aurora
Chicago
Friday, July 6, 1900
Cleveland, Ohio
Canton
Tuesday, July 17, 1900
St. Paul, Minnesota
Wednesday, July 18, 1900
Milwaukee, Wisconsin
Chicago, Illinois
Friday, July 20, 1900
Washington, DC
Monday, September 3, 1900
Chicago, Illinois
Tuesday, September 4, 1900
Saratoga, New York
Wednesday, September 5, 1900
Albany
Thursday, September 6, 1900
Detroit, Michigan
Friday, September 7, 1900
Bay City
Saginaw
Owosso
Lansing
Jackson
Eaton Rapids
Charlotte
Hastings
Grand Rapids
Saturday, September 8, 1900
Holland
Allegan
Kalamazoo

Benton Harbor

Niles

South Bend, Indiana

Hammond

Sunday, September 9, 1900

Chicago, Illinois (no campaign events)

Monday, September 10, 1900

La Crosse, Wisconsin

Tuesday, September 11, 1900

Flandreau, South Dakota

Egan

Madison

Dell Rapids

Sioux Falls

Canton

Hawarden, Iowa

Akron

Elk Point, South Dakota

Vermillion

Yankton

Wednesday, September 12, 1900

Chamberlain

Kimball

Plankinton

Mitchell

Woonsocket

Wolsey

Huron

De Smet

Brookings

Thursday, September 13, 1900

Castlewood

Watertown

Clark

Redfield

Faulkton

Aberdeen

Friday, September 14, 1900

Webster

Summit

Milbank

Wilmot

Sisseton

Ortonville, Minnesota

Graceville

Wheaton

Wahpeton, North Dakota

Abercrombie

Fargo

Saturday, September 15, 1900

Mapleton

Casselton

Buffalo/Wheatland

Tower City

Valley City

Sanborn

Jamestown

Dawson

Steele

Sterling

Bismarck

Sunday, September 16, 1900

Mandan

New Salem

Hebron

Richardton

Dickinson

Medora

Glendive, Montana

Miles City

Forsyth

Billings (overnight; events on Monday)

Monday, September 17, 1900

Columbus

Big Timber

Livingston

Bozeman

Manhattan

Logan

Townsend

Winston

Helena

Tuesday, September 18, 1900

Clancy

Basin

Boulder

Butte

Wednesday, September 19, 1900

Dillon

Lima

St. Anthony, Idaho

Rexburg

Market Lake

Idaho Falls

Blackfoot

Pocatello

Thursday, September 20

Cache Junction, Utah

Logan

Brigham City

Ogden

Friday, September 21

Salt Lake City

Saturday, September 22

Evanston, Wyoming

Green River

Rock Springs

Sunday, September 23

O'Neill Siding (visit to Bill Daley's Ranch)

Monday, September 24

Rawlins

Hanna

Medicine Bow

Laramie

Tie Siding

Cheyenne

Tuesday, September 25, 1900

Eaton, Colorado

Greeley

Fort Collins

Loveland

Berthoud

Longmont

Niwot

Boulder

Denver (events; overnight at a nearby estate, Wolhurst)

Wednesday, September 26, 1900
    Castle Rock
    Colorado Springs
    Colorado City
    Manitou Springs
    Divide
    Gillett
    Independence (Teller County)
    Victor
    Cripple Creek
Thursday, September 27, 1900
    Leadville
    Granite
    Buena Vista
    Salida
    Canon City
    Florence
    Pueblo
Friday, September 28, 1900
    Jennings, Kansas
    Norton
    Prairie View
    Phillipsburg
    Smith Center
    Mankato
    Belleville
    Clyde
    Clay Center
    Junction City
    Abilene
    Salina
    Lindsborg
    Hutchinson
Saturday, September 29, 1900
    El Dorado
    Eureka
    Yates Center
    Iola
    Chanute
    Cherryvale
    Parsons
    Cherokee

Weir

Pittsburg

Pleasanton

Paola

Olathe

Fort Scott

Armourdale

Kansas City, Missouri

Sunday, September 30, 1900

Kansas City (no campaign events)

Monday, October 1 and Tuesday, October 2, 1900

Falls City, Nebraska

Auburn

Tecumseh

Beatrice

Wilber

Crete

Fairmont

Minden

Holdredge

McCook

North Platte

Lexington

Kearney

Grand Island

Aurora

York

Seward

Lincoln

Ashland

Plattsmouth

Wednesday, October 3 and Thursday, October 4, 1900

Broken Arrow

Seneca

Hyannis

Alliance

Crawford

Chadron

Lead, South Dakota

Deadwood

Valentine, Nebraska

Ainsworth

Bassett

Atkinson

O'Neill

Clearwater

Neligh

Norfolk

West Point

Fremont

Blair

Omaha

Friday, October 5, 1900

Fort Dodge, Iowa

Iowa Falls

Waterloo

Cedar Rapids

West Liberty

Davenport

Rock Island, Illinois (event; overnight on train at Burlington Yard)

Saturday, October 6, 1900

Sterling

Dixon

Belvidere

DeKalb

Elgin

Chicago (two nights at the Auditorium Annex)

Sunday, October 7, 1900

Chicago (no campaign events)

Monday, October 8, 1900

Joliet

Streator

Minonk

Eureka

Peoria

Lincoln

Mount Pulaski

Springfield

Jacksonville

Litchfield

East Alton

East St. Louis

(Overnight at the Planters' Hotel in St. Louis)

Tuesday, October 9, 1900
> St Louis, Missouri
> (Overnight traveling on the train)

Wednesday, October 10, 1900
> Hammond, Indiana
> Rensselaer
> Monon
> Lafayette
> Frankfort
> Logansport
> Peru
> Wabash
> Huntington
> Fort Wayne
> (Overnight on the train at a siding outside Marion)

Thursday, October 11, 1900
> Marion
> Fairmount
> Summitville
> Alexandria
> Anderson
> Muncie
> Winchester
> Richmond
> Cambridge City
> Knightstown
> Greenfield
> Indianapolis (events and overnight)

Friday, October 12, 1900
> Plainfield
> Greencastle
> Brazil
> Terre Haute
> Lewis
> Linton
> Bee Hunter
> Marco
> Sandborn
> Edwardsport
> Bicknell
> Vincennes

Princeton

Evansville (events and overnight)

Saturday, October 13, 1900

   Henderson, Kentucky

   Madisonville

   Hopkinsville

   Guthrie

   Russellville

   Bowling Green

   Munfordsville

   Elizabethtown

   Louisville

Sunday, October 14, 1900

   Spring Station (visit to A. J. Alexander's farm))

Monday, October 15, 1900

   Lexington

   Winchester

   Mt. Sterling

   Morehead

   Ashland

   Greenup

   Vanceburg

   Maysville

   Covington (overnight at Cincinnati)

Tuesday, October 16, 1900

   Cincinnati, Ohio

   Hamilton

   Middletown

   Miamisburg

   Dayton

   Springfield

   Yellow Springs

   Xenia

   South Charleston

   London

   Columbus (events and overnight)

Wednesday, October 17, 1900

   Delaware

   Marion

   Upper Sandusky

   Carey

   Fostoria

Bradner
Pemberville
Toledo
Fremont
Clyde
Bellevue
Norwalk
Elyria
Cleveland (events and overnight)
Thursday, October 18, 1900
Akron
Canton
Navarre
Scio, West Virginia
Dillonvale
Long Run
Warrenton
Martin's Ferry
Wheeling
Benwood
Moundsville
New Martinsville
Sistersville
St. Mary's
Waverly
Parkersburg (events and overnight)
Friday, October 19, 1900
Ravenswood
Mason City
Point Pleasant
Huntington
Charleston
Hinton
(Overnight traveling on the train)
Saturday, October 20, 1900
Washington, DC (visit with President McKinley)
Baltimore
(Overnight traveling on the train)
Sunday, October 21, 1900
Oyster Bay, New York (no campaign events)
Monday, October 22, 1900
Weehawken, New Jersey

West Nyack, New York
Congers
Haverstraw
Cornwall
Newburg
Kingston
Tuesday, October 23, 1900
    West Hurley
    Shokan
    Phoenicia
    Pine Hill
    Shandaken
    Fleischmans
    Arkville
    Roxbury
    Stamford
    Bloomville
    Davenport Centre
    Oneonta
    Otsego
    Unadilla
    Sidney
    Norwich
Wednesday, October 24, 1900
    Earlville
    Cazenovia
    Canastota
    Oneida
    Rome
    Herkimer
    Utica
Thursday, October 25, 1900
    Camden
    Watertown
    Oswego
    Sterling
    Weedsport
    Auburn
    Syracuse
Friday, October 26, 1900
    Little Falls (scheduled; later canceled)
    Amsterdam

Schenectady
Albany
New York City
Saturday, October 27, 1900
    Jersey City, New Jersey
    Paterson
    Passaic
    Suffern, New York
    Hillburn
    Middletown
    Port Jervis
    Shohola, Pennsylvania
    Lackawaxen
    Cochecton, New York
    Callicoon
    Long Eddy
    Hancock
    Deposit
    Susquehanna, Pennsylvania
    Great Bend
    Binghamton, New York (events)
Sunday, October 28, 1900
    Binghamton (no campaign events)
Monday, October 29, 1900
    Cortland
    Ithaca
    Van Etten
    Elmira
Tuesday, October 30, 1900
    Corning
    Bath
    Wayland
    Livonia
    Avon
    Geneseo
    Canandaigua
    Geneva
    Penn Yan
    Rochester
Wednesday, October 31, 1900
    Brockport
    Holley

Albion

Medina

Lockport

Niagara Falls

North Tonawanda

Black Rock

Buffalo

Thursday, November 1, 1900

Batavia

Attica

Warsaw

Silver Springs

Ellicottville

Salamanca

Little Valley

Cattaraugus

Dayton

Dunkirk

Jamestown

Friday, November 2, 1900

Randolph

Olean

Friendship

Cuba

Wellsville

Hornellsville

Addison

Waverly

Oswego

Saturday, November 3, 1900

New York City

Monday, November 5, 1900

Oyster Bay

APPENDIX B
State-by-State Totals of Campaign Stops

Following is an alphabetical listing of the states visited by Theodore Roosevelt during his campaign for the vice presidency in 1900 showing the number of reported stops in communities large and small. If there were several speeches or events during a single stop (e.g., Salt Lake City), that community is counted once. If a community was visited multiple times during the campaign (e.g., Chicago), it is counted as a stop more than once in this list.

Colorado...25
Idaho..6
Illinois..39
Indiana..38
Iowa...8
Kansas...39
Kentucky...19
Maryland..1
Michigan...15
Minnesota...4
Missouri...4
Montana..19
Nebraska...38
New Jersey..4
New York...97
North Dakota...20
Ohio..30
Oklahoma (Territory)....................................3
Pennsylvania...4
South Dakota...31
Utah...5
West Virginia...19
Wisconsin...2
Wyoming...10
Total Number of Reported Stops..............480

(Note that there were also two visits by Theodore Roosevelt to Washington, DC, during the months of the campaign.)

APPENDIX C
Threats, Violence, and Organized Protests

This is a listing of incidents during the Roosevelt vice presidential campaign where the candidate and his party experienced extraordinary and untoward behavior—threats, violence, or brutal verbal protests by organized groups. While there were frequent instances of heckling or other disruptions by individuals, the incidents included in this list went beyond rudeness to the risk of serious physical confrontation.

Yankton, South Dakota (September 11, 1900)—as the Roosevelt procession approached the downtown area, a fire behind the Singer Sewing Machine Shop triggered an alarm and caused widespread confusion in the crowd. Newspapers reported that the fire was deliberately set by Bryan supporters to disrupt the Roosevelt rally. (At nearly the same moment, the horses of Roosevelt's carriage bolted but were brought under control before it became a problem.)

Victor, Colorado (September 26, 1900)—shouted insults during the Roosevelt rally by an organized mob of radical miners became a physically threating situation. Several of Roosevelt's party surrounded him to escort him from the meeting hall to the train, but noisy protestors marched alongside with Bryan banners. Fifteen hundred people were in the streets, and several fights ensued. One protestor assaulted Roosevelt by poking a two-by-four pole into his chest. He safely regained the train, but the next day there were reports that he had also sustained a knee injury. Also during the following days, the editor of the *Victor Daily* was assaulted in his office for writing an editorial critical of the protestors.

Flandreau, South Dakota (September, 1900; exact date uncertain)—another incident was reported as sidebar coverage to the events in Victor. In this small community visited on September 11, 1900, by Roosevelt, the local newspaper editor wrote a follow-up piece critical of one of the speakers, William Bell, the only South Dakotan to serve with the Rough Riders. Bell stormed into the newspaper office and shot the journalist.

Salida, Colorado (September 27, 1900)—an organized mob of fifty local youth circulated in and around the rally crowd shouting abusive epithets and other insults in an attempt to disrupt the Roosevelt meeting.

Pueblo, Colorado (September 27, 1900)—frequent insults were shouted at Roosevelt and his supporters in the streets. Police uncovered a plot to shut down the Republican rally with a Victor-style protest and arrested the ringleaders before the candidate's arrival.

Armourdale (Kansas City), Kansas (September 29, 1900)—an organized mob of men and boys shouted repeatedly from the crowd at a large outdoor rally; eventually, Roosevelt became engaged with them in a loud argument.

Omaha, Nebraska (October 4, 1900)—during a Roosevelt speech, several protestors scattered throughout the gallery became so loud and disruptive that they were removed by police.

Chicago, Illinois (October 7, 1900)—Roosevelt and a traveling companion attended Sunday worship. When they exited the church, a group of thirty or more newsboys, wearing hats that read *Chicago American,* shouted abusive and profane insults and chased Roosevelt's carriage screaming at him and throwing clods of mud. The publication they represented was a Hearst newspaper supportive of the Democratic ticket.

Ft. Wayne, Indiana (October 10, 1900)—as Roosevelt rode through the community in the procession planned by event organizers, stones pelted his carriage. He was hit in the side, and the stone glanced off him to hit another occupant of the carriage in the mouth. Warnings of problems in Ft. Wayne had led local police to round up several individuals and warn them against bad behavior.

Elizabethtown, Kentucky (October 13, 1900)—during the outdoor Roosevelt rally, coal haulers drove their filled wagons through the area at full speed, nearby steam whistles were blown repeatedly, Bryan supporters shouted continuously, and small boys carried Bryan banners through the crowd.

Ashland, Kentucky (October 15, 1900)—unkempt, wild-eyed mountaineers wearing Bryan buttons roved constantly through the audience during the speeches, speaking loudly to one another, and unsettling people.

Covington, Kentucky (October 15, 1900)—rumors of serious threats caused law-enforcement officials to add deputies. Protestors walked about, blew horns, and shouted insults. Roosevelt's supporters took him out a back door at the end of his speech to avoid physical confrontations.

Cleveland, Ohio (October 17, 1900)—laborers favoring Bryan arrived early and filled the front half of the seating in the large tent where the Roosevelt meeting was held. This contingent interrupted the speaking with shouts and hisses. As the campaign party left the tent, a young boy in a group of disrupters threw a stone that hit Roosevelt in the head. His hat kept him from serious injury.

St. Mary's, West Virginia (October 18, 1900)—twenty-five or more disrupters gathered on the outskirts of the crowd, intimidating people by their presence and shouting. At one point, McKinley supporters confronted the protestors and threatened them. Disruptions quieted.

Norwich, New York (October 23, 1900)—an organized gang of thirty or forty boys massed outside Roosevelt's dining car parked on a siding, shouting vile insults at the governor and his party as they ate dinner.

Rome, New York (October 24, 1900)—an organized group of young boys heckled Roosevelt throughout his speech.

Auburn, New York (October 25, 1900)—locals described by journalists as "roughs" poured out of nearby saloons, as Roosevelt arrived at the rally site, and they were generally threatening to people arriving for the event. These men so disrupted an outdoor meeting that the speakers had to give up addressing the large crowd and turn only to those standing nearby on a sidewalk.

Syracuse, New York (October 25, 1900)—reports of threats caused the local force to add extra police to the number guarding the campaign party. One policeman said their orders were to break the arm of any man who raised his hand in a hostile fashion.

Cohecton, New York (October 27, 1900)—when a Bryan supporter began shouting for his candidate during the speaking, another man slapped him in the mouth with a backhanded swing to quiet him.

Elmira, New York (October 29, 1900)—a gang was hiding in alleyways and ran out when Roosevelt's carriage passed. They surrounded the vehicle, shouted insults, and threw pictures of the Democratic gubernatorial candidate at him. Then they began pelting the carriage with sticks, eggs, and vegetables; Roosevelt was hit by a stick. Later the mob attacked two Republican clubs from Elmira and another from Corning as they marched in the parade. Five members of the Corning Club required medical attention. Finally, the protestors harassed and attacked individuals on the streets to the extent that police escorts were necessary for many of the visitors.

Geneva, New York (October 30, 1900)—incessant blowing of factory whistles and shouting through megaphones from windows made speaking nearly impossible at this outdoor rally.

Waverly, New York (November 2, 1900)—a large stone was thrown at Roosevelt's railcar. The window near where he was sitting was shattered.

APPENDIX D
Election Results in States on Roosevelt's Campaign Tours

(Note that all numbers are percentages of the popular vote)

McKinley won:

Illinois .... 52.83 to 44.44
Indiana .... 50.60 to 46.42
Iowa .... 58.04 to 39.46
Kansas...................... 52.56 to 45.96
Maryland .... 51.50 to 46.23
Michigan .... 58.10 to 38.89
Minnesota .... 60.21 to 35.69
Nebraska................. 50.46 to 47.22
New Jersey.............. 55.28 to 41.09
New York .... 53.10 to 43.83
North Dakota .... 55.25 to 39.64
Ohio .... 52.30 to 45.66
Pennsylvania .... 60.74 to 36.16
South Dakota........... 56.73 to 41.14
Utah .... 50.58 to 48.30
West Virginia........... 54.27 to 44.75
Wisconsin .... 60.06 to 35.97
Wyoming .... 58.66 to 41.17

Bryan won:

Colorado................... 55.43 to 42.04
Idaho .... 50.79 to 46.96
Kentucky.................. 50.21 to 48.51
Missouri................... 51.48 to 45.94
Montana .... 58.43 to 39.79

(Data from David Leip, "1900 Presidential General Election Results," National Election Results website from the reference Dave Leip's Atlas of U.S. Presidential Elections.)

NOTES

PROLOGUE

1. See an example of a contemporary telling of the legend in the *Cape Girardeau (MO) Democrat*'s June 30, 1900, report on the nominating speech of Senator Chauncey Depew.

2. All sixty-nine electors cast a vote for Washington, effectively giving him a unanimous victory, although there were votes for others because each elector was accorded two votes, with the runner-up becoming vice president.

3. For instance, the *St. Louis Republic* on June 23, 1900, p. 6, opined that "easterners know him as a shallow man" and the *Meade County (KS) News* on October 25, 1900, p. 2, termed him "an ambitious braggart."

4. Morris, *Rise of Theodore Roosevelt*, p. 541.

5. *New York Times*, September 29, 1900, p. 7.

CHAPTER 1: FROM HERO TO GOVERNOR

1. Mattson, "Politics Is Up."

2. Ibid., p. 303.

3. Ibid., p. 306.

4. Roosevelt, *Rough Riders*, p. 2.

5. Roosevelt, *Autobiography*, p. 295.

6. Ibid., p. 311.

7. Ibid., pp. 311-12.

8. Roosevelt, *Rough Riders*, p. 5.

9. Ibid., p. 6.

10. Ibid., p. 8.

11. Mattson, "Politics Is Up," p. 309.

12. Morris, *Rise of Theodore Roosevelt*, p. 874.

13. Ibid., p. 882.

14. Roosevelt, *Rough Riders*, p. 74.

15. Cresswell, "Richard Harding Davis."

16. *Anaconda (MT) Standard*, July 30, 1898, p. 2.

17. *San Francisco Call*, June 26, 1898, p. 2.

18. *St. Landry Clarion* (Opelousas, LA), July 2, 1898, p. 1.

19. *Anderson Intelligencer* (Anderson Court House, SC), July 6, 1898, p. 2.

20. *San Francisco Call,* June 25, 1898, p. 1.

21. Roosevelt, *Rough Riders,* pp. 48, 83.

22. *Times* (Washington, DC), July 9, 1898, p. 5.

23. *Williamsburg (VA) Gazette,* July 9, 1898, p. 1.

24. *Los Angeles Herald,* August 5, 1898, p. 1.

25. *Dalles (OR) Daily Chronicle,* August 10, 1898, p. 2.

26. *Wichita (KS) Daily Eagle,* August 16, 1898, p. 2.

27. Campbell, *Spanish-American War: American Wars and the Media in Primary Documents,* p. 6.

28. Morris, *Rise of Theodore Roosevelt,* p. 873.

29. Thayer, *Intimate Biography,* p. 129.

30. Morris, *Rise of Theodore Roosevelt,* p. 873.

31. Roosevelt, *Autobiography,* p. 390.

32. Pearson, *Theodore Roosevelt,* p. 68.

33. Morris, *Rise of Theodore Roosevelt,* p. 647ff.

34. Ibid., p. 648.

35. Auchincloss and Schlesinger, *Theodore Roosevelt,* p. 47.

36. Howland, *Theodore Roosevelt and His Times,* p. 44.

37. Morris, *Rise of Theodore Roosevelt,* p. 658.

38. *Sun* (New York City), September 24, 1898, p. 1.

39. *New-York Tribune,* September 24, 1898, p. 1.

40. *Sun* (New York City), September 24, 1898, p. 1.

41. Morris, *Rise of Theodore Roosevelt,* p. 658.

42. *Sun* (New York City), September 24, 1898, p. 1.

43. Ibid., p. 1.

44. Ibid., p. 1.

45. Ibid., p. 1.

46. *New-York Tribune,* September 24, 1898, p. 1.

47. Ibid., p. 1.

48. Morris, *Rise of Theodore Roosevelt,* p. 659.

49. *Sun* (New York City), September 27, 1898, p. 1.

50. Ibid., p. 1.

51. *New-York Tribune,* September 28, 1898, p. 1.

52. Goodwin, *Bully Pulpit,* p. 11.

53. Ibid., p. 276.

54. Thayer, *Intimate Biography,* p. 133.

55. Roosevelt, *Autobiography,* p. 280.

56. Morris, *Rise of Theodore Roosevelt,* p. 664.

57. Ibid., p. 664.

58. *New-York Tribune,* October 30, 1898, p. 1.

CHAPTER 2: FROM GOVERNOR TO VICE PRESIDENTIAL CANDIDATE

1. See Goodwin, *Bully Pulpit*, ch. 9.

2. Roosevelt, *Autobiography*, pp. 325-26.

3. This list of items relies upon biographical works by Auchincloss and Schlesinger, Goodwin, Howland, Morris, Pearson, and Thayer and the autobiography of Theodore Roosevelt. Full references are in the bibliography for this book.

4. Ibid.

5. Morris, *Rise of Theodore Roosevelt*, p. 685.

6. Ibid., p. 696.

7. Ibid., p. 685.

8. Ibid., p. 699.

9. Ibid., p. 701.

10. *Kansas City Journal*, June 24, 1899, p. 1.

11. *El Paso Daily Herald*, June 24, 1899, p. 9.

12. *Evening Herald* (Shenandoah, PA), June 24, 1899, p. 3.

13. *St. Paul Globe*, June 25, 1899, p. 1.

14. *Record-Union*, Sacramento, CA, June 25, 1899, p. 1.

15. *Wichita Daily Eagle*, June 25, 1899, p. 4.

16. *Salt Lake Herald*, June 26, 1899, p. 2.

17. *Evening Times* (Washington, DC), June 27, 1899, p. 2.

18. *Kansas City Journal*, June 28, 1899, p. 3.

19. Morris, *Rise of Theodore Roosevelt*, p. 570.

20. Thayer, *Intimate Biography*, p. 79.

21. Ibid.

22. Morris, *Rise of Theodore Roosevelt*, p. 581.

23. Theodore Roosevelt, Letter to Thomas Platt, February 1, 1900, printed in Thayer, *Intimate Biography*, p. 83.

24. Theodore Roosevelt, Letter to Norton Goddard, April 16, 1900, quoted in Roosevelt, *Autobiography*, p. 261.

25. Goodwin, *Bully Pulpit*, p. 273. (In a twist of fate, Alton Parker would become the Democratic nominee for the presidency in 1904 and run against Theodore Roosevelt.)

26. Morris, *Rise of Theodore Roosevelt*, p. 587.

27. The *Bismarck (ND) Daily Tribune*, June 18, 1900, p. 1.

28. *Evening Bulletin* (Maysville, KY), June 19, 1900, p. 1.

29. *San Francisco Call*, June 19, 1900, p. 1.

30. *Indianapolis Journal*, June 19, 1900, p. 1.

31. *Wichita Daily Eagle*, June 19, 1900, p. 1.

32. *San Francisco Call*, June 20, 1900, p. 1.

33. *Times* (Washington, DC), June 20, 1900, p. 1.

34. *Guthrie (OK) Daily Leader*, June 20, 1900, p. 1.

35. *Omaha Daily Bee,* June 21, 1900, p. 1.

36. *Scranton (PA) Tribune,* June 21, 1900, p. 1.

37. *Richmond Dispatch,* June 21, 1900, p. 1.

38. *St. Paul Globe,* June 21, 1900, p. 1.

39. *Rock Island (IL) Argus,* June 21, 1900, p. 1.

40. *El Paso Daily Herald,* June 21, 1900, p. 1.

41. For a detailed account of the convention, see Morris, *Rise of Theodore Roosevelt.*

42. Ibid.

43. The actual vote for Roosevelt's candidacy was one vote shy of unanimity. He nobly chose to abstain from voting for himself.

CHAPTER 3: CRAFTING IMAGE AND NEGOTIATING STRATEGY

1. *Puck,* May 16, 1900, p. 1.

2. Theodore Roosevelt, Letter to Seth Low, June 23, 1900, in Morison, *Letters of Theodore Roosevelt,* p. 1337.

3. Theodore Roosevelt, Letter to Anna Roosevelt Cowles, June 25, 1900, in Morison, *Letters of Theodore Roosevelt,* p. 1339.

4. Morris, *Rise of Theodore Roosevelt,* p. 588.

5. Roosevelt, *Autobiography,* p. 253.

6. Theodore Roosevelt, Letter to Dr. Lyman Abbott, June 27, 1900, in Morison, *Letters of Theodore Roosevelt,* p. 1344.

7. Theodore Roosevelt, Letter to President William McKinley, June 27, 1900, in Morison, *Letters of Theodore Roosevelt,* p. 1366.

8. Theodore Roosevelt, Letter to Alice Lee Roosevelt, July 14, 1900, in Morison, *Letters of Theodore Roosevelt,* p. 1356.

9. Roosevelt, Letter to Seth Low, June 23, 1900, in Morison, *Letters of Theodore Roosevelt,* p. 1356.

10. Theodore Roosevelt, Letter to Marcus Alonzo Hanna, June 25, 1900, in Morison, *Letters of Theodore Roosevelt,* p. 1340.

11. Theodore Roosevelt, Letter to Cecil Arthur Spring Rice, July 20, 1900, in Morison, *Letters of Theodore Roosevelt,* p. 1358.

12. Theodore Roosevelt, Letter to John Hay, July 30, 1900, in Morison, *Letters of Theodore Roosevelt,* p. 1368.

13. Theodore Roosevelt, Letter to Anna Roosevelt Cowles, August 18, 1900, in Morison, *Letters of Theodore Roosevelt,* p. 1387.

14. Theodore Roosevelt, Letter to Silas Wright Burt, July 14, 1900, in Morison, *Letters of Theodore Roosevelt,* p. 1356.

15. Theodore Roosevelt, Letter to Paul Dana, July 25, 1900, in Morison, *Letters of Theodore Roosevelt,* p. 1362.

16. Theodore Roosevelt, Letter to William Howard Taft, August 6, 1900, in Morison, *Letters of Theodore Roosevelt,* p. 1377.

17. Theodore Roosevelt, Letter to George Hinkley Lyman, June 27, 1900, in Morison, *Letters of Theodore Roosevelt*, p. 1345.

18. Roosevelt, Letter to Paul Dana, July 25, 1900, in Morison, *Letters of Theodore Roosevelt*, p. 1345.

19. Theodore Roosevelt, Letter to General Leonard Wood, August 22, 1900, in Morison, *Letters of Theodore Roosevelt*, p. 1389.

20. Theodore Roosevelt, Letter to John Hay, June 25, 1900, in Morison, *Letters of Theodore Roosevelt*, p. 1338.

21. Theodore Roosevelt, Letter to Winthrop Chanler, July 26, 1900, in Morison, *Letters of Theodore Roosevelt*, p. 1364.

22. See Morris, *Rise of Theodore Roosevelt*, p. 532ff.

23. Theodore Roosevelt, Letter to Elihu Root, August 16, 1900, in Morison, *Letters of Theodore Roosevelt*, p. 1384.

24. Theodore Roosevelt, Letter to Charles Henry Burke, August 16, 1900, in Morison, *Letters of Theodore Roosevelt*, p. 1385.

25. Theodore Roosevelt, Letter to Henry L. Turner, August 19, 1900, in Morison, *Letters of Theodore Roosevelt*, p. 1387.

26. Theodore Roosevelt, Letter to Charles Richard Williams, August 28, 1900, in Morison, *Letters of Theodore Roosevelt*, p. 1393.

27. Theodore Roosevelt, Letter to Marcus Alonzo Hanna, June 27, 1900, in Morison, *Letters of Theodore Roosevelt*, p. 1342.

28. Roosevelt, Letter to Marcus Alonzo Hanna, June 25, in Morison, *Letters of Theodore Roosevelt*, p. 1339.

29. Theodore Roosevelt, Letter to Marcus Alonzo Hanna, July 7, 1900, in Morison, *Letters of Theodore Roosevelt*, p. 1350.

30. Theodore Roosevelt, Letter to Henry Clay Payne, August 18, 1900, in Morison, *Letters of Theodore Roosevelt*, p. 1389.

CHAPTER 4: PARTY PLATFORMS AND PUBLIC POLICY

1. Roosevelt, *Autobiography*, p. 290.

2. Both the *Republican Party Platform* (June 19, 1900) and the *Democratic Party Platform* (July 4, 1900) are available from the American Presidency Project of the University of California, Santa Barbara. The documents may be examined online at www.presidency.ucsb.edu, and all quotations that follow are from one or the other of the party platforms as identified in the text.

3. *Republican Party Platform*, Ibid.

4. *Democratic Party Platform*, Ibid.

5. Morison, *Letters of Theodore Roosevelt*, note p. 1397.

6. Ibid., p. 1397.

7. Ibid., p. 1398.

8. Ibid., p. 1399.

9. Ibid., p. 1400.

10. Ibid., p. 1401.

11. Ibid., p. 1404.

12. Watts, *Rough Rider in the White House,* p. 143.

13. Dorsey, *We Are All Americans,* p. 92.

CHAPTER 5: JULY AND AUGUST TRAVEL

1. James Thorton, "When You Were Sweet Sixteen," popular song on wax cylinder issued by Columbia, George J. Gaskin, artist.

2. Campaign song, "McKinley and Roosevelt," mentioned in *Campaign Songs for 1900, New York Times,* October 21, 1900, p. 26.

3. *St. Louis Republic,* July 3, 1900, p. 11.

4. *Guthrie (OK) Daily Leader,* June 30, 1900, p. 5.

5. *Indianapolis Journal,* July 4, 1900, p. 9.

6. *Wichita Daily Eagle,* July 4, 1900, p. 2.

7. *Arizona Weekly Journal-Miner* (Prescott, AZ), July 4, 1900, p. 5.

8. *Hutchinson (KS) Gazette,* July 5, 1900, p. 4.

9. Morison, *Letters of Theodore Roosevelt,* p. 1508.

10. *Indianapolis Journal,* July 3, 1900, p. 4.

11. *Salt Lake Herald,* July 3, 1900, p. 3.

12. *Sun* (New York City), July 5, 1900, p. 4.

13. Historical marker #17-76 at the site of the McKinley home in Canton, Ohio, placed by the Ohio Historical Society.

14. *Stark County Democrat,* Canton, Ohio, Weekly Edition, July 6, 1900.

15. *San Francisco Call,* July 7, 1900, p. 7.

16. *Wheeling Daily Intelligencer,* July 7, 1900, p. 1.

17. Ibid.

18. *Evening Star* (Washington, DC), July 7, 1900, p. 10.

19. Morison, *Letters of Theodore Roosevelt,* pp. 1508-9.

20. *Minneapolis Tribune,* July 12, 1900, p. 1.

21. Ibid., July 18, 1900, p. 1.

22. Ibid., July 17, 1900, p. 1.

23. *St. Paul Globe,* July 18, 1900, p. 1.

24. *Minneapolis Tribune,* July 18, 1900, p. 1.

CHAPTER 6: MICHIGAN, INDIANA, ILLINOIS, AND WISCONSIN

1. These ideas have been discussed in several literary reviews and historical works over the years. See, for example, Henry M. Littlefield in *American Quarterly 16,* 1964, p. 47; Hugh Rockoff in *Journal of Political Economy 98,* 1990, p. 739.

2. *San Francisco Call,* July 3, 1900, p. 1.

3. *Jamestown (ND) Weekly Alert,* July 5, 1900, p. 8.

4. *Rock Island (IL) Argus,* September 4, 1900, p. 1.

5. Ibid.

6. *St. Louis Republic,* September 4, 1900, p. 6.

7. Ibid.

8. *Indianapolis Journal,* September 4, 1900, p. 1.

9. *Sun* (New York City), September 6, 1900, p. 3.

10. Ibid.

11. *Evening Times* (Washington, DC), September 6, 1900, p. 1.

12. *El Paso Daily Herald,* September 5, 1900, p. 1.

13. *Scranton (PA) Tribune,* September 6, 1900, p. 4.

14. *Kansas Agitator* (Garnett, KS), September 7, 1900, p. 4.

15. *Hocking Sentinel* (Logan, OH), September 6, 1900, p. 3.

16. *Albuquerque Daily Citizen,* September 6, 1900, p. 1.

17. *Times* (Washington, DC), September 7, 1900, p. 1.

18. *Sun* (New York City), September 7, 1900, p. 1.

19. Details from coverage in the *Rock Island (IL) Argus,* September 7, 1900, p. 1.

20. *San Francisco Call,* September 7, 1900, p. 4.

21. Ibid.

22. *New York Times,* September 9, 1900, p. 3.

23. *Times* (Washington, DC), September 8, 1900, p. 1.

24. *Omaha Daily Bee,* September 8, 1900, p. 2.

25. *Evening Bulletin* (Maysville, KY), September 8, 1900, p. 1.

26. *Times* (Washington, DC), September 8, 1900, p. 1.

27. *Omaha Daily Bee,* September 8, 1900, p. 2.

28. *Evening Bulletin* (Maysville, KY), September 8, 1900, p. 1.

29. *Omaha Daily Bee,* September 8, 1900, p. 2.

30. *Evening Bulletin* (Maysville, KY), September 8, 1900, p. 1.

31. *Omaha Daily Bee,* September 8, 1900, p. 2.

32. Ibid.

33. Ibid.

34. *New-York Tribune,* September 8, 1900, p. 2.

35. *Times* (Washington, DC), September 8, 1900, p. 1.

36. *New-York Tribune,* September 8, 1900, p. 2.

37. *Minneapolis Tribune,* September 9, 1900, p. 1.

38. *New York Times,* September 9, 1900, p. 3.

39. Ibid.

40. *Salt Lake Herald,* September 9, 1900, p. 2.

41. Ibid.

42. *New York Times,* September 9, 1900, p. 3.

43. *Indianapolis Journal,* September 7, 1900, p. 2.

44. *Indianapolis Journal,* September 9, 1900, p. 1.

45. Ibid.

46. Ibid.

47. Ibid., p. 2.

48. Ibid., p. 1.

49. *New York Times,* September 10, 1900.

50. *Minneapolis Tribune,* September 11, 1900, p. 1.

51. *Indianapolis Journal,* September 11, 1900, p. 1.

52. Ibid.

CHAPTER 7: SOUTH DAKOTA

1. *Aberdeen (SD) Daily News,* September 13, 1900, p. 1.

2. Roseboom and Eckes, *History of Presidential Elections,* p. 128.

3. U.S. Bureau of the Census, *Historical Statistics of the United States, Colonial Times to 1970,* bicentennial edition, pt. 2, Washington, DC, pp. 1076, 1097.

4. Roseboom and Eckes, *History of Presidential Elections,* p. 127.

5. *Yankton (SD) Press and Dakotan,* September 20, 1900, p. 1.

6. *Brookings (SD) Weekly Register,* September 13, 1900, p. 1.

7. *Yankton (SD) Press and Dakotan,* September 12, 1900, p. 1.

8. *Daily Argus-Leader* (Sioux Falls, SD), September 10, 1900, p. 1.

9. *Daily Argus-Leader* (Sioux Falls, SD), September 11, 1900, p. 1.

10. *Daily Argus-Leader* (Sioux Falls, SD), September 13, 1900, p. 1.

11. *Dakota Huronite,* Huron, SD, September 11, 1900, p. 1.

12. *Aberdeen (SD) Daily News,* September 12, 1900, p. 1.

13. *Aberdeen (SD) Daily News,* September 13, 1900, p. 1.

14. *Mitchell (SD) Daily Republican,* September 12, 1900, p. 1.

15. *Daily Argus-Leader* (Sioux Falls, SD), September 13, 1900, p. 1.

16. *Mitchell (SD) Daily Republican,* September 12, 1900, p. 1.

17. *Chamberlain (SD) Register,* September 13, 1900, p. 1.

18. *Daily Argus-Leader* (Sioux Falls, SD), September 11, 1900, p. 1.

19. *Aberdeen (SD) Daily News,* September 10, 1900, p. 1.

20. *Mitchell (SD) Daily Republican,* September 13, 1900, p. 1.

21. Source accounts for details of the Sioux Falls stop are from the *Daily Argus-Leader, Chicago Tribune, Mitchell Daily Republican,* and *Minneapolis Tribune.*

22. *Mitchell (SD) Daily Republican,* September 12, 1900, p. 1.

23. Source accounts for details of the Yankton stop are from the *Daily Argus-Leader,* Associated Press, *Mitchell Daily Republican, Yankton Press and Dakotan,* and *Yankton Weekly Gazette.*

24. *Yankton (SD) Press and Dakotan,* September 12, 1900, p. 1.

25. Ibid., p. 1.

26. *Daily Argus-Leader* (Sioux Falls, SD), September 10, 1900, p. 1.

27. Source accounts for details of the Brookings stop are from the *Daily Argus-Leader,* Associated Press, *Brookings Weekly Register, Mitchell Daily Republican,* and *New York Times.*

28. *Brookings (SD) Weekly Register,* September 13, 1900, p. 1.

29. *Daily Argus-Leader* (Sioux Falls, SD), September 10, 1900, p. 1.

30. *Brookings (SD) Weekly Register,* September 13, 1900, p. 1.

31. *Daily Argus-Leader* (Sioux Falls, SD), September 13, 1900, p. 1.

32. *New York Times,* September 13, 1900, p. 3.

33. Source accounts for details of the Aberdeen stop are from the *Aberdeen Daily News, Daily Argus-Leader, Chicago Tribune, Mitchell Daily Republican, Minneapolis Tribune,* and *New York Times.*

34. *Aberdeen (SD) Daily News,* September 13, 1900, p. 1.

35. *Aberdeen (SD) Daily News,* September 14, 1900, p. 1.

36. *New York Times,* September 14, 1900, p. 5.

37. *Aberdeen (SD) Daily News,* September 14, 1900, p. 1.

38. *Moody County Enterprise* (Flandreau, SD), September 13, 1900, *p. 1.*

39. *Minneapolis Tribune,* September 12, 1900, p. 1.

40. *Chicago Tribune,* September 12, 1900, p. 1.

41. *Mitchell (SD) Daily Republican,* September 12, 1900, p. 1.

42. Ibid.

43. Ibid. and *Daily Argus-Leader* (Sioux Falls, SD), September 12, 1900, p. 1.

44. *Mitchell (SD) Daily Republican,* September 12, 1900, p. 1.

45. *Minneapolis Tribune,* September 12, 1900, p. 1.

46. *Daily Argus-Leader* (Sioux Falls, SD), September 12, 1900, p. 1.

47. *Vermillion (SD) Plain Talk,* September 13, 1900, p. 1.

48. Ibid.

49. Source accounts for details of the Chamberlain stop are from the *Chamberlain Register, Daily Argus-Leader, Mitchell Daily Republican,* and *New York Times.*

50. *Chamberlain (SD) Register,* September 6, 1900, p. 1.

51. *Chicago Tribune,* September 13, 1900, p. 1.

52. *New York Times,* September 13, 1900, p. 3.

53. Source accounts for details of the Mitchell stop are from the *Daily Argus-Leader* and *Mitchell Daily Republican.*

54. *Mitchell (SD) Daily Republican,* September 12, 1900, p. 1.

55. Source accounts for details of the Huron stop are from the *Daily Argus-Leader, Dakota Huronite,* and *New York Times.*

56. *Daily Argus-Leader* (Sioux Falls, SD), September 10 and 13, 1900, p. 1 in each.

57. *Minneapolis Tribune,* September 14, 1900, p. 1.

58. *Daily Argus-Leader* (Sioux Falls, SD), September 14, 1900, p. 1; note also that the *Mitchell Daily Republican,* September 14, 1900, mistakenly reported that Shaw and Nelson spoke in Faulkton.

59. Source accounts for details of the Watertown stop are from the *Daily Argus-Leader,* Associated Press, *Daily Public Ledger,* and *Minneapolis Tribune.*

60. *Minneapolis Tribune*, September 14, 1900, p. 1.

61. Source accounts for details of the Clark stop are from the *Daily Argus-Leader* and *Minneapolis Tribune*.

62. *Daily Argus-Leader* (Sioux Falls, SD), September 10, 1900, p. 1.

63. *Daily Argus-Leader* (Sioux Falls, SD), September 10 and 14, 1900, p. 1 in each.

64. Associated Press wire report, September 14, 1900.

65. *Daily Argus-Leader* (Sioux Falls, SD), September 10, 1900, p. 1.

66. *Mitchell (SD) Daily Republican*, September 11, 1900, p. 1.

67. *Daily Argus-Leader* (Sioux Falls, SD), September 14, 1900, p. 1.

68. Ibid.

69. *New York Times*, September 15, 1900, p. 1.

70. *Daily Argus-Leader* (Sioux Falls, SD), September 14, 1900, p. 1.

71. *Chicago Tribune*, September 14, 1900, p. 1.

72. Link, "President as Progressive," in *Every Four Years*, p. 156.

73. *Yankton (SD) Weekly Gazette*, September 14, 1900, p. 1.

CHAPTER 8: NORTH DAKOTA

1. Roosevelt, *Autobiography*, p. 19.

2. Ibid., p. 27ff.

3. Ibid., p. 32.

4. Ibid., pp. 32-33.

5. Information from National Park Service (NPS), Internet site for Theodore Roosevelt National Park, "History of the Maltese Cross Cabin and the Elkhorn Ranch."

6. See these examples: Roosevelt, *Ranch Life and the Hunting Trail*; and Di Silvestro, *Theodore Roosevelt in the Badlands*.

7. National Park Service (NPS), Internet site for Theodore Roosevelt National Park, "History of the Maltese Cross Cabin and the Elkhorn Ranch."

8. Roosevelt, *Ranch Life and the Hunting Trail*, ch. 2.

9. Quotation drawn from Di Silvestro, *Theodore Roosevelt in the Badlands*, p. vi.

10. Morris, *Rise of Theodore Roosevelt*, p. 288.

11. Annenberg Learner (online), Biography of America, "TR and Wilson," p. 2.

12. *Bismarck (ND) Weekly Tribune*, August 24, 1900, p. 1.

13. Ibid.

14. *Minneapolis Tribune*, September 15, p. 1.

15. *St. Paul Globe*, September 11, p. 1. Also *Sun* (New York City), September 14, 1900, p. 1.

16. *Minneapolis Tribune*, September 15, 1900, p. 1.

17. *Sun* (New York City), September 15, 1900, p. 5.

18. Nicholas, *McGraw Electric Railway Manual*, p. 210.

19. *Sun* (New York City), September 15, 1900, p. 5.

20. *Omaha Daily Bee*, September 15, 1900, p. 5.

21. Source accounts for details of the Fargo stop are from the *Fargo Forum, Bismarck Weekly Tribune, Bismarck Daily Tribune, New York Times, Sun,* and *Minneapolis Tribune.*

22. *St. Paul Globe,* September 15, 1900, p. 3.

23. *Sun* (New York City), September 15, 1900, p. 5.

24. *Fargo (ND) Forum,* September 15, 1900, p. 1.

25. Ibid., p. 3.

26. Ibid.

27. Ibid., p. 11.

28. Ibid., p. 3.

29. Ibid., p. 11.

30. Ibid., p. 1.

31. *Minneapolis Tribune,* September 15, 1900, p. 1.

32. *Minneapolis Tribune,* September 16, 1900, p. 1.

33. *Bismarck (ND) Daily Tribune,* September 15, p. 1. This source and the following provided details for the stop in Bismarck: the *Bismarck Weekly Tribune, New York Times, Indianapolis Journal,* and *Minneapolis Tribune.*

34. *Bismarck (ND) Daily Tribune,* September 10, 1900, p. 1.

35. *Bismarck (ND) Daily Tribune,* September 17, 1900, p. 1.

36. *Indianapolis Journal,* September 16, 1900, p. 1.

37. *Bismarck (ND) Daily Tribune,* September 17, 1900, p. 1.

38. Ibid.

39. Ibid.

40. Ibid.

41. *Bismarck (ND) Weekly Tribune,* September 21, 1900, p. 1.

42. *Bismarck (ND) Daily Tribune,* September 17, 1900.

43. Ibid.

44. *Bismarck (ND) Daily Tribune,* September 15, 1900.

45. All details of the stops in North Dakota's small communities—including the direct quotations—are from the *Minneapolis Tribune* (September 15–17), *St. Paul Globe* (September 16), or *Bismarck Weekly Tribune* (September 21).

46. Di Silvestro, *Theodore Roosevelt in the Badlands,* pp. 255-56.

47. For an example of the advertisement, see the *Mexico Missouri Message,* September 13, 1900.

CHAPTER 9: MONTANA AND IDAHO

1. *Sun* (New York City), September 16, 1900, p. 5.

2. Theodore Roosevelt, Letter to Henry Clay Payne, August 18, 1900, in Morison, *Letters of Theodore Roosevelt,* p. 1389.

3. Theodore Roosevelt, Letter to Corinne Roosevelt Robinson, September 25, 1900, in Morison, *Letters of Theodore Roosevelt,* p. 1406.

4. *Deseret Evening News* (Salt Lake City, UT), September 18, 1900, p. 1.

5. *Red Lodge (MT) Picket,* September 21, 1900, p. 7.

6. *St. Paul Globe,* September 18, 1900, p. 5.

7. *Sun* (New York City), September 18, 1900, p. 2.

8. Ibid.

9. *St. Paul Globe,* September 18, 1900, p. 5.

10. *Red Lodge (MT) Picket,* September 21, 1900, p. 7.

11. Ibid.

12. *Omaha Daily Bee,* September 18, 1900, p. 3.

13. Ibid.

14. *Sun* (New York City), September 18, 1900, p. 2.

15. Ibid.

16. *Omaha Daily Bee,* September 18, 1900, p. 5.

17. *Sun* (New York City), September 18, 1900, p. 2.

18. *Omaha Daily Bee,* September 18, 1900, p. 3.

19. Jones, *American Red Cross,* p. 93.

20. *Evening Times* (Washington, DC), September 18, 1900, p. 1.

21. *Salt Lake Herald,* September 19, 1900, p. 2.

22. *Morning Astorian* (Astoria, OR), September 19, 1900.

23. *San Francisco Call,* September 23, 1900, p. 1.

24. *San Francisco Call,* September 19, 1900, p. 2.

25. *Bismarck (ND) Daily Tribune,* September 19, 1900, p. 1.

26. *San Francisco Call,* September 19, 1900, p. 2.

27. Ibid.

28. *Deseret Evening News* (Salt Lake City, UT), September 20, 1900, p. 2.

29. Ibid.

30. *San Francisco Call,* September 20, 1900, p. 2.

31. *Salt Lake Herald,* September 20, 1900, p. 2.

32. *St. Paul Globe,* September 18, 1900, p. 5.

33. Ibid.

34. *Sun* (New York City), September 18, 1900, p. 2.

35. Ibid.

36. *Salt Lake Herald,* September 19, 1900, p. 2.

37. Ibid.

38. *Salt Lake Herald,* September 20, 1900, p. 1.

39. *Sun* (New York City), September 20, 1900, p. 3.

40. *Indianapolis Journal,* September 20, 1900, p. 1.

41. *Salt Lake Herald,* September 20, 1900, p. 1.

42. *Sun* (New York City), September 20, 1900, p. 3.

43. Ibid.

44. Ibid.

45. Ibid.

46. Ibid.

47. *Salt Lake Herald,* September 20, 1900, p. 2.

48. *Sun* (New York City), September 20, 1900, p. 3.

49. *Salt Lake Herald,* September 20, 1900, p. 2.

50. Ibid., p. 4.

CHAPTER 10: UTAH AND WYOMING

1. *Barton County Democrat,* Great Bend, Kansas, September 21, 1900, p. 1.

2. *Deseret Evening News* (Salt Lake City, UT), September 20, 1900, p. 1.

3. Accounts are from these sources: the *Deseret Evening News, Salt Lake Herald, Indianapolis Journal,* and *San Francisco Call,* September 20-22, 1900.

4. *Deseret Evening News* (Salt Lake City, UT), September 20, 1900, p. 1.

5. *Sun* (New York City), September 21, 1900, p. 3.

6. *Salt Lake Herald,* September 22, 1900, p. 3.

7. *Salt Lake Herald,* September 20, 1900, p. 1.

8. *Sun* (New York City), September 21, 1900, p. 3.

9. *Sun* (New York City), September 22, 1900, p. 3.

10. *Times* (Washington, DC), September 23, 1900, p. 4.

11. *Deseret Evening News* (Salt Lake City, UT), September 21, 1900, p. 1.

12. *Salt Lake Herald,* September 22, 1900, p. 1.

13. Ibid.

14. *Sun* (New York City), September 22, 1900, p. 3.

15. *Indianapolis Journal,* September 25, 1900, p. 1.

16. *Deseret Evening News* (Salt Lake City, UT), September 22, 1900, p. 9.

17. Theodore Roosevelt, Letter to Alice Lee Roosevelt, July 14, 1900, in Morison, *Letters of Theodore Roosevelt,* p. 1356.

18. Quinn, *New Mormon History,* ch. 7, note 13, p. 133.

19. *Sun* (New York City), September 22, 1900, p. 3.

20. *Deseret Evening News* (Salt Lake City, UT), September 21, 1900, p. 1.

21. Theodore Roosevelt, Letter to Adelbert Moot, July 10, 1900, in Morison, *Letters of Theodore Roosevelt,* p. 1353.

22. *Salt Lake Herald,* September 22, 1900, p. 1.

23. *Deseret Evening News* (Salt Lake City, UT), September 21, 1900, p. 1.

24. *Salt Lake Herald,* September 22, 1900, p. 1.

25. Details and quotations from *Deseret Evening News* (Salt Lake City, UT), September 21, 1900, p. 1.

26. Ibid., p. 2.

27. *New York Times,* September 22, 1900, p. 3.

28. *Sun* (New York City), September 22, 1900, p. 3.

29. Details on the Beehive House visit and the organ concert from the *Deseret Evening News* (September 21) and *Salt Lake Herald* (September 22).

30. *Deseret Evening News* (Salt Lake City, UT), September 21, 1900, p. 2.

31. Information from "History: 1893 Coney Island of the West," website for the Great Saltair (www.thesaltair.com).

32. *Sun* (New York City), September 22, 1900, p. 3.

33. *Salt Lake Herald*, September 22, 1900, p. 2.

34. Ibid.

35. Ibid.

36. *Deseret Evening News* (Salt Lake City, UT), September 22, 1900, p. 9.

37. *San Francisco Call*, September 22, 1900, p. 3.

38. *Sun* (New York City), September 22, 1900, p. 3.

39. *Salt Lake Herald*, September 22, 1900, p. 1.

40. *Deseret Evening News* (Salt Lake City, UT), September 22, 1900, p. 9.

41. Ibid.

42. *San Francisco Call*, September 22, 1900, p. 3.

43. *New York Times*, September 22, 1900.

44. *Wichita Daily Eagle*, September 22, 1900, p. 1.

45. *Salt Lake Herald*, September 23, 1900, p. 4.

46. *San Francisco Call*, September 25, 1900, p. 3.

47. *Sun* (New York City), September 25, 1900, p. 3. See also the Wyoming Historical Society's website entry on "Francis E. Warren," as well as the *Lusk (WY) Herald*, November 28, 1929, available on the website of the Niobrara County Library.

48. *San Francisco Call*, September 25, 1900, p. 3.

49. *Wyoming Tribune* (Cheyenne, WY), September 25, 1900, pp. 1 & 4.

50. Ibid.

51. *Sun* (New York City), September 25, 1900, p. 3.

52. *Wichita Daily Eagle*, September 21, 1900, p. 1.

53. *Sun* (New York City), September 21, 1900, p. 3.

54. *Deseret Evening News* (Salt Lake City, UT), September 20, 1900, p. 1.

55. *Sun* (New York City), September 21, 1900, p. 3.

56. Ibid.

57. *Deseret Evening News* (Salt Lake City, UT), September 21, 1900, p. 2.

58. *Sun* (New York City), September 21, 1900, p. 3.

59. *Deseret Evening News* (Salt Lake City, UT), September 21, 1900, p. 1.

60. *Sun* (New York City), September 21, 1900, p. 3.

61. Details of the meeting are from the *Deseret Evening News* (Salt Lake City, UT), September 21, 1900, p. 2.

62. *Sun* (New York City), September 21, 1900, p. 3.

63. *Deseret Evening News* (Salt Lake City, UT), September 21, 1900, p. 1.

64. Information is from media reports on Roosevelt's visits in the *Sun* (September 24–25) and *Deseret Evening News* (September 24).

65. *Sun* (New York City), September 24, 1900, p. 3.

66. From the website Wyoming Places, entry: Daley Ranch.

67. *Indianapolis Journal*, September 25, 1900, p. 1.

68. *Sun* (New York City), September 25, 1900, p. 3.

69. Ibid.

70. *San Francisco Call,* September 25, 1900, p. 2.

71. *Sun* (New York City), September 25, 1900, p. 3.

72. *San Francisco Call,* September 25, 1900, p. 2.

73. *Sun* (New York City), September 25, 1900, p. 3.

74. Ibid.

CHAPTER 11: COLORADO

1. *San Francisco Call,* September 27, 1900, p. 1.

2. *Arizona Republican,* September 27, 1900, p. 1.

3. Langdon, *Cripple Creek Strike,* pp. 34-44.

4. *San Francisco Call,* September 27, 1900, p. 1.

5. September 27, 1900, editions (p. 1) of the *Akron Daily Democrat, Salt Lake Herald, San Francisco Call,* and *Marietta (OH) Daily Leader.*

6. Narrative sources are reports from these newspapers, editions of September 27-28, 1900: *New York Times, San Francisco Call, Akron Daily Democrat, Indianapolis Journal, Sun, New-York Tribune, St. Louis Republic, Wheeling Daily Intelligencer, Evening Bulletin, Marietta Daily Leader, St. Paul Globe, Salt Lake Herald, Morning Astorian, Colfax (WA) Gazette,* and *El Paso Daily Herald.*

7. *Indianapolis Journal,* September 28, 1900, p. 2.

8. Ibid.

9. *Akron (OH) Daily Democrat,* September 27, 1900, p. 1.

10. *Colfax (WA) Gazette,* September 28, 1900, p. 1, and *New-York Tribune,* September 28, 1900, p. 2.

11. *Indianapolis Journal,* September 27, 1900, p. 1.

12. Denver details are from the September 26, 1900, editions of the *Sun, Indianapolis Journal,* and *San Francisco Call.*

13. *Sun* (New York City), September 26, 1900, p. 5.

14. Ibid.

15. *San Francisco Call,* September 26, 1900, p. 2.

16. *Indianapolis Journal,* September 26, 1900, p. 1.

17. Ibid.

18. Pruett, *Mansions of Denver.*

19. *Biographical Directory of the United States Congress,* "Edward O. Wolcott" entry.

20. *San Francisco Call,* September 27, 1900, p. 1.

21. *Marietta (OH) Daily Leader,* September 27, 1900, p. 1.

22. Information from the website for the Historic St. Nicholas Hotel, link entitled "A Short History of Cripple Creek."

23. *Sun* (New York City), September 28, 1900, p. 1.

24. *New-York Tribune,* September 28, 1900, p. 2.

25. *Indianapolis Journal,* September 28, 1900, p. 1.

26. *Sun* (New York City), September 28, 1900, p. 1.

27. *Indianapolis Journal,* September 29, 1900, p. 1.

28. *Wheeling (WV) Daily Intelligencer,* September 26, 1900, p. 1.

29. *Sun* (New York City), September 26, 1900, p. 5.

30. *Wheeling (WV) Daily Intelligencer,* September 26, 1900, p. 1.

31. *Sun* (New York City), September 26, 1900, p. 5.

32. *Indianapolis Journal,* September 26, 1900, p. 1. (See also *Sun,* ibid.)

33. Details from the September 26, 1900, editions of the *Minneapolis Tribune* and *Wheeling (WV) Daily Intelligencer.*

34. *Sun* (New York City), September 28, 1900, p. 1.

35. Ibid.

36. *Indianapolis Journal,* September 29, 1900, p. 2.

37. *Indianapolis Journal,* September 28, 1900, p. 1.

38. *New York Times,* September 28, 1900.

39. Details from the *Sun,* September 28 edition, and *Indianapolis Journal,* September 29 edition.

40. *Sun* (New York City), September 28, 1900, p. 1.

CHAPTER 12: KANSAS AND NEBRASKA

1. Theodore Roosevelt, Letter to Corinne Roosevelt Robinson, September 25, 1900, in Morison, *Letters of Theodore Roosevelt,* p. 1406.

2. *Banner Democrat* (Lake Providence, LA), September 29, 1900, p. 2; and *Evening Bulletin* (Maysville, KY), September 29, 1900, p. 1.

3. On September 30, 1900, the Kansas Republican State Committee issued a statement on the success of Roosevelt's trip through the state. It said, in part: "Governor Roosevelt's train made thirty-one stops and at each he spoke, the time varying from one to forty minutes" (see *Sun,* October 1, 1900, p. 3). This discrepancy in the number of stops may mean the two brief stops went unreported by the media, or it may have been an exaggeration or error on the part of the state committee. One other possibility is that Roosevelt may have been credited with additional stops in those places where he gave speeches at more than one venue within a single community. Finally, the editor of Kansas's *Iola Register* mentioned that he would board the train at McPherson, which could have been the overnight stop between the first and second days (see note 41).

4. Eastern South Dakota was also an exception. The campaign special entered and left the state by the eastern border traversing the area west to the Missouri River with a southern/northern loop. However, nowhere other than Nebraska was a state covered twice border to border.

5. Population data from statistics at www.demographia.com. Information on Nebraska stops from the *Omaha Daily Bee,* October 1, 1900, p. 1.

6. *Sun* (New York City), October 1, 1900, p. 3, and *Custer County Republican* (Broken Bow, NE), October 18, 1900, p. 1.

7. *Omaha Daily Bee,* October 5, 1900, p. 3.

8. *New York Times,* September 30, 1900, p. 1.

9. *San Francisco Call,* September 30, 1900, p. 29.

10. *Sun* (New York City), October 1, 1900, p. 3.

11. *San Francisco Call,* September 30, 1900, p. 29.

12. *New-York Tribune,* September 30, 1900, p. 2.

13. *Sun* (New York City), September 30, 1900, p. 2.

14. *Sun* (New York City), October 1, 1900, p. 3.

15. *Cape Girardeau (MO) Democrat,* September 29, 1900, p. 1.

16. *Sun* (New York City), October 1, 1900, p. 3.

17. Ibid.

18. Ibid.

19. *San Francisco Call,* October 1, 1900, p. 3.

20. This phrase and the narrative on the events at Omaha are based on and occasionally quote coverage from the *Omaha Daily Bee,* October 5, 1900, pp. 1, 2, 3, and 7.

21. These crowd estimates are from the *Nebraska Advertiser,* October 19, 1900, p. 1.

22. *Wichita Daily Eagle,* September 25, 1900, p. 1.

23. *New York Times,* September 29, 1900, p. 7.

24. *Indianapolis Journal,* September 29, 1900, p. 1.

25. Ibid. and *San Francisco Call,* September 29, 1900, p. 2.

26. *Indianapolis Journal,* September 29, 1900, p. 1.

27. See "Dutch to Kansas: A Bibliography," on the website of the Kansas Historical Society.

28. *Indianapolis Journal,* September 29, 1900, p. 1.

29. Ibid.

30. Ibid.

31. *New York Times,* September 29, 1900, p. 7.

32. *Indianapolis Journal,* September 29, 1900, p. 1.

33. *Sun* (New York City), September 30, 1900, p. 2.

34. Ibid.

35. *Indianapolis Journal,* September 30, 1900, p. 1.

36. *Sun* (New York City), September 30, 1900, p. 2.

37. Ibid.

38. Ibid.

39. *Indianapolis Journal,* September 30, 1900, p. 1.

40. Ibid.

41. Recall, for instance, the Colorado newspaperman who was asked to leave the train, as mentioned in the previous chapter. Also, in Kansas, the editor of the *Iola Register* told

his readers in the September 28, 1900, edition that he would ride the Roosevelt train from McPherson to Cherryvale.

42. *Custer County Republican* (Broken Bow, NE), October 18, 1900, p. 3.

43. *Rapid City (SD) Journal*, October 4, 1900, p. 1.

CHAPTER 13: IOWA, ILLINOIS, AND MISSOURI

1. *San Francisco Call*, October 6, 1900, p. 2.

2. *Sun* (New York City), October 6, 1900, p. 3.

3. *Rock Island (IL) Argus*, October 6, 1900, p. 5.

4. Ibid.

5. *San Francisco Call*, October 6, 1900, p. 2.

6. Ibid.

7. *Wheeling (WV) Daily Intelligencer*, October 6, 1900, p. 1.

8. *Rock Island (IL) Argus*, October 6, 1900, p. 5.

9. *San Francisco Call*, October 6, 1900, p. 2.

10. *Rock Island (IL) Argus*, October 6, 1900, p. 5.

11. Ibid.

12. Ibid.

13. *Sun* (New York City), October 7, 1900, p. 1.

14. Ibid.

15. Details regarding Roosevelt's visit to Trinity and the demonstration afterward are from *San Francisco Call*, October 8, 1900, p. 1; *Sun* (New York City), October 8, 1900, p. 1; and *Indianapolis Journal*, October 8, 1900, p. 2.

16. *Indianapolis Journal*, October 9, 1900, p. 1.

17. *Rock Island (IL) Argus*, October 9, 1900, p. 1.

18. Ibid.

19. *Wheeling (WV) Daily Intelligencer*, October 9, 1900, p. 1.

20. *Indianapolis Journal*, October 9, 1900, p. 1.

21. *Sun* (New York City), October 9, 1900, p. 3.

22. Details on Roosevelt's day in St. Louis are from *Wheeling (WV) Daily Intelligencer*, October 9, 1900, p. 1; *Rock Island (IL) Argus*, October 10, 1900, p. 1; and *Indianapolis Journal*, October 10, 1900, p. 1.

23. *Indianapolis Journal*, October 10, 1900, p. 1.

24. Details of the Coliseum event in St. Louis are from *St. Louis Republic*, October 10, 1900, p. 2; *Times* (Washington, DC), October 10, 1900, p. 1; and *Indianapolis Journal*, October 10, 1900, p. 1. Although the *Times* estimated the crowd at 25,000, contemporary sources reported 12,000 as the maximum capacity of the Coliseum.

25. *Indianapolis Journal*, October 10, 1900, p. 1.

26. Ibid.

27. *St. Louis Republic,* October 10, 1900, p. 1.

28. Ibid.

29. Jonathon P. Dolliver was an Iowa Republican serving in the United States Senate. He had been one of the candidates promoted at the party's recent nominating convention to take the place on the ticket that went to Theodore Roosevelt.

30. *Omaha Daily Bee,* October 6, 1900, p. 2.

31. Details are from *Wichita Daily Eagle,* October 6, 1900, p. 1; and *Evening Bulletin* (Maysville, KY), October 6, 1900, p. 1.

32. *Sun* (New York City), October, 6, 1900, p. 3.

33. *San Francisco Call,* October 6, 1900, p. 2.

34. See www.nytimes.com for a Harpweek feature on the issue, "On This Day: October 6."

35. *Sun* (New York City), October 6, 1900, p. 3.

36. *Wichita Daily Eagle,* October 6, 1900, p. 1.

37. *Sun* (New York City), October 7, 1900, p. 1.

38. Ibid.

39. *Wheeling (WV) Daily Intelligencer,* October 9, 1900, p. 1.

40. *Indianapolis Journal,* October 9, 1900, p. 1.

41. *Sun* (New York City), October 9, 1900, p. 3.

42. *Rock Island (IL) Argus,* October 8,, 1900, p. 1.

43. *Sun* (New York City), October 9, 1900, p. 3.

44. Ibid.

45. *Indianapolis Journal,* October 9, 1900, p. 1.

46. *St. Louis Republic,* October 9, 1900, p. 1.

47. *Indianapolis Journal,* October 9, 1900, p. 1.

CHAPTER 14: INDIANA

1. Information on the *Indianapolis Journal* provided by the Indiana state library and made available on the website *Chronicling America* developed and supported by the National Endowment for the Humanities and the Library of Congress.

2. *Indianapolis Journal,* October 11, 1900, p. 1.

3. *San Francisco Call,* October 10, 1900, p. 1.

4. *Deseret Evening News* (Salt Lake City, UT), October 10, 1900, p. 1.

5. Fairbanks tried unsuccessfully for his party's presidential nomination in 1908, but Roosevelt supported William Howard Taft. In turn, Fairbanks supported Taft against Roosevelt in 1912, when Roosevelt ran on a third-party ticket. Both Taft and Roosevelt lost to Woodrow Wilson in that election. Finally, Fairbanks again appeared as the vice presidential candidate on the Republican national ticket in 1916, when Charles Evans Hughes failed to thwart Wilson's reelection bid.

6. *Indianapolis Journal,* October 11, 1900, p. 1.

7. Ibid.

8. Ibid.

9. Ibid.

10. Ibid.

11. Ibid., p. 4.

12. Ibid.

13. Ibid. (Note that "The Star-Spangled Banner" was not at the time the national anthem of the United States. The bill declaring it such was passed by Congress and signed by President Herbert Hoover in 1931.)

14. Ibid.

15. Ibid.

16. Ibid., pp. 1, 2, 11. (Note that while wording is verbatim to the source, the order of the edited narrative is slightly altered to tell the story logically.)

17. *Indianapolis Journal,* October 12, 1900, p. 1.

18. Ibid.

19. Ibid., p. 11.

20. Ibid.

21. Ibid.

22. Ibid.

23. Ibid.

24. Ibid.

25. Ibid.

26. Ibid.

27. Ibid.

28. Ibid., pp. 1, 3. (Note that while wording is verbatim to the source, the order of the edited narrative is slightly altered to tell the story logically.)

29. *Indianapolis Journal,* October 13, 1900, p. 1.

30. Ibid.

31. Ibid. (Note Roosevelt's clever pun on Bryan's 16-to-1 slogan.)

32. Ibid.

33. Ibid., pp. 1, 4.

34. Ibid., p. 4.

35. Ibid.

36. Ibid.

37. Ibid.

38. Ibid.

39. Ibid., pp. 1, 2. (Note that while wording is verbatim to the source, the order of the edited narrative is slightly altered to tell the story logically.)

40. Ibid., p. 1.

41. Ibid., p. 2.

CHAPTER 15: KENTUCKY

1. Principal source for the Goebel history is Walker, "Late Governor Goebel."

2. Material on Cobb's experience with the Goebel assassination is available at the Internet site www.kentuckyexplorer.com; Cobb's memoir, *Exit Laughing*, is the source.

3. *Indianapolis Journal*, October 16, 1900, p. 1.

4. *Sun* (New York City), October 16, p. 2.

5. Walker, "Late Governor Goebel."

6. *Hopkinsville (KY) Kentuckian*, October 16, 1900, p. 6.

7. *Sun* (New York City), October 16, p. 2.

8. Ibid.

9. *Kentucky Irish American*, October 13, 1900, p. 1.

10. *New-York Tribune*, October 14, 1900, p. 4.

11. *Indianapolis Journal*, October 14, 1900, p. 3.

12. Ibid.

13. *Wheeling (WV) Daily Intelligencer*, October 15, 1900, p. 1.

14. Information is from Greve's 1904 *Centennial History of Cincinnati*, www.nkyviews.com.

15. *Indianapolis Journal*, October 16, 1900, p. 1.

16. *Sun* (New York City), October 16, 1900, p. 2.

17. *Indianapolis Journal*, October 16, 1900, p. 1.

18. Ibid.

19. Ibid.

20. *New-York Tribune*, October 14, 1900, p. 4.

21. *Times* (Washington, DC), October 14, 1900, p. 1.

22. *New York Times*, December 14, 1900, p. 5.

23. *New-York Tribune*, October 14, 1900, p. 4.

24. Ibid.

25. Ibid.

26. Ibid.

27. Ibid.

28. *Deseret Evening News* (Salt Lake City, UT), October 16, 1900, p. 3.

29. *Indianapolis Journal*, October 15, 1900, p. 1.

30. *Wheeling (WV) Daily Intelligencer*, October 15, 1900, p. 1.

31. *Evening Bulletin* (Maysville, KY), October 16, 1900, p. 1.

32. *El Paso Daily Herald*, October 15, 1900, p. 1.

33. *Indianapolis Journal*, October 16, 1900, p. 3.

34. Ibid.

35. Ibid.

36. Ibid.

37. *Mt. Sterling (KY) Advocate*, October 16, 1900, p. 2.

38. *Sun* (New York City), October 16, 1900, p. 2.

39. *Daily Public Ledger* (Maysville, KY), October 16, 1900, p. 1.

40. *Evening Bulletin* (Maysville, KY), October 17, 1900, p. 2.

CHAPTER 16: OHIO, WEST VIRGINIA, AND MARYLAND

1. Everett Walters, *Ohio Fundamental Documents: Joseph P. Foraker,* Ohio Historical Society, available at www.ohiohistory.org.

2. Hake's *Americana Auction #209 Catalog,* 2013.

3. Fischer, *Tippecanoe and Trinkets Too,* p. 145. (Source of this quotation and the discussion that follows, except as otherwise noted.)

4. Fischer, *Tippecanoe and Trinkets Too,* p. 144.

5. Illustrations of the great variety of items from the 1900 presidential election may be seen in the following reference works: Sullivan and Fischer, *American Political Ribbons;* Sullivan, *Collecting Political Americana;* Wright, *Campaigning for President;* Hake, *Encyclopedia of Political Buttons;* Hake, *Political Buttons;* Collins, *Threads of History.*

6. Wright, *Campaigning for President,* p. 115.

7. Sullivan, *Collecting Political Americana,* p. 33.

8. *Evening Bulletin* (Maysville, KY), October 15, 1900, p. 1.

9. *San Francisco Call,* October 17, 1900, p. 1.

10. *Indianapolis Journal,* October 16, 1900, p. 1.

11. *Sun* (New York City), October 17, 1900, p. 5.

12. Ibid.

13. Ibid.

14. *Wheeling (WV) Daily Intelligencer,* October 17, 1900, p. 1.

15. *Sun* (New York City), October 17, 1900, p. 5.

16. *San Francisco Call,* October 17, 1900, p. 1.

17. Ibid.

18. *Sun* (New York City), October 18, 1900, p. 4.

19. *Sun* (New York City), October 18, 1900, p. 4.

20. *Marietta (OH) Daily Leader,* October 18, 1900, p. 1.

21. *Morning Astorian* (Astoria, OR), October 18, 1900, p. 1.

22. *Sun* (New York City), October 18, 1900, p. 4.

23. *Wheeling (WV) Daily Intelligencer,* October 18, 1900, p. 4.

24. *Indianapolis Journal,* October 19, 1900, p. 1.

25. West Virginia University, "About the *Wheeling Daily Intelligencer,*" available at the Library of Congress online service *Chronicling America.*

26. Unless otherwise noted, quotations and details regarding the stop in Wheeling are from *Wheeling (WV) Daily Intelligencer,* October 19, 1900, pp. 2, 4, 6.

27. *Indianapolis Journal,* October 19, 1900, p. 3.

28. The wording of the circular to which Theodore Roosevelt was responding was as follows: "Governor Roosevelt said in a speech in Cooper Institute, in New York City, in 1896: 'The way to get rid of Bryanism and its child, labor troubles, is to stand it up against the wall and shoot it to death.' And in a speech delivered in Chicago just after the great strike. 'Any person who would join a strike, or go near one, ought to be shot.' Will the man who earns his bread by labor support the Roosevelt ticket?" (Reference: *Wheeling (WV) Daily Intelligencer,* October 19, 1900, p. 4.)

29. *Marietta (OH) Daily Leader,* October 19, 1900, p. 1.

30. Ibid.

31. Ibid., p. 4.

32. Some newspapers on October 19 and 20 suggested there might be "other stops" in Maryland, but there were no details and these may never have materialized because of Roosevelt's fatigue and throat problems. On Sunday, October 21, newspaper space was consumed with lengthy features on the likely outcome of the election, and there were generally only brief reports on the Baltimore events. If there were additional, unscheduled stops, they went unreported by the national media.

33. *Der deutsche Correspondent* (Baltimore, MD), October 21, 1900, p. 4.

34. *Indianapolis Journal,* October 21, 1900, p. 1.

35. Ibid.

36. *New York Times,* September 5, 1900.

37. *Indianapolis Journal,* October 21, 1900, p. 2.

38. Ibid.

39. *San Francisco Call,* October 17, 1900, p. 1.

40. *Sun* (New York City), October 17, 1900, p. 5.

41. *San Francisco Call,* October 17, 1900, p. 1.

42. *Wheeling (WV) Daily Intelligencer,* October 17, 1900, p. 2.

43. *Sun* (New York City), October 17, 1900, p. 5.

44. *Sun* (New York City), October 18, 1900, p. 4.

45. Ibid.

46. Ibid.

47. Mayor Samuel M. Jones opened the Acme Sucker Rod Company, a firm that made iron pumping rods for the oil industry. These were known colloquially as "sucker rods."

48. *Sun* (New York City), October 18, 1900, p. 4.

49. *Marietta (OH) Daily Leader,* October 18, 1900, p. 1.

50. *Sun* (New York City), October 18, 1900, p. 4.

51. *Indianapolis Journal,* October 19, 1900, p. 3.

52. *Stark County Democrat* (Canton, OH), October 19, 1900, p. 1.

53. Ibid.

54. *Wheeling (WV) Daily Intelligencer,* October 19, 1900, p. 2.

55. *Wheeling (WV) Daily Intelligencer,* October 18, 1900, pp. 1, 3.

56. *Wheeling (WV) Daily Intelligencer,* October 19, 1900, p. 2.

57. *Wheeling (WV) Daily Intelligencer,* October 19, 1900, p. 6.
58. Ibid.
59. Ibid.
60. Ibid.
61. Ibid.
62. *Indianapolis Journal,* October 19, 1900, p. 1.
63. *Wheeling (WV) Daily Intelligencer,* October 20, 1900, p.
64. *Indianapolis Journal,* October 20, 1900, p. 1.
65. Ibid.
66. *Sun* (New York City), October 20, 1900, p. 3.
67. *Indianapolis Journal,* October 21, 1900, p. 2.

CHAPTER 17: NEW YORK, NEW JERSEY, AND PENNSYLVANIA

1. *San Francisco Call,* October 21, 1900, pp. 13, 14.
2. Ibid.
3. Ibid.
4. Ibid.
5. Ibid.
6. *St. Paul Globe,* October 21, 1900, p. 7.
7. Ibid.
8. *Indianapolis Journal,* October 21, 1900, p. 17.
9. Ibid.
10. Rhode and Strumpf, *Historical Presidential Betting Markets,* p. 2. (This study by two University of North Carolina professors is available online. Both authors are professors of economics at the university, and Dr. Rhode is also a research associate with the National Bureau of Economic Research, Cambridge, MA.)
11. Ibid., pp. 2, 3.
12. Ibid., table 1, p. 21.
13. Ibid., p. 1.
14. *Sun* (New York City), October 21, 1900, p. 1.
15. *New-York Tribune,* October 31, 1900, p. 5.
16. *Evening World* (New York City), October 22, 1900, pp. 1&2.
17. Ibid.
18. Ibid.
19. Ibid.
20. *New-York Tribune,* October 23, 1900, p. 1.
21. Ibid.
22. Details and quotations on Newburg—ibid.
23. Details and quotations on Kingston—ibid. (unless otherwise noted).
24. *Washington Weekly Post,* October 23, 1900, p. 1.

25. Ibid.

26. *San Francisco Call,* October 24, 1900, p. 9.

27. *St. Louis Republic,* October 23, 1900, p. 1.

28. *Sun* (New York City), October 24, 1900, p. 3.

29. *New-York Tribune,* October 24, 1900, p. 2.

30. *Omaha Daily Bee,* October 24, p. 5.

31. *New-York Tribune,* October 24, 1900, p. 2.

32. *Omaha Daily Bee,* October 24, p. 5.

33. *New-York Tribune,* October 24, 1900, p. 2.

34. *Omaha Daily Bee,* October 24, p. 5.

35. *New-York Tribune,* October 24, 1900, p. 2.

36. Ibid.

37. *Sun* (New York City), October 24, 1900, p. 3.

38. *New-York Tribune,* October 24, 1900, p. 2.

39. *Sun* (New York City), October 24, 1900, p. 3.

40. *Omaha Daily Bee,* October 24, p. 5.

41. *Sun* (New York City), October 24, 1900, p. 3.

42. *Omaha Daily Bee,* October 24, p. 5.

43. *Sun* (New York City), October 24, 1900, p. 3.

44. Ibid.

45. *New-York Tribune,* October 24, 1900, p. 3.

46. *New-York Tribune,* October 25, 1900, p. 3.

47. Ibid.

48. Ibid.

49. Ibid.

50. Ibid.

51. *Sun* (New York City), October 25, 1900, p. 1.

52. *New-York Tribune,* October 25, 1900, p. 3.

53. *Sun* (New York City), October 25, 1900, p. 1.

54. *New-York Tribune,* October 26, 1900, p. 2.

55. Ibid

56. *Sun* (New York City), October 26, 1900, p. 8.

57. *New-York Tribune,* October 26, 1900, p. 2.

58. *Sun* (New York City), October 26, 1900, p. 8.

59. *New-York Tribune,* October 26, 1900, p. 2.

60. *El Paso Daily Herald,* October 26, 1900, p. 1.

61. *Sun* (New York City), October 26, 1900, p. 8.

62. Ibid.

63. *Evening World* (New York City), October 26, 1900, p. 1.

64. *Sun* (New York City), October 27, 1900, p. 3.

65. *Evening World* (New York City), October 26, 1900, p. 1.

66. Ibid.

67. *Sun* (New York City), October 27, 1900, p. 3.

68. *New-York Tribune,* October 27, 1900, p. 12.

69. *Evening World* (New York City), October 26, 1900, p. 1.

70. *New-York Tribune,* October 27, 1900, p. 3.

71. Details of the events in New York City may be found in these sources: *New-York Tribune,* October 27, 1900, p. 1; *Sun* (New York City), October 27, 1900, p. 2; *San Francisco Call,* October 27, 1900, p. 1; *Marietta (OH) Daily Leader,* October 27, 1900, p. 1.

72. *St. Louis Republic,* October 28, 1900, p. 1.

73. *New-York Tribune,* October 27, 1900, p. 3.

74. *New-York Tribune,* October 28, 1900, p. 4.

75. Ibid.

76. *Sun* (New York City), October 28, 1900, p. 4.

77. *Indianapolis Journal,* October 28, 1900, p. 1.

78. *New-York Tribune,* October 28, 1900, p. 4.

79. Ibid.

80. *Sun* (New York City), October 28, 1900, p. 3.

81. Ibid.

82. Ibid.

83. *Indianapolis Journal,* October 28, 1900, p. 5.

84. Ibid.

85. *New-York Tribune,* October 28, 1900, p. 4.

86. Ibid.

87. *Sun* (New York City), October 28, 1900, p. 3.

88. Ibid.

89. *New-York Tribune,* October 28, 1900, p. 4.

90. *Sun* (New York City), October 28, 1900, p. 3.

91. Ibid

92. *New-York Tribune,* October 28, 1900, p. 4.

93. Ibid.

94. *Sun* (New York City), October 28, 1900, p. 3.

95. Ibid

96. *Indianapolis Journal,* October 28, 1900, p. 1.

97. *New-York Tribune,* October 30, 1900, p. 6.

98. Ibid.

99. Ibid.

100. Ibid.

101. Ibid.

102. *Indianapolis Journal,* October 30, 1900, p. 1.

103. *New-York Tribune,* October 30, 1900, p. 6.

104. *New-York Tribune,* October 31, 1900, p. 5.

105. *Sun* (New York City), October 31, 1900, p. 4.

106. Ibid.

107. *New-York Tribune,* October 31, 1900, p. 5.

108. *Sun* (New York City), October 31, 1900, p. 4.

109. *New-York Tribune,* October 31, 1900, p. 5.

110. *Indianapolis Journal,* October 31, 1900, p. 1.

111. Ibid. and *New-York Tribune,* October 31, 1900, p. 5.

112. *Sun* (New York City), October 31, 1900, p. 4.

113. Ibid.

114. *New-York Tribune,* October 31, 1900, p. 5.

115. *Sun* (New York City), October 31, 1900, p. 4.

116. *Sun* (New York City), November 1, 1900, p. 5.

117. *New-York Tribune,* November 1, 1900, p. 1.

118. Ibid.

119. *Sun* (New York City), November 1, 1900, p. 5.

120. *Indianapolis Journal,* November 1, 1900, p. 1.

121. Ibid.

122. Ibid.

123. *Sun* (New York City), November 1, 1900, p. 5, and *Indianapolis Journal,* November 1, 1900, p. 1.

124. *New-York Tribune,* November 1, 1900, p. 1.

125. Sources for details of the Buffalo stop include: *Sun* (New York City), November 1, 1900, p. 5; *Indianapolis Journal,* November 1, 1900, p. 2; and *New-York Tribune,* November 1, 1900, p. 1.

126. *Sun* (New York City), November 1, 1900, p. 5.

127. Ibid.

128. Ibid.

129. *Indianapolis Journal,* November 1, 1900, p. 2.

130. *New-York Tribune,* November 2, 1900, p. 1.

131. *San Francisco Call,* November 2, 1900, p. 1.

132. The *New-York Tribune,* November 2, 1900, p. 3.

133. *Sun* (New York City), November 2, 1900, p. 5.

134. Ibid.

135. *New-York Tribune,* November 3, 1900, p. 2.

136. Ibid.

137. *Sun* (New York City), November 3, 1900, p. 3.

138. Ibid.

139. *New-York Tribune,* November 3, 1900, p. 2.

140. Ibid. (Note that this account mistakenly locates the rock-throwing incident in Addison.)

141. Ibid. See also: *Sun* (New York City), November 3, 1900, p. 3.

142. *New-York Tribune,* November 3, 1900, p. 2.

CHAPTER 18: ELECTION

1. Numbers that were widely circulated near the end of the 1900 campaign reported that Roosevelt had visited 567 communities and made 673 speeches, and these totals have been repeated by many biographers through the years. While there may have been a few unreported stops in very small towns here and there, the number 567 was almost surely a Republican creation in answer to the Democratic claim that Bryan's campaign of 1896 held the record with 493 whistle stops. The total of 480 includes all stops on the trip to the second Rough Riders reunion, the trip to St. Paul for the National Republican League Convention, the Labor Day trip to Chicago, and the tour of western, midwestern, and border states, as well as the tour of New York and all other incidental campaign visits reported by regional and statewide newspapers across the nation.

2. *New-York Tribune,* November 4, 1900, p. 1.

3. *Sun* (New York City), November 4, 1900, p. 3.

4. *New-York Tribune,* November 4, 1900, p. 1.

5. Ibid.

6. Ibid. and *Indianapolis Journal,* November 4, 1900, p. 1.

7. *Indianapolis Journal,* November 4, 1900, p. 1.

8. *New-York Tribune,* November 4, 1900, p. 1.

9. *San Francisco Call,* November 4, 1900, p. 13.

10. *New-York Tribune,* November 4, 1900, p. 3.

11. *Sun* (New York City), November 6, 1900, p. 2.

12. *New-York Evening Journal,* November 5, 1900, as reported by *The San Francisco Call,* November 6, 1900, p. 1.

13. *San Francisco Call,* November 6, 1900, p. 1.

14. *Sun* (New York City), November 6, 1900, p. 2.

15. *Deseret Evening News* (Salt Lake City, UT), November 7, 1900, p. 1.

16. List from Hake, *Political Buttons,* p. 13. The *New-York Tribune* on October 21, 1900, ran a slightly different list, reporting Dr. S. C. Swallow as the candidate of the United Christian Party, terming Maloney's party as De Leon Socialist, calling Barker's party Middle of the Road Populists, and reporting that William Jennings Bryan was also the candidate of the Populist Party and the Silver Republican Party.

17. *Yankton (SD) Press and Dakotan,* September 12, 1900, p. 1.

18. *Deseret Evening News* (Salt Lake City, UT), September 21, 1900, p. 1.

19. *Sun* (New York City), November 3, 1900, p. 3.

20. *Sun* (New York City), November 8, 1900, p. 3.

21. Ibid.

22. Quote included in the narrative of Ward, *Roosevelts: An Intimate History,* p. 67.

23. Ibid.

24. Morris, *Rise of Theodore Roosevelt,* p. 595.

25. McCollough, *Mornings on Horseback,* p. 363.

26. *Sun* (New York City), November 9, 1900, p. 2.

BIBLIOGRAPHY

BOOKS AND JOURNAL ARTICLES

Auchincloss, Louis, and Arthur M. Schlesinger Jr. *Theodore Roosevelt.* (iBook electronic edition.) Published as part of the American Presidents series. New York: Times Books, 2002.

Collins, Herbert R. *Threads of History.* Washington, DC: Smithsonian Institution Press, 1979.

Di Silvestro, Roger L. *Theodore Roosevelt in the Badlands.* New York: Walker, 2011.

Dorsey, Leroy G. *We Are All Americans, Pure and Simple: Theodore Roosevelt and the Myth of Americanism.* Tuscaloosa: University of Alabama Press, 2007.

Fischer, Roger A. *Tippecanoe and Trinkets Too.* Urbana: University of Illinois Press, 1988.

Goodwin, Doris Kearns. *The Bully Pulpit.* (iBook electronic edition.) New York: Simon and Schuster, 2012.

Hake, Ted. *Encyclopedia of Political Buttons: United States 1896-1972.* New York: Dafran House, 1974.

Hake, Ted. *Political Buttons: Book 3, 1789-1916.* York, PA: Hake's Americana and Collectibles Press, 1978.

Howland, Harold. *Theodore Roosevelt and His Times.* (iBook electronic edition.) New Haven, CT: Yale University Press, 1921.

Jones, Marion Moser. *The American Red Cross from Clara Barton to the New Deal.* Baltimore: Johns Hopkins University Press, 2012.

Langdon, Emma Florence. *The Cripple Creek Strike.* Denver: Great Western, 1905.

Link, Arthur S. "The President as Progressive." In *Every Four Years.* Smithsonian Exposition Books. New York: W. W. Norton, 1980.

Mattson, Robert Lee. "Politics Is Up: Grigsby's Cowboys and Roosevelt's Rough Riders, 1898." *South Dakota History* 9, no. 4 (Fall 1979): 303-15.

McCollough David. *Mornings on Horseback.* New York: Simon and Schuster, 1981.

Morison, Etling E., ed. *The Letters of Theodore Roosevelt, Vol. 2.* Cambridge, MA: Harvard University Press, 1954.

Morris, Edmund. *The Rise of Theodore Roosevelt.* New York: Modern Library, 1979.

Nicholas, Frederic, ed. *McGraw Electric Railway Manual, Vol. 21.* New York: McGraw, 1914.

Pearson, Edmund Lester. *Theodore Roosevelt.* (iBook electronic edition.) New York: Macmillan, 1920.

Pruett, James Bretz. *The Mansions of Denver: The Vintage Years.* Denver: Pruett, 2005.

Quinn, D. Michael. *The New Mormon History.* Salt Lake City, UT: Signature Books, 1992.

Roosevelt, Theodore. *Ranch Life and the Hunting Trail.* New York: Century, 1896.

Roosevelt, Theodore. *An Autobiography.* (iBook electronic edition.) New York: Macmillan, 1913.

Roosevelt, Theodore. *The Rough Riders.* (iBook electronic edition.) New York: Charles Scribner's Sons, 1899.

Roseboom, Eugene H., and Alfred E. Eckes Jr. *A History of Presidential Elections,* 4th ed. New York: Collier Books, 1979.

Sullivan, Edmund B. *Collecting Political Americana.* New York: Crown, 1980.

Sullivan, Edmund B., and Roger A. Fischer. *American Political Ribbons and Ribbon Badges 1825-1981.* Lincoln, MA: Quarterman, 1985.

Thayer, William Roscoe. *Theodore Roosevelt: An Intimate Biography.* (iBook electronic edition.) Boston: Houghton Mifflin, 1919.

US Bureau of the Census. *Historical Statistics of the United States: Colonial Times to 1970.* Bicentennial ed., part 2. Washington, DC, 1976.

Walker, Marianne C. "The Late Governor Goebel." *Humanities: Journal of the National Endowment for the Humanities* 34, no. 4 (July/August 2013). Available online at www .neh.gov.

Ward, Geoffrey C. *The Roosevelts: An Intimate History.* New York: Alfred A. Knopf, 2014. (Companion volume to the PBS documentary film by Ken Burns.)

Watts, Sarah. *Rough Rider in the White House: Theodore Roosevelt and the Politics of Desire.* Chicago: University of Chicago Press, 2003.

Wright, Jordan M. *Campaigning for President.* New York: Harper Collins, 2007.

LETTERS OF THEODORE ROOSEVELT

February 1, 1900: To Thomas Platt
April 16, 1900: To Norton Goddard
June 23, 1900: To Seth Low
June 25, 1900: To Anna Roosevelt Cowles
June 25, 1900: To Marcus Alonzo Hanna
June 25, 1900: To John Hay
June 27, 1900: To Dr. Lyman Abbott
June 27, 1900: To Marcus Alonzo Hanna
June 27, 1900: To George Hinkley Lyman
June 27, 1900: To President William McKinley
July 7, 1900: To Marcus Alonzo Hanna
July 10, 1900: To Adelbert Moot
July 14, 1900: To Silas Wright Burt
July 14, 1900: To Alice Lee Roosevelt
July 20, 1900: To Cecil Arthur Spring Rice
July 25, 1900: To Paul Dana

July 26, 1900: To Winthrop Chanler
July 30, 1900: To John Hay
August 6, 1900: To William Howard Taft
August 16, 1900: To Charles Henry Burke
August 16, 1900: To Elihu Root
August 18, 1900: To Anna Roosevelt Cowles
August 18, 1900: To Henry Clay Payne
August 19, 1900: To Henry L. Turner
August 22, 1900: To General Leonard Wood
August 28, 1900: To Charles Richard Williams
September 25, 1900: To Corinne Roosevelt Robinson

NEWSPAPERS

(Note: Many of the following are available at the website *Chronicling America,* a service of
the National Endowment for the Humanities and the Library of Congress.)

Aberdeen (SD) Daily News
Albuquerque Daily Citizen
Akron (OH) Daily Democrat
Anaconda (MT) Standard
Anderson Intelligencer (Anderson Court House, SC)
Arizona Republican (Phoenix, AZ)
Arizona Weekly Journal-Miner (Prescott, AZ)
Banner Democrat (Lake Providence, LA)
Barton County (KS) Democrat
Bismarck (ND) Daily Tribune
Bismarck (ND) Weekly Tribune
Brookings (SD) Weekly Register
Cape Girardeau (MO) Democrat
Chamberlain (SD) Register
Chicago Tribune
Colfax (WA) Gazette
Colored American (Washington, DC)
Columbus (NE) Journal
Courier (Lincoln, NE)
Custer County Republican (Broken Bow, NE)
Daily Argus-Leader (Sioux Falls, SD)
Daily Public Ledger (Maysville, KY)
Dakota Huronite (Huron, SD)
Dalles (OR) Daily Chronicle
Der deutsche Correspondent (Baltimore, MD)

Deseret Evening News (Salt Lake City, UT)
El Paso Daily Herald
Evening Bulletin (Maysville, KY)
Evening Herald (Klamath Falls, OR)
Evening Herald (Shenandoah, PA)
Evening Star (Washington, DC)
Evening Times (Washington, DC)
Evening World (New York City)
Fargo (ND) Forum
Guthrie (OK) Daily Leader
Herald (Los Angeles, CA)
Hocking Sentinel (Logan, OH)
Hopkinsville (KY) Kentuckian
Houston Daily Post
Hutchinson (KS) Gazette
Indianapolis Journal
Iola (KS) Register
Jamestown (ND) Weekly Alert
Kansas Agitator (Garnett, KS)
Kansas City Journal
Kentucky Irish American
Los Angeles Herald
Lusk (WY) Herald
Marietta (OH) Daily Leader
McCook (NE) Tribune
Mexico Missouri Message
Minneapolis Tribune
Mitchell (SD) Daily Republican
Morning Astorian (Astoria, OR)
Moody County (SD) Enterprise
Mt. Sterling (KY) Advocate
Nebraska Advertiser (Nemaha City, NE)
New York Herald
New York Journal
New York Times
New-York Tribune
New York Evening Journal
Norfolk (NE) Weekly News
North Platte (NE) Semi-Weekly Tribune
Ohio Democrat (Logan, OH)
Omaha Daily Bee
Pacific Commercial Advertiser (Honolulu, Hawaiian Islands)

Rapid City (SD) Journal

Record-Union (Sacramento, CA)

Red Lodge (MT) Picket

Richmond (VA) Dispatch

Rock Island (IL) Argus

Salt Lake Herald

Scranton (PA) Tribune

St. Landry Clarion (Opelousas, LA)

St. Louis Republic

St. Paul Globe

San Francisco Call

Shiner (TX) Gazette

Stark County (OH) Democrat

Sun (New York City)

Times (Washington, DC)

Vermillion (SD) Plain Talk

Washington (DC) Weekly Post

Wheeling (WV) Daily Intelligencer

Wichita Daily Eagle

Williamsburg (VA) Gazette

Wyoming Tribune (Cheyenne, WY)

Yankton (SD) Daily Citizen

Yankton (SD) Press and Dakotan

Yankton (SD) Weekly Gazette

OTHER RESOURCES

Almanac of Theodore Roosevelt (website). www.theodore-roosevelt.com

American Presidency Project (website). *Republican Party Platform* (June 19, 1900) and *Democratic Party Platform* (July 4, 1900). University of California, Santa Barbara. www.presidency.ucsb.edu.

Annenberg Learner (online). "TR and Wilson." *Biography of America.* www.learner.org.

Campbell, W. Joseph. *The Spanish-American War: American Wars and the Media in Primary Documents.* Website of W. Joseph Campbell. www.academic2.american.edu.

Cobb, Irvin S. *Exit Laughing.* Excerpts from book available at the website kentuckyexplorer.com.

Cresswell, Ray. "Richard Harding Davis." *The Spanish-American War Centennial Website.* 1998. www.spanamwar.com.

Demographia.com. Resource for census/population data.

Greve's Centennial History of Cincinnati. Excerpts from 1904 reference work. www.nkyviews.com.

Hake, Ted. *Americana Auction #209 Catalog.* 2013.

Harpweek. "On this Day: October 6." nytimes.com.

Historic St. Nicholas Hotel. *A Short Cripple Creek History.* www.hotelstnicholas.com.

Indiana State Library. "The Indianapolis Journal." Information on the publication at the website *Chronicling America,* a service of the National Endowment for the Humanities and the Library of Congress. www.chroniclingamerica.loc.gov.

Kansas Historical Society. "Dutch to Kansas: A Bibliography." Electronic access at the website: kshs.org.

National Park Service. "History of the Maltese Cross Cabin and the Elkhorn Ranch." Website for Theodore Roosevelt National Park. www.nps.gov.

New York Times. "McKinley and Roosevelt." *Campaign Songs for 1900.* October 21, 1900.

Niobrara County (WY) Library. *Lusk Herald,* November 29, 1929. Entry: "Francis E. Warren." www.niobraracountylibrary.org.

Ohio Historical Society. William McKinley historical marker #17-76 at the home of William McKinley in Canton, Ohio. Electronic access at the website *Remarkable Ohio.* www.remarkableohio.org.

Poor's Manual of the Railroads of the United States. 1897. Selections available as Wikimedia Public Domain Documents.

Puck. Selected images. Literary and humor magazine published in New York City between 1871 and 1918.

Rhode, Paul W., and Koleman S. Strumpf. *Historical Presidential Betting Markets.* Chapel Hill: University of North Carolina. 2004. Available online.)

Saltair. "History: 1893 Coney Island of the West." *The Great Saltair.* www.thesaltair.com.

Theodore Roosevelt Center at Dickinson (ND) State University. Items from the collection as available on the center's website at theodorerooseveltcenter.org. (See also Theodore Roosevelt Digital Library, Dickinson State University.)

Thornton, James. "When You Were Sweet Sixteen." Popular song at the turn of the twentieth century; recorded by Columbia and released on a wax cylinder. George J. Gaskin, artist.

United States Congress. "Edward O. Wolcott." *Biographical Directory of the United States Congress.* bioguide.congress.gov.

Walters, Everett. *Ohio Fundamental Documents: Joseph P. Foraker.* ohiohistory.org.

West Virginia University. "The Wheeling Daily Intelligencer." Information on the publication at the website *Chronicling America,* a service of the National Endowment for the Humanities and the Library of Congress.

Wikimedia Public Domain Documents.

Wyoming Historical Society. "Francis E. Warren" entry. WyoHistory.org.

Wyoming Places. Entry: "Daley Ranch." www.wyomingplaces.org.

ACKNOWLEDGMENTS

American Cyclone was a germinating idea for twenty years from the moment I ran across a celluloid campaign button that promoted a visit by Theodore Roosevelt to Aberdeen, South Dakota, on September 13, 1900. Because most local libraries maintain archives of regional newspapers, I was able to begin fleshing out the details of a remarkable whistle-stop tour that brought the New York governor deep into the Midwest seeking votes for the Republicans' McKinley and Roosevelt national ticket. I acknowledge and thank librarians whose work means so much to scholarship on projects that otherwise would be impossible. I'm also grateful for the American Political Items Collectors, an organization of folks that share my interest in the material culture of presidential elections. My membership began around the time of the nation's bicentennial, and it was one of my fellow members who featured the Roosevelt button in an auction brochure during the 1990s.

Retirement gave me the chance to undertake research and writing on the project in earnest, and my wife, Pat, deserves credit for delaying her plans for us to travel and spend time with family and friends. She also helped immeasurably with inspiration, editing, and creative illustrations. Without her input, there would be no book. Our three sons and their wives and significant others joined Pat on an ad hoc editorial committee that kept me on the straight and narrow. There are eighteen college degrees—half of them master's or doctoral degrees—in our immediate family, so this committee's contributions were both scholarly and significant.

Resources available from the Theodore Roosevelt Center at Dickinson State University in North Dakota and from the Library of Congress were invaluable. The online database of newspapers from around the nation, *Chronicling America*, saved months of travel, untold hours of searching for primary sources, and thousands of dollars that would otherwise have been required to complete this project.

Last, but by no means least, I acknowledge and thank the University Press of Mississippi for accepting and publishing *American Cyclone*. Director

Leila W. Salisbury was encouraging and helpful from the moment we first discussed the project, peer reviewers had good suggestions for enhancements, and members of the board were generous in voting for publication.

I am grateful to one and all.

AUTHOR'S BIOGRAPHY

John M. Hilpert spent thirty-six years in higher education administration, serving most of two decades as a university president. During his career, he was elected to three terms as board chair for the Southern Association of Colleges and Schools (SACS), the accrediting organization for more than eight hundred institutions in the eleven southeastern states. He also served as the elected president of the Mississippi Associations of Colleges and the appointed interim associate commissioner of the Mississippi Institutions of Higher Learning. Hilpert holds a PhD degree from the University of Michigan, where he was awarded the 1985 John S. Brubacher Award for excellence in scholarship on the history of higher education. During his career, journals and magazines, as well as local and statewide newspapers, published more than one hundred of Hilpert's articles and columns. He married Patricia Tucker in 1971; she is an award-winning photographer who spent a thirty-year career as a nursing administrator. The couple has three adult sons and a growing number of grandchildren. They split their time between homes in Arkansas and South Dakota.

INDEX